Military Ethics

An Introduction with Case Studies

STEPHEN COLEMAN

New York   Oxford

OXFORD UNIVERSITY PRESS

Oxford University Press is a department of the University of Oxford.
It furthers the University's objective of excellence in research,
scholarship, and education by publishing worldwide.

Oxford   New York
Auckland   Cape Town   Dar es Salaam   Hong Kong   Karachi
Kuala Lumpur   Madrid   Melbourne   Mexico City   Nairobi
New Delhi   Shanghai   Taipei   Toronto

With offices in
Argentina   Austria   Brazil   Chile   Czech Republic   France   Greece
Guatemala   Hungary   Italy   Japan   Poland   Portugal   Singapore
South Korea   Switzerland   Thailand   Turkey   Ukraine   Vietnam

For titles covered by Section 112 of the US Higher Education Opportunity Act,
please visit www.oup.com/us/he for the latest information about pricing and
alternate formats.

Published by Oxford University Press
198 Madison Avenue, New York, NY 10016
http://www.oup.com

Oxford is a registered trademark of Oxford University Press.

Library of Congress Cataloging-in-Publication Data.
Coleman, Stephen. Military ethics : an introduction with case studies/Stephen Coleman.
    p. cm.
Includes bibliographical references and index.
    ISBN 978-0-19-984629-0
1. Military ethics—Case studies.   2. Soldiers—Conduct of life—Case studies.   3. War—Moral
and ethical aspects—Case studies.   4. Just war doctrine—Case studies.   5. Humanitarian
intervention—Moral and ethical aspects—Case studies.
I. Title.
U22.C552 2012
172'.42—dc232012014522

For the three main women in my life,
my daughters, Jacqui and Hannah
and my wife, Nikki.

CONTENTS

6. POWER AND AUTHORITY—ISSUING AND FOLLOWING ORDERS   121

7. DISCRIMINATION AND PROPORTIONALITY I: TRADITIONAL ISSUES OF *JUS IN BELLO*   148

PREFACE

⌒

AIMS, CONTENT, AND STRUCTURE

Imagine you are a fighter pilot in the British Royal Air Force (RAF), flying one of the most advanced fighting machines in the world over the sands of Libya. You are flying a reconnaissance mission, with the aim of locating enemy forces on the ground below, but always with eyes alert for any sign of enemy planes in the skies. If you manage to locate the enemy and return to base without being shot down, then the troops and tanks of the British Eight Army will be able to use the information you have gained to close with the enemy forces you have located and engage them in battle. It is 1941 and Britain and her Commonwealth allies are at war with Germany and Italy.

Fast forward 70 years, to 2011, and once again imagine that you are a fighter pilot in the RAF, flying one of the most advanced fighting machines in the world over the sands of Libya. You are not flying a reconnaissance mission in support of your state's ground forces; this time you are engaged in attacks on the equipment of the Libyan state military forces. Strictly speaking, you do not have any "allies" on the ground, but if you did they would not be the military forces of your own state, or indeed the military forces of any state; they would be rebel forces engaged in an uprising against their own government. Britain is not actually at war with Libya but is part of "Operation Unified Protector," an operation mounted to enforce resolutions passed by the United Nations Security Council (UNSC). Strictly speaking, those UNSC resolutions do not support either side in the conflict, but rather are designed, in accordance with the doctrine of "Responsibility to Protect," to prevent Libyan civilians from being harmed during the ongoing clashes.

For you as the pilot in 1941, the enemy is both clearly identified and, by and large, clearly identifiable. German and Italian pilots, soldiers, and sailors will be trying to kill you and other members of the British and Commonwealth armed forces. You and other members of these British and allied forces will be trying to kill the members of the German and Italian armed forces. In 1941, war is technically difficult and physically dangerous, but not especially ethically challenging.

The situation in 2011, on the other hand, would probably be unimaginable to someone from 1941. The job of a pilot is certainly still technically difficult, but now there are layers of ethical complexity woven into that difficulty as well. As was the case in 1941, in 2011 attacks will be mounted against military targets, but now, unlike in 1941, those targets will routinely be located in the midst of civilian areas and must be attacked while causing as little damage to those civilians and their property as possible. The overall aim of the operation is not to militarily defeat an enemy, but to protect civilians from harm. Some pilots flying aircraft over Libya in 2011 are no longer in any physical danger at all, for the aircraft they are flying are unmanned aerial vehicles (UAVs) being flown remotely by pilots located an enormous distance away from the combat zone, in some cases on the other side of the world.

Of course, although the example I have drawn on here is an Air Force one, it is not only pilots who face these ethical complexities in modern operations. Troops on the ground used to only engage in combat with armed forces from other states. Now they can expect to be involved in counterinsurgency operations, counterterrorism operations, in conflict against irregular forces, in peacekeeping operations, peacemaking or peace enforcement operations, and armed interventions launched for purely humanitarian purposes. Naval forces, as well as being involved in and/or supporting all of these aforementioned land and air operations, may also be involved in operations at sea that combat piracy, or deal with boatloads of refugees, or attempt to protect their state against drug smugglers, people smugglers, or illegal fishermen, among other things.

As well as being more ethically complex, the situation for military personnel has also become more legally complex. Whatever operation they happen to be involved in at the time, military personnel are required to abide by the Law of Armed Conflict (LOAC), also known as International Humanitarian Law (IHL). Almost all of the international treaties which make up LOAC (listed in the Appendix to this book) have come into effect since the end of World War II. Given the intimate relationship between law and ethics, which is discussed in Chapter 1, this legal complexity is also extremely important in ethical terms.

My aim in writing this book has been to assist those members of the military who have to deal with all of the ethical issues raised by complex modern operations. In particular, I have focussed on the problems faced by those charged with the day-to-day conduct of such operations, usually relatively junior military leaders, rather than the problems faced by the more senior military commanders who must deal with the strategic issues such operations raise.

The Structure and Contents of This Book

In writing this book I have tried to keep the focus on the practical issues that military personnel will face in modern military operations. As I mentioned a moment ago, my aim in writing the book was to provide practical ethical guidance to those military personnel involved in field operations, rather than to senior military commanders. Therefore, the ethical decisions I discuss in this book are mainly of the type likely to be made be relatively junior military leaders, such as junior officers and noncommissioned officers, who also need to be able to give guidance on such issues to those under their command. Such decisions are largely tactical, rather than strategic, in that they are focused on individual battles and engagements, rather than on the whole campaign. Of course, in the modern world, decisions made by low ranking military personnel within individual engagements can have a reverberating effect on the whole campaign; such is the world of the "strategic corporal."[1]

Each chapter within this book addresses a specific topic of relevance to military personnel involved in field operations. Although the book can, of course, be read from cover to cover (something I would encourage everyone to do if they have time!), I have attempted, so far as this is possible, to make each individual chapter also stand on its own. So, for example, if an Army Sergeant was about to be deployed on a peacemaking mission and wanted to read some material that discussed the ethical problems likely to be encountered in such a context, he or she could simply read Chapter 9 of this book, which discusses such issues.

Instructors who are using this book as a text in a formal educational environment will find some useful extra materials on the associated website. I hope, and expect, that those using this book in this way will not feel constrained to work through the book from cover to cover. Some instructors, for example, might feel that there is too much ethical theory included in Chapters 1 and 2 and so might tell their students to skip straight through to Chapter 3. Other instructors might feel that there is not enough ethical theory and so will want to supplement the material here with additional readings from other sources. In my own teaching I have found the amount of material presented here to be appropriate, but I have aimed to not force such a view onto others who wish to use this book as a text in their own courses.

The Case Studies

There are over 50 case studies highlighted within the pages of this book, and this number does not include various other examples and analogies discussed within the text itself. Other case studies are available through the website associated with this book. The case studies are intended to illustrate particular issues and to stimulate thought and discussion. In so far as it has been possible, I have tried to keep the case studies short while also including all the relevant information a person would need to know to understand the main issues raised by that case, even if that person knew nothing else about the event being discussed. My aim was always to produce a short and clear case study, which could be read and understood by all the participants in a discussion within a couple of minutes. The main reason for this is to allow readers of this book to use the case studies as a basis for discussion wherever and whenever they might be useful: in a university lecture or classroom; a presentation; a training course; or even for discussion among members of a deployed unit.

The case studies are of three main types. There are a few obviously fictional case studies, none more than a few sentences long, all of which illustrate theoretical points. There are a very large number of case studies based on historical events, some better known than others. When creating these case studies, as I mentioned earlier, I have tried not to assume any background knowledge on the part of the reader. The remaining case studies, scattered throughout the book, are all stories related to me by serving military personnel, about actual events in their own lives. These case studies have been fictionalized to some extent to help protect the identities of the people involved, all of whom remain nameless at their own request. When I have used these case studies in my own teaching in the past, some readers have found it hard to believe that some of these events actually occurred (a sentiment also expressed by more than one of the experts who reviewed this manuscript before publication). Nonetheless, the events described in these cases did occur, more or less as described, in the lives of real people. This certainly illustrates the ethical complexity of military service.

The Structure of Each Chapter

Other than the introduction and conclusion, each chapter in this book commences with one or two case studies. The aim in starting each chapter in this way is to introduce, through some concrete examples, the sorts of issues that will be discussed in that chapter. Other cases studies are then introduced throughout the chapter as a means of illustrating other ideas of importance. Occasionally, case studies used in previous chapters are also referred to, but since every case study is both highlighted in the text of the book and listed in the table of contents, finding and reading these case studies should not provide any difficulty for those who are only interested in reading certain chapters of the book. Each chapter also concludes with some additional readings, for those who wish to pursue the matter further, as well as some questions for reflection and/or discussion. Further materials, including lecture notes, additional case studies, and discussion questions, can be found on the website associated with this book, www.oup.com/us/coleman.

The Content of Each Chapter

Chapter 1 introduces ethics as a general field of study, a field that everyone, whether they realize it or not, is already familiar with to some extent. The chapter also discusses the relationship between law and ethics, which, as I mentioned earlier, is of particular importance to those who serve in the military. The last section of this chapter examines ethical problems people may face and divides them into two main categories: tests of integrity and ethical dilemmas. Tests of integrity and ethical dilemmas may be equally difficult to deal with, but the difficulty in each of these situations lies in a different area. In the case of an ethical dilemma, the difficulty is in deciding what the right thing to do is. In the case of a test of integrity, the difficulty lies not in deciding what the right thing to do is, but in actually doing it.

Chapter 2 provides a brief overview of the main theories of ethics. It highlights the sort of considerations that need to be taken into account when making ethical decisions and discusses the way in which these principal considerations have led into the formulation of the three main theories of ethics: consequentialism, including the various types of utilitarianism; deontological theories, including natural law theories, social contract theories, and Kantian ethics; and virtue theory, sometimes referred to as Neo-Aristotelianism. As each theory is discussed, major criticisms of the theory are also mentioned, along with some responses to those criticisms that might be made by a defender of the theory. In this context there is some discussion of the doctrine of double effect (DDE), which has had a significant influence on some aspects of LOAC. The last part of the chapter attempts to refute some general criticisms of ethical theory and explains how the main theories of ethics might be integrated together to help people when dealing with practical problems.

Chapter 3 examines some of the particular moral requirements placed on those who serve the state as members of the military. It discusses the "profession of arms" and the "role morality" which is required of military personnel, as well as discussing some of the virtues, and possibly vices, that military personnel may need to develop to carry out their role in society.

Chapters 4 and 5 discuss issues related to that aspect of just war theory known as *jus ad bellum*, which examines when it is ethically right to resort to war. Chapter 4 looks at these issues in a traditional context, of armed conflict between sovereign states. This includes some discussion of the main ideas of realism, a major alternative to just war theory, as well as explicit discussion of whether it can be ethical to engage in preemptive or preventative wars. Chapter 5 looks at issues of *jus ad bellum* in the context of modern armed conflicts, such as insurgencies, counterinsurgencies, and armed humanitarian interventions of various sorts. The aim is to see whether the traditional ideas of just war theory can be applied to these conflicts, or whether there is a need to modify the theory to deal with such issues.

Chapter 6 examines ethical problems related to power and authority within the military, in particular the problems associated with giving and following orders. Ethical issues can easily arise in the process of issuing or following orders, both in combat zones and in peacetime operations, especially since those in positions of command within the military can be issuing orders that literally raise issues of life and death. The chapter also examines some other topics that arise in this context, such as what makes a person an effective or ineffective leader and why it is important for leaders to set a good moral example. Some readers may question why a discussion about giving and following orders would include these sorts of comments about leadership. The simple answer is that command and leadership are not the same thing, in that people obey commanders, but follow leaders. In the years I have been teaching prospective military officers, I have never come across anyone who was happy to simply command others: they all wanted to be leaders. Thus, the discussion about the ethical issues of command, of giving and following orders, also includes discussion of issues related to leadership as well. Problems discussed in this chapter include issues of whether there are orders a military commander should not issue, whether there are orders that should not be followed, and what a member of the military ought to do when given two sets of orders that conflict with each other.

Chapters 7, 8, and 9 discuss the second traditional aspect of just war theory, known as *jus in bello*, which examines right conduct during war. The two fundamental principles of *jus in bello* are discrimination and proportionality. The principle of discrimination asserts that the only appropriate targets are those concerned with the enemy's war effort, and the principle of proportionality claims that the damage that is done in prosecuting such targets needs to be in line with the actual military value of the target itself. Chapter 7 discusses these ideas in the context of traditional conflicts between sovereign states; Chapter 8 discusses these same principles in the context of insurgencies, counterinsurgency operations, and conflicts involving irregular forces; and Chapter 9 discusses these principles in relation to armed humanitarian interventions, peacekeeping operations, and peace enforcement operations.

Chapters 10 and 11 discuss problems that may arise for military personnel in relation to surrender and detention, particularly with regard to the treatment of those who are taken into custody during counterterrorism operations. Chapter 10 examines what surrender actually means, as well as how people may be treated once they are taken into custody by military personnel. Chapter 11 extends this discussion by looking at terrorism, and in particular examining the principle that has come to be known as "supreme emergency," since this principle suggests that terrorism may be ethically justified in extreme situations. This leads into examination of some of the problems related to counterterrorism, especially how alleged terrorists ought to be treated if and when they are taken into custody and whether the principle of supreme emergency might provide justification for torturing such people, at least in extreme cases, as a counterterrorism tactic.

Chapter 12 provides a conclusion for this overall discussion. In particular, this final chapter attempts to demonstrate how the various different issues relate to each other, as well as reexamining the professional duties and role morality of military personnel.

ACKNOWLEDGMENTS

It has taken me a long time to write this book, as my immediate family would no doubt attest. I first felt the need for such a book in 2006, when I started teaching in the School of Humanities and Social Sciences at the University of New South Wales (UNSW) Canberra, at the Australian Defence Force Academy (ADFA). It was then that serving military personnel started to tell me their stories, and so my initial collection of case studies in military ethics began. I simply cannot thank enough all the anonymous members of the military, from more different countries and services than I care to name, who have shared their stories with me over the last 5 years.

I finally started the actual writing process while on study leave from UNSW. From September 2009 to May 2010, I served as Resident Fellow in Ethics at the Vice Admiral James B. Stockdale Center for Ethical Leadership at the U.S. Naval Academy in Annapolis, Maryland. During that time I received a great deal of help from a large number of people, who fall into three main groups: people associated with the Stockdale Center; people associated with the Department of Leadership, Ethics and Law, located on the same floor in Luce Hall as the Stockdale Center; and my neighbors in Perry Circle, who were always willing to discuss things with me.

Among the many people associated with the Stockdale Center, I would like to thank the following: the Director, COL Art Athens (U.S. Marine Corps, Ret) and the Administration staff, Marge Bem and Jaclyn Danna, for making me feel so welcome; the nonresident fellows Pat Lin, Brad Allenby, and Max Mehlman for lively and interesting discussions particularly on issues related to new military technologies (which, unfortunately, mostly did not make it into this book); the other semiresident fellow, Brig. Gen. Rick O'Meara (U.S. Army, Ret) for many useful discussions, especially regarding the relationship between law and ethics; Ed Barrett (aka LTCOL Barrett—U.S. Air Force Reserve) for his many insightful thoughts; the other Center staff who were happy to discuss issues with me whenever I poked my head into their respective offices, including LTCOL Dan Healey (U.S. Marine Corps), Shaun Baker, and Betsy Holmes; and in particular, Professor George Lucas, who helped arrange for me to come to the Stockdale Center in the first place, and who gave me such strong encouragement to write this book. Of the people associated with the Department of Leadership, Ethics and Law, particular thanks go to Deane-Peter Baker, with whom I discussed issues of military ethics almost every day; Brad Johnson, who gave great encouragement to my writing; Joe Thomas, who provided some excellent ideas and examples on leadership; CAPT Bill DiFilippo (U.S. Navy, Ret), who happily discussed ethical problems related to orders; CAPT Rick Rubel (U.S. Navy, Ret), who greatly assisted me in writing readable case studies; and CAPT Steve Trainor (U.S. Navy), Patricia Cook, Larry Lengbeyer, Michael Skerker, and Chris Eberle, who were all willing to have me interrupt them to discuss specific issues and problems.

I know my family would join me in thanking our wonderful neighbors in the housing in Perry Circle, military families all, who made us feel very welcome. I would especially like to thank all the serving military officers among our neighbors, who were all more than happy to talk about any problem in military ethics which I cared to name. In no particular order, thanks to Ben Leming (U.S. Marine Corps Reserve); Sarah Leming (U.S. Marine Corps Reserve); Aaron Leong (U.S. Air Force); Chuck Crosby (U.S. Army); Mike Ferns (U.S. Navy); Paul White (U.S. Navy); Carla Pappalardo (U.S. Navy); Russ Pesut (U.S. Navy); Jordan McCaleb (U.S. Navy); and John Owen (U.S. Navy).

In Australia, my work has been well supported by the School of Humanities and Social Sciences, UNSW Canberra, in particular by my Head of School, Professor David Lovell; the administration staff, Jo Muggleton, Shirley Ramsey, Marilyn Anderson-Smith, and Bernadette McDermott; Ned Dobos, who provided particularly helpful comments for Chapters 4 and 5; and Peter Balint, who has been a very useful sounding board (and has also made me ridiculous amounts of coffee). I also must thank the Vincent Fairfax Ethics in Leadership Foundation for supporting my position at UNSW Canberra.

I have had some very useful discussions with a large number of Australian Defence Force staff here at ADFA, in particular Jamie Cullens, who provided a lot of insight as well as a number of useful case studies; and Lieutenant Commander Richard Adams, whose ideas have encouraged me to reexamine a lot of my ideas on command and leadership. Thank you to all the students I have taught, particularly in ZGEN2240, who have forced me to think hard about these issues, and to the staff who have helped me to teach that course, who have also shared their thoughts with me, in particular Nikki Coleman, Ned Dobos, Richard Adams, Nick Evans, Shannon Ford, Dean Cocking, Rebecca Hosking-Young, and Adam Gastineau. Thanks also to those other people in military education around the world who have encouraged me along the way, especially George Lucas; Martin Cook; Shannon French; David Whetham; Richard Schoonhoven; Daniel Lagacé-Roy; and Deane-Peter Baker. Thanks to my friends Michael and Suzanne Clark for providing me with a quiet place to work when the going got tough. Thanks to Robyn Veugen, Anton Veugen, Milton Coleman, and Patsy Coleman for helpful and encouraging comments, and to Nikki Coleman for helping with the research for this book. Special thanks to my friend, Mark Jennings, who tried to make sure that I got things right when discussing international law; obviously any false statements that may have crept in are my fault and not his.

Thank you to all those at Oxford University Press for their help with this project, in particular Robert Miller, Kristin Maffei, and Christina Mancuso. Thanks also to the many people who reviewed either the book proposal or parts of the manuscript on behalf of OUP: Cian O'Driscoll, University of Glasgow; Martin Cook, U.S. Naval War College; Eric Heinze, University of Oklahoma; an anonymous reviewer, University of Queensland; Reed Bonadonna, U.S. Merchant Marine Academy; Richard Schoonhoven, U.S. Military Academy; Christopher Cullen, Fordham University; Oak DeBerg, University of Texas at San Antonio; Daniel Lagacé-Roy, Royal Military College, Canada; Carl Ficarrotta, U.S. Air Force Academy; George Lucas, U.S. Naval Academy; Shannon French,

Case-Western University; Bryan Bearden, U.S. Marine Corps War College; Mark Jensen, U.S. Air Force Academy; Arnold Piper, Norwich University; Chris Mayer, U.S. Military Academy; Erik Wingrove-Haugland, U.S. Coast Guard Academy; Jeffrey Wilson, U.S. Military Academy; James Cook, U.S. Air Force Academy; and David Whetham, King's College, London.

My special and heartfelt thanks to all those people who have read through the entire manuscript and whose comments have made this a much better book than would otherwise have been the case: Nikki Coleman; Deane-Peter Baker; Mark Jennings; Richard Schoonhoven; Jeffrey Wilson; Arnold Piper; Shannon French; George Lucas; and Kierryn Higbed.

Finally, I have to thank my wife, Nikki, and my daughters, Hannah and Jacqui, who have put up with so much while I have been writing this book. Now that it is finished, I promise I will be home more often. This book is for you.

NOTE

1. A term coined by U.S. Marine General Charles C. Krulak in "The Strategic Corporal: Leadership in the Three Block War," *Marines Magazine* 28(January 1999), 28–34.

ABBREVIATIONS

The following is a list of abbreviations used in this book. I have not provided explanations for any abbreviations that are only used within a single case study. With regard to the abbreviation for the military rank of Captain, different states (and even different services within a state) use different abbreviations for this rank. In the interests of consistency I have used the abbreviation CAPT throughout this book, regardless of the state or service being referred to at the time.

ANC	African National Congress
CAPT	Captain (Military Rank)
CDR	Commander (Military Rank)
CO	Commanding Officer (Officer in Command of a unit, e.g. an infantry battalion)
CPL	Corporal (Military Rank)
DDE	Doctrine of Double Effect
FRY	Federal Republic of Yugoslavia (Sovereign State)
GCIII	Geneva Convention (III) relative to the Treatment of Prisoners of War. August 12, 1949.
GCIV	Geneva Convention (IV) relative to the Protection of Civilian Persons in Time of War. August 12, 1949.
IAEA	International Atomic Energy Agency
ICRC	International Committee of the Red Cross
ICTY	International Criminal Tribunal for the former Yugoslavia
IDF	Israel Defense Forces
IED	Improvised Explosive Device
IHL	International Humanitarian Law
KFOR	Kosovo Force (UN mission)
KVM	Kosovo Verification Mission (NATO Mission)
KLA	Kosovo Liberation Army
LCDR	Lieutenant Commander (Military Rank)
LOAC	Law of Armed Conflict
LT	Lieutenant (Military Rank)

LTJG	Lieutenant—Junior Grade (Military Rank)
MHAT	Mental Health Advisory Team
MK	*Umkhonto we Sizwe* aka the Spear of the Nation (militant resistance group of the ANC)
NATO	North Atlantic Treaty Organization
NCO	Non-Commissioned Officer
OC	Officer Commanding (Officer in Command of a sub-unit, c.g. an infantry company and under the authority of the CO)
OOD	Officer of the Deck
PLO	Palestine Liberation Organization
POW	Prisoner of War
RAF	Royal Air Force (U.K.)
ROE	Rules of Engagement
RPF	Rwandan Patriotic Front
RPG	Rocket Propelled Grenade
SEAL	U.S. Navy Sea, Air and Land Team aka Navy SEALs
UAV	Unmanned Aerial Vehicle
UCMJ	Uniform Code of Military Justice (U.S. military regulations)
U.K.	United Kingdom (Sovereign State)
UN	United Nations
UNPROFOR	United Nations Protection Force (Balkans)
UNSC	United Nations Security Council
UNTSO	United Nations Truce Supervision Organization (Middle East)
U.S.A.	United States of America (Sovereign State)
U.S.	United States (aka U.S.A.) (Sovereign State)
U.S.S.R.	Union of Soviet Socialist Republics (Sovereign State)
WMD	Weapons of Mass Destruction

1

‒○

Introduction
What Is Ethics? What Is an Ethical Decision?

Ethical decision making is something that everyone is familiar with, whether they are aware of it or not, and the process of making ethical decisions is something that everyone is engaged in on a regular basis. An ethical decision is one which has an ethical component to it, such as a decision about what is right or wrong, good or bad, fair or unfair, just or unjust. A decision to bribe a government official is an ethical decision, as is a decision to lie to a friend in order to avoid an awkward situation, as is a decision to keep a promise to go to an unpleasant relative's birthday party, as is the decision to go to war.

Some people will do what they believe to be right as a matter of course, others will know what they plan to do is wrong but will do it anyway; regardless of what they actually do these people are engaged in the process of ethical decision making. Like everyone else, military personnel, even junior personnel, are involved in making ethical decisions. In fact because of the positions that they hold and the responsibilities that they have, the ethical decisions made by military personnel are particularly serious ones, for such decisions often have a dramatic effect on the lives of others. The aim of this book is to aid military personnel in understanding the ethical decisions that they will have to make; to help them to clarify their thinking; to enable them to get a better grasp of the issues involved in making ethical decisions; and ultimately, to help them make better ethical decisions when they are in positions of authority.

WHAT IS ETHICS AND WHY SHOULD I STUDY IT?

In technical terms, ethics is that branch of philosophy that addresses questions about morality; thus, ethics is sometimes known as moral philosophy. In simpler terms, ethics is the study of the sorts of moral concepts I mentioned earlier, such as good and bad, right and wrong, and so on. On hearing this, students often ask what the difference between ethics and morality is. The English word "ethics" is derived from the Greek term *éthos*, best translated as "character," whereas the English word "morality" is derived from the Latin term *mos*, which refers to personal character or habits and is essentially the same concept.[1] Although there are arguments in philosophical circles that suggest that the terms have somewhat different meanings (with "ethics" usually seen to be the broader term), in everyday discussions people often use the terms "ethics" and "morality" interchangeably, and since this is not a technical philosophical discussion, I will use the terms interchangeably in this book.

It is generally accepted that there are three broad branches of ethics: (1) metaethics, which seeks to understand the nature of ethical concepts and asks questions like "what do the terms 'good,' 'bad,' 'right,' and 'wrong' actually mean?" or "are answers to ethical questions universal or relative to a particular time and place?"; (2) normative ethics (or moral theory), which attempts to find a rule or set of rules that can be used in all situations to determine what the right and wrong thing to do is; and (3) applied ethics, which applies the ideas of normative ethics to individual situations, often with a focus on a particular aspect of human life—medical ethics, environmental ethics, and business ethics are thus all branches of applied ethics.[2] As an examination of military ethics, this book is a work in applied ethics, and is focused on practical rather than theoretical issues. Although ethical theory will be discussed in Chapter 2, it will only be discussed to the extent necessary for an understanding of the practical ethical issues faced by military personnel in general and by junior military leaders in particular.

Students who study ethics, particularly those who do so in compulsory courses, often complain that there seem to be no right answers in ethics. Some also complain that it is insulting that they are required to study ethics, believing that such a requirement shows a lack of faith in their personal character. I would argue that such statements come down to a lack of understanding of the purpose of studying ethics. Getting a good grade in an ethics course does not mean that one is a good person; I'm sure that there have been self-confessed murderers serving life sentences who have done very well in ethics courses. The fact that a person understands ethics, or even that they are able to differentiate right from wrong, certainly does not mean that person will actually **do** the right thing. Knowing what is the right thing to do and actually doing the right thing are two very different things, as I will discuss later in this chapter. Studying ethics, especially in an applied ethics course, allows a person to gain an understanding of ethical principles and ideas—especially those principles that are relevant to those persons in specific roles or occupations, such as the military—and to learn how those principles and ideas ought to be applied in practice.

Unfortunately (and I am probably risking the wrath of a goodly number of theorists in normative ethics by claiming this) there is no one ethical theory that applies to every situation and supplies a perfect answer to every ethical question—at the very least there is no one theory that all ethicists (or even the vast majority of ethicists) agree on. This is certainly one way in which the study of ethics differs from the study of a science like physics. The reason that many students feel that there are no right answers in ethics is that courses in applied ethics usually focus on the difficult problems in life, and these are precisely the sorts of cases where ethical theories tend to disagree. Having said that, I will argue in the next chapter that all the main ethical theories agree on what is right and wrong in the vast majority of situations, and even in cases where ethical theories ultimately disagree about what the right thing to do is, there is usually substantial agreement on some aspects of those same cases. Thus in a particular case where a doctor might be able to act in ten different ways, even if two ethical theories disagree about which of those ten options is ultimately the right one, with one theory claiming option A is correct and the other claiming option B is correct, they at least agree that options C through J are incorrect.

Studying the ethics applicable to a particular profession often resolves at least some of these problems, since professions have their own norms and regulations of practice that tend to limit the options available to a member of that profession in any particular situation. Thus if an ordinary person is confronted on the street by a wild-eyed man who is wielding a knife, it might be perfectly acceptable for that person to run away, but it is fairly obvious that it would not be acceptable for an armed on-duty police officer to do the same thing. Since military personnel are generally considered to be members of the profession of arms, professional considerations will often be important in the ethical decisions that military personnel have to make. Some of these considerations will be discussed in Chapter 3, and will form the foundation for discussion of the issues which arise in later chapters.

LAW AND ETHICS

I have found during my years of teaching that many people conflate law and ethics, thinking that everything that is legal must therefore be ethical, and everything that is illegal must therefore be unethical. Such thoughts are particularly common among people who work within the legal system itself but they are also frequently found among members of occupations whose actions are greatly restrained by law, such as members of the military. While law and ethics are often closely related, they are far from being the same thing, and it is not difficult to find examples of situations where law and ethics come into conflict. Laws can be perfectly well framed and pass through all the required government processes that are necessary for those laws to come into effect, thus making them perfectly valid in a legal sense, yet at the same time those laws can be morally abhorrent. The laws that allowed the persecution and execution of millions of Jews, gypsies, and minority peoples under the Nazi German regime are a good example of this sort of situation, as are the apartheid laws that applied in South Africa for much of the latter part of the twentieth century, the laws enforced by the Taliban during their period of effective control of Afghanistan, or even the segregation laws that applied in the Southern United States until the 1950s and 1960s. It is also not terribly difficult to imagine situations in which it is ethically correct to break the law. Suppose I have in my car a person who has been bitten by a deadly snake and I am racing against time to get them to the hospital to receive the antidote for the venom that is now moving through their bloodstream. If I am a well-trained driver travelling on a quiet stretch of freeway then it would seem to be entirely ethical for me to exceed the speed limit by a reasonable margin. While these circumstances would almost certainly be seen by a court as a reasonable excuse for my exceeding the speed limit, the fact remains that in exceeding the speed limit I would be breaking the law. It is also fairly simple to find situations in which there is near universal agreement that a certain action is right, but there is no law requiring people to act in that way. Nearly everyone agrees that parents ought to love their children, for example, but there are no laws that require it, nor could there be any such laws.[3]

Of course although the demands of law and ethics do sometimes conflict with each other, it is far more usual for them to coincide, and this is only to be expected. While some laws are enacted simply to maintain stable social interactions or provide social goods, many laws, especially criminal laws, articulate ethical principles that are deemed to be particularly important. Laws against murder, rape, assault, theft, and so on exist because of a prior ethical view that it is wrong to murder, assault, or steal from other people. It is also generally agreed that members of society have a duty to follow the laws of the land, which means that there is a *prima facie* ethical requirement to follow the law. Thus any decision to break the law will always be a decision of ethical significance, which will be important to remember when considering some of the problems discussed later in this book.

Military conduct is usually heavily regulated by both domestic law and international law. Members of the military forces of a particular country will be subject to the domestic laws of that country, and it is common for such laws to place specific requirements on those serving in the military, such as demanding that they always follow orders. Military conduct during international conflict is also subject to international law, most importantly to the Law of Armed Conflict (LOAC), also known as International Humanitarian Law. While LOAC has mostly been created as a result of the signing of international treaties or through long-standing customs of international relations, it should be recognized that these treaties and customs also have an ethical basis in that they are founded on the requirements of an ethics of war that has been discussed and defined over the centuries and has come to be known as just war theory. The ethical basis and requirements of just war theory will be examined at length in later chapters.

ETHICAL DILEMMAS AND TESTS OF INTEGRITY

When discussing ethical problems and ethical decision making, I have found that it is often helpful to divide problems into two distinct groups. There is certainly an overlap between the groups, and problems can shift from one group to the other, but I find that dividing ethical problems up into these two groups aids in understanding the issues raised in specific situations. I refer to one group of ethical problems as ethical dilemmas and to the other group as tests of integrity.[4] Ethical problems falling into either one of these groups can be very difficult for the people involved to deal with, but they are difficult for completely different reasons. What I call an ethical dilemma (or sometimes, a test of ethics) is a situation in which the difficulty lies in knowing what the right thing to do actually is. It is a situation in which a person is faced with a number of choices, often a number of bad choices, and has to work out what is the right thing to do in that particular situation. Situations like this may arise in a number of ways, such as when differing values come into conflict, or when helping one person is likely to cause harm to another. What I call a test of integrity is a situation in which it is reasonably obvious, or even perfectly obvious, what the right thing to do is, but for whatever reason, it is difficult for the person involved to actually do the right thing.

Tests of integrity and ethical dilemmas may be equally difficult to deal with, but the difficulty in each of these situations lies in a different area. In the case of an ethical dilemma, the difficulty is in deciding what the right thing to do is. In the case of a test of integrity, the difficulty lies not in deciding what the right thing to do is, but in actually doing it.

It is important to understand the various sorts of reasons why it may be difficult for a person to do what they know to be the right thing in a situation where they are faced with a test of integrity. It may be that doing the right thing is unpopular, either with that person's friends, family, or peers, or with the community at large. It might be that there is a lot of pressure, in one way or another, placed on that person to not do the right thing, in that they might be bribed, bullied, or blackmailed. The person might have a lot to gain from not doing the right thing; perhaps there are financial or other rewards to be gained from not doing the right thing in this particular case. It may be that those close to this person will have a lot to lose from the person doing the right thing in this case. It may be that to fail to do the right thing in this situation would simply be to go along with the crowd, since many other people are already doing the wrong thing. Or it may be that failing to do the right thing in this situation doesn't seem to cause harm to anyone.

Consider the situation where a military officer who has been deployed overseas is offered a substantial (and untraceable) bribe to ensure that a supply contract with a particular company is renewed. The company is really the only one in a position to fulfill the contract anyway so there will be no questions asked if the contract is renewed; the company is also aware of this but offers the officer this payment as a form of insurance. There is no doubt that it would be wrong for the officer to accept a payment like this, but there may be considerable temptation for the officer to accept it, particularly if this officer's family is facing serious financial difficulties at the time. A situation such as this is a clear example of a test of integrity.

There are many historical examples of tests of integrity, such as the case of Warrant Officer Hugh Thompson, who acted to stop the massacre of Vietnamese civilians at My Lai in 1968. When Thompson realized that U.S. troops were shooting unarmed civilians, he landed his helicopter and confronted Lieutenant (LT) William Calley, the army officer in charge. Soon afterward he protected another group of wounded Vietnamese by landing between them and the U.S. troops and ordering his door gunners to train their weapons on the U.S. soldiers until the civilians had been evacuated. His complaints about U.S. actions that day eventually led to a full inquiry, at which he gave evidence. Though his actions were vilified by many people in the years after the incident, in 1998 Thompson and his crew were awarded the Soldier's Medal, the U.S. Army's highest award for bravery not involving direct contact with the enemy, for their actions at My Lai. Thompson knew that what the U.S. soldiers were doing was wrong, and displayed great moral courage in acting to stop them, rather than taking the easy way out and simply ignoring what the soldiers were doing. LT Calley, on the other hand, clearly failed a test of integrity and was later convicted of murder for his actions at My Lai.

Understanding why it is that people fail tests of integrity—why they do something even when they know it is the wrong thing to do—is an extremely interesting issue in terms of moral psychology. Since subordinates will find it easier to stand up for what they know is right if their leaders provide a good moral example, those who want to be good leaders need to be able to both recognize, and deal appropriately with, tests of integrity when they arise. However, tests of integrity are much less interesting when considered purely in terms of applied ethics. Since this book is primarily intended to assist junior military leaders and prospective junior military leaders in their study of ethics and in dealing with the ethical dilemmas they will face in their future careers, it therefore focuses primarily on ethical dilemmas rather than tests of integrity, on those cases where the difficulty lies not in doing the right thing in the face of pressure to do otherwise, but rather in working out what the right thing to do is in the first place.

To understand the sorts of considerations that military personnel ought to take into account when faced with these ethical dilemmas, it is necessary to first examine the general theories of ethics that are thought to govern the actions of all rational people before examining the specific duties and obligations military personnel face when dealing with these situations.

NOTES

1. It might be hard to imagine that the word "morality" comes from the Latin term *mos*, but it is much easier to understand when one considers that when used as an adjective *mos* became *moralis*, and when used as a noun it was *moralitas*.

2. To put this in really simple (albeit slightly inaccurate) terms (1) is about what good and bad actually mean, (2) is about what rules define good and bad, and (3) is about how to apply those rules.
3. This example comes from Seumas Miller, John Blackler, & Andrew Alexandra, *Police Ethics*, 2nd ed. (St. Leonards, NSW: Allen and Unwin, 2006), p. 27.
4. This issue is discussed in more detail in my paper "The Problems of Duty and Loyalty," *Journal of Military Ethics* 8(2009), 105–115.

FURTHER READING

Coleman, Stephen. "The Problems of Duty and Loyalty." *Journal of Military Ethics* 8(2009), 105–115.

Ficarotta, J. Carl. "A Higher Moral Standard for the Military." In George Lucas et al. (eds.), *Ethics for Military Leaders*. 5th ed. (Boston: Pearson Custom, 2002), pp. 93–103.

Whetham, David. "The Challenge of Ethical Relativism in Coalition Operations." *Journal of Military Ethics* 7(2008), 302–316.

DISCUSSION QUESTIONS

- Are there certain types of cases where the distinction between tests of integrity and ethical dilemmas might be particularly blurred?
- Do the types of ethical problems a person tends to face change in character as a person moves up the chain of command within a military organization? Are lower ranked personnel more likely to face tests of integrity than more senior personnel? Is it the other way around? Or do all military personnel tend to face the same sorts of ethical problems, regardless of their rank?

2

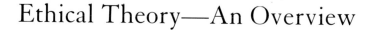

Ethical Theory—An Overview

CASE STUDY 2.1

The Runaway Railway Car

A railway car is running out of control down a track. In its path are five railway workers. They are working on the tracks in a narrow cutting, which means they will not be able to get out of the way of the car. Fortunately, you can flip a switch, which will lead the trolley down a different track. Unfortunately, there is a single worker, again in a narrow cutting, working on that track. You are certain that whichever way the car goes, anyone caught in its path will be killed. Should you flip the switch?

SOURCE: Based on a case by Philippa Foot, "The Problem of Abortion and the Doctrine of the Double Effect," *Oxford Review* 5(1967), 5–15.

CASE STUDY 2.2

The Spare Parts Surgeon

Imagine a truly great transplant surgeon, the best in the world. At the moment this surgeon has five patients who need organs. One needs lungs, one needs a liver, two need a kidney each, and the fifth needs a heart. If they do not get those organs today they will all die but if the surgeon can find organs for them today then transplant operations can be performed and they will all live. But there are no suitable organs available for transplant and all five deaths seem inevitable. The time is almost up when a report is brought to the surgeon that a homeless young man, with exactly the right blood and tissue types to be the perfect donor, has just come into the clinic for a delicate, but not particularly difficult, life-saving operation. One small slip of the surgeon's scalpel will mean this man dies and the surgeon will have the organs that are needed to save the other five patients. Should the surgeon operate normally, save this man and let the other five die, or should the surgeon kill him during the course of the surgery to ensure the other five patients live?

SOURCE: Based on a case by Judith Jarvis Thomson, "The Trolley Problem," *Yale Law Journal* 94(1985), 1395–1415. Thomson discusses Foot's already famous case (hence the name of her article) and then goes on to extend the discussion in various ways. This case comes from that discussion.

ETHICAL CONSIDERATIONS

The aim of this chapter is not to present a comprehensive overview of ethical thought, since such an undertaking would in itself fill an entire book. What I intend to do here is simply to sketch out the main considerations that are generally thought to be important in making ethical decisions, and to see how they relate to each other with regard to the sorts of ethical decisions that are made in the military context. In addition I will also introduce some key terms that are of particular interest in discussions of ethics. Since this chapter only provides a bare bones account of ethical theory, I have no doubt many readers will want to delve more deeply into the intricacies of the various theories discussed here. I would encourage those readers to examine some of the further readings suggested at the end of the chapter.

A lot of thought is required for a person to make consistently good decisions, and ethical decisions are no different in this respect. The main issue in making good ethical decisions is to understand what sorts of things need to be taken into account, and what importance various ethical considerations might have in relation to each other. One way that philosophers examine such issues is by means of thought experiments, imaging a particular situation and then thinking about its implications. When used to examine issues in ethics, thought experiments are sometimes referred to as "intuition pumps," since they are often designed to make clear the intuitions that people have about particular situations.[1]

Cases 2.1 and 2.2 are examples of philosophical thought experiments. Over the last 10 years I have used cases very similar to these ones to introduce literally thousands of students to ethical concepts, for these two cases when examined together bring out all the main considerations that are usually thought to be important in ethical decision making. The two cases obviously have some similarities; in both cases five people will die if no action is taken, but in both cases an action can be taken which will save those five people, but at the cost of another person's life. When asked about Case 2.1 (The Runaway Railway Car), the overwhelming majority of my students think that the right thing to do is to throw the switch and save the five people on the track, even though this means that the other person will die. On the other hand, when asked about Case 2.2

(The Spare Parts Surgeon), the overwhelming majority of my students think that the surgeon ought to operate normally on the homeless man and allow the other five patients to die.[2]

Such widely differing responses might seem a little surprising given the surface similarity between the cases, but the fact that people consistently demonstrate those intuitions suggests that there are in fact ethically important differences between these two situations. There are a number of suggestions as to what the differences between the two cases might actually be. One possibility is that directly killing the homeless man violates a principle, do not murder, which is not violated in the runaway railway car case, where while the death of the one worker might be seen as a terrible accident, it is not a case of murder. Having said this, it must be acknowledged that the small minority who do not think it right to throw the switch to turn the runaway railway car almost always think that it would be the wrong thing to do because it means that you are directly contributing to that man's death, in much the same way as the surgeon killing the homeless man. While many people see this principle as applying in one case and not the other, not everyone agrees, although I will argue, later in the chapter, that there are coherent ways of showing that throwing the switch to divert the train is morally permissible.

A second possibility is that the intentions of the people in the two cases are different, in that only one actually intends to cause a death. The surgeon intends to kill his patient, and it is this death that is the very means by which the lives of the other patients will be saved. If the surgeon's scalpel slips but the patient survives, then the surgeon will have to take another action to kill this patient, and if the other five patients are to be saved then the surgeon will have to keep making "mistakes" until the homeless man finally dies. On the other hand, the person who throws the switch to divert the railway car is trying to minimize the destruction caused by a terrible situation and does not in any way intend to kill the railway worker who will now be hit by the runaway railway car. If there was a miracle, and this railway worker was to somehow survive, then the person who threw the switch would be happy, and wouldn't say "You ought to be dead!" and run over and bash the worker's brains out with a shovel!

A third possibility is that there is an implied social contract involved in these cases (and possibly an actual contract in the surgeon case). Hypothetically, if all the people in society were to be questioned in advance then they would probably all agree that any runaway train (or railway car, or tram, or bus, or car) ought to be steered in the direction where it will cause the least loss of life. Thus the worker who will be killed in the runaway railway car case could be thought to have given hypothetical consent to the actions of the person who pulled the switch in Case 2.1. However it is highly unlikely that people would give similar consent to the idea of a doctor deliberately killing a patient to benefit others, even though, statistically speaking, each individual in society is more likely to benefit from such an arrangement than be harmed by it. Thus hypothetical consent could not be thought to exist in Case 2.2.

A fourth possibility, somewhat related to the third, suggests that considering all the consequences in both cases would lead a person to act differently in the runaway railway car case than they would in the surgeon case. Turning the train achieves the best possible consequences in that situation, where we are dealing with a fairly isolated incident and want to minimize the damage the runaway railway car causes. But the idea that it is acceptable for a surgeon to deliberately kill a patient to benefit other patients has wider ramifications, especially if news of the case became public. There would be a lot of people who would now be too scared to go to the hospital, worried that they might be chopped up for the benefit of others, and this would have serious implications for health care across the whole of society.

One final possibility, which I will not discuss further here but will examine in general terms in the next chapter, is the suggestion that the surgeon, as a member of the medical profession, has a particular professional obligation that would be violated by killing the homeless man, even if this benefits other people.

I would suggest that these various possibilities are in fact all correct, to greater or lesser degree. What is most important is that they highlight the sorts of considerations that are important in making ethical decisions. Specific principles are important; as was mentioned in the previous chapter, a lot of specific ethical principles are thought to be so important that they have come to be incorporated into law. There are various ways in which such principles might be thought to be derived, and the idea of a social contract is in fact one way of deriving such principles, so the first and third suggestions (mentioned in the preceding discussion) might be thought to be related in that respect. Consequences are obviously also an important consideration in ethical decisions; after all, the only reason to throw the switch in Case 2.1 (Runaway Railway Car) is to try to achieve better consequences, to save five lives at the expense of one. The intentions, or character, of moral agents are also an important consideration; some people might think that the actions of the surgeon in killing the homeless man are excusable given that the surgeon's intention was to try to save the lives of five other people, but I think few people would excuse the surgeon's actions if the surgeon's intention in killing the homeless man was merely to reduce the number of people living on the streets.

The big question is how these considerations can be brought together into a coherent ethical theory. The first step is to recognize what the various requirements of a good ethical theory actually are. An ethical theory is a consistent and transferable guide to action, which means that it must be able to explain why certain actions in the past were right or wrong and also aid in deciding whether particular actions are right or wrong in the future. With this in mind it is clear that a good ethical theory ought to agree with any "known" results, that is, explain why certain actions that are obviously right or wrong are in fact right or wrong; and in cases where the results of the theory disagree with these "known" results, there must be a clear and logical explanation for this disagreement. To meet the requirement of consistency a good ethical theory will also have to treat like cases alike, though it may well be the case that situations that look similar in fact differ in some important respects, as was the situation with Cases 2.1 (Runaway Railway Car) and 2.2 (Spare Parts Surgeon). A good ethical theory will also need to be able to provide clear answers to new and difficult cases, otherwise it is not a useful guide to action. Finally, and perhaps most important, a good ethical theory will need to be able to be universalized. An ethical theory is one that could, in principle, be adopted by everyone to guide their actions, so whatever actions it allows or requires must be reciprocal in an important sense; a theory that allowed some people to act in particular manner would have to allow everyone to act in that manner in the same circumstances. As a practical example of this in terms of warfare, adopting a universal theory of ethics means that any actions that may legitimately be taken by one party in the conflict may also legitimately be taken by any other parties to the conflict in the same circumstances. In simple terms, if it is OK for you to do it, then it is OK for your enemy to do it in the same circumstances. This is something I will discuss in much greater detail in later chapters.

In practice, the main types of ethical theory take one of the ethical considerations mentioned previously, that is, consequences or principles or character, elevate that consideration to being of primary importance and then universalize it to everyone by arguing that every person ought to act in a manner which recognizes the primacy of that particular consideration. In this way we get the three main types of modern ethical theory: consequentialist theories, which require everyone to act in a manner that achieves the best possible consequences for all; deontological or principle/duty based theories, which require everyone to follow universal rules of behavior; and virtue based theories, which focus on the character of the moral agent (intentions being an important aspect of character) and which require everyone to act in a manner that best exemplifies a virtuous character. Since some further understanding of these main types of ethical theory is required, even if only to allow us to understand what other writers on military ethics are actually saying, I will briefly explain the fundamentals of each of these types of theory. Before doing this, however, I want to make note of an important distinction, between theories of ethics and what might be termed theories of value.

THEORIES OF VALUE AND THEORIES OF ETHICS

When people first start to examine issues in ethics, or even when they argue about ethical issues in public debates, they often fail to recognize that there is a distinction between the two different types of theory that apply to those issues. What I term a theory of value is a theory about who or what counts in ethics; in other words, a theory of what is morally considerable. A theory of ethics, on the other hand, is a theory about how one ought to deal with those people or things that are morally considerable; in other words, a guide to ethical decision making. People may agree on a theory of value, but disagree on a theory of ethics or may agree on a theory of ethics, but disagree on a theory of value. Failure to recognize the important distinction between theories of value and theories of ethics often leads to people talking past each other in debates about ethical issues. For example, imagine Jane, who claims that abortion is always ethically equivalent to murdering an adult human being and Anna, who is arguing with her and claiming that early abortion is never ethically equivalent to murder. Despite appearances, their argument is not about the ethics of murder or about ethical theory (even though Jane and Anna probably think that is what they are arguing about); it is in fact an argument about theories of value, in this case specifically about the moral value of the human fetus in the early stages of pregnancy.

So let us examine in a little more detail the issue of moral considerability, before moving on to theories of ethics. There are essentially two ways in which something might be thought to be morally valuable. It may be either of intrinsic value, which roughly speaking means that it is valuable in and of itself, or it might be of instrumental value, which roughly speaking means it is valuable because it helps to achieve something that is intrinsically valuable or because of its relationship to something of intrinsic value. So for example, it can be argued that the pleasures experienced in living a normal human life are intrinsically valuable, but money is only of instrumental value; money might assist a person in living a pleasurable life if there are worthwhile things that can be bought with it, but money is essentially worthless if there is nothing that can be bought.

For the purposes of discussing military ethics it is unnecessary to delve too deeply into what gives something intrinsic value; although it is something that is argued about, most people will agree that life is valuable, and the more mentally complex the creature that is experiencing that life is, the more intrinsic value that life has. The commonsense view might suggest a hierarchy of things of intrinsic moral value; in other words various types of beings might possess intrinsic moral value without all being equally morally valuable. Thus the most complex creatures, such as those capable of making moral decisions, might be considered to have the highest intrinsic moral value, followed by what we might call near persons (such as higher mammals), then other living things that are capable of experiencing pain in a manner similar to humans (such as lower mammals and birds), followed by other living and moving creatures (e.g., insects and fish), and finally other living things such as plants.

So what of instrumental value? While some might argue that particular non-living things possess intrinsic value, I think this is a difficult argument to make, and thus I would suggest that any nonliving thing that is valuable possesses instrumental value rather than intrinsic value. Having said that, it should be recognized that some things that are of "merely" instrumental value may still be extremely valuable, and in some cases things of instrumental value may be considered more valuable than things of intrinsic value. Thus given a choice between rescuing something of intrinsic value, such as a person, from danger and saving something of instrumental value, it might actually be the right thing to do to abandon the person and save the object of instrumental value. This may seem an outrageous claim to make, and in any ordinary circumstance it seems obvious that we ought to safeguard people rather than things, but this may not always be the case. Consider the following cases. Suppose there was a fire at a sporting stadium and the stadium employees have to decide whether to rescue people or sporting equipment from the fire. This is what we might call the "ordinary" case, and it seems obvious that employees of the stadium ought to ensure the safety of the people present before trying to rescue the sporting equipment threatened by the fire. But suppose the fire was not at a sporting stadium but instead was at the Louvre, possibly the world's greatest art gallery and museum. It seems far less obvious that employees of the Louvre ought to ensure that all the people visiting the gallery are safe before even attempting to safeguard artistic masterpieces such as the Mona Lisa and the Venus de Milo. This is what we might call the "extraordinary" case, where such artistic treasures might well be seen to have such high value that they ought to be safeguarded before ensuring the safety of all the people, despite the people being of intrinsic, rather than mere instrumental, value.

ETHICAL THEORY—CONSEQUENCES

Having discussed theories of value, it is now time to return to theories of ethics. As I mentioned earlier, the main types of ethical theory usually elevate one of the ethical considerations to primary importance and then universalize it to everyone. Out of the three main theories, perhaps the most logically simple is consequentialism, which argues that consequences are the only ethically significant consideration and that each person should act so as to ensure the best possible consequences for everyone. For a consequentialist, whether an act is ethically right or not depends solely on the consequences of the action. Thus neither principles nor intentions are directly relevant in determining whether an act is ethically correct, though such things may assist in determining what will have the best overall consequences.

The first question that a consequentialist must answer is how the best consequences are to be defined; some criteria for defining what is good and what is bad will be needed before it is possible to decide what the best consequences are. Early consequentialist thinkers like Jeremy Bentham (writing in the late eighteenth century) argued that pleasure was the only good, thus acting to achieve the best possible consequences meant maximizing pleasure and minimizing pain. Bentham called acting in this manner "maximising utility"[3], which led to the theory itself being known as utilitarianism. These days utilitarianism is easily the most important and well-known variety of consequentialism, to the extent that quite a number of people use the terms interchangeably, discussing utilitarianism when they are actually referring to all types of consequentialist theory.

For the classical (or hedonistic) utilitarian, an act X is morally good only insofar as it maximizes the total pleasure/happiness (= utility). In other words, of all the available alternatives, act X is the one that produces the greatest possible increase of happiness over pain for all moral beings. It is particularly important to recognize that a utilitarian is maximizing utility for "all moral beings," thus in the modern world a committed utilitarian would need to consider the consequences of their actions on every person on the planet, and quite possibly on a large number of nonhuman animals as well. A person cannot legitimately claim to be a utilitarian while prioritizing the needs of one select group of people, such as the citizens of one's own country, over the needs of others.

Assessing the overall consequences in line with utilitarian principles is sometimes known as performing a "utilitarian calculus." This sort of consequentialist reasoning is especially clearly demonstrated in some of the larger scale decisions of warfare. Consider the following case, for example.

CASE STUDY 2.3

First Use of the Atomic Bomb

By the beginning of August 1945, World War II was coming to an end. Germany had been defeated by the Allies, and the forces of the United States and the other allied states were now in position to launch a direct assault on their only remaining adversary, Japan. However, in recent battles Japanese forces had inflicted heavy losses on the Allies, particularly through the use of *kamikaze* (suicide) attacks. United States nuclear scientists had recently completed work on a new weapon, the atomic bomb, perhaps the first true "weapon of mass destruction," which was massively more powerful than any other weapon known to the world at the time. United States President Harry Truman had to decide whether or not to order the use of this new weapon against Japan, knowing that it would have a massive area of effect and thus would have to be used against an entire city, civilian population included, rather than against a purely military target.

One of the people advising Truman was the Secretary of War, Henry L. Stimson, who later wrote about his part in the decision:

> The ultimate responsibility for the recommendation to the President rested upon me, and I have no desire to veil it...I felt that to extract a genuine surrender from the Emperor and his military advisers, they must be administered a tremendous shock which would carry convincing proof of our power to destroy the Empire. Such an effective shock would save many time the number of lives, both American and Japanese, that it would cost...Our enemy, Japan, commanded forces of somewhat over 5,000,000 armed men. Men of these armies had already inflicted upon us...over 300,000 battle casualties...had the strength to cost us

a million more...Additional large losses might be expected among our allies and...enemy casualties would be much larger than our own...My chief purpose was to end the war in victory with the least possible cost in lives...The face of war is the face of death; death is an inevitable part of every order that a wartime leader gives. The decision to use the atomic bomb was a decision that brought death to over a hundred thousand Japanese...But this deliberate, premeditated destruction was our least abhorrent choice.[4]

Truman decided to order the use of the bomb, and two Japanese cities were attacked, Hiroshima on August 6, and Nagasaki on August 9. The exact number of casualties caused by these bombings is difficult to calculate, but most estimates suggest that around 120,000 people, mostly civilians, were killed immediately by the two bombs, with as many more dying from injuries and radiation sickness in the weeks and months that followed. Unconditional Japanese surrender followed a few days later.

One reason that Stimson's discussion about the decision to use the Atomic Bomb on Japan is interesting is because he talks not only about the bombing saving American lives but also, somewhat obliquely, about it saving Japanese lives as well. While this might be seen to simply be justification after the fact, the idea of achieving the greatest good for the greatest number of people does come through very clearly. Of course, the conclusion that Stimson reached is debatable and many ethicists, particularly those who are not utilitarians, might argue that it was wrong for the United States to use nuclear weapons on Japan, particularly in an attack that deliberately targeted noncombatants, as the attacks on Hiroshima and Nagasaki did. It is also interesting to note that even if the sorts of casualty figures that Stimson quotes are accurate, thus leading to the conclusion that these bombings did actually save a lots of lives that would otherwise have been lost, some utilitarians might still think it was wrong to use the bomb, as there are other longer term consequences that could also be factored into the decision. For example, would the world have been a better place if nuclear weapons have never been used? Whether or not one actually agrees with this particular decision, one thing that Stimson alludes to here is clearly true; that sometimes ethical decisions are about finding the least abhorrent option among bad choices.

Criticizing Consequentialism

Classical utilitarianism has been criticized in a number of ways. One early criticism was that utilitarianism reduces humans to the level of animals, as mere seekers of basic gratification, a criticism which had some bite in the late eighteenth century. However this criticism is seen as much less important today when it is recognized that we are in fact animals. Another good response to this criticism is that for most people the greatest pleasure tends to come from lasting things, like family relationships, rather than simply from passing pleasures like sex and drugs and rock & roll.

A second objection to utilitarianism proceeds by means of a thought experiment. It argues that if maximizing pleasure and minimizing pain is all that matters, if it were to become possible to connect a person to a "virtual experience machine," which maximized pleasure and minimized pain, then a utilitarian ought to hook themselves up to such a machine and stay connected for the rest of their life, even though they would be achieving nothing.[5] Since most people would hate the idea of being connected to such a machine for the rest of their lives, then there must be something wrong with classical utilitarianism. The response to this counterexample was to develop a slightly more sophisticated version of the theory, known as preference utilitarianism, which suggests that maximizing utility means maximizing the preferences of moral agents rather than merely seeking to maximize pleasure and minimize pain. This is now the most widely accepted form of utilitarianism. Since preferences will generally be maximized by respecting people's autonomy, that is, by allowing people to do what they want to do as long as this does not overly affect others, autonomy is seen as an important value by most preference utilitarians.

Another problematic objection to utilitarianism is the difficulty of actually knowing what the consequences of an action will be. One answer to this objection is the fact that for many actions the consequences are reasonably obvious. But this objection has led some modern utilitarians to develop a slightly different version of the theory, known as rule utilitarianism, which argues that a person ought to act in accordance with rules that are likely to bring about the best overall consequences; such a position is somewhat different from the more traditional view, now known as act utilitarianism, which demands that people assess the consequences of each individual action. The move to rule utilitarianism solves what might be termed the "calculation problem," in that a rule utilitarian no longer has to try to calculate what the consequences of every single action will be. But this move comes at a cost, since although the rules that will be followed will generally bring about the best consequences, a rule utilitarian must accept that following such rules will mean, in at least some cases, that the overall consequences will not be maximized.

The modifications provided by rule utilitarianism and preference utilitarianism go some way to defending the theory against another major objection, which is the claim that a theory of ethics that demands that we always act to achieve the best consequences requires too much of ordinary people, since it would require people to be totally selfless in many, if not most, situations. A utilitarian cannot, for example, prioritize the needs of themselves or their friends and family over the needs of complete strangers, which is an idea that many people find extremely hard to accept. Thus, these sorts of objections have led many theorists to seek a somewhat less restricted theory of ethics.

ETHICAL THEORY—PRINCIPLES AND DUTIES

Ethical theories based on a set of universal principles or duties are, at least to some extent, not as demanding as consequentialist theories since they do not require a person to always act in a manner that achieves the best possible outcome. Under a theory of this sort, whereas some acts are impermissible, and some acts are obligatory, many acts are permissible, and a person following such a theory will usually be able to act in a number of ways while still acting in an ethically appropriate manner. However, since ethical theories of this type see some acts as obligatory and some as impermissible in all circumstances, it can be argued that in at least some circumstances they are more demanding than consequentialist theories since they do not permit exceptions even in extreme cases.

There are a variety of different types of principle or duty based ethical theories, but the most important are probably natural law theories, social contract theories, and Kantian theories of ethics. These sorts of theories are collectively known as deontological theories (from the Greek *deon*, meaning "duty"). One big advantage of deontological theories is that they are often expressed in the form of prohibitions, and thus are relatively simple to understand.

Natural law theories represent the earliest type of articulated ethical theory; such theories argue that certain moral "laws" are intrinsic to the world or to human nature. Many versions of natural law have a religious basis, suggesting that the natural laws were put in place (and sometimes revealed to human beings) by a higher power.[6] The U.S. Declaration of Independence actually articulates human rights, which are based on natural law theory, as is evident in the famous quotation: "We hold these truths to be self-evident, that all men are created equal, that they are endowed by their Creator with certain unalienable rights, that among these are life, liberty, and the pursuit of happiness."

Social contract theories suggest that human behavior must comply with the demands of a hypothetical "contract" to allow people to regulate their social contact and interaction. This type of theory was made famous by Thomas Hobbes, who argued that the rights of humans flow out of the constraints necessary for mutually beneficial cooperation.[7] John Rawls used a type of social contract theory to argue for the existence of human rights.[8] His argument is that the social contract must be negotiated from a position of equality, which he called the "Original Position." Rawls claimed that people who had to decide what moral laws they would live under while negotiating from behind "a veil of ignorance," which prevented them from knowing what sort of position they would occupy in society, would inevitably agree on a social contract that included respect for human rights.

The most widespread and well-known deontological theory is derived from the work of Immanuel Kant, who claimed that morality begins with the rejection of nonuniversalizable principles, a concept which Kant called "The Categorical Imperative."[9] Kant presented the categorical imperative in three forms, which he felt were equivalent to each other, though at least some Kantian scholars disagree with him on this point. Kant's three forms were the following: (1) Act as if the maxim of your action were to become by your will a universal law of nature;[10] (2) Act that you use humanity, whether in your own person or in the person of any other, always at the same time as an end, never merely as a means,[11] and (3) Act as though you were through your maxims a law-making member of a kingdom of ends.[12]

In simple terms Kant's first and third formulations of the categorical imperative suggest that before acting a person should ask themselves the question "Would it be possible for everybody to do this?" If the answer is no, then acting in that way is ethically wrong. While this may sound quite simplistic, in fact it is not, since what Kant suggested people ought to be considering before they acted was not whether the consequences of everyone acting in this manner would be good or bad, but rather whether everyone could actually act in such a manner without this leading to a logical contradiction. One example that Kant actually discusses is a case where a man borrows money from another man without ever intending to pay the money back. Kant says that this would be wrong, not because it would produce bad consequences if people were to borrow money without ever intending to pay it back, but because universalizing such a practice would lead to a logical contradiction; no one would ever lend money to others if they knew it would never be paid back, which would mean that the entire process of borrowing and lending money would cease to exist and our hypothetical man who wants to borrow money without ever intending to pay it back would therefore have no one to borrow money from. This particular example is part of a larger discussion within Kant's writing about lying. Kant believed that lying was always wrong, since if everyone was to lie then the entire process of communication would break down, as no one would ever be able to believe what they were being told. When criticized on this point, Kant was willing to "bite the bullet," and said that it would be wrong to lie even if you were approached by a known murderer who asked if you knew where he could find his next victim. Kant did not think that there was a moral duty to actually answer the murderer's question, it would be acceptable to say nothing at all in response, but Kant did say that even under those circumstances it would be wrong to tell a lie.[13] Some modern Kantian scholars don't agree with Kant on this point, and they tend to take greater account of the circumstances under which lying occurs to determine if lying in that particular type of situation is something that could be universalized.

Kant's second version of the categorical imperative demands that people act with respect for other people, which means not simply using those people without the possibility of their consent. This does not mean that it is always impermissible to use other people as a means to achieving things; merely that it is not permissible to do so without the possibility of their consent. So if, for example, Bob borrows some money from his rich Uncle Ed to buy a car, Bob is using Ed as a means to get what he wants, which in this case is a car. However, by borrowing the money and repaying it later (possibly with interest added) he is also respecting

Ed as an end in himself, since Ed has a choice about whether he will lend the money or not. This is very different from Bob stealing the money from Ed to buy the car, since that would use Ed merely as a means without respecting him as an end as well. Stealing the money from Ed would obviously also breach the other formulations of the categorical imperative as well, as the idea of theft cannot be universalized without resulting in a contradiction; if it would be acceptable for every person to take the property of any other person without asking, then the very idea of ownership of property would collapse.

The following case is an interesting example of how such deontological principles can operate in a military context.

CASE STUDY 2.4

Shooting the Downed Pilot

A World War II fighter pilot told the following story:

> Three ME-109s came at us from out of the sun. It was one hell of a dogfight. Jimmy Craig was hit and bailed out. He was up there in his chute, settling down easy, when this Kraut pulls away and takes dead aim at Jimmy. I couldn't believe it. You never shoot a guy hanging in a chute. But that's what he did. He cut him in half. I swung round on that bastard's tail and picked at him until he bailed out. His chute opened. I watched him floating there just like Jimmy. I wanted to see his eyes. But he had goggles on. Then I shot that son of a bitch out of the sky."
> "How'd it feel?"
> "It felt good."
> "Really?...Well, you were there."
> "No...Okay...I cried."

SOURCE: As told to Dr. Peter French and reproduced in Shannon E. French, *The Code of the Warrior* (Lanham, MD: Rowman and Littlefield, 2003 p. 241.)

While some people may claim that "all is fair in love and war," most cultures have in fact placed various formal or informal restrictions on the conduct of those who fight in wars. One of the modern restrictions on warfare is mentioned in this case; that you don't shoot a pilot who is floating helplessly to earth by parachute. While this idea was not formally incorporated into international law until after the end of World War II, it was a principle which was widely accepted during that war. The pilot telling this story clearly knows this, and is shocked and angered when the German pilot shoots Jimmy Craig after Jimmy had bailed out of his plane. The Allied pilot responded to the German's actions by breaching the principle himself, but his confession at the end of the case reveals that he knew that what he had done was wrong. This highlights another important point about deontology; that deontological principles are absolute, and thus they have to be followed even if there are costs in doing so, and even if the enemy does not abide by those same principles. Killing a person who is helpless, is no longer a threat, and is unable to defend themselves in any way, is clearly not something that can be universalized, thus it clearly violates Kant's categorical imperative. It also violates an important principle of essentially every other deontological system.

The pilot in this story wanted revenge; to kill the man who had machine-gunned Jimmy Craig while he was helpless and unable to protect himself. But after the German pilot had bailed out of his plane, the only way to take revenge was to violate the same deontological principle that the German had already violated. I would argue that what the pilot in this story faced was a test of integrity. The principle at stake here was not one that permitted exceptions to the rule, for as the pilot himself said the idea was that "you **never** shoot a guy hanging in a chute," not that "you don't shoot a guy hanging in a chute **unless** he has done something wrong." The pilot knew he was doing the wrong thing but the cost of doing the right thing, of obeying the principle that you don't shoot a guy hanging in a chute, was that the German would get away with what he had done. So the pilot did what he knew was wrong and shot the helpless German pilot. However, it does appear that he realized after the event that doing the wrong things has costs as well, for he obviously still felt guilty about what he had done more than 40 years after the event. As Shannon French points out in her book, while warriors train to take lives, they also learn to "take only certain lives in certain ways, at certain times, and for certain reasons,"[14] and perhaps it is by examining who they do **not** kill that we can most easily distinguish the warrior from the murderer.

Criticizing Deontology

There are various problems with deontological theories, some more specific to particular versions of deontology. The most obvious problem for any theory based on a series of rules is the issue of what ought to happen when those rules come into conflict. Are some rules always more important than others, with one rule being the most important and thus never able to be broken? Or is it the case that the rules all have basically equal strength and the particular rule that ought to be followed if the rules come into conflict will vary depending on the situation? Kant apparently thought that principles derived from the categorical imperative could never come into conflict, but few people would agree with him.

Another problem with deontological theories is that they seem to produce counterintuitive results in some situations; straightforward Kantian ethics, for example, would demand that you not throw the switch to divert the runaway railway car in Case 2.1 since this would involve acting in a manner that would directly bring about a person's death, which Kant believed was not in accord with the categorical imperative.

This sort of counterintuitive result is certainly not unique to Kantian ethics since some other types of deontological theory, particularly some types of natural law theory, also seem to come up with the same result in such a case. These sorts of counterintuitive problems have long been recognized in deontological theory, and the attempt to deal with these sorts of issues has resulted in an idea known as the doctrine (or principle) of double effect (DDE), first formulated by Thomas Aquinas in the mid-thirteenth century.[15] This doctrine has become so important in military ethics, particularly with regard to things like the permissibility of collateral damage, that it has been incorporated into various international laws that govern armed conflict. Thus it is worth taking some time to examine when the DDE does and does not apply.

The Doctrine of Double Effect

The fundamental claim of the DDE is that there is a moral difference between those things that a person intends to bring about when acting and those things that a person foresees will happen as a consequence of their actions, but does not intend to happen. Although it was originally formulated in fairly general terms, the DDE has been refined over the years and now it is understood that for an act to be justified under the DDE it must meet four specific conditions, all at the same time.[16]

1. The action taken must be morally good or morally indifferent (i.e., the action taken can't be something that is ruled out by the particular version of deontological theory in question);[17]
2. The intention of the agent must be to bring about the good effect and not the bad one. If the agent could attain the good effect without the bad effect, then that is what is required;
3. The good effect must be produced directly by the action, not by the bad effect (i.e., it is not permitted to use a bad means to achieve a good end);
4. The good effect must be sufficiently desirable to compensate for the allowing of the bad effect (i.e., the good that is achieved must be proportional to the bad that is allowed).

Thus the DDE would allow a deontologist to throw the switch in Case 2.1 (The Runaway Railway Car), since this action meets all four conditions: (1) the act of throwing the switch does not in itself violate any of the rules of the theory; (2) the intention in throwing the switch is to save the lives of the five workers who will otherwise be killed by the runaway railway car, while the death of the other worker is foreseen but not intended, and the only way to save the five workers is to throw the switch; (3) the lives of these workers will be directly saved by turning the runaway railway car; and (4) saving five lives is a good enough effect to compensate for the one death, which will be allowed to occur. On the other hand, stopping the runaway railway car by pushing a bystander under its wheels would not be allowed under the DDE, since this would violate Condition 3, in that it uses a bad means to achieve a good end. In really short and simple terms, the DDE may be applied where a person can see that their actions will bring about both good and bad effects if, and only if, the action taken is itself morally permissible, is undertaken with good intentions, achieves the good directly, and is proportionate to the bad that can be foreseen will also occur.

Some deontologists, including Aquinas, refer to the same principle as a means of justifying killing in self-defense; the intention is for you to protect yourself, though you foresee that this will result in the death of your attacker.[18] One possible problem with the DDE is that it relies, through its proportionality condition, on an assessment of the consequences of the action. This is somewhat problematic since deontological theory is supposed to be solely concerned with principles and duties, and not with consequences. Nonetheless, the DDE is hugely important in military ethics, as shall be seen in some of the discussions in later chapters.

Despite the problems with deontological theories, the lesser demands that they place on people in comparison to consequentialist theories[19] as well as the ease of understanding deontological theories makes them very popular. In fact deontological theories are the only form of ethical theory that can be said to be the subject of something approaching universal agreement. All deontological theories can be expressed in terms of rights; either negative rights (a right not to have something done to you; e.g., the right not to be tortured) or positive rights (a claim to something; e.g., a right to freedom of opinion and expression). An appeal to rights is now widely understood and accepted within most world cultures, especially since the adoption of the Universal Declaration of Human Rights by the General Assembly of the United Nations in 1948. This declaration has since been affirmed, in one form or another, by almost every nation on the planet, thus it can be claimed that rights are the moral currency of our time. The biggest problem with theories of rights, as with all deontological theories, is the issue of knowing what to do when rights come into conflict with each other. Sometimes it is justified to infringe on people's rights, but the question of when it is justified is often difficult to answer.

One suggestion is the idea that people may forfeit certain rights as a result of the actions they have taken. Thus, if someone commits a crime and is later arrested and imprisoned for that crime, then this appears to violate their right to liberty, but one way of understanding why this might be justified is to say that by their actions in committing that crime this person has forfeited their right to liberty and thus imprisoning them does not actually violate their rights.[20] This idea of forfeiture of rights will be discussed in Chapter 7 in the context of arguments about why all enemy combatants, regardless of location, might be legitimate targets in warfare.

Another common answer to the question of when it is justified to infringe on other people's rights revolves around the intentions of the person who is infringing on the right. The problem with such an answer is that deontological theories are supposed to be about principles or duties, not about intentions. This has led some ethicists to suggest another sort of theory, which has come to be known as virtue ethics, which is based on the character of the moral agent and thus takes account of intentions while still considering other factors like consequences, principles, and duties.

ETHICAL THEORY—CHARACTER

Virtue Ethics focuses on the character of the moral agent. For a virtue theorist the intention of the moral agent will be important, but consequences, principles, and duties may also be important depending on the situation. According to virtue ethics theories an action is right if, and only if, it is what a moral agent with a virtuous character would do in the circumstances.

Virtue ethics has a long history; it was prominent in ancient Greece, particularly in the writings of Aristotle. Though it came to be supplanted by natural law theories, especially after the rise of Christianity, it was revived in the latter part of the twentieth century. Given its basis in the writings of Aristotle, virtue ethics is often referred to as Neo-Aristotelianism.

Aristotle believed all things in the universe had a particular function, and living things in particular had potential, which must be developed for that living thing to fulfill its function in the universe. He believed that humans were unique in having the ability to reason, and it is this faculty that had to be developed to allow humans to fulfill their function. Aristotle believed that the ultimate good for human beings was *eudaimonia*, which is commonly translated into English as "happiness," or more commonly in recent years as "flourishing," and means living a fulfilling, satisfying life.[21] Aristotle believed a person needed to develop certain virtues of character, necessary to achieve *eudaimonia*. These virtues included courage, self-restraint, justice, temperance, honesty, benevolence, love of knowledge, generosity, and so forth. Most important Aristotle thought it was necessary to develop *phronesis*—practical wisdom and the capacity for reasoning and wrestling with problems—which guided one as to when the particular virtues were appropriately displayed.[22] Aristotle also suggested that for at least some character traits, the ideal was not to possess that particular trait in absolute abundance, but rather to possess it at an appropriate level: not too little, not too much. This idea is sometimes referred to as "The Golden Mean."[23] Consider courage, for example. Too little courage is cowardice, which of course the Greeks recognized as a bad thing. But Aristotle pointed out that too much courage leads to recklessness, which is also a bad thing. In the same way, lack of honesty is a vice, but being too honest is also a vice, for this can shade into callousness. To be virtuous required the character trait to be displayed at the appropriate level between these two extremes.

Modern Virtue Theory universalizes virtue as the basis of the theory and argues that all moral agents should seek to develop a virtuous character. Right action is based on what a person with a virtuous character would do in those circumstances. Virtue theorists argue that the correct answers to moral problems can only be obtained through understanding of the virtues. Consequences and principles are tools that aid the moral agent but can never reveal the whole picture.

There are a number of obvious benefits of virtue theory. It has intuitive appeal to many people, for it is very flexible and is more obviously adaptable to different situations than other ethical theories. It also includes reference to the values of other theories like consequences and principles, which adds to its intuitive appeal. Virtue theory also seems better able to accommodate "agent-centered" values like friendship, which consequentialism and deontology often struggle with. Virtue theory can also be easily generalized through appeal to an "Ideal Agent" or an actual moral exemplar. So a virtue theorist who is unsure of the right thing to do in a particular situation can ask themselves something like "WWJD—what would Jesus do?" or "WWAD—what would Aristotle do?" or even "WWGWD—what would George Washington do?" to help to solve the ethical dilemma that they face. This idea of an ideal agent makes the theory relatively easy to apply in some military situations as well.

CASE STUDY 2.5

Marines Don't Do That

While Lieutenant (LT) Parks wasn't entirely convinced about the justification for the Vietnam War, he did know that as a member of the U.S. Marines he was part of a proud military tradition. It was that tradition, which he had tried hard to instill in all of his men, that he called on when he came across a young Private from his command with his rifle pointed at the head of a Vietnamese woman. This Private had only been in Vietnam for a short period of time, but had already seen several of his buddies killed in combat with the Vietcong, or by booby traps they had set. Parks was now sure these things had pushed the Private right to the edge of reason.

It was clear that this Private was mere moments away from shooting an unarmed civilian, but LT Parks didn't yell at him, didn't remind him of the requirements of the Law of Armed Conflict, or the Uniform Code of Military Justice, or even the orders they had been given before the engagement to protect noncombatants. He simply walked up to the Private and said to him, very clearly, "Marines don't do that." That was enough; the Private shuddered for a moment, then stepped back, and lowered his weapon.

SOURCE: This is an expanded and somewhat fictionalized version of a case mentioned by Mark J. Osiel in *Obeying Orders: Atrocity, Military Discipline and the Law of War* (New Brunswick, NJ: Transaction, 1999), p. 23. Osiel credits the original case to W. Hays Parks, hence the name of the Lieutenant in this story.

One of the reasons why virtue theory is often appealing to members of the military is that it does not simply reduce to a list of rules that must be applied without exception in every situation. To say that "Marines don't do that" is to say a lot more than simply that Marines don't breach the law, in this particular case by killing unarmed civilians. There may be, and in fact probably are, a lot of things that "Marines don't do," which would actually be permitted by international law and by the Uniform Code of Military Justice (UCMJ), as well as a lot of things which "Marines must do," which are not required by either international law or the UCMJ. It is also perfectly possible for there to be some things that "Marines don't do" in one situation but that "Marines must do" in another; one of the advantages of virtue theory is that it takes account of the circumstance of the particular situation in a manner in which deontological theories, in particular, do not. Virtue theory also recognizes that the ideals of one group may not be the same as another; and thus, although some rules might apply to all military personnel, such as the prohibition against killing a helplessly parachuting pilot (Case 2.4), other rules or principles, quite plausibly, do not. So whereas any member of a particular tradition within the military might be able to gain guidance from a phrase that applied to them, like "Marines/Submariners/SAS operators/Fighter Pilots/ SEALS don't do that," the ideals expressed by these phrases are not all the same. Thus although the military roles of U.S. Marines and U.S. regular army soldiers may be similar, "Marines don't do that" does not mean exactly the same thing as "Soldiers don't do that."

There is another, perhaps less obvious reason, why something like virtue theory may be attractive to those who serve in the military. One of the claims of virtue theory is that not only should each person act in a virtuous manner, but also that each person should constantly strive to continue to develop the virtues of character in themselves. When a person is faced with a difficult ethical dilemma it may be just as difficult for a virtue theorist to work out the right thing to do as it is for a consequentialist or a deontologist. However, because a virtue theorist has worked hard to develop virtues of character in themselves, it can plausibly be argued that it should be easier for the virtue theorist to actually **do** the right thing than it would be for a consequentialist or a deontologist, especially in cases where actually doing the right thing is difficult or costly. Or to use the terminology that I presented earlier in this book, virtue theory, unlike consequentialism or deontology, might actually help a person to deal with tests of integrity as well as ethical dilemmas. Therefore, virtue theory might well be attractive for a person who knows that they are likely to face a significant number of tests of integrity and who wants to be prepared for those situations when they arise.

Although many military personnel find it attractive, there are several fairly obvious problems with virtue theory. Virtue theorists can and do disagree about what the virtues of character actually are, and thus they also disagree about the conclusions that come out of the theory. The theory may also not give clear answers to problems, particularly if an agent relies on using a moral exemplar in decision making, since in many cases it may not be obvious what a particular moral exemplar would do. Even in cases where it is obvious what a certain moral exemplar would do, it will often be the case that the actions of different moral exemplars do not agree with each other. So it may be the case, for example, that WWJD ≠ WWAD in much the same way that "Marines don't do that" ≠ "Soldiers don't do that."

IS ETHICS SIMPLY RELATIVE?

There are some clear problems that arise out of this discussion; there is no one theory of ethics that is universally agreed on, and a particular ethical theory may not give definite answers in all situations. It is also clear that some things that we now consider wrong, such as slavery, have been accepted in Western society in the past, and things that were once almost universally condemned in the same society, such as homosexual relations between consenting adults, are now generally considered acceptable. Some things that Western society considers wrong are also accepted within other societies, such as polygamy, restrictions on women, and child labor. These issues have led some people to question whether in the end ethics is simply a matter of opinion.

The theory that claims that moral values are relative to different cultures is known as relativism. It is important not to be confused about what is being discussed here. I am not talking about descriptive (or cultural) relativism, which is a factual claim (often made by anthropologists) that cultural practices can only be understood relative to that particular culture. What I am talking about is ethical (or normative) relativism, which is the claim that all values, including moral values, are only cultural, and that there are no universal values. Ethical relativists claim therefore that one ought to be tolerant of the moral practices of other cultures and not judge them.

There are various aspects of relativism that people often find attractive. Both descriptive and ethical relativism promote tolerance of cultural differences, which helps ease animosity and judgmentalism. But what many people find particularly attractive about ethical relativism is that it resolves the difficulty of finding an overall theory of ethics, for the simple answer is that there is no overall theory of ethics, since everything is relative. This seemingly makes ethics easy, because everything is simply a matter of opinion.

However, there are a number of problems with ethical relativism. Ethical relativism gives an excuse for avoiding hard ethical judgments, since all ethical judgments can simply be claimed to be a matter of opinion. In addition it destroys any concept of moral progress, since we can only progress against an absolute standard, not a relative one, and ethical relativism also prevents any criticism or praise of other cultures, societies, or countries. Ethical relativism also seems to have a number of significant deficiencies from a theoretical standpoint. It appears illogical to move from the observation that there is disagreement about ethical issues to the conclusion that there are no correct answers to ethical questions, especially since this is not an argument that we would accept in other contexts. People used to disagree about whether or not the earth was round, for example, but this does not mean that there was no right answer. Ethical relativism also seems to be based on some false observations, since many apparent ethical differences between cultures actually involve disagreement about facts rather than values; two cultures can have equal respect for their dead even though one culture buries their dead and the other cremates their dead in the local volcano.

The claim that there are only relative standards in ethics across cultures is also false, for many cultural practices can be judged against objective standards. For example, if a culture engages in a particular practice because such a practice develops courage, yet when examined the practice turns out to not promote courage but rather to promote lying and deception, then that practice can be condemned since it does not promote the values it is intended to promote. This is judging the practice against an objective standard, not a relative one. Another problem with ethical relativism is that it seems incoherent on its own standards; one cannot suggest that there are no universal moral values and then advocate universal tolerance, for tolerance is itself a moral value. A particular problem for the relativist in this regard would be a culture that actually regards intolerance as a moral virtue; it is extremely difficult to see how such a culture could be incorporated into the overall theory of relativism.

In the end, for most people the biggest problem with relativism is that a relativist cannot condemn **anything**, not genocide, slavery, pedophilia, torture, or any sick, twisted, depraved practice you might care to name, for everything is relative. This is a position that in the end very few people are prepared to accept.

INTEGRATING THEORIES OF ETHICS

Having spent some time discussing the ways in which the main theories of ethics differ, it is time to draw things back together again and to explain how these differences might be dealt with in a coherent manner. The first thing to note, which I have mentioned before, is that for the vast majority of situations all ethical theories agree about what is the right and the wrong thing to do. This should not be surprising since a good ethical theory needs to agree with "known" results, and there is actually significant agreement over the right thing to do in a majority of cases, despite the fact that this is often obscured by the way that most courses on ethical theory focus on the differences between the theories, and on the hard cases where the theories tend to produce different results from each other. A second point to note is the fact that although there is significant disagreement between theories about why particular values are important, the most defensible modern versions of all of the main ethical theories in fact share many common values, such as respect for individuals and their rights. A preference utilitarian might believe rights are important since they are derived from autonomy, a deontologist might believe they are important since they can be universalized, a virtue theorist might argue they are important because they are something a virtuous person would respect and that a rights-respecting community is essential to human flourishing; but in the end this is a point on which modern versions of all the major theories agree.

Whereas various theories might disagree about why it is important, all the major theories of ethics agree that people in democratic societies ought to obey the law, at least in the vast majority of cases.[24] This is not surprising, since, as has already been mentioned, the criminal law enforces values that are considered especially important. It is noteworthy in this respect that the criminal law actually takes into account all the moral considerations we have discussed. The law considers consequences; a clear example of this is the fact that in every major jurisdiction driving under the influence of alcohol is considered a much more serious offense when it leads to injury to others. The criminal law upholds some things as a matter of principle; invading someone's privacy is wrong, whether they know about it or not. The law also considers intentions to be important; the intentions of the guilty party are the difference between murder and manslaughter.

Military personnel are subject to various laws, both domestic and international, as well as the standards of the profession of arms, to which they belong. These laws and professional standards impose certain overriding duties on military personnel, as well as requiring them to take account of consequences, principles, and intentions when making ethical decisions. In most circumstances rather than relying on general theories of ethics, it is these laws, the most important of which is International Humanitarian Law, along with professional military standards, which guide the ethical decision making of military personnel. Since these laws and professional standards are so important in guiding the ethical decisions of military personnel, it is necessary to examine them in some detail. This is the topic of the next chapter of this book.

NOTES

1. See Daniel Dennett, *Elbow Room: The Varieties of Free Will Worth Wanting* (Cambridge, MA: MIT Press, 1984), p. 12.
2. I have always presented that runaway railway car case first, so there is undoubtedly some bias in the responses given to the surgeon case from people who want their answers to be consistent; I suspect that if I presented the surgeon case first that there would hardly be anyone who thought it was the right thing to do to kill the homeless man to harvest his organs.

3. Jeremy Bentham, *An Introduction to the Principles of Morals and Legislation* (Oxford: Clarendon, 1907). The book was first published in 1789, and reprinted with corrections by the author in 1823. The 1907 edition is a reprint of the 1823 version. Chapter 1 of the book discusses the principle of utility.

4. "The Decision to Use the Atomic Bomb," *Harper's Magazine* 194, no. 1161 (February 1947), pp. 101, 102, 106, 107. It should be noted that Stimson's projected casualty figures for an invasion of Japan have been disputed. For a relatively recent discussion of this and other issues see J. Samuel Walker, "Recent Literature on Truman's Atomic Bomb Decision: A Search for Middle Ground," *Diplomatic History* 29(2005), 311–334.

5. A machine of this sort is at the heart of the Matrix films (*The Matrix, The Matrix Reloaded,* and *The Matrix Revolutions,* written and directed by the Wachowski Brothers), but the objection was proposed a long time before those movies were made.

6. Divine Command theory, which suggests that the right thing to do is what God commands, can be considered a type of natural law theory, though some scholars would put it into a class of its own.

7. See Thomas Hobbes, *Leviathan* (Oxford: Oxford University Press, 1965), originally published in 1651.

8. See John Rawls, *A Theory of Justice* (New York: Oxford University Press, 1971).

9. See Immanuel Kant, *Foundations of the Metaphysics of Morals* (New York: MacMillan, 1990), originally published in 1785.

10. Ibid., p. 38.

11. Ibid., p. 46.

12. Ibid., p. 54.

13. This problem is discussed in Kant's essay, "On a Supposed Right to Tell Lies from Benevolent Motives," first published in 1797.

14. Shannon E. French, *The Code of the Warrior* (Lanham, MD: Rowman and Littlefield, 2003), p. 3.

15. *Summa Theologica* (II-II, Qu. 64, Art.7).

16. Based on the formulations given by Joseph Mangan, "An Historical Analysis of the Principle of Double Effect," *Theological Studies* 10(1949), 41–61, p. 43, and by F. J. Connell, "Double Effect, Principle of," *New Catholic Encyclopedia* (New York: McGraw-Hill, 1967) pp. 1020–22, vol. 4.

17. So if the DDE is being applied by a Kantian, the action taken can't be something which in and of itself violates the categorical imperative, if the DDE is being applied by a natural law theorist then the action taken can't be something which in and of itself violates natural law, and so on.

18. This was the problem Aquinas was addressing in his original formulation in *Summa Theologica*.

19. In saying this I simply mean that deontological theories do not insist, in the way that consequentialist theories do, that there is always one, and only one, right thing to do in any set of circumstances. Nor do deontological theories insist, in the way that consequentialist theories do, that agents ignore the special ties of friendship and family

when considering what they ought to do. However, since deontological theories tend to not allow exceptions to the rules, even under special circumstances, these theories can seem extremely demanding in such cases.

20. This idea is discussed by Stephen Kershnar in "*The Structure of Rights Forfeiture in the Context of Culpable Wrongdoing,*" *Philosophia,* 29(2002)57–88.
21. See *The Nichomachean Ethics,* Book I, Chapter 7.
22. *The Nichomachean Ethics,* Book VI, Chapter 5.
23. *The Nichomachean Ethics,* Book II.
24. I have limited this particular claim to democratic societies, since in such societies it can be assumed that the law will have been established through some reasonable consultative process. In non-democratic societies the situation may well be very different, and it may in fact be ethically appropriate for people to break the law in a large range of circumstances. Some cases along these lines will be considered in later chapters.

FURTHER READING

Cahn, Steven M. (ed.). *Exploring Ethics: An Introductory Anthology.* 2nd ed. (New York: Oxford University Press, 2010).

Sterba, James P. *The Triumph of Practice over Theory in Ethics.* (New York: Oxford University Press, 2004).

United Nations. *Universal Declaration of Human Rights.* Adopted and proclaimed by United Nations General Assembly resolution 217 A (III) of December 10, 1948. (http://www.un.org/Overview/rights.html).

Singer, Peter (ed.). *A Companion to Ethics* (Oxford: Blackwell, 1991).

DISCUSSION QUESTIONS

- Is it reasonable to criticize consequentialist theories as being too demanding of ordinary human beings?
- Is it reasonable to criticize deontological theories as being too inflexible to deal with difficult moral problems?
- Is it reasonable to claim that virtue-based theories do not give exact answers to moral problems?

3

✦◯

Professional Ethics, Duties, and Obligations

┌─────────────── CASE STUDY 3.1 ═══════════════┐

The HMAS *Westralia* Fire

BACKGROUND This case discusses a fire that broke out onboard HMAS *Westralia* on May 5, 1998. This narrative of the events on board was compiled from the public version of the report of the Department of Defence Board of Enquiry into the fire[1] and from the report of the findings of the Western Australian Coronial Inquest into the deaths of the four crew members who were killed.[2]

HMAS *Westralia* departed Fleet Base West at 0900 on Tuesday May 5, 1998. The ship was scheduled to transfer some of its approximately 20,000 tons of diesel fuel cargo to HMAS *Success* and then to proceed to northern waters. At approximately 1030, during a routine roving check of the Main Machinery Space (MMS), Petty Officer (PO) Hollis discovered a serious fuel leak coming from the port main engine, spraying onto the catwalk between the main engines, into the bilge, and flowing under the starboard main engine. PO Hollis immediately reported the leak to the Engineer, Lieutenant Commander (LCDR) Crouch, who relayed the report to the bridge; in response both engines were stopped, some 30 seconds after the leak was first reported. The ship was sent to "emergency stations," and the Sea Standing Fire Brigade (SSFB) were ordered to report for action as a precaution.

A few minutes later, fire erupted from the top of the starboard main engine, apparently from another, as yet undetected, fuel leak. Lieutenant (LT) Walters, who observed the outbreak of the fire, gave evidence that the flame resembled a blowtorch, with a flame approximately 6 meters (20 feet) high. Eight members of the crew were in the MMS at this time, all either on the middle or lower catwalks: three laying out fire hoses or extinguishers as a precaution; four, including LT Walters, dealing with various aspects of the repair of the fuel leak from the port main engine; and one, a midshipman attached to the engineering staff for training, apparently observing the repairs.

The fire had several immediate effects. Various electrical cables directly above the main engines were quickly burnt in the fire, severing power supplies for machinery, communications to the bridge, and the MMS evacuation siren. Smoke and toxic gases being given off by the burning insulation covering the cables added to the quantity of gases being generated in the MMS.

LT Walters immediately raced to the Machinery Control Room (MCR) and reported the fire. Some of the personnel in the MMS attempted to fight the fire using handheld and trolley mounted foam extinguishers, but their efforts had little to no effect. Visibility in the MMS rapidly dropped to zero, since the entire area was filling with thick black smoke. At this point, since the starboard ladder was engulfed in flames, there was only one means of escape from the MMS; up the port ladder to the MCR. Some personnel did indeed escape this way, but this escape was rendered extremely hazardous by the heat and smoke, and by occasional fireballs that washed over the port ladder, apparently drawn upward by the draft of air up the funnel immediately overhead. Knowing that there were still personnel unaccounted for and believed to be trapped in the MMS, the team leader of the SSFB asked LCDR Crouch for permission to send two members of the SSFB (who were equipped with breathing apparatus, anti-flash gloves, and hood, but not full fire-protection suits) into the MMS to search for missing personnel, but permission was refused. Within minutes it became necessary to order the evacuation of the MCR due to the buildup of smoke. At this point it was still uncertain how many personnel were unaccounted for.

After evacuating the MCR, LCDR Crouch telephoned the bridge and spoke with the Commanding Officer (CO), recommending an immediate CO_2 drench, which would flood the MMS with carbon dioxide gas, thus cutting off the oxygen supply that the fire needed to continue to burn. The CO declined to activate the CO_2 drench at this point and directed that a hose team be sent into the MMS to search for missing personnel. When giving evidence to the Board of Inquiry, the Engineer explained:

> Now, I …said to the commanding officer, recommended the CO_2 drench, I knew what his answer was going to be because that's the answer that I would have given me if I was the CO and someone had rung me up and (said) that to (me), "No, go in and search for them," but that's the advice I had to offer him because that's what I felt at the time. I didn't believe I had the time or that the commanding officer would be prepared to spare the time to listen to me explain …the reasoning behind my wanting to CO_2 drench and I can't reiterate enough that I honestly believed the commanding officer's decision was correct in saying, "Do not CO_2 drench. Search."[3]

Having determined that four people were unaccounted for, LCDR Crouch advised the aft Damage Control team to prepare a team in full firefighting gear to enter the MMS as soon as possible. Ten minutes later Hose Team 1 entered the MMS, and reporting finding nothing, with visibility zero and temperatures extremely high. The CO left the bridge and went to the main Damage Control station to discuss the status of the fire with LCDR Crouch. There was still a major concern over the missing personnel, but also a realization that the personnel in the MMS were unlikely to be alive. Command priority thus shifted to saving the ship. The CO ordered the hose team to continue searching the MMS for a further 5 minutes and then to activate the CO_2 drench.

Firefighting teams reentered the MMS some 25 minutes after the activation of the CO_2 drench and reported intense heat and zero visibility in the dense smoke. Firefighting efforts were directed by the use of thermal imaging scanners, which allowed the hoses to be directed at all hot spots. During these efforts, the firefighting teams discovered the bodies of Leading Seaman Bradley Meek, Petty Officer Shaun Smith, Able Seaman Phillip Carroll, and Midshipman Megan Pelly. One hour after teams reentered the MMS, and almost exactly 2 hours after the first fuel leak had been reported, the CO was informed that the fire had been extinguished.

DISCUSSION

Those who serve their country as members of the defense forces perform a role that is essentially unique in society. Consider, for example, the following differences between those who are serving in the armed forces of their country and those who work in civilian employment within that country. Those in military service are required to do things that few, if any, other members of society are expected or even able to do. Those who serve in the military do so knowing that they may be killed while doing their duty. In some special circumstances a member of the defense forces could be routinely and lawfully ordered by their superiors to act in a manner that places their life at risk, another demand placed on few members of the civilian community; only those in the emergency services face anything like this situation. Members of the military are subject to laws and restrictions that are not imposed on other members of society. Members of the military are also called on to act in ways which would, under other circumstances, be considered to be seriously ethically wrong, in that they may be required to kill other people and/or engage in acts that cause widespread destruction of property to further the interests of the state. What this means, in the end, is that it is impossible to discuss how members of the military ought to act in particular situations without first understanding the specific ethical and legal requirements of the military role.

Therefore, in this chapter I will discuss the nature of professions in general, and of the profession of arms in particular, to better understand the demands this places on the ethical decisions of those in the military. Since the actions of military personnel will also be constrained by international law in many situations and this will often have a significant and direct impact on their decision making, particularly with regard to their conduct in combat operations, the nature and origin of international law will also be discussed at times in this and subsequent chapters.

THE PROFESSION OF ARMS

The terms "professional" and "profession" are used so often these days that few people are clear about their true meanings. The word "professional" is now used in quite a number of contexts. Sometimes it is used to simply refer to someone who is being paid for their work, as is the case when we talk about a professional sports person. Sometimes the term is used to recognize someone who is particularly good at their job; if I was to suggest that a carpenter did "a really professional job," then I would be using the term in this manner. But the base meaning of the term "professional" is simply to indicate that the person being referred to is a recognized member of a particular profession. So what is a profession? There is some dispute about the term, but most attempts to define a profession incorporate a number of common features in that they suggest that the members of a particular profession must (a) provide an important public service; (b) possess special knowledge and/or expertise; (c) exercise autonomous professional discretion in their practice; and (d) be governed by a body made up of members of that profession and subject to a specific code of conduct—in other words the members of the profession govern and regulate themselves (at least to a large extent) according to standards not required of those not within the profession.[4] The traditional professions were divinity, medicine, law, and (possibly) the profession of arms. It could be argued that professions were originally defined simply by virtue of being respectable occupations for the sons of gentlemen, but all of the traditional professions do seem to capture the features just mentioned, a fact which separates the traditional professions from other occupations of the time. Members of the professions have traditionally enjoyed high social standing and were often seen as leaders among their communities, possibly because early professionals were in fact often the younger sons of lesser nobility. It is probably this fact that has led to the use of the term "professional" as a term of praise, as in my earlier example of the carpenter who does a professional job, and has also led to many other varieties of employment seeking to be formally endowed with the status of a profession. It is true, however, that the range of modern occupations that can legitimately be termed professions is quite broad, since a modern list of professions is likely to include things such as dentistry, veterinary science, accountancy, engineering, architecture, optometry, physical therapy, and so on, alongside the traditional professions.

Members of professions are often granted special rights or privileges as a result of their professional status. Members of certain medical professions, for example, have the right to prescribe medications, a right not given to ordinary members of the community. However, along with these special rights come moral obligations beyond those held by ordinary members of the public. For example, a medical doctor has historically been considered to have a moral obligation to assist those in medical need wherever and whenever such encounters occur, although modern litigation has tended to modify this in a number of jurisdictions.

While it might be suggested that the profession of arms no longer exists in modern times, I think that at least some members of the defense forces do qualify as members of a profession; this would include at least those who are members of the officer corps as well as senior noncommissioned officers.[5] The public service that members of the military perform is obvious, in that they protect the whole of society from external threats. In addition it is obvious that this service to society is not simply self-serving, as members of the military often serve society at detriment to their own self-interest. Since one of the hallmarks of a traditional profession is the requirement that the needs of those served come above the needs of the professional, the selfless service of military members certainly suggests that military service is a professional service, provided that other requirements for professionalism can be met.

Military officers clearly possess special knowledge and expertise, which in many cases is expertise that is not available to those outside the military and can only legitimately be practiced within the bounds of the military profession. Most significantly in terms of the professional status of military officers, the special knowledge they are required to possess and apply is not simply applied in a routine fashion; they exercise professional discretion in their practice. It is perhaps this factor that separates what is expected of officers from what is expected of the enlisted personnel that they lead, in much the same way that it separates architects, who are usually considered to be members of a profession, from draftsmen, who are not. However, I am inclined to think that senior noncommissioned officers are also expected to exercise similar discretion in their military practice and would thus suggest that it is not simply officers who are members of the profession of arms, though one might question exactly how far down the command structure such membership extends.

The governance of the profession of arms is obviously rather different from the governance of the other traditional professions, in that the government has direct control over the military in a way that does not occur with other professions. Consider the difference between government control of medicine and government control of the military, for example. Whereas a government might employ a lot of medical personnel in hospitals and regulate the practice of medicine in various ways, members of the various medical professions still have the opportunity to work for other people or even for themselves, and thus may no longer work at the direction of the government. Military personnel do not have this option since a country's military, at least in any true democracy, will always work under the direct control of the civilian government. In years gone by the government was also the only possible legitimate employer for a member of the military profession, but in modern times the rise of private military companies has changed this situation, at least to some extent.

Overall there is justification for claiming that the profession of arms still exists as a profession, and thus I will refer to the duties of military personnel as professional duties; I hope that those who disagree about the professional status of military officers will at least accept my use of the term as useful shorthand. However, whether one accepts the professional status of military personnel or not, it is clear that the role that they play brings with it certain particular, and somewhat unusual, moral duties.

ROLE MORALITY

Certain roles within society, especially professional roles, seem to create unique moral obligations at odds with ordinary morality. Consider, for example, the moral duty of a lawyer who is defending a person that they know is guilty of a serious crime. Ordinary morality would suggest that if you know that a person is guilty of a serious crime then you ought to do all that you legally can to ensure that person is convicted for their crime. Yet despite knowing that this client is guilty the lawyer is obliged to do his or her best to ensure that this client is not convicted; the lawyer's professional duty to ensure the integrity of the criminal justice system requires lawyers in such situations to act in a manner that would be considered wrong by ordinary morality. Lawyers are not alone in facing these sorts of situations. Priests are duty-bound to honor the sanctity of the confessional, even in cases where penitents confess to serious crimes. This priestly duty has long been respected in law, though recent changes in legislation have been made in some jurisdictions that would require priests to reveal details of such confessions in certain situations, such as in child sex abuse or murder cases.

People who occupy specific roles in society may also be required to do things that would be supererogatory (i.e., going beyond the call of duty) for ordinary people in an identical situation. Consider the response to the attacks on the Twin Towers in New York on September 11, 2001, for example. There is a famous photograph showing long lines of people filing down the emergency stairs to get out of the towers in the immediate aftermath of the attacks, which also shows the New York firefighters climbing up those same stairs to get to the fires on the upper floors. These firefighters were required by their role to head into the danger that basically everyone else was heading away from; on that day it cost over three hundred and forty of them their lives.

People who occupy specific roles in society may also find it necessary to develop skills and character traits that would normally be considered vices, rather than virtues. Undercover agents, for example, need to be convincing liars. So for someone in such a position the ability to lie to others would be a virtue, even though an ability such as this would not usually be considered virtuous in normal circumstances. When considering the role military personnel perform, the ability and willingness to harm others in the pursuit of important objectives might well be considered to be a virtue, though under normal circumstances I think most people would consider this to be, at the very least, a significant flaw in a person's character, even if they were not willing to go so far as to call this a vice.[6]

In general terms, people who occupy particular roles may sometimes be morally required to (1) routinely do things that would normally be wrong, (2) do things that would be supererogatory for ordinary people in an identical situation, and (3) do things in specific situations that would be wrong for ordinary people in an identical situation.

The duties of military personnel flow out of the oath(s) of office military personnel take, and out of the mission of such state military forces. Modern military oaths obviously vary from one country to another. In the United States, all military personnel swear an oath to uphold and defend the Constitution; in the United Kingdom and in most other Commonwealth countries, military personnel swear an oath to be faithful and bear true allegiance to the current monarch (and their heirs and successors); Polish officers swear an oath to bear faithful allegiance to the Republic of Poland; and so on.

Although these oaths may be different, the oaths of all genuine modern democracies seem to share at least one important feature in common. All these various oaths, despite their differing emphases and phrasings, require military personnel to swear their loyalty to the state as a whole, or to some idealized representation of the state such as the Constitution, rather than to the governing body, to a specific individual, or even to a specific elected office.[7] The duties encapsulated by an oath to serve the state as a whole are subtly different than would be captured by an oath to simply serve the needs of the elected government of the day. This is an important distinction, since it means that even though there is civilian control of the military within a democracy, there are some limits to that control, which are actually incorporated into the military oath itself. Thus if the civilian government of the day was to order the military to do something that was clearly at odds with the interests of the state as a whole, then military personnel could legitimately refuse to obey such an order. Consider the U.S. situation as an example here. There might seem to be little difference between (a) swearing an oath to uphold the Constitution, when that Constitution establishes the President as the Commander in Chief of the armed forces; and (b) simply swearing an oath to be faithful to the orders of the President who is the Commander in Chief. In nearly all situations the two oaths would be identical in effect, but in some extreme situations the two oaths could have dramatically different implications. If, for example, a President were to lose an election and then order the military to impose martial law across the country to allow that President to retain power, then the military, having sworn an oath to uphold the Constitution, could quite obviously, and legitimately, refuse such an order since such an order would violate the Constitution they have sworn to uphold. If the military simply swore to obey the orders of the President, on the other hand, they might well **want** to refuse to obey an order to impose martial law, but it is no longer so obvious that they can do this without breaking the oath that they have sworn.[8]

Given that military personnel promise to serve the state, the mission statements of state military forces will obviously also be very important in determining the role morality of military personnel. Most Western democracies have fairly similar mission statements for their military forces, which amount to defending the country, including its people and its national interests. The role morality required of military personnel thus flows out of the oath of service taken by them, out of the general mission of military forces, and out of the command structure of those military forces, which has been established in order to better fulfill the overall mission of the defense forces. Members of the military will have a duty to (1) deal out death and destruction, often not in strict self-defense, in accordance with international law and the legitimate demands of the civilian government that controls the military; (2) follow all legal orders; (3) risk their own life and health in dangerous missions where this is necessary in order to fulfill the overall defense mission, which in some cases might also include a duty to sacrifice friends and/or colleagues in the fulfillment of those missions; (4) deploy when required, again in accordance with international law and the legitimate demands of the civilian government that controls the military; and (5) accept a curtailment of the usual right to free speech, especially with regard to public criticism of the civilian government.

Specific aspects of some of these duties will be explored in later chapters. For example, the legitimate demands of civilian government with regard to making war will be discussed in Chapters 4 and 5, and the duty to follow orders, including discussion of what orders ought to be given, will be specifically discussed in Chapter 6 as well as being examined during discussions of other issues in later chapters. However, at this point it should already be clear that examining issues in military ethics requires consideration of the role morality entailed by military service. This often means that what military personnel are ethically required to do will be different from what is required of others in similar situations.

MILITARY VALUES AND MILITARY VIRTUE

The defense forces of most modern democracies have a statement of values or list of military virtues that is intended to remind members of the military what is considered important and thus how they are expected to behave, both in peacetime and at war. Unfortunately, such lists are often somewhat confused over the distinction between values (the ideals a community cherishes, such as freedom and equality) and virtues (desirable characteristics of individuals, like courage and honesty).[9] As Paul Robinson notes, most such lists are inward looking in that they focus only on the individual member of the military and perhaps on their relationship with other members of the military, and on what is necessary to make those military personnel functionally effective; to ensure they will follow orders and efficiently use deadly force when required. "They seem to ignore the fact that the purpose of military ethics is not solely to produce soldiers who will be efficient, but also to limit the use of force and to protect others from the power that soldiers wield."[10]

Equally problematically, whereas some military services do devote a substantial amount of time to training their members about these values and their meanings, in many cases these lists seem to be presented with little in the manner of explanation. In training establishments and recruitment centers in many countries around the world one can find posters displaying the values of one military service or another, apparently with the assumption that the terms included on such lists will be clearly understood by all those who read them. While this may be true of some virtues, it is certainly not the case with others. Even when examining virtues that appear to be obvious, like courage, for example, most military personnel are likely to think of this virtue in terms of physical courage, say in the face of the enemy, rather than moral courage; doing what you know to be right even when this is unpopular.

Given the wide range of military organizations across the world, and the differing values that they have, it would be foolish of me to attempt to discuss in detail all of the various virtues that seem to be expected of military personnel in all these different countries. However, there are some military virtues that seem to be almost universally accepted: courage, which as I have already mentioned ought to be taken to include moral as well as physical courage; honesty, which in some lists of military values may be subsumed under the headings of credibility, or integrity, or honor; and loyalty, to both the state and to other members of the military. These virtues, being so widely accepted but also, in at least some circumstances, so problematic, deserve closer examination. All three of the major military virtues I have mentioned are important in the following case, though each is important in a different way.

CASE STUDY 3.2

Leave No One Behind

Many military organizations use the code, "Leave no one behind." This phrase creates a deep individual commitment among fighters which will, in turn, strengthen the fighting spirit and morale of a unit. It helps to assure the families of the fighters that their relative will not be left behind/alive or dead, they will be brought home. But this code also places a heavy moral burden on the Commanding Officer. He or she must ask: How many healthy fighters will I risk to bring home one wounded fighter or a body? This becomes one of the most difficult moral decisions of Command; losing an unknown number of lives of your people to uphold the important code, "Leave no one behind." This case is a peace-time scenario, which probably occurs much more frequently than the war-time scenario, and has the exact same moral decision at its core.

He was one of those rare naval aviators who were universally admired. In both social and official situations, he always seemed to ask the right question, and he seemed to find that balance between being friendly and professional at the same time. When he walked into the squadron ready-room people would sit up a little straighter; not because he required it, but because they admired him, and they wanted his respect.

As Commanding Officer of Helicopter Antisubmarine Squadron NINE, (HS-9), CDR James "Fox" Davis knew his men and women, and he understood his mission. The Squadron's many missions included Anti-submarine/Anti-surface operations, Combat Search and Rescue (CSAR), and logistics support for the Carrier Battle Group. Clearly, their everyday embedded mission was Search and Rescue (SAR). As CDR Davis used to say with pride, "On a **good day** we catch a submarine. On a **great day** we save a life." The SAR mission and particularly the CSAR mission were well respected in the fleet; not only because the HH-60H "Seahawk" would be there to pick you up out of danger, but because the aircrew would often (selflessly) risk their lives to make the dangerous pick-up.

CDR "Fox" Davis knew the fine line between bravado and professionalism. He instilled in his Squadron the idea that if you have to take risks, make sure you understand, plan for, and minimize those risks while performing your duty.

HS-9 was three months into a six-month deployment on the Carrier, and they had established a superb record with the Carrier Air Wing Commander (CAG). The CAG is the Commander of all the aircraft squadrons and is responsible for aircraft operations to the Battle Group Commander. The squadron CO worked for the CAG, and although the CAG was an F/A-18 "fighter-jock," he treated his HS skipper with private and public respect. "Fox" Davis's squadron was also respected by the CAG and Battle Group staffs not only for getting the job done, but also for taking care of their people, and even getting the routine admin paperwork in on time (a trait not all that common among naval aviators).

Every Tuesday at 13:30 during the deployment, the Squadron skipper held training with his pilots and crews. They would review basic procedures (NATOPS), and talk about operational and emergency flight parameters. In aviation terms, they discussed normal and emergency "envelopes"—the parameters of safe flight—and which of these areas a pilot could trade off in emergency situations of mechanical failure or weather conditions. His pilots felt comfortable enough with their skipper to ask hypothetical questions, such as, "Skipper, what if we were in the situation where...."

During normal flight operations, an HH-60H would be airborne in a "Primary Search and Rescue" position to immediately rescue a downed pilot or man overboard. On this day, they were transiting the North Atlantic, and as was often the case in October, the weather was terrible and unpredictable. Depending on where you were in relation to the land masses and islands, you could find a sudden change in the weather in both wind speed and wave height.

With winds at 45 knots (gusts to 55), and waves and swells over 25 feet (40 feet crest to trough), all aircraft were either struck down to the hanger bay, or tied down on the flight deck. The Air Boss had just called CDR Davis and asked him to keep HH-60H, call sign "Troubleshooter 615," on the flight deck in an Alert 30 launch status, but with double tie downs, and extra straps on the wildly bouncing rotor blades. Davis complied, but knew that if the helo were needed it would take quite a bit longer to make it ready.

"Fox" Davis was in his stateroom trying to do paperwork while the carrier rolled and pitched. His Squadron Duty Officer, LT "Puck" Evans, had just reported to him that the Alert 30 was set with Troubleshooter 615 and LCDR "Chipper" Morrison as Aircraft Commander. The Alert 60 was also set with Troubleshooter 722, with LT "Pigpen" Phillips and his crew.

On his desk, CDR Davis had a small communications panel with several phones. At that moment, two of the phones rang at the same time. Davis was startled a bit, because one call appeared to be coming from the Air Boss and the other from his squadron ready room. "This can't be good!" he thought.

He answered the Air Boss call first.

"Davis, here."

"Fox, we have a confirmed man overboard from the USS *Mahan*. They have a DR (Dead Reckoning) plot on his position, 5 miles from us."

"What are the weather conditions?" CDR Davis asked, as he tried to turn on his closed circuit TV to see the topside camera picture. He tried all channels, but could not get a picture on the screen.

"That's the problem," said the Air Boss, "We have about zero-zero conditions (visibility) and 45-knot winds and 25-foot swells." (This explained why he couldn't get a picture on his closed circuit TV.)

CDR Davis knew he would be asked for a recommendation at the end of this call, so his mind began to go through the flight envelopes, helicopter launch and recovery parameters, the hypothermia tables (how long a person can survive in this water), and the qualifications of his crew. After reviewing all those considerations, the image of the sailor in the water trying to survive caused him to quickly say, "Let's launch 615 and reset 722 as an Alert 15 standby. I'll assemble the rescue coordination team in CVIC."

Within seconds, "Now launch the alert helo!" came over the 1MC.

By the time CDR Davis got down the passageway to the ready room, LCDR "Chipper" Morrison, his co-pilot, the hoist operator and rescue swimmer in full water survival gear ran past him with flight helmets in hand. CDR Davis didn't want to stop them with a long talk, because he knew that they were trying to focus on the rescue mission, and they were well trained; they knew what to do. They knocked three sailors and a supply officer off their feet as they ran to the flight deck.

Within 12 minutes, and 18 minutes ahead of schedule, Troubleshooter 615 lifted off the flight deck with almost zero-zero visibility, disappearing into the fog at about 30 feet of altitude. Every second counts. They established radio communication with the USS *Mahan* and were directed to the estimated position of the man in the water. They radioed back that the visibility was about 50 feet and there was no ceiling. In other words, they could see less than 50 feet around them and that was it. In the calculus of finding a lone sailor in 20 foot waves, high winds, and reduced visibility, the odds for success on this mission were very low, but there was a chance. This mission was well out of safe flight parameters, but a human life was at stake. Davis sent his XO to the CVIC, and he went to the ready room to be with his pilots. In the ready room, time sort of stood still, as they waited for news from 615. The "Alert 15" crew of Troubleshooter 722 was standing by in the aircraft, with their fingers on the engine start buttons. CDR Davis tried to look calm for his squadron pilots, but he knew this mission was at (or beyond) the limit of his crew's and aircraft capabilities.

He thought to himself, "With these conditions, they are working very hard just to stay out of the water themselves, making finding the man overboard very difficult." After all, he'd done this himself several times before—each time not finding the survivor despite his best efforts. But, "We have to do everything we can."

Then the phone in the Ready Room rang, "Fox, this is the Air Boss." His voice was steady but very serious. "Mahan says that 615 spotted something in the water, and on the way down to a hover, caught a gust or a large wave, and they believe 615 went in the water. Mahan hasn't heard from them in over 2 minutes."

This is every squadron Commanding Officers' nightmare call.

There was a long pause on the phone, as the Air Boss understood that Davis would need a few seconds to assess the information. After a few seconds came the inevitable question,

"Skipper, do you want to launch 722 to go after them?"

As CDR Davis focused on this question, all the sounds in the ready room were filtered out by his concentration. Time seemed to stop as he considered what to do. Should he risk another flight crew to save the first crew in the water? Maybe he should "cut his losses" and declare that it's unsafe to fly. He knew he was well outside safe flight parameters. He had many people to answer to, including his CAG, his pilots, and their families. CAG certainly wouldn't want to lose another plane or crew. But his squadron pilots would certainly want to make another rescue attempt. His squadron would want to launch every flyable helicopter to save a life. (Often, in these situations, the CO will be the only one to hold them back from a high-risk rescue. They are trained to save lives, and he knew they would be ready to go in an instant.). What about the families, he thought. How can I tell them I didn't try to save their husbands and sons? But if I send another crew, and **they** go down, how will I explain to **their** families that we flew in these conditions—twice?

All his years of flight training allowed him to stay cool and think calmly under stress. But his flight training never prepared him for this decision. In vivid detail, he thought, "Every second counts for survivability. A perfectly good helicopter went down because of the weather. Will 722 have a better chance or could they go down too?"

While the Air Boss waited on the phone for an answer, CDR "Fox" Davis was trying to decide: **What is the right thing to do?**

SOURCE: Case written by CAPT W. Rick Rubel, U.S. Navy (Ret), and reprinted with permission from W. Rick Rubel, "Leave No One Behind," *Journal of Military Ethics* 3(2004), 252–56.

Courage: To attempt a rescue in these conditions requires physical courage. However, as was mentioned in the context of Aristotelian virtue theory in Chapter 2, courage is a virtue but recklessness is not. If the flying conditions are so bad that rescue would be essentially impossible, then CDR Davis will have to possess the moral courage to restrain his squadron and prevent them from attempting an impossible rescue.

Honesty: One military virtue that is especially important, but often not well recognized, is the virtue of honesty. In one form or another it appears on virtually all lists of military virtues or military values, sometimes on its own, sometimes tied into other terms like "credibility," or as an aspect of more overarching terms. Some lists of military virtues include honor, for example, which is usually taken to mean an allegiance to one's duty and to doing what is right; this clearly also includes an expectation of honesty. "Integrity," which is also often found on lists of military virtues, is almost always defined in terms of soundness of character and also clearly includes an expectation of honesty.[11]

The reason that honesty is so important as a military virtue is that military decisions often put lives at risk, especially in war but also in peacetime, and an incredible number of those decisions are based on trust; trust that the information being supplied from the field is correct, trust that the readiness reports are an accurate indication of the unit's ability to operate, trust that the individuals involved are actually trained to the required standard. Trust is fundamentally dependent on honesty. If it is learned that someone is being dishonest then that trust starts to break down, and even if the dishonesty is not discovered, decisions are being made with inaccurate information, which often means an increased risk for those being ordered into action. If a pilot's training records have been falsified, for example, and that pilot is ordered to do something that he is, on paper, capable of doing but that he has not actually been trained to do, then this will mean that he and the people around him are going to be placed at more risk. Consider the situation in Case 3.2 (Leave No One Behind). When CDR Davis decided to launch a helicopter to try to find the man overboard, his assessment of the risk involved was based on quite a few assumptions, foremost among them being that he was launching a perfectly good helicopter with a skilled and fully trained pilot at the controls. If this is not actually true, then he is putting lives in even more danger than he believed, perhaps placing them at so much risk that the operation should not reasonably be carried out at all. CDR Davis's assumptions are based on trust and honesty: trust that the maintenance personnel have not cut corners and then lied in their maintenance reports; trust that the pilot's past training and operational records honestly reflect the pilot's capabilities; trust that the pilot who will fly the mission is not lying when he says he is fully fit and up to the task, as opposed to actually feeling extremely sick and having reported for duty simply because he didn't want to let anyone down; and so on. The actions of his subordinates are also based on trust: trusting that CDR Davis won't risk their lives by sending them out on this dangerous mission if there is simply no prospect of being able to successfully carry it out, and also trusting that he is being honest with them about their chances of accomplishing a rescue.

Loyalty: One particularly problematic virtue is loyalty, which needs to be especially well understood in the context of the military because it is so commonly regarded as a military virtue. In his chapter on ethics education in the military, Paul Robinson notes that loyalty (in one form or another) appears on 8 out of the 12 lists of military virtues included in his discussion.[12] But loyalty often poses problems for military personnel because the demands of loyalty can easily come into conflict with the duties required by military service. A good example of this is when a soldier finds out that another soldier in his section has been engaged in some form of misconduct. In such a situation loyalty seems to demand one course of action, in this case to help the other soldier to avoid punishment for his misconduct, while the duties of military service seem to require that the misconduct be reported.[13]

Everyday understandings of loyalty tend to see it as an all or nothing concept; that if one is loyal to another person then this requires supporting that person in every way, and failing to do so is demonstrating disloyalty. Anyone who understands loyalty in this way will thus almost certainly believe that "genuine loyalty" will place essentially unlimited demands on a person, a concept that seems neatly in parallel with the idea of military service itself being an unlimited liability contract, a contract under which military personnel may have to go into harm's way, perhaps even die, in the course of their duty.[14] Seeing loyalty in this way might be quite reasonable in some circumstances, such as in combat situations where military personnel place their lives in each others' hands and where they almost routinely take great risks, even extreme risks, to protect the lives of their colleagues. However, viewing loyalty in this "all or nothing" manner will be much more problematic in the much more common, even mundane, noncombat situations in which duty and loyalty seem to come into conflict.

What is not often recognized, unless it is specifically discussed, is the fact that people actually have many loyalties, to family, friends, colleagues, organizations, countries, and to themselves, and these loyalties can sometimes come into conflict with each other. With this in mind it is important to understand what it actually means to be loyal and to be disloyal. Some loyalties are generally seen to be more important than others; some loyalties even have legal protection. A judge or lawyer may be thought to have a loyalty to the law (or perhaps more specifically to the criminal justice system), but even if they have taken an oath to uphold the law this does not mean that loyalty cannot be legitimately overridden by another loyalty, such as their loyalty to their spouse. Suppose, for example, that the spouse of a judge was accused of a crime, and the judge was believed to possess evidence about that crime. The judge has loyalties both to the law and to their spouse, but we would not say that they were being disloyal to the law if they were to refuse to testify against their spouse, and in fact in most jurisdictions the right to refuse to give testimony against one's spouse is protected by law.

When loyalties come into conflict, a person can chose to act on one loyalty rather than another, but this does not mean that they are as a consequence being disloyal. I would argue, along with John Kleinig, that a person is only disloyal if they abandon the bonds of loyalty for reasons that are self-serving.[15] When loyalties come into conflict, acting in accordance with one loyalty does not necessarily mean disloyalty to another, though of course it may well be perceived as such. Thus, in many cases where a person chooses to act in accordance with one loyalty and not another, although they may be accused of being disloyal, this is often an inappropriate accusation. Of particular interest in this regard are those situations where a person who has done something wrong requests (or even demands) in the name of loyalty that another person place themselves at some risk to either correct the problem or attempt to ensure that it will not be discovered.

CASE STUDY 3.3

The Training Course

Captain Cupples's battalion was scheduled for deployment to the Middle East in the near future and he was trying to squeeze in as much time with his newborn son as possible. Consequently he was rather unimpressed to be informed, on very short notice, that he and three other officers from the battalion would be required to attend a week-long course on the use of new technology in multinational operations. He was even less impressed when he was informed that the course was in another country, since this added to the length of time he would be away, and meant that he would also have to cope with jet lag as well. Cupples knew his battalion wasn't expected to be engaging in any coalition operations during the deployment, and he had attended a similar course in his own country only a few months earlier, so he thought this course was a waste of time and money, especially since it was apparently all taking place in a fairly expensive hotel.

When Cupples arrived for the start of the course he was rather surprised to realize that he and the three other officers from his battalion were the only officers from their country present; all the other course participants were foreign military personnel. All were scheduled to be deployed to the Middle East around the same time, and this course was apparently part of a new effort at international cooperation in the area. Cupples was also both surprised and happy to see that one of the main instructors was an old friend of his from the Academy, Marc Schwartz, a recently retired Army officer who was now working for AIM Robotics, a private military company right at the cutting edge of new technology. Marc's last deployment before retirement had been to the Middle East, and the course proved to be very down to earth and much more useful than Cupples had expected both in terms of teaching him about the latest technological developments and making good contacts with officers in the military forces of other countries.

Marc proved to be very knowledgeable about the best local restaurants as well as new military technologies, and he decided that it was his "patriotic duty" to look after the four Army officers. He took them to a different restaurant every night and even paid for all their food and drink, waving away every one of their attempts to contribute with a cheerful cry of "It's all on the AIM expense account. My boss told me to take people out every night—it's why I'm running this course in the first place."

After returning home, Cupples had the luxury of a couple of days off before having to report for duty again, time that he enjoyed spending with his family. When he returned to duty the following week, Cupples was walking down the corridor when he met Captain Gruen, one of the other officers from his battalion who had attended the course. Gruen informed him that since the accounting period had closed off the previous day, the CO had ordered Gruen (technically the senior officer of the four who had attended the course, and the only one on duty in any case) to submit the expense claims for all four course attendees.

"I just submitted forms for the usual daily allowance for meals and incidentals" said Gruen. "You can stop by the CO's office sometime today to sign it. Everything with this course happened so fast he wasn't sure what expenses the unit would get stuck with, maybe even our flights and accommodation, so he's happy that everything else was taken care of."

Cupples nodded absently, his mind on other things, and then he paused as a thought struck him; he hadn't spent a cent all week. The hotel they were staying in had provided free airport transfers, both breakfast and lunch had (somewhat unexpectedly) been provided to all participants in the course, and Marc had paid for everything else. "I don't think that's right. I'm pretty sure the book says we can only claim for meals and incidentals if we actually paid for them, and I know I didn't pay for anything at all this last week."

Gruen grinned knowingly. "Maybe. It's one of the quirks of the new defense expense system that you get the full day's expenses if you only pay for one "major" meal, and since you don't have to keep receipts anymore, no one will ever be able to check up on it. Anyway, it's too late now, the claim's gone in and everyone else has signed it. The way I figure it, since the boss is happy with the cost, it must be OK. Consider it compensation for being away from your family."

Cupples felt a little uncertain, but he knew if he didn't sign the form that had already been submitted in his name, then the others would all get into trouble. Since they were being deployed soon and would have each other's lives in their hands, Cupples didn't want to cause any problems; he signed the form in the CO's office later that day. Four weeks later the battalion deployed to the Middle East.

There are several aspects of this case that could be considered problematic; for example, accepting food and drinks on the AIM expense account could be an issue, especially if these officers will later have to make recommendations about purchasing technology from that company. However, the issue I want to focus on for the purposes of this discussion is the clearly inaccurate expense claim that Gruen has submitted, apparently with the collusion of the other officers who attended this course. Submitting an expense claim like this is a straightforward case of fraud, at least in every jurisdiction that I can think of. Thus when Gruen suggests that Cupples ought to go along with the others and submit a form claiming expenses that Cupples is not entitled to, Gruen is actually asking Cupples to collude with him in defrauding the government (and by extension every taxpayer in the country). Acting in such a manner is clearly wrong, since it is both illegal and in obvious violation of the officer's duty to serve the state. Thus this is a test of integrity. It is obviously wrong to submit a fraudulent claim but there is temptation to do so since there is little likelihood of being caught. However, when I have discussed situations like this one with military personnel, they have often suggested that this is not a simple test of integrity, but rather that it is an ethical dilemma, since Cupples's loyalty to Gruen and the other officers will mean that Cupples should not reveal their wrongdoing and thus he should go along with them in submitting an inaccurate expenses claim. In other words it would be disloyal of Cupples to reveal the wrongdoing of the other officers by refusing to submit a similar expense claim. To be clear, what these people are suggesting is not that the loyalty that Cupples feels towards Gruen and the other officers makes this a more difficult test of integrity (i.e., that it gives him even more reason to do something that he knows is wrong), but that consideration of the virtue of loyalty, a virtue so often emphasized to military personnel, actually changes this situation enough so that it is no longer clear what the right thing to do is, and turns it into a genuine ethical dilemma.

This sort of thinking reveals two big problems. The first problem is the way in which such thinking seems to elevate the virtue of loyalty to a status far above any of the other military virtues; that when questions of loyalty arise, other military virtues, such as moral courage and honesty/integrity/honor, simply go by the wayside. The second problem this sort of thinking reveals is a lack of understanding of what loyalty actually means, as well as when and how it ought to be appropriately displayed.

When a military officer engages in misconduct and then asks another officer to help cover things up, if the second officer agrees to help cover up the misconduct, then this will itself be a form of misconduct, and thus entails a level of risk for the second officer. If they refuse to help cover up the misconduct, then they will often be accused of being disloyal, in many cases not only by the officer who engaged in the misconduct in the first place but also by other military colleagues, even those who thoroughly disapprove of the original act of misconduct. Given that the original act of misconduct is itself a form of disloyalty, in that it is disloyal to the officer's oath of office and to the aims and ideals of the military, it seems odd in such a case to accuse the second officer of being disloyal; odd to even suggest that their loyalty could or should be requested or even demanded by someone who is actually demonstrating a lack of loyalty at the time, as well as displaying a lack of other important military virtues such as honesty or integrity.

What I have just described here is a more general version of the situation with which Cupples was faced; Gruen has done the wrong thing and asks Cupples to demonstrate loyalty to him and the other officers by not revealing their misconduct, which in this particular situation actually requires Cupples to become complicit in that misconduct himself. It is difficult to see how the loyalty that Cupples is demonstrating to Gruen and the other officers, by colluding in their submission of an inaccurate expense claim, can truly be thought to be virtuous, given that Gruen is demonstrating a lack of virtue in several respects, in that he is showing a lack of honesty, a lack of loyalty to his oath of service to his country, and even a lack of loyalty to Cupples, since he is asking Cupples to engage in illegal activity. Cases like this one demonstrate that loyalty, especially unthinking loyalty, is not always a military virtue, but that it can actually be a vice if the loyalty is displayed in inappropriate ways or inappropriate situations.

Loyalty, as a virtue, is only ever an instrumental virtue, in that loyalty is only good as a consequence of the effects that it brings about and not good in and of itself. This means that the character (or characteristics) of the person or object of loyalty will be extremely important in determining whether loyalty is in fact a virtue; if the object of loyalty is a worthy one, then loyalty will be a virtue, but if a person is loyal to a malevolent ideal or to an evil person, then they are not demonstrating a virtue at all. Thus someone who is intensely loyal to the ideals of the Klu Klux Klan, for example, cannot in any sense be considered to be virtuous as a result of that loyalty; whereas someone who is loyal to the ideals of a benevolent organization, such as the International Red Cross, is demonstrating a virtue as a result of that loyalty. What this means in military terms is that it is virtuous to demonstrate loyalty to those people who are upholding the values and mission of the defense force, but loyalty to those who are acting in ways that undermine those values, and the overall mission, is not virtuous and might even be considered to be a vice.

When loyalty is poorly or wrongly understood, this can have the effect of making fairly straightforward tests of integrity look like genuine ethical dilemmas. In most military cases a better understanding of loyalty reveals that this is in fact a false impression, and that loyalty, appropriately displayed, does not act as a significant modifier of ethical action in such situations. If a situation is one that would usually be seen as a test of integrity, but on this occasion loyalty seems to suggest that a different course of action might be the ethically correct option, then this can really only mean that one's duty in such a situation appears obvious but that the apparent obligations of loyalty in the case mean that it seems like doing one's duty may not be the ethically correct thing to do. In other words, duty pulls in one direction and loyalty in another, as was the situation for Captain Cupples in Case 3.3 (The Training Course). It is hard to think of a single military situation like this that does not involve the decision maker (A) becoming aware of the wrong doing of another person (B), who they feel some bond of loyalty with, and then A either (1) ignoring, (2) covering up, or (3) colluding in the wrongdoing of B because of the loyalty that they feel. Doing any one of these three things will usually be wrong, though they are not all equally wrong, since colluding in the wrongdoing will almost always be worse than simply ignoring it. What is clear though is that in any situation like this B really cannot be demonstrating loyalty to A; it is simply a case where loyalty is being demanded by someone who by the very act of demanding loyalty is in fact demonstrating their own disloyalty. When properly understood, in any situation like this considerations of loyalty are not sufficient to turn what would normally be a test of integrity into an ethical dilemma.

To be clear, I am certainly not suggesting that the situation that Cupples had to deal with was an easy one. Tests of integrity can perhaps, at least in some cases, be even more difficult to deal with than ethical dilemmas, especially when doing what is right will involve significant costs or other harms to those a person is close to. Given the particularly close, almost familial, bonds that exist in many military units, especially combat units, it is no surprise that the pull of loyalty in such units will be very strong indeed.

One specific area where military commanders need to consider the issues posed by duty and loyalty is with regard to the issue of military personnel reporting the misconduct of others.[16] It is quite common for military personnel to be ordered to report the misconduct of others, and the mere duty to follow orders might be thought to be sufficient to ensure that the personnel receiving such orders would see any situation like this as a test of integrity. However, unless the demands of loyalty are properly understood by the personnel involved, then such situations are much more likely to be viewed as genuine ethical dilemmas. It is only in recognizing the disloyalty inherent in a demand by a colleague to help to cover up their misconduct, despite the duty to report it, that military personnel are likely to start to view such a situation as a test of integrity. Of course this does not guarantee that the person will actually report the misconduct of their colleague, since even when a person knows they are facing a test of integrity they may still do the wrong thing. However, there is another difference between tests of integrity and ethical dilemmas that is important here. In some cases a person who has to deal with an ethical dilemma may never actually know whether they did the right thing or not, since they might not know whether things would have turned out better if they had taken a different course of action. A person who knows that they are facing a test of integrity, on the other hand, knows what the right thing to do is, even if they do not actually do it. Thus it is no small thing for a military officer to be able to educate those under their command to recognize the difference between a test of integrity and an ethical dilemma, especially in situations where loyalty may come into play. If Captain Cupples thinks the situation he faces is a genuine ethical dilemma then he might go along with the actions of Gruen and the other officers all the while believing that he is actually doing the right thing. On the other hand, if he sees the situation as a test of integrity he might still go along with the actions of Gruen and the other officers, but at least he would now recognize that he is doing the wrong thing, and this is significant in itself. Of course some people in the military will do the wrong thing, but it will always be better if they **know** they are doing the wrong thing than for them to act wrongly but think what they are doing is actually ethically correct.

THE TRIANGULAR BALANCE

Commanders must balance three responsibilities when engaged in any form of operations, in war or in peacetime.[17] These are (1) the responsibility to achieve the mission; (2) the responsibility to protect their own forces; and (3) the responsibility to protect other persons, which in peacetime operations will mean any bystanders or other innocent parties and in wartime operations will include all noncombatants and their property. This triangular balance can be difficult to maintain, especially in combat operations, since it will often be the case that two of the considerations will come into conflict with the third one.

CASE STUDY 3.4

Military Dispute Over Casualties in Afghanistan

In mid-June 2006, images captured by an Australian unmanned aerial vehicle (UAV) led to a clash between a senior Australian officer and U.S. defense force officials over the issue of civilian casualties. The UAV was apparently engaged in an unrelated mission, but was in a position where it was able to record the results of a U.S. missile strike on a compound that was allegedly a Taliban stronghold. The attack was part of the U.S.-led Operation Mountain Thrust, which was being conducted in Southern Afghanistan at the time. In public comments after the operation, the U.S. military said its missile strikes had been successful and had killed scores of Taliban fighters.

What was apparently of concern to the senior Australian officer in this case was the fact that the images captured by the UAV appeared to show a number of civilians, including children, being blown up during the strike. Australian Defence sources suggested that this officer, stationed at the military headquarters in Bagram, had confronted a senior U.S. officer over the operation and the level of collateral damage that it had caused. He also threatened to relay his concerns back to the Australian Department of Defence, an action that may well have caused the Australian government to reevaluate its cooperation with the U.S. in Afghanistan. The Australian officer was particularly concerned that the U.S. had decided to attack the Afghan compound with missiles from a ground-based rocket system without asking for more information about the target from the Australian forces, who were in a much better position than U.S. troops to carry out more detailed reconnaissance on the compound, which was located near the Australian area-of-operations.

However, this dispute between allies over the issue of civilian casualties did not become public until 2009, at a time when both the Afghan government and international observers expressed major concerns about the level of collateral damage caused by U.S. air and missile strikes against apparent Taliban and Al-Qaeda targets.

SOURCE: Based on Australian Defence Force reports and Nick Mackenzie, "Military Dispute over Casualties," *Sydney Morning Herald*, May 18, 2009.

The apparent aim of the U.S. operation in Case 3.4 was to kill a large number of Taliban fighters, and the means used for the attack—a ground-based rocket system—ensured that the lives of U.S. personnel would not be risked in an assault. However, employing this form of attack meant that there would probably be a higher number of noncombatant casualties than would be the case if another form of assault had been chosen. It appears that the senior Australian officer mentioned in the case felt that the U.S. commander had placed too much emphasis on two factors, achieving the mission and protecting U.S. forces, and not enough emphasis on protecting the lives of noncombatants. The Australian officer obviously believed that other avenues of assault should at least have been investigated before a rocket assault of this type was launched. Learning to balance the competing considerations when making decisions of this type is such an important issue that I cannot consider it in detail at this point, but it will form the basis of the discussions in Chapters 7, 8, and 9 where these problems will be discussed in much greater depth.

In peacetime operations the third point of the triangle, the responsibility to protect other persons, may sometimes be essentially nonexistent, but the other two points, fulfilling the mission and protecting military lives, can still come into conflict. Consider Cases 3.2 (Leave No One Behind) and 3.1 (HMAS *Westralia* Fire) in this regard. In Case 3.2, the CO had to balance completing the mission, in this case the rescue of those lost at sea, with the risk to the lives of those who would be trying to complete that mission, the personnel in the second helicopter. A further complication for the CO is the fact that most of the people that he is trying to rescue, the crew of helicopter 615, are also under his direct command, which will almost inevitably lead to a sense of responsibility to protect them as well. In Case 3.1, the Captain of the *Westralia* had to balance completing the urgent mission that had arisen as a result of the outbreak of fire, which was the mission of protecting the ship, with the risk to the crewmembers trapped by fire in the MMS. The best course of action to protect the ship would be to engage in an immediate CO_2 drench of the MMS, and this is almost certainly the action the Captain would have chosen were it not for the fact that some crewmembers were unaccounted for. In this case the Captain chose to delay the CO_2 drench to attempt a rescue of those trapped in the MMS, a decision that almost certainly put the ship at greater risk.

The problems associated with maintaining this triangular balance can also be exacerbated by other factors. One of these is the need for military personnel, on occasion, to operate in roles for which they have not been trained or in environments where the usual standards and procedures of military operations may not be appropriate.

CASE STUDY 3.5

Esequiel Hernandez Shooting

Eighteen-year-old Esequiel Hernandez was shot and killed during a government antidrug operation conducted near the U.S.-Mexican border town of Redford on the evening of May 20, 1997. There was little dispute about the basic facts of the case; Hernandez was shot and killed by Clemente Banuelos, an employee of the Federal government. However, while controversy is not unusual in cases where an American citizen has been killed by personnel in the employ of the government, this particular situation was almost unique, for Banuelos was not a police officer, FBI agent, or Border Patrol officer, but a U.S. Marine Corporal.

The Posse Comitatus Act (a U.S. Federal law passed in 1878) generally prohibits federal military personnel from acting in a law enforcement capacity within the United States, but specific exceptions can be approved by Congress. One such exception, prompted largely by concerns over drug smuggling across the U.S.-Mexican border, allowed the Department of Defense to set up "Joint Task Force Six," which from 1989 to 1997 deployed troops to the border to assist with Border Protection. One task that these troops engaged in was covert surveillance of certain sites where U.S. Border Patrol officers believed drugs might be smuggled across the border. Corporal Banuelos was in charge of a squad of four Marines involved in such surveillance on the evening when Esequiel Hernandez lost his life. Given the covert nature of the operation, the Marines were dressed in ghillie suits (special camouflage clothing augmented with artificial foliage) in addition to their usual equipment. They also carried communications gear and their standard issue M-16 rifles.

When Hernandez left his home that afternoon to tend to the family's goats, which generally roamed the area near the border, he took with him a World War I vintage bolt action .22 caliber rifle as protection against local predators such as coyotes, wild dogs, and snakes. While herding the goats his route took him within some 200 meters of the Marine observation point, and he apparently became aware that someone or something was in the area, and fired two shots in the general direction of the Marines. Banuelos ordered his men to lock and load, and proceeded to maneuver the squad so as to keep Hernandez under observation and to ensure that their position could not be flanked. The Marine command team was informed by radio that the unit had taken fire, and local law enforcement personnel were informed and requested to attend the scene. Over the next 20 minutes the Marines kept Hernandez under surveillance, while he moved a short distance through the low scrub, apparently trying to ascertain whether there was still something watching him. When Hernandez raised his rifle again, apparently pointing in the direction of one of the Marines, Corporal Banuelos fired a single shot from his M-16, hitting Hernandez in the torso. The Marines cautiously approached the location, unsure whether Hernandez might be lying in wait for them, but Hernandez was dead when they found him.

Various investigations into the shooting began as soon as the local law enforcement officers arrived on the scene. Eventually a Texas grand jury decided no criminal charges would be laid against Corporal Banuelos, a Federal civil rights investigation declined to charge any of the Marines, and a Marine Corps investigation found that the Marines had acted properly in following both their orders and the standing rules of engagement during the incident. However, in 1998 the U.S. Government paid $1.9 million to the Hernandez family to settle the wrongful death case that the family was pursuing through the civil courts.

SOURCES: Major General John T. Coyne, "Investigation to Inquire into the Circumstances Surrounding the Joint Task Force-6 (JTF-6) Shooting Incident that Occurred on 20 May 1997 Near the Border Between the United States and Mexico" (the U.S. Marine Corps investigation of the incident); S. C. Gwynne, Charlotte Faltermayer, and Mark Thompson, "Border Skirmish," *Time Magazine*, August 25, 1997; and Thaddeus Herrick, "Family to Receive $1.9 Million in Border Shooting / Grand Jury Again Refuses to Indict Marine," *Houston Chronicle*, August 12, 1998, pp. A1, A3.

Case 3.5 illustrates some of the problems that can occur when military personnel are required to perform operations that would routinely be the role of the police. While there certainly are some similarities in the professional roles of police officers and military personnel, there are also some stark differences. Police officers are trained specifically to work to maintain law and order within the community and they operate by and large with the consent of the community in which they work. Military forces, on the other hand, exist to protect a country from external threats and aim to force those threatening the country into submission. Police usually work in pairs, in very small groups, or sometimes even by themselves, while military forces are trained and organized so as to be able to coordinate the actions of thousands of people. Police are usually equipped with a range of less than lethal weaponry, and in most jurisdictions are only empowered to use deadly force as an absolute last resort. Military personnel, on the other hand, are not routinely equipped with less than lethal weapons, but often carry a range of lethal weaponry, and are trained to use such weaponry in a wide range of circumstances. I certainly do not mean to imply that these differences between police and military personnel are a bad thing, they are simply a result of the differing roles these two professions undertake and of the situations they routinely encounter while engaged in that role. However, these differences in role, training, and equipment become particularly important considerations in situations where those from one profession are required, for whatever reason, to perform the functions of the other. It is rare for police officers to have to take on military roles, and this will usually only happen in extreme circumstances, such as when one country has actually been invaded by another and the police of the invaded country try to mount some sort of last ditch defense against an the invader.[18] Historically it has been far more common for military personnel to be required to take on various policing roles, both within their own country and during operations abroad, and it is here where problematic issues can easily arise.

The Marines involved in Case 3.5 (Esequiel Hernandez Shooting) acted exactly as they had been trained to do, and as they had been ordered to do in this situation. When fired on they did not reveal their presence, instead they remained concealed and followed Hernandez. When Hernandez raised his weapon and pointed it in the direction of one of the Marines, he was shot and killed, in accordance with the U.S. Marine Corps Standing Rules of Engagement (SROE). The major problem with acting in this manner is that the Marines were essentially engaged in a domestic policing operation, and it is highly unlikely, to say the least, that police officers who were facing a similar set of circumstances would have shot and killed Hernandez without ever identifying themselves as law enforcement officers and/or giving him the opportunity to surrender. Because these Marines were being deployed for an operation that was outside the usual sphere of military expertise, the Marines were faced with a situation they had not been trained to deal with, and for which their usual training and SROE were seen to be inappropriate. Indeed, when assessing the actions of the Marines in this case, an attorney and an internationally recognized expert on military operational law, Colonel W. Hays Parks, noted that the SROE "May be legally correct for the purposes for which it is intended, but it is an inappropriate set of terms of reference for military support to domestic law enforcement operations"[19] and that the ROE card issued to JTF-6 personnel, including the Marines involved in this operation, "May be consistent with (the SROE) and the JTF-6 commander's intent, but it is not an accurate statement of U.S. domestic law relating to the use of deadly force."[20]

Perhaps the easiest way to deal with the sorts of problems that arise when military personnel are tasked with policing operations would be to simply ensure that military personnel do not do these sorts of jobs. However, as we shall see in later chapters, although it **may** be possible to avoid placing military personnel in policing roles within a country's purely domestic context, this is not the case for many military personnel who are deployed overseas. This is because there are many places around the world where military personnel are being forced to engage in counterinsurgency operations, which are at the very least police like in their nature and, in those contexts, situations like Case 3.5 (Esequiel Hernandez Shooting) cannot simply be avoided, and thus military personnel will have to be prepared to deal with them when they arise.

Having examined some of the requirements of military professionalism and some of the virtues military personnel are expected to display, it is now time to turn to the business of armed conflict itself. To do this, it is best to start by examining when it is actually ethically appropriate to become involved in such a conflict. This is the topic of the next two chapters, which examine such issues in the context of traditional conflicts, and then in less traditional modern conflicts.

NOTES

1. Commonwealth of Australia, *Report of the Board of Inquiry into the Fire in HMAS WESTRALIA on 5 May 1998* (Canberra: Defence Publishing Services, 1998).
2. Western Australia State Coroner, *Inquest into the Deaths of Shaun Damien Smith; Phillip John Carroll; Megan Anne Pelly and Bradley John Meek (HMAS Westralia)* (Perth: Government of W.A., 2003).
3. *Report of the Board of Inquiry into the Fire in HMAS WESTRALIA*, p. 50.
4. For some discussion of these issues see Jessica Wolfendale, *Torture and the Military Profession* (New York: Palgrave MacMillan, 2007), especially Chapters 1, 2, and 3.
5. Of course some members of the military profession, such as engineers or medical personnel, may also be members of other professions as well. Some writers, such as Samuel Huntington, have argued that only officers are members of the military profession, whereas others, such as Jessica Wolfendale, argue that all military personnel are members of the profession. See Samuel Huntington, "Officership as a Profession" in Malham M. Watkin (ed.) *War, Morality and the Military Profession*, 2nd ed. (Boulder, CO: Westview, 1986); and Jessica Wolfendale, *Torture and the Military Profession* especially Chapter 3, "Professional Ethics and the Military," pp. 47–76.
6. My thanks to Lieutenant Colonel Chris Mayer for suggesting this example.
7. As an aside here, I should perhaps note for those unfamiliar with the legal situation in Commonwealth countries, and indeed in many other countries which operate as constitutional monarchies, the fact that military personnel swear to serve the monarch (albeit the monarch and their heirs and successors) is not at odds with what I have said here, despite surface appearances. In such countries the monarch has symbolic power only, and while the monarch may be the symbolic head of the armed forces, they are not actually in the chain of command. Similarly, while laws in such countries might be enacted "in the name of the Crown" and require the assent of the monarch, who is technically the Head of State in such countries, before they can come into effect, many many years of tradition dictate that this assent is purely ceremonial. This is in marked contrast to the real power wielded by those elected to the position of President (and thus Head of State) in republics like the U.S.A. Thus in countries operating as constitutional monarchies, swearing to serve "the Crown" is in some respects a convenient legal fiction, and simply reflects a commitment to serve the state as a whole, rather than the government of the day.
8. In this context it is interesting to note that in 1934, after Adolph Hitler's rise to power, the German military oath was changed. It had previously been an oath of

loyal service to the German people and the country (rather like the modern oaths that I have been discussing here) but was changed so that German military personnel were now swearing to render unconditional obedience to Adolph Hitler, the Fuhrer of the German Reich and people, and Supreme Commander of the armed forces. Since the end of World War II German military personnel have again sworn an oath to serve the state.

9. See Paul Robinson, "Introduction: Ethics Education in the Military" in Paul Robinson, Nigel de Lee, & Don Carrick (eds.), *Ethics Education in the Military* (Aldershot, U.K.: Ashgate, 2008), pp. 1–12, especially pp. 5–7.

10. Ibid., p. 6.

11. Dictionary definitions of these terms are often even more explicit about the link to honesty. The definition of "honour" in the *Oxford English Dictionary*, for example, mentions "an abhorrence of perfidy, falsehood and cowardice"; and the definition of "integrity" is "soundness of moral principle…especially in relation to truth and fair dealing; uprightness, honesty, sincerity" (Oxford: Clarendon, 1989).

12. See Robinson, "Introduction: Ethics Education in the Military". Included in the list are countries such as the U.S.A., the U.K., Australia, Canada, Israel, Germany, and France.

13. The U.S. Army's Mental Health Advisory Team IV conducted surveys of soldiers and marines serving in Iraq between August and October 2006. The results were presented to the Commandant of the Marine Corps in a briefing which can be found at http://militarytimes.com/static/projects/pages/mhativ18apr07.pdf. As well as the usual questions related to mental health, this particular survey also included questions about battlefield ethics, broken up into sections on attitudes, behaviors, reporting, and training. In the section on reporting, those surveyed were asked whether they would report a member of their unit for various offenses. The results, which are included in Case Study 11.1 (The Petraeus Letter to the Troops), were perhaps unsurprising given the extremely strong bonds of loyalty that exist between members of a combat unit, but they were nonetheless of concern to the U.S. military hierarchy.

14. Such a claim is made by various authors, notably by Martin L. Cook in *The Moral Warrior: Ethics and Service in the U.S. Military* (Albany: State University of New York Press, 2004), p. 74.

15. John Kleinig, "The Blue Wall of Silence: An Ethical Analysis," *International Journal of Applied Philosophy* 15(2001), 1–24, p. 10. Kleinig's analysis focuses on the loyalties that form the "blue wall" of police, but he notes that one might also talk about a "white wall" (physicians), a "grey wall" (prison officers), a "red wall" (firefighters), and others. See Kleinig's Note 8, pp. 15–16. In this context perhaps we might talk about the "camouflaged wall" of military personnel. This issue is discussed in more detail in my paper "The Problems of Duty and Loyalty," *Journal of Military Ethics* 8(2009), 105–115.

16. Reporting the misconduct of others is sometimes referred to as "whistle-blowing," or by colloquial terms such as "dobbing," "ratting," "snitching," "grassing," and so on.

17. I owe this idea to discussions with Captain W. Rick Rubel (U.S. Navy, Retired), Distinguished Military Professor of Ethics at the U.S. Naval Academy, Annapolis, MD.

18. Even when a country has actually been invaded, it has been rare for police to attempt to directly take on opposing military forces, since most modern police forces would be massively outgunned by even a relatively underequipped modern army.
19. Colonel Hays Parks was a retired Colonel in the U.S. Marine Corps Reserve. Quoted in Coyne, "Investigation to Inquire into the Circumstances Surrounding the Joint Task Force-6 (JTF-6) Shooting Incident that Occurred on 20 May 1997 Near the Border Between the United States and Mexico," paragraph 762.
20. Ibid., paragraph 763.

FURTHER READING

Coleman, Stephen. "The Problems of Duty and Loyalty." *Journal of Military Ethics* 8(2009), 105–115.

Cook, Martin L. "The Normative Dimensions of Military Professionalism." In *The Moral Warrior* (Albany, NY: State University of New York Press, 2004), Chapter 3.

Journal of Military Ethics 6(4)(2007). Special Issue. "Military Virtues."

Stockdale, James B. "A Vietnam Experience, Duty—Address to the Class of 1983, United States Military Academy." In Christopher Cox (ed.), *West Point's Perspectives on Officership*. (West Point, NY: Thomson Custom Publishing, 2002), pp. 261–266.

Thrasher, Zachary D. "Truth vs Loyalty: The Case of the Missing Flashlight." In W. Rick Rubel & George Lucas (eds.), *Case Studies in Ethics for Military Leaders*. 3rd ed. (Boston: Pearson Custom, 2009), pp. 125–127.

Wolfendale, Jessica. *Torture and the Military Profession* (New York: Palgrave MacMillan, 2007). Chapter 1: "Professions and Professional Ethics"; Chapter 2: "Virtue Ethics and Professional Roles"; Chapter 3: "Professional Ethics and the Military."

DISCUSSION QUESTIONS

- What does it mean for someone to be a member of the "profession of arms"?
- What does it mean for a military officer to act "professionally"?
- Are the virtues required of a member of the military different from those required of other people?

✦◯

4

Just War Theory—Traditional Issues of *Jus Ad Bellum*

┌──────────── CASE STUDY 4.1 ════════════┐

The 1991 Gulf War

On August 2, 1990, the military forces of Iraq invaded the neighboring state of Kuwait, an attack that Iraq claimed was justified by previous actions of Kuwait, notably its "refusal to resolve the border disputes with Iraq, its rejection of Iraqi demands that its multi-billion dollar debt be cancelled, and its insistence on pumping oil exceeding the OPEC production quotas," all actions Iraq claimed were "tantamount to military aggression."[1]

International condemnation of the invasion was swift; that very day the United Nations Security Council (UNSC) passed Resolution 660, condemning Iraqi aggression, the first of 12 UNSC Resolutions on the issue. On August 6, Resolution 661 was passed, which imposed immediate economic sanctions on Iraq, most notably in terms of oil sales, the lifeblood of the country. The U.S. government was concerned that Iraq might move against Saudi Arabia, and with the explicit permission of the Saudi government began moving troops to the Middle East in Operation Desert Shield. On November 29, 1990, the UNSC passed Resolution 678, which imposed on Iraq a deadline for withdrawal from Kuwait of January 15, 1991, after which member states were authorized to use force to expel Iraqi forces from Kuwait. By the time this deadline arrived a coalition of 34 states had amassed an army of nearly a million personnel ready to move against Iraq.

The war began at 0300 on January 17, 1991, with massive coalition air strikes that continued until the commencement of the ground assault on February 23. These ground forces liberated Kuwait and started a push into Iraqi territory, but this was ended by a cease-fire agreement that came into force on February 28, one hundred hours after the ground war started.

In a speech made to the annual convention of religious broadcasters in Washington, DC, on January 28, while the air campaign against Iraq was underway,

U.S. President George Bush made explicit mention of just war theory in defending the war.

> The first principle of a just war is that it support a just cause. Our cause could not be more noble. We seek Iraq's withdrawal from Kuwait—completely, immediately, and without condition, the restoration of Kuwait's legitimate government and the security and stability of the Gulf. We will see that Kuwait once again is free, that the nightmare of Iraq's occupation has ended and that naked aggression will not be rewarded....But a just war must also be declared by legitimate authority. Operation Desert Storm is supported by unprecedented UN solidarity, the principle of collective self-defense, twelve Security Council resolutions and, in the Gulf, twenty-eight nations from six continents united—resolute that we will not waiver and that Saddam's aggression will not stand....
>
> A just war must be a last resort. As I have often said, we did not want war....From August 2, 1990—last summer, August 2—to January 15, 1991—166 days—we tried to resolve this conflict. Secretary of State Jim Baker made an extraordinary effort to achieve peace. More than 200 meetings with foreign dignitaries, ten diplomatic missions, six congressional appearances. Over 103,000 miles travelled to talk with, among others, members of the United Nations, the Arab League and the European Community. And sadly, Saddam Hussein rejected out of hand every overture made by the United States and by other countries as well. He made this just war an inevitable war.

CASE STUDY 4.2

The 2003 Invasion of Iraq

The cease-fire imposed on Iraq through UNSC resolution 687 following the 1991 Gulf War set quite stringent conditions, which included requirements for Iraq to (1) destroy all its stocks of chemical and biological weapons along with any ballistic missiles with a range greater than 150 kilometers; (2) hand over any and all existing nuclear materials to the International Atomic Energy Agency (IAEA), as well as committing not to develop or acquire any nuclear weapons or nuclear weapon components; and (3) submit to complete and unfettered inspection by agents of the IAEA and other United Nations (UN) weapon inspection teams to ensure that all cease-fire conditions were being complied with. During the decade following the Gulf War, Iraqi officials had impeded the work of UN inspectors on numerous occasions, and the UNSC had passed 16 resolutions calling on Iraq to take seriously its disarmament obligations and demanding its cooperation with weapons inspections.

Concerns about the situation in Iraq increased after the September 11 attacks in the United States and the subsequent war in Afghanistan. In January 2002, U.S. President George W. Bush singled out Iraq, Iran, and North Korea, claiming that "States like these, and their terrorist allies, constitute an axis of evil, arming to threaten the peace of the world."[2] The U. S. threatened to use force to overthrow the government of Iraq if it did not fully comply with all UNSC resolutions and rid itself of all weapons of mass destruction (WMD) and convince the UN that it had done so. On November 8, 2002, the UNSC unanimously passed resolution 1441, which found Iraq in breach of its obligations under resolution 687. It offered Iraq a final opportunity to comply with its disarmament requirements and threatened serious consequences if Iraq did not comply and fully cooperate with inspectors from the United Nations Monitoring, Verification and Inspection Commission (UNMOVIC) and the IAEA. Iraq agreed with the resolution on November 13, and inspectors from the UNMOVIC and the IAEA entered Iraq 2 weeks later. These inspectors entered sites where WMD were suspected to be held, but no weapons were discovered apart from a few, apparently out-of-date chemical rockets, which were destroyed under UNMOVIC supervision. The UN Chief weapons inspector, Dr. Hans Blix, made a number of reports to the UN in early 2003 that suggested that Iraq was cooperating only reluctantly with inspections, but that this cooperation was welcome and that moves by Iraq toward increased cooperation were apparent. He stated that the weapons inspection would be completed in months, rather than years.

In 2002 and 2003, the U.S. and British governments made repeated claims that intelligence information that they had obtained proved that Iraq was still in possession of WMD. It was also claimed that Iraq had links to terrorist groups, and it was insinuated that the Iraqi President, Saddam Hussein, was involved in the September 11 attacks. In a presentation to the UNSC in February 2003, U.S. Secretary of State Colin Powell stated:

> We know that Saddam Hussein is determined to keep his weapons of mass destruction; he's determined to make more. Given Saddam Hussein's history of aggression...given what we know of his terrorist associations and given his determination to exact revenge on those who oppose him, should we take the risk that he will not some day use these weapons at a time and the place and in the manner of his choosing at a time when the world is in a much weaker position to respond? The United States will not and cannot run that risk to the American people. Leaving Saddam Hussein in possession of weapons of mass destruction for a few more months or years is not an option, not in a post-September 11 world.[3]

In early March the U.S. and the U.K. began pushing for a new resolution from the UNSC that would authorize war against Iraq. However, when it became apparent that France would veto any resolution that would immediately lead to war, the states stopped pressing for a further resolution. On March 17, 2003, the U.K. Attorney General, Peter Goldsmith, laid out his government's legal case for the invasion of Iraq. He claimed that the use of force against Iraq had been authorized in 1990 by resolution 678 and that this authority had been suspended but not terminated by resolution 687, which had been passed by the UNSC in 1991. Since resolution 1441 found Iraq to be in breach of resolution 687, the authority for the use of force under resolution 678 was thus revived.[4] Similar claims were advanced by representatives of the government of the U. S., which had passed a congressional resolution authorizing the use of force against Iraq in late 2002. However, most other member states of the UNSC made it clear that in their view resolution 1441 did not in any way include an authorization for the use of force and did not revive the authority under resolution 678.

Nearly 250,000 U.S. troops and 45,000 British troops, supported by contingents from Australia, Spain, Denmark, and Poland, massed in Kuwait in preparation for the invasion of Iraq, which began on March 20, 2003. Overall the invasion was a success; massive air strikes disrupted Iraqi military control and most of the Iraqi army was quickly overwhelmed. Baghdad was occupied on April 9, and Saddam Hussein and his central leadership soon went into hiding. Major combat operations concluded on May 1, and the occupation of Iraq formally began.

DISCUSSION

The debate over the justification for the 2003 invasion of Iraq (Case 4.2) created very high levels of interest in the ethics and legality of war, with many people seriously questioning whether war against Iraq was justified. Domestically, there were heated debates about the justification for war, most notably within the U.S.A., the U.K., and Australia, all of whom would later participate in the invasion. At an international level there were marked differences of opinion between those in power in the states favoring war, such as the U.S.A. and the U.K., and those in other states who believed that war, if not completely unjustified, was at least premature. The overall situation in 2003 provides something of a contrast to the situation in 1991 (Case 4.1), where there seemed to be near universal agreement, at least at an international level, that war was justified. Despite some debate within states such as the U.S.A., the U.K., and Australia, the level of domestic support for war in 1991 was considerably higher than it was in 2003. These sorts of debates, as well as the differences between the justifications for these relatively recent wars, mean that these wars serve as excellent case studies to introduce ideas about the justification for going to war.

Decisions about whether to go to war or not are made in the upper echelons of government, with military input usually only coming from the very highest levels of command. So it might seem a little odd that a book aimed at prospective and junior military leaders would include discussion of the issues of what has come to be known as just war theory, given that the decisions being discussed are way above that pay grade. However, there are a number of reasons why it is important that all military leaders understand these higher level issues. Just war theory encompasses much more than simply discussion of when it is justified to go to war; much of the theory is concerned with conduct at a much lower level of command and thus will be directly relevant to decisions that will be made by junior military leaders. But the aspects of the theory that do directly apply to the lower levels of command cannot be fully understood without some grasp of the overall reach of the theory. It is also important for junior military leaders to understand these debates since they may need to answer questions about them raised by the personnel they command. The junior lieutenant who is asked by a private, "Why are we here, isn't this war illegal?," needs to have a better answer than to simply say "We're here because we are following orders," especially since that same private has already been told that he can be charged with a war crime if he follows illegal orders (an issue that I will discuss in Chapter 6). In rare cases it might also be the case that a junior military leader may become convinced that the war itself is actually illegal, and therefore refuses orders to serve in that war, as was the situation in the case of Ehren Watada, who refused to serve in Iraq in 2006 (Case 6.1). Such a decision cannot be made without an understanding of when war is legal and/or justified, and indeed an understanding that the morality and the legality of a war might in fact not coincide, so that a war might actually be legal while not being ethical and vice versa. The overall aim of this chapter will be to explain both just war theory and the relevant aspects of international law to gain an understanding of when it is and is not justified to engage in a conventional or traditional war. These issues will be expanded on in the following chapter, which examines similar issues for what might be called nontraditional wars, such as humanitarian interventions, insurgencies, and counterinsurgency operations.

ALTERNATIVE THEORIES ON WAR

Just war theory argues that in some cases states (and some non-state groups) are justified in engaging in armed conflict, provided certain conditions are met before the use of armed force is resorted to, and provided that certain limitations, which are designed to limit the destructiveness of this armed force, are followed. It is just war theory that is the main focus of this book. But before I begin any detailed discussion of just war theory, I will very briefly explain why I am focusing on it and not on what are recognized to be the two main theoretical alternatives to it in discussing issues of war, the ideas of pacifism and realism.

Pacifism

At the heart of pacifism is the idea that war is always wrong. Such a view can be based in various sorts of frameworks, such as a purely religious one; a consequentialist one, which claims that engaging in warfare will never bring about the best possible consequence; or a deontological one, which suggests that warfare will always be unjust since it will always infringe on inviolable rights. Whereas many people outside the military do hold serious pacifist views, it is difficult to construct a credible argument that leads to the conclusion that war is **always** wrong, and anything less than this will not do for the pacifist. Someone who argues that war will in fact be justified in certain circumstances has already abandoned outright pacifism and moved to a version of just war theory.[5] In any case, since this book is aimed at prospective and junior military leaders, it seems unlikely to be a view held by such readers, since it is hard to believe that a pacifist would want to join the military in the first place.

Realism

Realists claim that it is simply a mistake to apply moral concepts to international affairs. They see the international arena as an anarchic contest, where all states act in their own self-interest and moral rules simply do not apply. Strong states will (and do) take advantage of weaker ones and so to protect themselves, states need to ensure that they are powerful enough to protect their own national security. Within such an arena wars will inevitably occur and so states need to prepare for this; they ought to resort to war if (and only if) engaging in war makes sense in terms of national security, and once a war has begun the state ought to do whatever is necessary to win. Ideas like just war theory may be useful in giving some guidance as to when war is actually going to be worthwhile, but these principles, and even international laws, should be ignored if they are not in accordance with the interests of the state. Perhaps unsurprisingly, most, if not all, of the defenders of realism have come from stronger states.

I certainly don't have time to fully refute the claims of realism here,[6] but some comments about these ideas are in order. Most realists do not argue that there is no such thing as morality, but rather that morality simply does not apply to international relations. This seems to me to be a very odd claim to make. One thing that realists often seem to ignore when discussing the actions of states on the international stage is the simple fact that states are not independent beings capable of thoughts or actions; it is the thoughts and actions of the people who govern the state that determine how that state acts internationally. To describe something as the actions of a state is simply to use a convenient shorthand term that describes the collective actions of this group of people. The people who govern a state have moral duties to others in every other aspect of their lives, including moral duties to people who are not fellow citizens of the state, so it seems somewhat implausible to suggest, as realists do, that in the field of international relations, but nowhere else, the people governing a state have moral obligations only to citizens of their state and have no duties at all to noncitizens. I agree that as representatives of the state these people may have special duties toward citizens of that state, but it is hard to see how this would override every other moral duty, such as the obligation to respect the fundamental rights of all people, no matter where they come from. A lot of writers argue that the right to national self-defense is derived from the right to individual self-defense.[7] If this is the case then it follows that the only actions that a national government can ethically engage in while exercising that right to self-defense are those actions that individual citizens could also justifiably engage in while defending themselves as individuals. Thus, if an individual cannot justifiably violate the basic human rights of another person simply because it will bring them some benefit, then equally a national government cannot justifiably violate the basic human rights of citizens of other states simply because this is in the national interest.

Another analogy that is of use here is that of an agent, such as a lawyer, who is authorized to act on behalf of someone else. This is a useful analogy because the duly elected government of a democracy can be considered to be the agent of its people, authorized to act on their behalf but with a moral responsibility to pursue the best interests of those people. At the individual level, a lawyer acting on behalf of a client has these same responsibilities, but this certainly does not mean that the lawyer does not have any responsibilities at all to people who are not the lawyer's clients. Nor does this mean that the lawyer is entitled to do absolutely anything that would further the interests of their client; the lawyer is not morally entitled to do things that their client is not morally entitled to do. As Orend notes, the lawyer is not morally (or indeed legally) permitted to bribe a judge or murder a damaging witness.[8] If such limitations apply at the individual level when one acts as an agent for others, it seems reasonable to think that these same limitations apply at the international level and thus that the state, as agent of its citizens, is not morally entitled to do things in the interests of those citizens that the citizens themselves are not morally entitled to do.

Nevertheless, some claims realists make are clearly important ones, such as urging that states should be cautious about the possible costs and likely benefits of a war, and arguing that states ought to examine other plausible alternatives before resorting to war to resolve a problem. However, such claims are not exclusive to realism, since they are an important part of just war theory as well.

A VERY BRIEF HISTORY OF JUST WAR THEORY

Despite the rhetoric of some people and the innumerable images from movies, television, and video games, the fundamental reality remains: War is not a game. War always causes death and suffering, usually on both sides, although sometimes only, or primarily, on one side of a conflict. Death and suffering are bad according to all ethical theories; therefore, war always requires justification. As was mentioned in Chapter 2, the most defensible versions of modern ethical theories all refer to universal principles, such as fundamental human rights possessed by all people; such principles require us to take into account the suffering to both sides involved in a war when considering whether that war is justified. These are the problems with which just war theory attempts to grapple. Although just war theory is often discussed as if it is a coherent whole, in fact there are a range of theories that address various aspects of warfare and share enough commonality that they can be grouped together under the general heading of just war theory. In this chapter, I will only discuss those parts of this family of theories that are agreed on by all. However, it should be noted that since just war theory is not a scientific theory it is perfectly possible for two people to agree on the theory but disagree on the results it produces in a particular case. So while we might expect that two physicists who both apply the theory of special relativity to the same problem with the same data ought to come up with the same answer, this is not always the case with just war theory, where two experts on the theory can look at the same data but, because they assign different weight to particular aspects of that data, come up with different answers to the question of whether the war is justified or not.

People have been writing about the moral issues faced by soldiers going to war for literally thousands of years; Greek writers such as Plato and Aristotle discussed these issues, as did ancient Chinese thinkers and writers in India. Modern just war theory is part of a long historical tradition that stretches back through the centuries, with roots in various intellectual traditions around the world. However, the earliest writings that link directly to the modern understandings of just war theory probably come from the work of Augustine in the late fourth and early fifth centuries, which synthesized a lot of previous ideas in Greco-Roman thought. Christianity had up until this time been marginalized in Roman society and a lot of Christians did not serve in the Roman army, some because of their convictions about the value of pacifism, some because they were concerned about heathen religious practices that commonly occurred during army service and in which they would be expected to participate, and some because they were concerned about the relatively indiscriminate manner in which the Roman Empire waged war.

When Christianity became the official religion of the Roman Empire, such convictions were problematic, to say the least; how could an empire, even a peaceful empire, be maintained if the official religion suggested that people not join the army? Augustine argued that not all wars are wrong, and that some wars can be ethically justified. In particular, Augustine emphasized the idea of war only being just if it is being fought with the right intention, suggesting that the evil in war was not so much the deaths that it caused but the desire to harm and the lust to dominate. He also suggested that war required a just cause, in that those who are to be attacked must have engaged in some moral wrong before an attack on them would be ethically justified. This is an essential part of modern just war theory, which insists that an ethical war can only exist if it is being fought for an appropriate reason, such as self-defense. Within the Christian tradition these thoughts were further developed by later writers such as Thomas Aquinas in the thirteenth century, who added other ideas that have survived to modern times, particularly in regard to just conduct during war and the applicability of the doctrine of double effect to conflict; some of his ideas will be discussed in later chapters when these issues are examined in more detail.

In the 1600s Hugo Grotius developed the ideas of just war theory outside such an exclusively Christian tradition by placing them within a more legalistic framework. The just war tradition assumed more importance after the Peace of Westphalia in 1648, which is usually seen as the birth of the era of the modern nation-state and the beginning of the modern system of international diplomatic relations. As Europe came to be seen as the center of world affairs through the seventeenth, eighteenth, and nineteenth centuries, the traditions of relationships between major European states, including the ideas of just war theory, came to be taken as a norm for relations between all the states of the world. In modern times the most comprehensive statement of the ideas of just war theory is Michael Walzer's book *Just and Unjust Wars*, which is referred to by almost all other writers on this topic.

Just war theory is traditionally taken to have two aspects: *jus ad bellum* (justice of war), which deals with when it is right to resort to war rather than attempting to resolve a dispute by other means; and *jus in bello* (justice in war), which deals with the conduct of those who are actually fighting the war, be they soldiers, sailors, airmen, marines, or even civilians who have taken up arms. In recent times there has also been considerable discussion of a proposed third aspect of just war theory known as *jus post bellum* (justice after war), which deals with peace agreements and ending wars; essentially the business of moving from war back into peace, especially with the aim of producing a just and lasting peace after war.

Jus ad bellum consists of six conditions that must all be met before a state is ethically justified in going to war: (1) there must be just cause for going to war; (2) those deciding to go to war must do so with appropriate intentions; (3) war must be used as a last resort; (4) the war must be publicly declared and authorized by the appropriate authority; (5) there must be a reasonable probability of success in the war; and (6) the overall cost of the war, not merely the financial cost but the harm involved, must be proportional to the benefit that will be obtained by going to war. *Jus in bello* consists of two main principles by which the participants in the war must abide: (1) discrimination and (2) proportionality.

Although there is some dispute about the issue, most just war scholars argue that the two main standards of just war theory, of *jus ad bellum* and *jus in bello*, are logically distinct and it is therefore perfectly possible for a war to meet one of these standards without meeting both of them. So unjust or illegal wars, which fail to meet the criteria of *jus ad bellum*, may be conducted in a justifiable manner, that is, in accordance with *jus in bello*. Similarly, wars that are justified, in that they meet the criteria of *jus ad bellum*, may be conducted in a nonjustifiable manner, in that they fail to meet the criteria of *jus in bello*. Issues of *jus post bellum* are also added into the mix in the same sort of way, in that it is possible, for example, for a state to go to war in compliance with the principles of *jus ad bellum* and to comply with the principles of *jus in bello* in conducting the war, but then fail to meet the principles of *jus post bellum* after the war has ended.

However, having noted that the three aspects of just war theory are logically distinct, they are clearly practically related in at least one important aspect. Those who engage in warfare, even those who do so for clearly immoral reasons such as the lust for conquest or the desire for revenge against a bitter foe, always look forward to enjoying the fruits of what that war will bring. In other words, it is what one aims to achieve which explains **why** one goes to war, **when** one thinks that war is justified, and usually **how** one conducts the war as well. In basic just war terms, the **why** equates to *jus post bellum*, the **when** to *jus ad bellum*, and the **how** to *jus in bello*. Thus a state that engages in an aggressive war with an immoral aim, such as seizing control of the resources of a neighboring state, will be doing so in violation of the principles of *jus ad bellum*; and if it wins the war, it will obviously be unlikely to apply the principles of *jus post bellum* to any subsequent peace agreement. On the other hand, a state that only goes to war in appropriate circumstances and for the right reasons, such as to defend itself from aggression, and is thus in compliance with the principles of *jus ad bellum*, is much more likely to be interested in achieving a peace in line with the ideals of *jus post bellum*, and is therefore likely to want to limit the destruction of war through following the principles of *jus in bello*, since doing so will tend to limit the ill-will of the enemy and reduce the likelihood of war reoccurring in the future. One important thing to note here though is that although the **why** and **when** aspects of warfare will almost inevitably be closely linked, the **how** is probably a little more separable. In part this is because in the modern world the **why** and **when** of warfare will be political issues that will be determined by those who govern, whereas **how** a war is fought is largely determined by the military. Essentially this means, in democratic states at least, that violations of the principles of *jus ad bellum* and *jus post bellum* will largely be the responsibility of politicians, while violations of the principles of *jus in bello* will be the responsibility of military personnel.

Thus since military personnel are involved in the business of fighting a war, rather than in deciding when to go to war or how peace agreements ought to be drawn up after the war has ended, the most important aspect of just war theory for these personnel is clearly that of *jus in bello*, and these principles will thus be examined at length in later chapters of this book. That discussion will include examination of how these principles apply to both traditional wars and modern irregular conflicts, such as insurgencies, counterinsurgencies, and humanitarian operations. To deal appropriately with these topics it is important to explore the issues of *jus ad bellum* more deeply, since doing this will highlight some important points of relevance to the ideas of *jus in bello*.

Although I have mentioned *jus post bellum* only briefly, I will not discuss it in any depth in this book, despite the fact that a lot of the issues raised in this area are very interesting. There are two main reasons for this: (1) probably the most important ideals of *jus post bellum*, the ideas about what the appropriate aims of war actually ought to be, are in fact captured in *jus ad bellum* discussions about principles such as just cause and right intention; and (2) the issues properly discussed under the heading of *jus post bellum* are largely outside the scope of matters dealt with by military personnel, and certainly by junior military personnel.

This claim requires a little clarification, since some people might argue that the topic of *jus post bellum* relates to everything that occurs after the official end of a war, including all subsequent military operations. A person who subscribes to this idea would therefore claim, for example, that all U.S. and allied military operations that took place in Iraq after President George W. Bush's famous "Mission Accomplished" speech on May 1, 2003, ought to be discussed under the category of *jus post bellum*. I don't think this is actually a helpful idea, since most of the practical problems related to issues of *jus post bellum* arise, as I suggested earlier, at the political level rather than the military level. Thus although I will discuss some of the problems faced by military personnel engaged in post-conflict stabilization operations in places like Iraq and Afghanistan, I will consider them simply as *jus in bello* problems in nontraditional wars.

So why am I actually discussing *jus ad bellum* in such depth, given that I have already claimed that the issues of *jus ad bellum*, like *jus post bellum*, will largely be decided at the political, rather than military, level. One reason for discussing *jus ad bellum* in depth is that in at least some cases, arguments about issues related to *jus ad bellum* have a direct effect on what is considered to be appropriate with regards to *jus in bello*. This is particularly the case with arguments related to the concept of supreme emergency, which are of great importance in the modern world and which will be discussed in depth in Chapter 11.

Armed conflicts almost inevitably involve death and destruction on a reasonably large scale, so decisions about when it is ethically appropriate to **start** an armed conflict are almost always going to be more serious than decisions about when it is ethically appropriate to **stop** one, and this is another reason for examining *jus ad bellum* in detail but not examining *jus post bellum*. It is also plausible to suggest that *jus ad bellum* decisions are actually more ethically significant to military personnel than *jus post bellum* decisions are, since *jus ad bellum* decisions will involve ordering military personnel to start engaging in activities that under normal circumstances would be seriously morally wrong; that is, activities that will cause death and destruction. *Jus post bellum* decisions, on the other hand, are ones that involve ordering those same military personnel to stop engaging in those activities. As will be discussed in Chapter 6, there have been recent and well-publicized cases where military personnel have refused to obey orders to go to war on the grounds that they believe the war to be illegal (e.g., Case 6.1: Ehren Watada and Iraq). However, I know of no cases where military personnel have refused orders to stop fighting because they believed these orders were illegal and/or immoral.

ETHICS AND INTERNATIONAL LAW

As I mentioned in Chapter 1, there is a close relationship between law and ethics, and this relationship is often especially apparent in the international laws that deal with the international use of military force. As it turns out, as well as being important in ethics, just war theory is also extremely important in international law. Since this is partly because of the manner in which international law is derived, it is worth taking a moment to examine where international law actually comes from.

The two sources of international law are treaties and customary law. A treaty is a formal written agreement, a contract, which has been entered into by two or more states with the intention of creating specific rights and obligations. A relatively straightforward example is a peace treaty, which, as well as formally ending a conflict, will commonly place specific obligations on the previously warring parties, such as a requirement to not move troops within a certain distance of their mutual border. These sorts of formal agreements between states have become more and more common over the years and regulate international conduct in a wide range of situations, such as international armed conflict, trade, diplomatic conduct, and so on. Formal agreements between states are known by many different names, such as charter, convention, note, protocol, and so on, but all have the same force under international law. However, an important distinction to be aware of in this context is that between signing a treaty and ratifying a treaty. When a treaty is signed by an appropriate representative of a state, such as the President, Prime Minister, or Foreign Minister, this simply indicates that the state intends to accept the treaty; however, the treaty has no legal force until it has been ratified.[9] This is a process that is internal to the state, and will vary depending on the constitution of that state. In states with a Westminster system of government, such as the U.K., Canada, and Australia, ratifying a treaty does not require parliamentary approval. In the U.S.A., on the other hand, a treaty cannot be ratified until the President receives the "advice and consent" of two thirds of the members of the Senate, a fact that probably goes some way to explaining why the U.S.A. has ratified relatively few international treaties in comparison to most other major democratic states.

The second main source of international law is a largely informal and unwritten body of laws derived from the established practice of inter-state relations and from the reactions of states to the statements and actions of other states. This has become known as customary international law. At its simplest the idea is that if there is a consensus among states regarding what the law ought to be, then this becomes the law, even though it is not written down. So if states consistently act in a particular manner, especially if they act in that manner because they believe that international law requires them to act that way, then this actually establishes the law even more firmly. Most important, customary international law is binding on all states, not simply on those states whose consensus created the law in the first place. Many long-standing international laws have been derived in this way. However, since treaties take precedence over the requirements of customary international law, most of the more important aspects of international law have now been codified through treaties, though many were originally part of customary international law. The rules contained within a treaty that were not part of customary international law, if agreed to by a sufficient number of states, can also become part of customary international law and thus become binding even on those states who are not party to the original treaty. A good example of this is the ban on the use, in warfare, of so-called dum-dum bullets (technically, bullets that expand easily or flatten in the body[10]). Only a relatively small number of states signed the original treaty banning the use of such ammunition, but this ban fairly rapidly became a part of customary international law and is now considered binding on all states.

Given the influence that the ideas of the ethics of just war had on the rulers of the major European states, it is really no surprise that law and ethics are so closely related in this area. The ethical principles of just war theory were followed (most of the time in any case) by European leaders after Westphalia, at least in their relations with each other, if not in their relations with peoples from other parts of the world. These principles were followed because the European leaders felt both that the principles ought to be followed and because they felt they were required to follow them. Thus the ethical principles of just war became part of customary international law, later codified into a number of international treaties governing both *jus ad bellum* and *jus in bello*. Of all of these treaties, the United Nations Charter is by far the most important in terms of *jus ad bellum*. This treaty, which founded the United Nations (UN) in 1945, is important for several reasons. Article 2(4) of the UN Charter effectively bans the use of force in international relations, except under certain special circumstances:

> All Members shall refrain in their international relations from the threat or use of force against the territorial integrity or political independence of any state, or in any other manner inconsistent with the Purposes of the United Nations.[11]

Article 103 makes it clear that the UN Charter overrides all other treaty obligations, and Article 102 of the Charter bans secret treaties, requiring that all treaties be lodged with, and published by, the UN Secretariat. These provisions make it impossible for any state to justifiably claim that its obligations to uphold the principles of the UN can be overridden by another treaty. Since essentially every state in the world has ratified the UN Charter, nearly the entire world falls under its jurisdiction, making it the most important piece of international law in history.[12] The Charter also establishes the UN Security Council (UNSC) as the institution within the UN charged with upholding international peace and security.

IMPLEMENTING THE PRINCIPLES OF *JUS AD BELLUM*

So how do these principles of *jus ad bellum* work in practice, both in law and in ethics? I will now examine each of the principles in detail, illustrated with various examples, to demonstrate what each principle is intended to achieve and also to see whether each principle is actually effective in practice.

Just Cause: The most basic aspect of *jus ad bellum* insists that a state may only engage in warfare for an appropriate reason. Ancient writings on just war suggested a number of "just causes" that are no longer recognized as such today, such as Aristotle's claim that it was permitted to engage in warfare to gain slaves for your community as long as those who were to be targeted for such a war were "naturally servile" to begin with, and Cicero's claim that it was permissible for Rome to engage in wars that were necessary for her to defend her honor and glory. However, in modern times it is generally accepted, as Michael Walzer argues, that the only just cause for war is the resistance of aggression.[13] The clearest examples of this are the defense of one's own country from aggressive attack and the defense of another country from aggressive attack. In more recent times it has also been suggested, rather more controversially, that protection of innocent citizens from the aggressive attack of their own government would also amount to a legitimate cause for war, an issue which will be examined in the next chapter.

The suggestion that the only just cause for war is resistance to aggression has one vitally important and immediate implication. Logically, it is only possible for one side in a conflict to actually have just cause on their side. Of course, although only one side can actually have just cause on their side, it is very common for both sides to claim they are the wronged party and thus fighting for a just cause. Unfortunately, what is even more common in reality is that neither side is actually justified in going to war, and both are in the wrong, ethically speaking.

As a matter of international law, self-defense is recognized as an appropriate ground for war in article 51 of the UN Charter:

> Nothing in the present Charter shall impair the inherent right of individual or collective self-defence if an armed attack occurs against a Member of the United Nations, until the Security Council has taken measures necessary to maintain international peace and security.[14]

The right to action in self-defense is a long-standing principle in customary international law, and this is recognized in the wording of Article 51 with its mention of the "inherent right of individual or collective self-defence." This allows a state to respond if it is attacked and also applies in cases where a third state has been aggressively attacked and other states come to their aid, particularly in cases where there is a mutual defense treaty between the state that is attacked and the aiding state or states, as is evident in the "collective self-defence" phrasing. However, even in cases where an aggressive attack is underway it has often been the case that states have refrained from acting until they are backed by the authority of the UNSC.

```
┌─────────────────════════════   CASE STUDY 4.3   ════════════─────────────────┐
```

The Korean War

The Korean peninsula had been under the full control of the government of Japan since 1910, with millions of Koreans conscripted into forced labor; hundreds of thousands of these laborers ended up working in Japan or in parts of its overseas empire. As the end of World War II approached, the Western allies, without any input from the Koreans, decided that Korea would be divided, at the 38th parallel, into American and Soviet spheres of influence.

As tensions grew between the U.S.A. and the U.S.S.R. in the years following World War II, both states established governments in their zones of influence: the right-wing Republic of Korea in the American, or southern, zone (commonly known as South Korea) and the communist Democratic Republic of Korea in the Soviet, or northern, zone (commonly known as North Korea). Both governments wished to reunify Korea under their own political system and armed clashes along the border were common. On June 25, 1950, forces of the North Korean People's Army (KPA) crossed the 38th parallel and headed south. The government of North Korea claimed that they were responding to an attack by the army of South Korea (the Republic of Korea, or ROK), and that their intent was to arrest and execute the South Korean President Syngman Rhee, who they labeled a bandit and a criminal.

Within hours of the invasion the UNSC adopted Resolution 82, which condemned the actions of the KPA as a breach of the peace, and called on those forces to immediately withdraw to the 38th parallel, which was the established border between North and South Korea. On June 27, 1950, the UNSC adopted Resolution 83. This resolution noted the failure of North Korea to comply with Resolution 82 and concluded that urgent military measures were required to restore international peace and security. With this in mind the UNSC recommended that "members of the United Nations furnish such assistance to the Republic of Korea as may be necessary to repel the armed attack and to restore international peace and security in the area".[15]

North Korean forces advanced rapidly into South Korea, and by September 1950, the UN-supported ROK army controlled only a small area in the south around the city of Pusan. However, U.S. and UN forces continued to arrive in significant numbers, and the KPA, with their stretched supply lines, lacked air and naval support. An amphibious landing at Inchon on September 15 allowed a breakout from Pusan, and KPA forces were rapidly pushed back beyond the 38th parallel. ROK forces pursued them over the border in early October and U.S. and UN forces joined them a few days later, and almost all of North Korea was captured over the next few weeks. But the Communist People's Republic of China entered the war on the KPA side in November and the fighting rapidly moved southward again. Seoul fell to North Korean forces for the second time in January 1951 before being recaptured by the ROK in March. After a number of offensives by both sides, the front lines finally stabilized in July 1951 near the original border at the 38th

parallel. The Korean War ended in an armistice in July 1953, which established a
demilitarized zone between North and South Korea, drawn essentially along the
original border between the two countries. Since a permanent peace treaty was
never signed, the two states have technically been at war ever since.

Various states could have acted to aid South Korea in the name of self-defense
since the North Korean attack was a form of illegal aggression. Customary law
principles would have allowed other states to assist South Korea in defending
itself against this attack, even if North Korea's attack was not a direct threat to the
interests of those other states, since defending another state from an aggressive
attack is always just cause for war. However, in this particular situation, those
states who wished to aid South Korea, like the U.S.A., did not rely on those principles of customary law. Instead they sought authorization for such action through
the UNSC.

At this time the UNSC consisted of eleven members; the five permanent
members with veto power (U.S.A., U.S.S.R., U.K., France, and China) and six
rotating members.[16] This structure, now recognized as awkward and unwieldy,
had been established by the victorious powers at the end of World War II. There
were seven votes in favor of Resolution 82 and one against, with three states not
participating in the voting. The U.S.S.R., which could have (and probably would
have) vetoed the resolution, was not present, having boycotted meetings of the
UNSC as part of their protest that the Republic of China (i.e., Taiwan, at the
time governed by ousted Chinese leader Chiang Kai-shek) held the seat on
the UNSC rather than the People's Republic of China (i.e., the communist government of Mao Zedong that controlled mainland China). The U.S.S.R. was also
not present to vote on Resolution 83, which authorized military measures, or on
two subsequent resolutions regarding this military action. At the time many
assumed that U.S.S.R.'s failure to vote on the resolution acted as a veto, but the
fact that most states treated the resolution as valid established a new customary
law, that a veto must be explicitly registered at the UNSC.

The veto power made it extremely difficult for the UNSC to perform its
intended function of upholding international peace and security, and this was
especially obvious during the Cold War, since any vote in the UNSC that
adversely affected one of the veto-holding states would inevitably fail. While the
Chinese seat was held by the Republic of China, the U.S.S.R. was isolated on the
UNSC and used its veto frequently. Prior to 1965 the U.S.S.R. vetoed more than
100 resolutions, while the other four states vetoed only seven; the U.S.A. did not
actually use its veto power until 1970. In 1971 the People's Republic of China was
awarded China's seat in the UN (and consequently on the UNSC) by United
Nations General Assembly Resolution 2758. Since that time the U.S.A. has
vetoed more than 80 resolutions, far more than the other four states combined.[17]

The 1991 Gulf War (Case 4.1) is another interesting example of states deeming it more prudent to gain the authority of the UNSC rather than relying on claims of self-defense. The attack by Iraq on Kuwait in 1990 was unquestionably an act of international aggression and many states could have responded to it as they did to the German invasion of Poland in 1939; by immediately declaring war on Iraq and thereby declaring their intention of assisting Kuwait to defend itself. However, rather than taking this option, the international community condemned the Iraqi aggression through the UNSC, which eventually authorized the use of military force to expel the Iraqis from Kuwait. This case is particularly interesting in terms of the discussion of the ethical aspects of just war theory. In terms of international law there was no doubt about the status of a war against Iraq; UNSC Resolution 678 unquestionably made war against Iraq legal under international law. But in claiming that the war was justified in the speech he made in January 1991, then President George Bush appealed to the ethical aspects of just war theory, rather than to international law. It is perfectly possible for a war to be legal but unethical, or ethical but illegal. In this case President Bush emphasized that war against Iraq was both legal and ethical.

Another extremely important issue that arises in the context of self-defense is the question of whether a state is permitted, either legally or ethically, to engage in pre-emptive and/or preventative attacks. There is a considerable amount of dispute about how the terms "pre-emptive' and "preventative" ought to be used in this context, but for the purposes of this discussion I will use the term "pre-emptive attack" in cases where enemy aggression is imminent,[18] and the term "preventative attack" in cases where enemy aggression is expected at some time in the future. In simple terms the big question being asked here is whether a state can strike first as a defense against aggression, or whether the act of striking first entails that state is the aggressor.

CASE STUDY 4.4

The Six Day War

Actual fighting in the Six Day War between Israel and the neighboring Arab states of Egypt, Jordan, Syria, and Iraq began on June 5, 1967, with an Israeli air strike against Egyptian air fields. The Egyptian air force was by far the largest and most modern of the Arab world with about 450 combat aircraft, all Soviet built and including a significant number of MiG-21 fighters, at the time considered one of the best in the world. Virtually the entire Israel air force was involved in the surprise attack in which Israeli planes bombed and strafed Egyptian planes on the ground, as well as dropping tarmac shredding bombs on the runways, leaving them unusable. The strike destroyed over 300 planes and virtually guaranteed Israeli air superiority in the subsequent war.

Events in the Arab states over the previous few weeks had caused great anxiety in Israel, leading the Israeli military hierarchy to believe that war was inevitable.

On May 14 the Egyptian government had put its forces on maximum alert, and a few days later it had expelled the United Nations Emergency Force (a peace-keeping force that had been stationed in the Sinai peninsula since the 1956 Suez crisis) and began massing troops and equipment in the Sinai peninsula, near the Israeli border. On May 22 the Egyptian government announced that the Straits of Tiran, previously considered an international waterway, would be closed to Israeli shipping and to any other vessels carrying strategic materials to Israel. On May 26, Egyptian President Gamal Abdel Nasser announced in a major speech that in the event of war the Egyptian aim would be nothing less than the destruction of Israel. On May 30, King Hussein of Jordan signed a treaty that placed the Jordanian army under Egyptian command in the event of war; given the existing alliance between Egypt and Syria, who had signed a mutual defense pact in 1966, this meant that in the event of war Israel would face enemies on three fronts.

With troops massed on her borders, Israel was in a difficult position. The Israeli regular army numbered only about 50,000 and although over 200,000 reserves had been called up to supplement this force, they could not be kept on duty for a lengthy period without totally paralyzing the Israeli economy. The Arab states on the other hand could call on some 250,000 regular soldiers who could be kept in place more or less indefinitely, providing a constant threat to Israel's security; between them the Arab states also possessed nearly three times as many tanks and aircraft as Israel. In such circumstances the Israeli government argued that a pre-emptive strike was justified since this was the only way in which the survival of Israel could be assured.

The Six Day War ended when a cease-fire was signed on June 11. By that time, despite the numerical superiority of the forces deployed against her, Israel had captured the entire Sinai Peninsula and the Gaza Strip from Egypt, the West Bank region from Jordan, and the Golan Heights from Syria. Israel's territory had increased by a factor of three, and one million more Arabs came under Israeli control in the newly captured territories.

Various articles in the Charter of the UN seem relevant to the question of whether pre-emptive attacks can be legal under international law. Of particular interest is Article 2(4), which seems to rule out the possibility of a pre-emptive attack by forbidding the use or threat of force. Yet the situation is made less clear by the wording of Article 51 which discusses "the inherent right of individual or collective self-defence if an armed attack occurs." The phrase "if an armed attack occurs" implies that pre-emptive attacks are illegal and that a state cannot defend itself by the use of armed force until it is actually attacked. However, the "inherent right" also mentioned in the article tends to cloud this issue, for prior to the UN Charter customary international law did recognize a right to engage in pre-emptive attacks in certain circumstances, but only in cases "in which the necessity of that self-defense is instant, overwhelming, leaving no choice of means, and no moment of deliberation".[19] However, preventative attacks, as opposed to pre-emptive attacks, are illegal under the UN Charter.

The situation with regard to the ethical status of pre-emptive attacks is somewhat clearer. Michael Walzer argues at some length that pre-emptive attacks are justified in some circumstances, and he explicitly includes the Israeli pre-emptive attack in the Six Day War (Case 4.4) as an example. Walzer's specific claim is that:

> States may use military force in the face of threats of war, whenever the failure to do so would seriously risk their territorial integrity or political independence. Under such circumstances it can fairly be said that they have been forced to fight and that they are the victims of aggression.[20]

In illustrating this point, consider an individual case as an analogy. Suppose I am facing a heavily armed attacker (say he has a gun and several knives) who has threatened to kill me, and there is no one else around to help me. If I have no doubt that he is going to kill me and the only way I can defend myself is to attack him before he attacks me, then my engaging in a pre-emptive attack against him seems to be perfectly reasonable. In the same way it can be argued that a state has an ethical right to engage in a pre-emptive attack if this is the only way to ensure that the state survives against an attacker who clearly means harm.

There is a problem with fully applying this analogy to the defense of a state, since in the individual case, it doesn't seem reasonable to kill the attacker unless this is absolutely necessary to my survival. Thus if I could escape the situation by kicking my attacker in the groin and then running away while he is incapacitated, then this is what I ought to do; I would not be justified in grabbing his gun and killing him while he was rolling around in pain (though taking his gun from him before running away seems quite reasonable). It is rather difficult to imagine what, on the nation-state level, would equate to kicking an attacker in the groin and then disarming him.

Whereas an argument from analogy can be posed in favor of pre-emptive attacks, it is much much more difficult to find a good ethical argument in favor of preventative attacks. Even if we could find a case where there appears to be a good cause for a preventative attack, which is far from easy, such attacks will always run into difficulty with regard to another just war principle, that of last resort, which I will discuss shortly.

Right Intention: The second principle of *jus ad bellum* is that a state must intend to fight a war only for the sake of its just cause. The basic idea is that if a war is going to be ethically justified, it is not sufficient to simply have an excuse to declare war; the intention behind going to war must also be ethically appropriate. This requirement rules out ulterior motives such as securing new territory or gaining control over resources as well as other ethically problematic motives for conflict, such as revenge or ethnic hatred.

I should make it clear at this point that this "right intention" principle is an important part of the ethical theory of just war but is not included as a provision in international law. Since intention is a mental state and it is not possible to get inside another person's mind to see what their intentions actually are (at least not at this point in time anyway), a person's intentions can only be inferred from their actions, which is often a difficult task even in ordinary criminal cases.

When we are talking about the "intentions of a state" in going to war it is rare that we are talking about the intentions of only one person, though this might be the case if a state ruled by an absolute dictator goes to war. Generally what we are actually talking about are the individual intentions of a number of people, including senior political leaders and military commanders, who may be (and probably are) acting from a range of motives, some of which even they may not be fully aware of. An additional problem with including the right intention principle in international law is the fact that if the law is going to be able to be used to determine if a particular war is legal or not, then international law with regard to the use of force must be able to be used before a war actually begins. However, the true intentions of a person or a state are often only able to be discerned in hindsight, since from an external standpoint the preparations for a purely defensive war will probably look the same as the preparations for a war that is launched with a apparently legitimate excuse, but is actually intended to secure access to new territory or resources.

This brings me to the possible problem with Israel's conduct in the Six Day War. While their intention was to protect themselves against the threatened attacks of their allied Arab neighbors, one result of the war was that the amount of territory under direct Israeli control expanded dramatically. It can be argued that this expansion of territory was a military necessity to protect against the possibility of future attacks, since Israeli military planners were concerned that an offensive launched against Israel from the West Bank could see Jordanian tanks reach the Mediterranean Sea within half an hour, cutting Israel in two. However, acquiring territory by military conquest is illegal under international law, so Israel's continued occupation of territory conquered in the Six Day War at the very least places question marks over the legitimacy of the intentions of Israel's leaders in terms of just war theory.

Last Resort: The third principle of *jus ad bellum* asserts that war is only justified as a last resort, which in modern times will usually mean that diplomatic pressure and other forms of international pressure, such as economic sanctions, will have failed to resolve the situation. While this principle is a legal one to some extent, it is much more important in the ethics of just war theory than it is in international law. The last resort principle also applies much more to a state that is thinking of starting a war than to a state responding to an attack; it will obviously always be reasonable to use military force when your own borders have been breached by an invasion force, but even in cases where the military incursion by enemy forces is much smaller, a military, rather than diplomatic response, will generally be seen as appropriate. Strictly speaking, the principle is not so much one of last resort as last reasonable resort, since there is almost always something else which could be tried before resorting to war. In the 1991 Gulf War

(Case 4.1), for example, war was not, strictly speaking, a last resort. A deadline for compliance had been given by the UNSC and Iraq had failed to comply with any of the UNSC's demands, but this does not mean that war was the only option, since further diplomatic pressure could have been applied in various ways. However, in this case it is fairly clear that further negotiation was unlikely to succeed and thus although war was not actually the last resort, it can be seen to be the last reasonable resort.

The situation is rather different with the 2003 invasion of Iraq (Case 4.2). While it was apparent that Iraqi officials were only reluctantly cooperating with the UN weapons inspectors, they were in fact cooperating, and moves toward increased cooperation were apparent. The chief UN weapons inspector also suggested that the time necessary to complete the process of UN inspections could be measured in months, rather than years. Certainly war was not a first resort in this case since a number of other steps had been taken before the use of armed force. However, it is difficult to argue that war was really a last resort. Despite this fact, even if war was not a last resort that does not mean the war was actually illegal, since, as I mentioned earlier, the principle of last resort is much more important in the ethics of just war theory than it is in international law. This is apparent in the argument that Lord Goldsmith presented with regard to the legality of war (see Case 4.2); his argument talks about the various resolutions passed by the UNSC but doesn't address in any way other steps apart from war that could be taken to secure Iraqi compliance with these resolutions, since in international law the main focus is on just cause rather than last resort.

The principle of last resort also has important implications for pre-emptive and preventative attacks, and it is here where the principle probably has the greatest implications for international law. If a state engages in a pre-emptive attack against another state, even in a case where this is fully justified by the events leading up to the pre-emptive strike, launching such a strike rules out the possibility of any options other than war for resolving the dispute. Engaging in a pre-emptive strike might still be justified since it might be obvious that no other options will actually resolve the situation. In the Six Day War (Case 4.4) all of Israel's attempts to resolve the situation by diplomatic means had failed; Walzer suggests that these attempts actually increased Israel's sense of isolation rather than decreasing tensions, and it is plausible to argue that a pre-emptive attack was in fact the last reasonable resort in this situation.[21]

CASE STUDY 4.5

Israeli Attack on Iraq's Osirak Nuclear Reactor

On June 7, 1981, the Israeli air force launched an attack on the Iraqi nuclear reactor that was being constructed at Osirak, outside Baghdad. The attack was performed by a flight of eight Israeli F-16s, each armed with a pair of 2,000-pound delayed action bombs, who were accompanied by six F-15s for fighter support. The aircraft flew, apparently undetected, more than 800 kilometers through Jordanian, Saudi Arabian, and Iraqi airspace before dropping their bombs on the unfinished reactor and returning to Israel without loss. The reactor complex was heavily damaged; ten Iraqi soldiers and one French civilian researcher were killed in the attack.

Israel claimed that the attack was a justified act of self-defense because a nuclear armed Iraq, which was at the time under the control of Saddam Hussein, would be an unacceptable threat to the existence of Israel. In addition, Israel claimed that it had taken all necessary measures to ensure that the damage would not be disproportionate; the attack had been launched before the nuclear fuel rods were installed, thus ensuring that there would be no fallout over Iraq, and the attack had been launched on a Sunday so that foreign workers involved in the installation of the reactor would be less likely to be present.

The UNSC rejected Israel's claims to self-defense. Resolution 487, which was unanimously approved on June 19, strongly condemned the attack as a violation of the Charter of the UN and a violation of international law. In addition, the resolution noted (1) that Iraq's nuclear facilities had been inspected by the International Atomic Energy Agency, and found to comply with Iraq's obligations under the Treaty on the Non-Proliferation of Nuclear Weapons; (2) that Israel had not adhered to the Treaty on the Non-Proliferation of Nuclear Weapons; and (3) that the UNSC believed that Iraq was entitled to compensation from Israel for the damage caused.

While the principle of last resort poses difficulties for pre-emptive attacks, those difficulties are relatively minor compared to the ones it poses for preventative attacks. A pre-emptive attack is launched against an enemy who is fully expected to launch his own attack in a very short period of time, perhaps a few days at the most. A preventative attack is launched against an enemy who is expected to be a threat at some stage in the future, possibly not for a number of years. It is extremely difficult to argue that such an attack is really a last resort. The attack by Israel on Iraq's unfinished nuclear facilities was clearly a preventative, rather than a pre-emptive, attack. Even if these Iraqi facilities were capable of producing weapons grade nuclear material, a claim at odds with the findings of the IAEA and the French suppliers of the reactor, there was no possibility of it being used in such a manner for a considerable period of time, probably many years, and it would take even longer for Iraq to develop an effective nuclear weapon from that material. The military strike that Israel engaged in was clearly not a last resort and as well as being contrary to international law, it cannot be ethically justified under just war theory.

Proper Authority and Public Declaration: The fourth principle of *jus ad bellum* is that the decision to go to war must be made by the appropriate authorities and according to the proper process, and must be publicly announced to both the citizens of the state going to war and to citizens of the enemy state. In general, the issue of appropriate authority was more problematic in the Middle Ages than it has been in the era of modern nation-states. Since the rise of the modern state, wars have usually been waged by one state against another, and it has usually been reasonably clear within a state as to where the authority to wage war actually resides. But in earlier times a large number of people, such as princes, lords, and knights, might engage in warfare in the name of the king or of the church and there was no guarantee that the person in whose name the war was being conducted even knew about it.

The situation with regard to the legitimate authority to wage war has become rather more complicated since the rise of the UN. While states still have an inherent right to engage in warfare in self-defense, the UN Charter establishes the UNSC as the only body legally allowed to authorize warfare in other cases. However, the distinction between what is legal and ethical may again be important here. While the UNSC might be the only legitimate authority under international law, this does not mean that others might not also have the ethical, rather than legal, authority to authorize a war, especially in cases where the UNSC fails to act due to the self-interest of one of the permanent members with their ability to veto action. I will discuss this issue again in the next chapter.

The traditional idea of the public declaration of war was mainly to help ensure that war was actually being used as a last resort. If war was publicly declared then this in effect gave a last opportunity to avoid it; a weaker opponent might decide at this point to capitulate to the demands of a stronger one without having to face the costs of a war, knowing as they now did that war was inevitable. In fact, few wars in the modern era have been publicly declared, and international law does not require war to be declared for a state of war to exist and thus for those laws that apply to a state of war (such as the Geneva Conventions) to come into effect.

Probability of Success: The fifth *jus ad bellum* principle is another principle that applies in ethics but not in international law. It is the principle that a state is not justified in going to war if the war will not have a significant chance of improving the situation, or in other words that violent action will not be justified if that action is going to be largely futile. Perhaps the reason that this requirement is not part of international law is because it is seen to be biased in favor of larger states and against smaller states, but I think there is rather more going on here. Suppose a large state was intent not simply on conquering a small neighboring state, but on genocide. The large state has a huge and well-equipped army, while the small state barely has an army at all. The government and people of the small state thus face a choice; they can die fighting a war that would inevitably end extremely rapidly in their utter defeat, or they can submit and be slaughtered. At its simplest, the principle of success seems to suggest that the people of the small state ought to simply allow themselves to be slaughtered, which does seem far too much to demand of anyone.

A problem here is the definition of success; the people of the small state might justifiably feel that success in such a case involves actively resisting the will of the larger state, rather than going meekly to their deaths. Another problem is the tendency to look at "success" in purely military terms; in fact there are many cases through history where the armed struggle of a small group against overwhelming odds has eventually resulted in them achieving their aims without actually achieving military superiority. Sometimes their opponents have wearied of the struggle. Sometimes others have allied themselves to the cause of the smaller group, as was the situation with Kuwait's resistance to the Iraqi invasion in 1990 (Case 4.1). In modern times it has also been the case on occasion that other forms of international pressure have been applied by other states to end the conflict favorably for the smaller group, something that I will discuss in more detail in the next chapter.

Proportionality: The sixth principle of *jus ad bellum* is important in ethics and, to a lesser degree, in law. It is the idea that war is not justified if the costs will clearly outweigh the benefits. This is obviously closely related to the probability of success principle and in fact it is not uncommon to find the two principles grouped together as one. The proportionality principle does differ somewhat from the probability of success principle, however, in that it is properly applied to the costs to all sides, not just to "our" side. It should also be clear, on reflection, that the probability of success principle and the proportionality principle might well give different answers about whether it is just to go to war. It is not too hard to imagine a case where a state will be certain it will be able to win a war, but where the costs will be so large that the war will not be worth fighting.

Applying this principle obviously involves a measurement problem in that war involves so many unforeseeable factors and thus determining the likely costs and benefits of a war will often be difficult. Perhaps the best that can be said is that the principle will be easy to apply in extreme cases: where the costs will be small and the benefits large or where the costs will be large and the benefits small. Other cases are rather more difficult.

CASE STUDY 4.6

The Falklands War

The U.K. and Argentina have been engaged in an extremely long-running sovereignty dispute over the Falkland Islands in the South Atlantic (known to the Argentines as *Islas Malvinas*). Disputes began in the 1700s when both Britain and Spain asserted sovereignty over the islands, but the Falklands have been under British rule since the expulsion of Argentine forces from the islands in 1833 (Argentina having gained its independence from Spain some years earlier). There were many disputes over sovereignty of the Falklands and other British holdings in the South Atlantic, including South Georgia Island and the South Sandwich Islands over the ensuing years, with the Argentine government lodging a number of formal protests over the British presence in the islands during the 1800s.

Argentine efforts to secure sovereignty over the islands increased after World War II when the power of the British Empire was in obvious decline; Argentina raised the issue of the Falklands at the UN in 1945. The U.K. proposed on several occasions that the issue be settled by the International Court of Justice in The Hague, but each time Argentina declined. In 1964, the UN passed a resolution that called for a peaceful resolution to the sovereignty question, which would be "in the best interests of the population of the Falkland Islands";[22] the U.K. continued to assert that since the population were determined to remain British, the principle of self-determination (one of the foundational principles of the UN Charter) required that the Falklands remain under British sovereignty.

In April 1982 Argentina attempted to secure its claim to sovereignty by invading the Falkland Islands and other British possessions in the South Atlantic. The invasion was condemned by the UNSC, which passed Resolution 502 calling for the withdrawal of Argentine forces from the islands, an end to further military operations, and urging the two states to seek a diplomatic resolution to the dispute. However, diplomatic attempts at a resolution failed, and the U.K. dispatched a task force to retake the islands by amphibious assault. The British successfully recaptured all the territory seized by Argentina and the war ended with Argentine surrender on June 14. While they remain a British possession, Argentina has never relinquished its claim to sovereignty over the islands.

The Falklands case can be examined from both a legal and an ethical standpoint. The Argentine invasion of the Falkland Islands was clearly illegal under international law in that it violated the Charter of the UN. The British response was clearly legal under the principle of self-defense, since British territory had been invaded and British subjects had been forcibly placed under foreign rule. The British assault to reclaim the islands does not constitute an act of aggression under international law, despite the fact that it took place several weeks after the Argentine invasion, since the British military responded as quickly as could be expected given the difficulties of organizing the operation and the distance across the seas that the British taskforce had to travel; the ongoing occupation of the islands can also be considered a continuing act of aggression.

When examined from an ethical standpoint it is fairly clear that the Argentine invasion of the Falkland Islands failed to meet the necessary criteria for a just war; there was no just cause for war and war was not a last resort in this case. The British response obviously meets most of the criteria for a just war, but two criteria appear somewhat problematic: probability of success and proportionality. British forces did in fact succeed in retaking the Falkland Islands, so with hindsight it is clear that the mission could succeed. However the British government was apparently advised by a number of well-informed sources, including the U.S. Navy and elements of their own Ministry of Defence, that a counterinvasion was extremely unlikely to be successful.

Perhaps more problematic is the question of proportionality, especially given the questionable likelihood of success of the British operation, which should have suggested a high possible cost at the outset. The war cost a total of nearly 900 lives, with a further 1,800 servicemen wounded. Between them Argentina and the U.K. lost one cruiser, two destroyers, two frigates, one submarine, two landing ships, one cargo ship, various smaller transport craft and some 140 aircraft. Estimates of the total financial cost of the war vary quite wildly, and I can find no estimates of the financial cost to Argentina, but it appears that the war cost the U.K. at least 2,000 million pounds (approximately 3,640 million US dollars) when the cost of replacing the sunken ships is taken into account. One can certainly question whether a sovereignty argument over some relatively isolated islands with a total population of only 1,800 people is worth such a cost, both in lives and money.

ASSESSING THE TWO GULF WARS

Having delved into the various legal and ethical criteria of just war theory, we can now return to where we started, with the Gulf Wars of 1991 (Case 4.1) and 2003 (Case 4.2). The Gulf War of 1991 is perhaps the classic case of a legal war; the only war authorized by the positive votes of all five permanent members of the UNSC. It is also a good example of a modern war that fits all the ethical criteria of just war theory, and in fact would have done so even without the authorization of the UNSC. Even the right intention criteria seems to be satisfied, as evidenced by the fact that the war ended as soon as Iraqi forces had been expelled from Kuwait and Iraq had agreed to comply with the resolution of the UNSC.

The war against Iraq in 2003, however, is considerably more problematic. It is true that scholars in international law disagree over the legality of the war, and that arguments can be supplied both for and against the legality of the invasion of Iraq. However, it is the ethical case for war which is the most dubious; one could take issue with the justification for war on the basis of several criteria, including right intention and last resort. The just cause criterion also looks rather shaky, given the controversies that have arisen since 2003 regarding the reliability of the intelligence used to underpin the assertion that Saddam Hussein possessed WMD and was attempting to acquire more. Even if the war is considered as a pre-emptive or preventative attack, its ethical foundations are dubious at best. Given the fact that many people tend to confuse the legal and ethical aspects of just war theory, I suspect that a large number of non-lawyers who argue that the war was illegal, which might well include a number of politicians from states who were vocal in their opposition to the war at the time, are in fact confused about that very distinction in this case. The fact that the war against Iraq in 2003 failed to meet the ethical requirement that war be the last reasonable resort does not make the war illegal, for last resort is not an essential requirement of international law.

In the end, whereas the legal case in favor of the war can be argued about, I do not think that the same can be said about the ethical case; if the war against Iraq in 2003 is considered simply in terms of an act of self-defense, then it clearly did not meet all the requirements of just war theory, and thus was an unethical war. But perhaps the justification for war can be salvaged on other grounds, since after the event there were claims that the war was justified as a humanitarian intervention, or even, given Saddam Hussein's alleged links to terrorist groups, as part of the overall war on terror. Perhaps these modern sorts of conflicts require some modification of the principles of *jus ad bellum*, and the 2003 war against Iraq might therefore be ethically justified. These are issues that will be considered in the next chapter, which examines *jus ad bellum* in the context of these modern wars, including humanitarian interventions, insurgencies, and counterinsurgency operations.

NOTES

1. Quoted in Michael R. Gordon & Bernard E. Trainor, *The General's War* (New York: Little, Brown, 1995), p. 14.
2. State of the Union address to the United States Congress, delivered January 29, 2002.
3. "Transcript of Powell's UN Presentation," February 6, 2003, http://www.cnn.com/2003/US/02/05/sprj.irq.powell.transcript.10/index.html (accessed March 30, 2010).
4. "A Case for War; written advice by Lord Goldsmith," March 17, 2003, http://www.guardian.co.uk/world/2003/mar/17/iraq2 (accessed March 30, 2010).
5. See, for example, J. Sterba, "Reconciling Pacifists and Just War Theorists," *Social Theory and Practice* 18(1992), 21–38.
6. Brian Orend is one writer who has argued at length against the claims of realism. My brief comments here owe much to the arguments he presents in his book, *The Morality of War* (Peterborough, ON: Broadview, 2006), especially Chapter 8, "Evaluating the Realist Alternative."
7. For example, Michael Walzer, *Just and Unjust Wars* (New York: Basic, 1977). However, for a contrary view, see David Rodin, *War and Self-Defense* (New York: Oxford University Press, 2003).
8. Orend, *Morality of War*, p. 237.
9. If a state wishes to become a party to a treaty that is already in force between other states, although the process is exactly the same, it is referred to as accession rather than ratification.

10. Hague Convention of 1899, Declaration III. This is a *jus in bello* example rather than a *jus ad bellum* one, but the point is clear in any case.

11. United Nations Charter, Article 2(4), http://www.un.org/en/documents/charter/chapter1.shtml (accessed April 2, 2010).

12. As of September 30, 2011, the only sovereign state with general international recognition that is not a member of the UN is the Holy See (i.e., Vatican City), which has permanent observer status within the UN. There are a number of other states that claim independence but lack full international recognition and are not members of the UN. Of these the most important are probably Taiwan, which competes with the People's Republic of China for recognition, and Palestine, which has observer status in the UN but is not recognized by a significant number of UN member states.

13. This is the central argument of Walzer's masterwork, *Just and Unjust Wars*.

14. United Nations Charter, Article 51, http://www.un.org/en/documents/charter/chapter7.shtml (accessed April 2, 2010).

15. UNSC Resolution 83, June 27, 1950.

16. An extra four rotating members were added to the UNSC in 1966, thus increasing the total number of members from eleven to fifteen.

17. Between 1966 and 2008, the U.S.A. vetoed the most resolutions (82), followed by the U.K. (29), U.S.S.R./Russia (18), France (14), and China (6). On many occasions a resolution has been vetoed by more than one state; the U.S.A., the U.K., and France in particular often voted together to veto a resolution, especially in the late 1970s and early 1980s.

18. Brian Orend uses the term "anticipatory attack," rather than "pre-emptive attack" to avoid any confusion about the distinction between pre-emption and prevention. See, for example, *The Morality of War* (Peterborough, ON: Broadview Press, 2006), p. 75.

19. This quotation from Daniel Webster, U.S. Secretary of State, forms the basis of the idea of anticipatory self-defense in customary international law. He was writing to the British Government in regard to a claim for compensation regarding the destruction of the U.S. steamboat *Caroline,* which had, while in U.S. waters, been destroyed by British troops who were engaged in putting down a rebellion in Upper Canada (now Ontario). See Michael Byers, *War Law: Understanding International Law and Armed Conflict* (New York: Grove, 2005), pp. 53–54.

20. Walzer, *Just and Unjust Wars*, p. 85.

21. Walzer, *Just and Unjust Wars*, p. 84.

22. UN General Assembly Resolution 2065, December 16, 1965.

FURTHER READING

Cook, Martin L. *The Moral Warrior* (Albany, NY: State University of New York Press, 2004). Chapter 1: "The Moral Framework of War."

Coppieters, Bruno & Fotion, Nick (eds.). *Moral Constraints on War: Principles and Cases* (Lanham, MD: Lexington, 2002).

Journal of Military Ethics 6(2)(2007). Special Issue. "Just and Unjust Wars: Thirty Years On."

McMahan, Jeff. "Preventive War and the Killing of the Innocent." In Richard Sorabji & David Rodin (eds.), *The Ethics of War: Shared Problems in Different Traditions* (Aldershot: Ashgate, 2006).

Orend, Brian. *The Morality of War* (Peterborough, ON: Broadview, 2006). Chapter 2: "Resisting Aggression."

Rodin, David. *War and Self-Defense* (New York: Oxford University Press, 2003).

Walzer, Michael. *Just and Unjust Wars* (New York: Basic, 1977).

Zupan, Daniel S. *War, Morality and Autonomy: An Investigation in Just War Theory* (Aldershot, U.K.: Ashgate, 2004).

DISCUSSION QUESTIONS

- Is all fair in love and war, or are there rules that must be followed in war, even if that means losing the war?
- Is it ever ethically permissible for a state to engage in a pre-emptive attack?
- Is it ever ethically permissible for a state to engage in a preventative attack?

5

Just War Theory—Modern Issues of *Jus Ad Bellum*

❦

Humanitarian Intervention, Insurgency, and Counterinsurgency

CASE STUDY 5.1

Operation Cast Lead

The Gaza Strip is a territory that is, at least theoretically, under the control of the Palestinian Authority. It lies on the eastern coast of the Mediterranean Sea. As of mid-2009 the territory had a population of approximately 1.5 million people, in an area of about 360 square kilometers (139 square miles). This makes the Gaza strip one of the more densely populated areas of the planet; the population density in Gaza City itself is much higher.[1] The Gaza Strip has a short border with Egypt in the southwest, while the rest of the Gaza Strip is bordered by Israel. The United Nations partition plan of 1947 would have included the Gaza Strip in an Arab state, but this plan was never implemented, and the Gaza Strip was controlled by Egypt until it was captured by Israel in the Six Day War in 1967. The strip was under Israeli military occupation until 1994, when a phased handover of governmental authority to the Palestinian Authority commenced, as required by the Oslo Accords.

In 2005 Israel undertook a unilateral withdrawal and on September 12 the Israeli cabinet formally declared an end to Israeli military rule in the Gaza Strip. Since that date the Israeli government has insisted that the Gaza Strip is no longer occupied territory, because Israel has no involvement in government in the region. However, the UN, Human Rights Watch, and many other international organizations still consider Israel to be the controlling power under international law,[2] since Israeli military forces control Gaza's land and sea borders and its airspace and do not allow the free movement of people or goods into or out of Gaza by land or by sea.[3]

Tensions between the two main Palestinian parties, Fatah and Hamas, began to rise following the 2004 death of Yasser Arafat, who had been the first President of the Palestinian Authority and the longtime leader of the Palestinian Liberation Organization (PLO). These tensions intensified when Hamas won the Palestinian Authority Elections in 2006, a result which caused Israel and many Western governments to cut off foreign aid to the Palestinian Authority since Hamas, unlike Fatah, refused to recognize the state of Israel and still avowed terrorism as a legitimate tactic. Fighting between Fatah and Hamas in 2007 resulted in an effective split in Palestine, with Fatah establishing a government in the West Bank and Hamas retaining control in the Gaza Strip. This result caused Israel to close the border entry points into the Gaza Strip to all goods except immediate humanitarian aid. Egypt's closure of its only crossing into the Gaza Strip meant virtual isolation for the population there.

Between 2005 and 2007, Palestinian groups in Gaza fired about 2,700 locally-made Qassam rockets into Israel, killing 4 Israeli civilians and injuring 75 others. During the same period, Israel fired more than 14,600 155-mm artillery shells into the Gaza Strip, killing 59 Palestinians and injuring 270. In mid-2008 Egypt brokered a *lull*: a semiformal deal between Israel and Hamas in which Hamas agreed to end the firing of rockets into Israel, Israel agreed to end military incursions into the Gaza Strip and to loosen the controls on goods passing into the Gaza Strip (mainly in terms of increasing the humanitarian aid passing into the territory), and Egypt agreed to stop the smuggling of weapons from its territory into Gaza.[4]

In November 2008 the Israeli military made its first significant incursion into the Gaza Strip since the beginning of the *lull*, with bulldozers and tanks crossing the border apparently to destroy a tunnel, which they alleged was being dug by agents of Hamas to allow them to infiltrate Israel and kidnap Israeli soldiers; Israel claimed its actions were a legitimate attack to deal with an immediate threat and not a violation of the truce. Rocket attacks into Israel increased dramatically following the raid, and as the end of the *lull* approached rocket attacks from Gaza into Israel began to approach pre-truce levels. While both Israel and Hamas claimed they wanted to extend the truce, both also claimed that this was dependent on a genuine commitment from the other side to comply with its terms; Hamas wanted Israel to allow significantly more traffic through the border crossings and Israel wanted Hamas to prevent anyone from launching rockets into Israel from the Gaza Strip. On December 25 Israeli Prime Minister Olmert issued a warning to Hamas to stop the attacks on Israel; the following day Israel reopened five border crossings allowing about 100 trucks of humanitarian supplies into Gaza; the same day militants fired about a dozen rockets and mortars into Israel from northern Gaza.

On December 27 Israel commenced "Operation Cast Lead" against Hamas, beginning with waves of air strikes against preplanned targets. The air strikes continued for several days, until Israeli ground forces entered the Gaza Strip on January 3. These forces were apparently attempting to achieve several interrelated objectives: to seize control of areas from which rockets had been fired into Israel, thus preventing further attacks; to destroy all the arms and ammunition dumps they could locate, thus disarming radical militants; and to destroy the military command and control apparatus of Hamas. Ground forces penetrated deep into Gaza City in engagements with Hamas fighters; although they encountered many booby traps and improvised explosive devices the Israeli troops generally suffered few casualties while inflicting heavy losses on Hamas. Israel announced a unilateral cease-fire on January 17 and completed the withdrawal of troops from the Gaza Strip on January 21.

CASE STUDY 5.2

The 1999 NATO Intervention in Support of Kosovo

On March 24, 1999, the North Atlantic Treaty Organization (NATO) launched an air campaign against the Federal Republic of Yugoslavia (now known as Serbia). This was the first time in its 50-year history that NATO had attacked an internationally recognized sovereign state. The campaign was apparently expected to swiftly achieve its objectives, but eventually lasted for 78 days before an agreement was reached, which allowed the deployment of an international peacekeeping force into the region.

Yugoslavia was relatively stable during the Cold War period from 1945 through to 1989, with ethnic tensions within its constituent republics largely held in check by the power of its charismatic leader, Josip Tito, who had led the Yugoslav Partisans in World War II. However, a new constitution, which was passed in 1974, gave a great deal of autonomy to the provinces of Kosovo and Vojvodina, which had formerly been controlled by the Socialist Republic of Serbia. Serbian nationalists were particularly upset by the loss of control over Kosovo, which had once been considered the heartland of the Serbian empire; the province is home to many of Serbia's most sacred churches and monasteries and was also the site of the famous Battle of Kosovo against the Ottoman Turks, an event central to Serbian nationalism. Despite its historic importance to Serbia, Kosovo's population was overwhelmingly composed of ethnic Albanians. Approximately 25% of the population of Kosovo was Serbian in 1961, and their numbers continued to decrease due to various factors; by the late 1990s, Serbs made up only about 10% of the population of the province.[5] Serbian nationalism began to swell in the 1980s, particularly under the leadership of Slobodan Milosevic, who became the leader of the Serbian communist party in 1986. When he became President of Yugoslavia in 1989 he proceeded to strip Kosovo's autonomy, shutting down the Albanian media, firing Albanians from state jobs, and suppressing the Albanian language.

In the early 1990s, the Yugoslav confederation began to fall apart, with some republics aiming to secure independence, while Serbia tried at the same time to strengthen federal authority. Slovenia and Croatia declared independence in June 1991, with Macedonia following in September. Disputes over the sovereignty of various parts of the former Yugoslavia erupted into conflict, particularly in areas of mixed ethnicity in Bosnia and Croatia during the period from 1992 to 1995, and a new concept entered in the public consciousness in the Western world, the idea of ethnic cleansing: "a purposeful policy designed by one ethnic or religious group to remove by violent and terror-inspiring means the civilian population of another ethnic or religious group from certain geographic areas".[6] Although similar acts had been carried out in other times and places in history, the deliberate attempt to remove certain sections of the population from particular territories through the use of murder, violence, and intimidation had not been seen on such a scale in Europe since the Nazi Holocaust in World War II. Most acts of ethnic cleansing were apparently carried out by Serbian troops of one form or another, though similar acts carried out by other ethnic groups against Serbian civilian populations were also reported.

Open conflict in most of the rest of the region ended in 1995; however, disputes within Kosovo continued. While the Yugoslav government (essentially Serbia) continued to officially control Kosovo, the Albanian majority set up its own parallel government that established social services for Albanians, funded by money from Albanians within the province and from abroad. This elected, but unofficial, government in Kosovo was headed by Ibrahim Rugova, who advocated nonviolent resistance to Serbian rule. Not all Kosovars were satisfied with this approach, and a guerrilla group known as the Kosovo Liberation Army (KLA) was established. In 1996, the KLA claimed responsibility for a number of violent attacks against Serbian police stations and government officials, triggering warfare with Serbian troops and forcing thousands of refugees to flee. This conflict continued into 1999, despite international calls for peace and internationally brokered cease-fires; although Serbian military personnel working for the Yugoslav government were later blamed for massacres of Albanian civilians in Kosovo, one aim of the KLA's actions did seem to be to encourage ethnic Serbs to leave Kosovo. British Defence Secretary George Robertson stated in Parliamentary testimony that up until January 1999 "the KLA were responsible for more deaths in Kosovo than the Yugoslav authorities had been".[7]

On January 16, 1999, unarmed international personnel from the Kosovo Verification Mission (KVM) discovered the bodies of 45 dead Albanians in the Kosovo village of Racak. KVM personnel had attempted to enter the village the day before, when the deaths had taken place, but had been prevented from entering by Yugoslav security forces. William Walker, the Head of the KVM, immediately proclaimed it an atrocity, and accused the Yugoslav security forces of engaging in a massacre. Several later investigations of the incident produced various contradictory findings; investigations conducted by the Yugoslav government and by Belarus (which at the time was an ally of the Milosevic regime) concluded that all those killed were members of the KLA, who did almost certainly have a base in Racak. Other investigations, such as those conducted on behalf of the European Union by a Finnish forensic team and a later investigation by the International Criminal Tribunal for the former Yugoslavia (ICTY), concluded that the dead were civilians. Many of the bodies in Racak had been mutilated; the Yugoslav government claimed this had been done by members of the KLA who wanted to drum up sympathy in the West, whereas the KLA claimed the mutilations had been carried out by special Serbian antiterrorist police forces. Many in the West saw the massacre as evidence that Serbian forces were engaged in ethnic cleansing in Kosovo.

The news from Racak and other accounts of fighting in Kosovo convinced NATO leaders of the need for intervention, and international pressure forced Yugoslav government officials and Albanian Kosovars into peace talks, held in Rambouillet, France. Notably one of the main aims of the proposed peace accord was a verifiable stop to **all** military action and violence in the province, whether carried out by Yugoslav forces or by the KLA, with the situation to be monitored by a UN task force. Two rounds of negotiations in February ended with the ethnic

Albanians signing the peace accord, but Milosevic rejecting it, despite the threat of military action by NATO. Milosevic may have been encouraged in his actions by the fact that the Russians, who shared cultural and religious ties with the Serbians, had indicated they would veto any UNSC resolution authorizing the use of military force against the Federal Republic of Yugoslavia.[8]

NATO began its air strikes on March 24, now convinced not only that Milosevic and the Yugoslav government were the main barriers to peace in Kosovo, but also that Serbian forces in the province had re-commenced a campaign of ethnic cleansing, accelerating their actions after the withdrawal of KVM personnel from the province on March 22. After 78 days of bombing, and under diplomatic pressure from Russia, the Federal Republic of Yugoslavia signed an agreement on June 9 that allowed for the withdrawal of their forces from Kosovo and the entry of a UN mandated international peacekeeping force, known as KFOR (Kosovo Force). By this time over 800,000 ethnic Albanians had fled the province into surrounding countries, with over 200,000 remaining as internally displaced persons in refugee camps within Kosovo. International observers almost universally claim these massive displacements were the result of the Serbian ethnic cleansing campaign; these claims were backed up by later investigations by the ICTY, and the discovery of mass graves of ethnic Albanian Kosovars in various secret locations in Serbia. These claims were denied by the Yugoslav government, which argued that the refugees were instead fleeing from the threat posed by the NATO strikes.

DISCUSSION

In the previous chapter, I examined what I have called the traditional issues of just war; cases where a war is being fought between two or more states (or state-like entities). However, many of the wars of recent history do not fit readily into this category. Since the end of World War II many states have faced insurgent groups of one type or another, often within their own country but sometimes within the borders of another country, and thus questions have been asked about the applicability of just war theory to insurgency and counterinsurgency warfare. Case 5.1, where the military forces of the state of Israel are being used against the irregular military forces of Hamas, is a good example of this type of situation.

The applicability of just war theory to a second type of international military action, military intervention on humanitarian grounds, has also been the subject of a great deal of discussion. Essentially unknown before the end of the Cold War, this type of intervention became increasingly common in the 1990s, and it could be argued that there is actually a moral imperative for powerful nations to engage in humanitarian interventions to prevent massive human rights abuses, such as in cases of attempted genocide. Case 5.2, where the military forces of the NATO intervened in Kosovo in 1999, is an example of this sort of conflict.

The problems raised by these two nontraditional types of conflicts are the focus of this chapter. While insurgencies and humanitarian interventions seem very different on the surface, these two types of conflicts do in fact raise many similar ethical problems in terms of just war theory. Both also raise problems in international law, though these two types of military intervention are probably less similar in terms of law than they are in terms of ethics.

OF COUNTRIES, STATES, AND NATIONS

When talking about war and international relations there is a tendency among lay people (i.e., those not seriously involved in the study of international relations or political science) to use terms like "nation," "country," and "state" more or less interchangeably. However, these terms all have specific meanings and in international relations terms, in fact not all countries are actually nations, not all nations are states, and referring to a country is not actually the same thing as referring to a state.

In technical terms, a country is a geographical region. The term is often applied to a political division but can be used in a less specific manner to refer to any sort of geographical area. In simple terms, a country is what can be found on a map. Thus, if I refer to the country of France, then technically what I am talking about is the actual physical region, and not its people or its government, though in everyday usage the term is often used to refer to all three.

In international relations, the term state usually refers to the institutions that actually govern a particular country, area or region, though it can often have other meanings as well since the term can also be used to refer to a political division within a country (such as the 50 states which make up the U.S.A.) or can be shorthand for "sovereign state," which refers to the political association that has sovereignty, that is, supreme authority, over a particular geographical area and its population. Thus when we talk about something like the negotiations between the U.S.A. and the U.S.S.R. that took place during the Cold War, in technical terms we are talking about negotiations between states, that is, the people from the institutions that governed the U.S.A. and the U.S.S.R., and not negotiations between countries, since the actual geographical areas can't talk. It is also important to recognize that the state and the government are not the same thing. The state is the ongoing set of institutions that govern a given political entity, whereas the government refers to the people who actually occupy the positions within those institutions. Since it is usual in democracies for these people to be elected to their positions, the term government is often used as a synonym for "elected government." While governments may change on a regular basis, the state (usually) endures. Italy, for example, has had more than fifty different governments since the end of World War II, but has still been the same state throughout this period.

A nation is a grouping of people who share a common history, culture, language, and ethnic origin. Since multiple national groups can exist within a sovereign state, it makes sense to talk about a country that is made up of several nations. Historically, nations have often worked hard to acquire political independence and achieve self-governance, which is one of the major reasons why the number of recognized independent countries in the world has increased so much over the last hundred years or so. However, it should be noted that the term "nation" is so often used as a synonym for a sovereign state that the term actually gets used this way in international treaties. The members of the United Nations Organization are actually sovereign states, not nations, and the same was true for its predecessor the League of Nations. This means that the context of the use of the term "nation" will always be extremely important in understanding what the term actually means when it is used.

In political science there is often talk about nation-states. Since the state is a political entity and the nation is a cultural or ethnic entity, to say that some particular political entity is a nation-state is to suggest that the people governed by a particular state share a common cultural and/or ethnic heritage, and that there are few people who do not share that heritage living within the geographical area that is controlled by that state. People commonly talk as if all the recognized countries in the world are nation-states, but technically this is not true. Most of the citizens of the country of Japan, for example, share a common language and ethnic heritage; thus Japan might well fit the technical definition of a nation-state. But the same cannot be said of the citizens of the U.S.A., which clearly contains people of many nations within its geographical borders.

There are a number of reasons why it is important to understand the distinctions between these various terms. If you don't understand the difference between a nation and a state, for example, then it is extremely difficult to understand the concept of an insurgent struggle for national liberation, which was the stated intent of the KLA in Case 5.2 (The 1999 NATO Intervention in Support of Kosovo). Understanding what it means for something to be considered a state also aids in understanding concepts in international law, where the actors involved are usually states, although some non-state entities are also important in this arena, such as the International Red Cross. The concept of a sovereign state is also hugely important in understanding the ramifications of the Peace of Westphalia, which is usually seen as the beginning of the modern system of international relations, and is vital in understanding some of the problems in applying the principles of *jus ad bellum* to things such as humanitarian interventions.

The various treaties that make up the Peace of Westphalia established several key principles, which have tended to underpin the practice of international relations ever since the signing of these agreements between the various European states in 1648. The most important of these are the ideas that individual states are sovereign entities and more or less legally equal regardless of their relative sizes; states have the right to govern their internal affairs as they see fit; and states have no inherent right to interfere in the internal affairs of any other state. Prior to this time, the international and internal affairs of the European states, all of them Christian, were governed by a fairly vague religious hierarchy. Larger states, or those governed by rulers who were seen to be of a higher religious standing, were considered to be justified in intervening in the internal affairs of other smaller or less important states, more or less whenever they felt like it. These ideas were, to a large extent, overturned by the Peace of Westphalia, which, among other things, guaranteed the right of each ruler to determine which Christian denomination (Catholic, Lutheran, or Calvinist) his own state would follow, as long as members of the population who followed one of the other religions were free to practice their religion in public at certain times and whenever they wished in private. Since the issue of religion had been the main cause of external interference, granting each ruler the right to determine the religion of his state introduced the principle of absolute sovereignty of states and the principle of noninterference in the affairs of other states. These are principles that can be found in many of the treaties that establish modern international law, including the Charter of the United Nations.

THE BASICS OF *JUS AD BELLUM* AND INSURGENCY

There is no universally accepted definition of insurgency, and consequently there is no universally accepted definition of counterinsurgency either. Fortunately, an absolutely precise definition of insurgency and counterinsurgency isn't really required for my discussions of these issues in this chapter. So in the course of this discussion, when I refer to an insurgency I am talking about an armed rebellion against a formally constituted authority, that is, a government recognized by a formal authority such as the United Nations as the legitimate ruler of a country, by forces that don't represent a foreign government and don't represent some other formally constituted rebelling authority.[9] Following from this definition of insurgency, the term counterinsurgency will be used to refer to the actions taken by government military or paramilitary forces against such insurgents. This definition does of course capture a wide range of situations, from operations against large and well-organized forces through to operations against very small and loosely organized terrorist cells, but this is simply a reality when discussing insurgency and counterinsurgency operations. However, it should be noted that although I will refer to the conflicts I am discussing as insurgencies and the operations to deal with the insurgents as counterinsurgency operations, many other terms might also be used; in recent times, for example, the terms "asymmetric war" or "irregular war" are often used to describe exactly the types of situations I am discussing here.

If it is possible to use just war theory to determine whether a particular traditional war between states is ethically justified or not, then it seems reasonable to suggest that it should also be possible to use just war theory to determine whether or not a particular insurgency is ethically justified. For unless we make the very big assumption that all insurgencies must be immoral in principle, then at least some insurgencies must be ethically justified, and we ought to be able to determine that in advance. Basically, what this means is that a person who is considering starting (or joining) an insurgency ought to be able to work out, in objective terms, whether or not that insurgency is ethically justified. If it is possible to determine whether or not an insurgency is ethically justified, then it ought to be equally possible to determine whether or not counterinsurgency operations are ethically justified, since just war theory can always be applied to assess the justness of both sides in a conflict.

There is, of course, an enormous legal difference between a traditional war and an insurgency. A traditional war, being international, must comply with international law, while an insurgency, at least in the vast majority of cases, occurs inside a single country, and thus both starting an insurgency and actually fighting an insurgent war fall under the umbrella of domestic law. International law recognizes that wars may be legitimate and thus a particular conflict can be legal according to international law, as we saw in the previous chapter. In fact, because of the manner in which international law came into existence, any traditional war that is ethically justified under just war theory will almost inevitably be legal under international law. Domestic law is another situation entirely, and I know of no domestic jurisdiction in which it would actually be legal to engage in an insurgency, whether or not that insurgency was ethically justified.

As was mentioned in Chapter 2, since people have a *prima facie* duty to follow the law, many people think that the mere fact that something is illegal gives an additional ethical reason to avoid doing it, so something that would be ethically permissible in other circumstances might well be ethically impermissible if it is against the law. Drinking alcohol is probably a good example here. In most countries of the world, adults are legally allowed to consume alcohol and so, all other things being equal, drinking alcohol is ethically permissible in those countries. However, in some countries, it is illegal for anyone to consume alcohol, and thus in those countries, unless some extraordinary circumstances dictated otherwise, it would be ethically impermissible to drink alcohol. The fact that it is illegal to do something does not mean that it will always be wrong to do it, but it does mean that much stronger reasons will be required for an illegal act to be the ethically right thing to do than would be the case if that action were not illegal. A straightforward example of this, at the individual level, is exceeding the speed limit. All other things being equal, the ethically correct thing for me to do will be to obey the speed limit, and I wouldn't be justified in breaking the speed limit simply because I was running late for a party. But there are times when it will be ethically justified to break the speed limit; as was mentioned in Chapter 1, if I found someone who had been bitten by a poisonous snake and was rushing them to hospital, then this does seem to be a case where it is ethically justifiable to break the speed limit, but only by a reasonable amount depending on the conditions and my skill as a driver. Having said this, it is clear that the argument that people are ethically required to follow the law is most applicable to those living in states where their basic human rights are protected and/or they actually have some say in what the law will be, such as in liberal democracies. People living under dictatorships, or other states that pass laws that are morally abhorrent, will often have much less reason to think that there is an ethical requirement to follow the law in general, and morally abhorrent laws in particular.

Given that engaging in an insurgency will almost certainly be illegal, it seems that the standard that must be reached before we can say that it is ethically justified to engage in an insurgency is going to be somewhat higher than that which would be required for a traditional war to be justified. However, given how stringent the conditions of *jus ad bellum* actually are, and given the high moral cost of engaging in any sort of warfare, the ethical standard required to justify an insurgency will only be slightly higher than the standard required to justify a traditional international war. In the end the level of ethical justification required is probably much more dependent on the type of government a country has than on any intrinsic difference between insurgencies and traditional international wars; it will be much harder to justify engaging in an insurgency in a true democracy than it will be in a state controlled by a dictatorship, since in the democracy there will be many more avenues of peaceful protest than there are likely to be under a totalitarian regime.

Some writers, such as Alex Bellamy[10] and Daniel Zupan,[11] claim that just war theory can be applied to insurgencies and other asymmetrical wars without modification, while others, such as Nick Fotion,[12] claim that the theory needs to be modified to deal with such cases. The easiest way to address this discrepancy is to simply look at the arguments presented by Fotion and like-minded theorists and look at the possible problems with their suggestions. Doing so illustrates some of the differences between traditional and nontraditional wars and also allows me to make more general claims about the various ways in which just war theory might be applied to modern wars such as insurgencies, counterinsurgencies, and humanitarian interventions.

Fotion argues that just war theory needs to be modified in various ways if it is to be useful for examining the ethics of modern irregular wars. Specifically, he suggests that in "asymmetric wars" the ethical principles of just war theory may also apply asymmetrically, in that some of the usual *jus ad bellum* principles don't actually apply to insurgents, and other principles don't apply to counterinsurgency operations. He also claims that some *jus in bello* principles may apply less rigorously in irregular wars than they do in traditional wars, a point to which I will return in Chapter 8.

Fotion claims that for an insurgency to be justified it must only fulfill four out of the usual six conditions of just war theory: just cause, right intentions, last resort, and proportionality. He believes that the other two criteria, legitimate authority and probability of success, are conditions that no insurgency could ever fulfill and so he claims that an insurgency can be justified without meeting these conditions.

I think there is something deeply problematic in the idea that a non-state entity could be justified in going to war without any consideration at all of whether those starting such a war have any authority to do so, or any need to calculate their chances of actually succeeding in their aims. If Fotion's argument here is taken to its extreme, then it would be ethically justifiable for a single individual to declare war against a state, assuming that this individual was able to demonstrate a just cause, right intention, proportionality, and last resort, something that I for one do not think is actually as improbable as it might sound. Fotion's rejection of both of these principles does seem to be rather hasty.

Consider the likelihood of success principle. Fotion's argument here is that it will almost always be the case that a rebel or insurgent group will, at least at the start of their revolution, have to assess their chances of success as realistically as possible, and will almost always conclude that their chances of success are very low; and thus, according to Fotion, beginning their revolutionary activity would be acting unjustly according to traditional just war theory: "Rebellions would automatically be immoral even if just cause were gloriously on their side."[13] I think the problem with Fotion's claim here is the manner in which he assesses the likelihood of success of revolutionary groups. Even while he is examining cases of irregular war, he seems to fall into the trap of examining them in terms of traditional war. If a hypothetical nation "Aydania" is contemplating going to war with another nation "Bedania," then just war theory requires Aydania's leaders to assess their likelihood of success, which in a situation like this will involve calculations of the number of troops, tanks, ships, and planes each side has; the terrain where battles are likely to take place; and so on. But assessing the chances of success of a revolutionary struggle is, I believe, quite a different calculation.

CASE STUDY 5.3

The Fight Against Apartheid

Apartheid (from the Afrikaans word for separateness) was a policy of legal racial segregation enforced in South Africa during the period of National Party rule, from 1948 until 1994. Under this policy, the rights of the majority of the population were curtailed and continued rule by the white minority was maintained.

Racial discrimination had long been a part of life in South Africa, with most non-whites not being permitted to vote and requiring special permits to travel (the infamous "pass laws"), but apartheid was only introduced as an official policy following the 1948 general election. Laws passed by the new government following the election enshrined the principles of racial segregation in that people were forced to live in specific areas based on their race; marriage between races was prohibited, followed shortly after by the prohibition on any interracial sexual relations; and amenities were separated by law, which led to whites and non-whites having separate schools, universities, hospitals, buses, beaches, public toilets, and even park benches. Later laws formalized racial discrimination in other areas, such as employment. The government services provided to whites were of a much higher standard than those provided to non-whites, and those provided to blacks were of the lowest standard of all. As John Kane-Berman, a journalist for the South African business magazine *Financial Mail*, wrote in 1974

> Discrimination...governs every facet of our lives from the cradle to the grave—and even beyond, since even our cemeteries are racially segregated. It is enforced where we live, where we work, where we play, where we learn, where we go when sick, and on the transport we use. Not only does the government condone it; it systematically pursues it, preaches it, practices it, and enforces it. It is enshrined in our Constitution, written into our laws, and enforced by the courts.[14]

The African National Congress (ANC) started a program of strikes, boycotts, and protests against the policy of apartheid, but these campaigns achieved little, in part because the government continually passed new laws that criminalized such campaigns and attempts to organize them. In 1959 a new organization called the Pan-Africanist Congress (PAC) was formed by a group of disenchanted ANC members. One of the PAC's first actions was to organize nationwide protests against the pass laws. One of these protests was held at Sharpeville, where a crowd of several thousand gathered and offered themselves up for arrest for not carrying their pass books. The police apparently panicked and opened fire on the crowd, killing 69 people and injuring 186; all the casualties were black and most were shot in the back as they attempted to run away. Shortly after the Sharpeville massacre both the ANC and PAC were banned by the government.

Faced by an unwavering government and the continued strengthening of apartheid laws, various opposition groups turned to armed resistance. The ANC formed its own militant resistance group, *Umkhonto we Sizwe*, the Spear of the Nation (also known as MK), under the leadership of Nelson Mandela. In November 1961, MK issued the following statement:

> The time comes in the life of any nation where there remain only two choices: submit or fight. That time has now come to South Africa. We shall not submit and we have no choice but to hit back by all means within our power in defence of our people, our future, and our freedom. The government has interpreted the peacefulness of the movement as weakness; the people's non-violent policies have been taken as a green light for government violence....We are striking out along a new road for the liberation of the people of this country.[15]

As part of its armed struggle against apartheid, MK engaged in a program of sabotage of government military installations, power plants, telephone lines, and transportation links. One of the aims of MK was to avoid bloodshed, so these acts of sabotage were carefully planned so as to minimize the chances of loss of life. However the campaign virtually died out after the arrest and imprisonment of many of the leaders of the movement, including Mandela, in late 1962 and early 1963.

International condemnation of the policy of apartheid began to increase as a result of the publicity generated by the protests and attacks by MK, and the UN General Assembly passed Resolution 1761 condemning South Africa's policies in November 1962. In August 1963 the UNSC passed a resolution calling for a voluntary arms embargo on South Africa, and the International Convention on the Suppression and Punishment of the Crime of Apartheid came into force in 1976.[16] Various other international sanctions were imposed on South Africa in the 1960s and 1970s, including exclusion from the Olympics Games as well as other sporting and cultural sanctions. In 1977 the voluntary arms embargo became mandatory after the passing of UNSC Resolution 418. The UN condemned South Africa at the World Conference Against Racism in 1978 and 1983, and significant economic sanctions began to be imposed by various countries in the late 1980s.

Within South Africa, after years of relative quiet, mass protests began again with the Soweto uprising in 1976, where black students protested against compulsory lessons in Afrikaans, which young blacks associated with apartheid. Police again opened fire on demonstrators; the official death toll was only 23, but most estimate hundreds were killed in the protests and subsequent riots against police actions. As the plight of non-white South Africans gathered international attention, money began to flow into the coffers of resistance organizations like the ANC. Violence and protests grew in size over the years; 20,500 people were killed in political conflict in South Africa between 1984 and 1994, and the government began to enter into secret negotiations with the ANC, and in particular with the still-imprisoned Nelson Mandela. In 1990, the ban on the ANC and PAC was lifted, and Mandela was released after more than 27 years in prison. The President, F.W. de Klerk of the National Party, entered into public and active negotiations with the ANC to grant full rights to all people in the country, and to prepare for free and fair elections. In 1993, de Klerk and Mandela were jointly awarded the Nobel Peace Prize for their work toward bringing a peaceful end to apartheid and toward a new and democratic South Africa.

In 1994, free elections under universal suffrage were held in South Africa for the first time. The ANC won more than 60% of the vote, and Nelson Mandela was elected President. The National Party, which had ruled the country since 1948, became the official opposition. A new National Unity Government was formed in the wake of the elections, with the three major parties represented in the new cabinet, and both the ANC deputy leader, Thabo Mbeki, and de Klerk appointed as Deputy Presidents.

The case of the struggle for the rights of black people in South Africa, which was led primarily by the ANC, is a good example of a justified insurgency according to Fotion's theory, in that it clearly fills his four conditions of just war theory in irregular wars. The ANC had a just cause for war, in that the vast majority of the people of South Africa were being unjustly disenfranchised, discriminated against, and deprived of fundamental human rights. The ANC had the right intentions in mounting an insurgency, since they wanted to create a country in which the rights of everyone, whatever their race, would be respected. The damage that would be caused by the insurgency was clearly proportional to the gains that would be achieved by success, and the last reasonable resort condition was also fulfilled, as evidenced by the years of attempts to reach a peaceful resolution to the dispute between the disenfranchised non-whites and the South African government. Since the insurgency meets these four conditions, Fotion would argue that it is justified, without the requirement for the insurgency to fulfill the probability of success or legitimate authority criteria. However, I think Fotion is much too hasty in claiming that no insurgency could possibly fulfill these last two conditions, for on closer examination it seems clear that the insurgency against apartheid actually does meet these conditions as well.

As well as being a good example of a justified insurgency, the struggle against apartheid is also a good example of the problems of relying on military assessments in determining the probability of success of an insurgency. When the ANC made the decision, in 1961, to engage in military actions in support of their struggle for equal recognition, any objective observer would have had to assess their likelihood of military success as being very small. The South African military was well-trained and well-equipped, and despite having the support of the majority of the population, the ANC had little prospect of ever being able to muster the military might to tackle them in open combat. Thus, according to Fotion's assessment, their likelihood of success was very small, despite just cause being "gloriously on their side." But of course it was never the intention of the ANC to engage in open combat, nor was this necessary for their revolutionary struggle to succeed. Violent action was only one aspect of the ANC strategy, and other tactics, such as mass strikes and international lobbying, were also integral parts of the revolutionary conflict. An independent assessment of the likelihood of success in 1961 that ignores all of these nonmilitary factors, especially an assessment that ignores the fact that just cause was quite clearly on the ANC's side—a fact highly relevant in terms of swaying international opinion against the government's apartheid policies—gives a highly unrealistic answer on the question of likelihood of success.

Fotion's other main claim with regard to insurgencies is that since non-state entities cannot, in principle, meet the requirement of legitimate authority, they do not need to do so for them to be engaged in a just war. This is an issue that has been addressed by various other writers, such as Alex Bellamy. Bellamy suggests there are three tests that must be passed for a non-state actor to demonstrate legitimate authority to wage war.[17] First, the non-state entity must be able to demonstrate that they enjoy high levels of political support within an identifiable community. Second, they need to be able to demonstrate that this community shares the political aspirations of the non-state entity, including the strategy of violence that is being adopted. Third, they need to be able to make and uphold agreements with other organizations, as well as control the members of their organization, especially with regard to ensuring that those members abide by the principles of *jus in bello*.[18]

It could be argued that Bellamy's principles could not work in practice, since it is possible that they might grant legitimate authority to more than one leader within a particular community. However, I don't think that this is an enormous objection to the idea, since it might well be the case that the leaders of several different groups engaged in irregular war against the same enemy all have legitimacy granted to them by the different sections of the population they represent, a situation analogous to what occurs in traditional just war theory in cases where a coalition of nations all engage in a war against a common foe. One obvious example of this sort of situation in irregular wars would be the range of different resistance groups who engaged in guerrilla and underground war against the German Occupation of France in World War II. Each one of these different resistance groups had the support of some identifiable section of the population, and it seems perfectly reasonable to suggest that each group had legitimacy as a result of having the backing of that section of the population.

It could also be argued that all these conditions are extremely difficult for a non-state entity to meet, especially given that legitimate authority is a *jus ad bellum* requirement that ought to be assessed before any war commences. However, there have certainly been non-state entities who could claim to have legitimate authority under these criteria, and to have had it for a considerable time before they engaged in insurgency warfare against a state. The ANC, as the main voice of the disenfranchised people of South Africa, is one organization that does seem to have legitimacy under such criteria, and there are other plausible examples as well, such as the Palestinian Liberation Organization (PLO). Given the fact that some insurgent groups are able to acquire legitimacy in such a manner, and in fact appear to have done so, it does not seem unreasonable to maintain that this is a necessary requirement for any groups to meet for their insurgency to fulfill the conditions of *jus ad bellum*.

In many ways the struggle against apartheid is an easy case to assess because the violations of human rights by the Nationalist government were so blatant and so widespread. A simple example of this can be found in comparing the voting figures from the "whites only" 1992 referendum, which voted to end apartheid, and the 1994 general election, which was held under universal suffrage. For the referendum there were nearly 3.3 million registered voters, 2.8 million of whom participated in the voting. There was no formal voter registration process before the 1994 election, but over 19.5 million people cast ballots over the three days of voting. Simple extrapolation from these figures suggests that over 85% of the adult population was disenfranchised under apartheid; when combined with all the other restrictions on non-white people in South Africa, like the restrictions on land ownership, residential and educational segregation, and so on, it is obvious that the rights of the majority of the population were massively violated. But other cases are not so simple to evaluate, such as situations where a group within an existing state seeks independence, as was the case with the ethnic Albanian population in Kosovo in Case 5.2 (The 1999 NATO Intervention in Support of Kosovo).

JUS AD BELLUM AND DIFFICULT INSURGENCY CASES

When discussing the justice of an insurgency against apartheid, I suggested that it was an easy case to assess because the violations of human rights by the Nationalist government were so widespread and blatant. To put this in more general terms, the apartheid regime in South Africa did not qualify as what Brian Orend calls a minimally just state. Orend suggests that a minimally just state

1. is recognized as legitimate by its own people and most of the international community;
2. avoids violating the rights of other legitimate states; and
3. makes every reasonable effort at satisfying the human rights of its own citizens.[19]

As Orend recognizes, there are various problems with determining whether a state actually meets all these criteria. With regard to Condition 1, for example, in the absence of regular free and fair elections it may be hard to tell whether a state is recognized as legitimate by its own people. A peaceful and apparently stable society might be evidence of the people's recognition of the legitimacy of the state, though this could also be evidence of a significant amount of state coercion. With regard to Condition 3, there is a difference between a state that is unwilling to satisfy the human rights of its citizens and a state that is willing to satisfy these rights but is for some reason unable to do so, yet this difference may not be easily discerned. It is also possible for some of these conditions to overlap with each other, since a state that fails to meet Condition 3 is unlikely to be recognized as legitimate by its own people and thus will probably also fail to meet Condition 1. Nevertheless, the three conditions for a minimally just state are quite helpful in determining whether there is just cause to engage in an insurgency against the state.

I suggested earlier that the ANC had a just cause for war, in that the vast majority of the people of South Africa were being unjustly disenfranchised, discriminated against, and deprived of fundamental human rights. This can be expressed more simply through the use of Orend's conditions; the Nationalist regime in South Africa that upheld apartheid did not qualify as a minimally just state in that it failed Conditions 1, since it was not recognized as legitimate by its own people,[20] and 3, in that it did not make reasonable efforts to satisfy the human rights of its citizens.[21] In fact it is possible to generalize from this case and from Orend's conditions; the existence of a state that is not minimally just is sufficient to provide just cause for war. In cases where the regime fails to meet Condition 3, for example, this will provide just cause for an insurgency by a group within that state. Failure to meet Condition 2 is the sort of situation that is examined in traditional conceptions of *jus ad bellum* as discussed in the previous chapter, for this simply equates to engaging in acts of aggression against other states and will thus provide a just cause for other states to go to war against the unjust state. It is important to remember, however, that simply having just cause for war is not sufficient for a war to be justified, since the other conditions of *jus ad bellum* will still need to be met.

Another important point to remember when discussing whether a state qualifies as a minimally just state, is that a state might be minimally just with regard to its treatment of some of the people it governs but not of others. This is especially the case when one state controls the territory of a number of national groups. For a reasonable part of the twentieth century, for example, many parts of Africa and Asia were controlled by colonial powers, primarily from Europe. The states who controlled these colonial territories may have been minimally just with regard to their treatment of those in Europe, but not with regard to their treatment of the indigenous populations of these colonial territories. For example, the British government, which controlled India, was minimally just in its treatment of those within Great Britain itself, but was not minimally just in its treatment of the people of India, since as well as not being considered legitimate by the indigenous peoples (Condition 1), it also did not make reasonable attempts at satisfying many of the basic human rights of those same people, such as giving them a voice in their own government (Condition 3). Therefore, although there may have been just cause for Indian nationalist groups to mount an insurgency against the British state in India, there would not have been just cause for some Scottish nationalist group to mount an insurgency against the British state in Scotland.

Cases 5.1 (Operation Cast Lead) and 5.2 (The 1999 NATO Intervention in Support of Kosovo) at the beginning of this chapter, both involve situations where there appears to be just cause for an insurgency because the state in control of the disputed territory is not a minimally just state with regard to the local population.[22] In both cases the state fails to meet both Condition 1, by not being recognized as legitimate by the local population, and Condition 3, by not making reasonable efforts to satisfy the human rights of the citizens within the disputed territory. Again, to be clear, the existence of just cause does not mean that an insurgency is immediately justified, since the other conditions of *jus ad bellum* will still need to be met. And even if an insurgency is fully justified under *jus ad bellum*, the tactics adopted by that insurgency may cause problems under *jus in bello*, a point to which I will return shortly.

One significant difference between traditional war and irregular war is that in irregular wars it is often difficult to know whether a state of war exists or not. A good example was the conflict that occurred between the Tamils and the

Sinhalese in Sri Lanka from the mid-1970s through to 2009.[23] The levels of violence in the country fluctuated dramatically over a long period of time, and thus if an attack occurred after a long period of relative calm, it was difficult to know whether to characterize this as a new war or a continuation of the old one. This is in marked contrast to the Arab-Israeli conflicts, where despite ongoing disputes, it is quite clear that the 1973 war, for example, was a new war and not simply a resumption of the hostilities from 1967.

This problem has implications for the justice of the Palestinian insurgency in Case 5.1 (Operation Cast Lead). Moves by Israel to create the Palestinian Authority and allow more autonomy for the Palestinian people suggested that the Israeli state was moving toward being a minimally just state with regard to the Palestinian Territories. Therefore, a person's opinion about whether a continuing insurgency against the Israeli state is justified might depend on their view of whether the current conflict is seen as a continuation of the long conflict between Palestine and Israel, or a new conflict that has begun more recently, after the creation of the Palestinian Authority. An armed insurgency against the Israeli state did seem to be justified in the period before the creation of the Palestinian Authority, so someone who thinks that the continuing insurgency is justified might well suggest that it is simply a continuation of this long conflict. I think that position is one that is difficult to sustain, however, since the signing of a formal agreement between Israel and the PLO marks a very clear change in the relationship between the Israeli government and the people of the Occupied Territories.

If an armed insurgency is to be justified in the Palestinian territories today, then the insurgents need to show that all the conditions of *jus ad bellum* have been met at some point after 1994. In other words, that there is just cause because Israel still fails to fulfill Orend's conditions with regard to being a minimally just state in its treatment of Palestinians; those pursuing the insurgency have legitimate authority, granted to them by the Palestinian people; armed resistance is the last reasonable resort in dealing with the Israeli state; and so on.

Case 5.2 (The 1999 NATO Intervention in Support of Kosovo) presents a somewhat different issue. The Serbian government seems to have been a minimally just state with regard to Kosovo before the Presidency of Slobodan Milosevic.[24] The actions of his government clearly provided just cause for an insurgency, but it is questionable whether all the other conditions of *jus ad bellum* were met before the Kosovo Liberation Army (KLA) began its attacks. In particular, it could be argued that such actions did not meet the principle of last resort, since further nonviolent measures could still have been undertaken, and also that the KLA lacked legitimate authority to conduct their insurgency campaign, especially since the elected leader of the ethnic Albanians in Kosovo, Ibrahim Rugova, endorsed nonviolent protest against Serbian rule.

As a final comment on the ethics of insurgency, I wish to briefly return to the *jus in bello* problems that may be raised by the tactics adopted by an insurgent group. As I noted in the previous chapter, most writers have suggested that *jus ad bellum* and *jus in bello* are completely separate considerations, and therefore, even if a war is fought unjustly, this cannot affect the issue of whether it was just to go to war in the first place. However, other writers have suggested that these two aspects of just war theory are more closely connected. For example, Alex Bellamy argues that if an insurgent organization consistently resorts to tactics that violate *jus in bello* considerations, such as the deliberate targeting of noncombatants through acts of terrorism, then the additional harm this causes changes the consideration of proportionality, which may undermine the *jus ad bellum* case for war.[25] The strategic reliance on tactics that violate the principles of *jus in bello* seems to be far more common in insurgencies than in other types of conflict, which is why the issue is so important in this context. Some of these issues will be discussed in later in this book, in particular in Chapters 8 and 11.

JUS AD BELLUM AND COUNTERINSURGENCY

When discussing whether a state is justified in engaging in counterinsurgency operations, there are a number of things that must be kept in mind. The first thing to remember is that launching military operations against an insurgency is unlikely to be the only direct counterinsurgency option available to a state; since insurgencies are usually subject to domestic law, rather than international law, they are almost inevitably illegal. A state will therefore be legally justified in engaging its law enforcement agencies in counterinsurgency efforts. Although there are a number of ethical issues that may be raised by employing the police in such a manner, since this book is focused on military rather than police ethics, I won't be examining those issues here. However, if the military are employed in domestic counterinsurgency operations, there may be difficult legal issues involved, since many countries have laws that limit the manner in which military personnel may be utilized in domestic situations.[26]

A second important point to note is the difference between law and ethics in these sorts of cases. Even though it will almost always be legally justified, whether the state is ethically justified in engaging in counterinsurgency is quite a different matter. As I mentioned in the previous chapter, it is only possible for one side in a conflict to fulfill the criteria for a just war. Thus in simple terms, if the insurgency is ethically justified, then it would not be ethically justified for the state to engage in counterinsurgency. The previously mentioned problems related to *jus in bello* considerations also come into play here; if the insurgency relies on tactics that violate the principles of *jus in bello*, then it is plausible to suggest that the state may be ethically justified in engaging in military counterinsurgency even if the insurgency was previously fully justified under *jus ad bellum*.

A state will almost inevitably feel that it is justified in engaging in counterinsurgency operations if it is dealing with an insurgency, whether that insurgency is justified or not. However, another state asked to provide assistance in these counterinsurgency operations may well be better placed to impartially assess the justice of the cause of the insurgents and in cases where that state recognizes that justice lies with the insurgents, it may be able to aid in negotiating a settlement between the two sides; the refusal of an external state to provide counterinsurgency assistance may well cause the state dealing with the insurgency to reassess their position.

When looking at whether Israel was justified in going to war to deal with the problems caused by Hamas in Case 5.1 (Operation Cast Lead), there are several issues that must be grappled with. From a legal perspective, one thing that must be considered is the actual status of the Palestinian Territories, in particular, the Gaza strip. Questions of the legality of the attack under international law only arise if this is considered to be an assault on a sovereign state, but these issues don't even arise if the Gaza Strip is considered to be occupied territory, since then the only law that would apply when determining whether or not it was legal for Israel to launch an attack on the Gaza Strip would be the domestic law of Israel.[27] On the other hand, the ethical issues are essentially the same whether this is considered an international assault or an attack on a domestic insurgency, since in either case such an attack needs to meet the conditions of *jus ad bellum*. Of these six criteria, the one that is the most problematic for this assault is the issue of proportionality.

The manner of the Israeli assault meant that it was always going to cause significant damage in the Gaza Strip, and despite the Israeli measures intended to reduce collateral damage, the assault was still likely to cause of a large number of civilian casualties. Given that the rocket attacks from the Gaza Strip had caused a relatively small number of casualties since 2005, far less than even the most conservative estimates of the likely number of collateral casualties from the planned Israeli assault, it would appear that the only way in which the attack can be seen as proportionate is to assign massively more weight to Israeli civilian casualties than to Palestinian ones. This, of course, runs against every idea of the universality of ethics, as well as the fundamental ideas of just war theory. However, the proportionality condition is one where considerations of *jus ad bellum* and *jus in bello* are fairly closely related. The major problem for the *jus ad bellum* proportionality condition in Operation Cast Lead was the number of collateral casualties likely to be caused by Israel's planned, full-scale military assault. If the same military objectives could be achieved without this level of collateral damage, say by using a different strategy in the assault, then the *jus ad bellum* proportionality condition might be fulfilled, and in fact this is what would be ethically required under *jus in bello*. This is an issue that will be examined more closely in Chapter 8, particularly during discussion of Case 8.1 (Casualties in the 2008–2009 Gaza War), which looks at this same conflict from the perspective of *jus in bello*.

Another issue that has also arisen in counterinsurgency is whether a state is justified in using its armed forces to protect its citizens from insurgency or other violence, when those citizens are within the borders of another country.

CASE STUDY 5.4

Israel, Uganda, and the Entebbe Incident

On 27 June 1976, an Air France jet left Israel with 251 passengers and a crew of twelve on board. After a brief stop in Athens, pro-Palestinian hijackers seized control of the plane and forced it to land in Entebbe, Uganda. The hijackers threatened to kill the hostages unless 53 pro-Palestinian terrorists were released from jails in France, Israel, Kenya, Switzerland and West Germany. On the third day of the hijacking, forty-seven non-Jewish passengers were released. On the fourth day another 100 were let go. The Government of Uganda, led by the dictator Idi Amin, took no apparent steps to secure the release of the remaining, mostly Israeli, passengers or the crew.

On 3 July 1976, shortly before the deadline set by the hijackers, Israeli commandos conducted an audacious and highly successful rescue operation. Without notifying the Ugandan government, a small force landed at Entebbe airport, stormed the plane and killed the hijackers. They saved the lives of all but three of the hostages and flew them back to Israel. Jonathan Netanyahu, the leader of the commando unit and the brother of Israeli politician Binyamin Netanyahu, was the only Israeli soldier to die in the raid. A number of Ugandan soldiers were also killed and several Ugandan military aircraft destroyed.

SOURCE: Taken from Michael Byers, *War Law: Understanding International Law and Armed Conflict* (New York: Grove, 2005), p. 57.

This case illustrates a situation that has become increasing common in the modern world, but which had been almost unprecedented up until that time. Israel claimed that international law gave it the right to use its military forces to protect its nationals abroad, if the government of that foreign state was unwilling or unable to do so. Some states vehemently protested the Israeli response, but overall the diplomatic response to the Israeli action in the case was fairly muted, and it has established a new precedent in international law. In the actual Entebbe incident, the pro-Palestinian terrorists were apparently acting not only with tacit approval from the Ugandan government but with active support. Ugandan troops were actually protecting the airport, and the reason why several Ugandan military planes were destroyed was because the Israelis thought it possible, even likely, that Israeli aircraft would be pursued, or shot down, by the Ugandan Air Force as they attempted to leave Ugandan airspace after the raid.

The precedent that this raid set in international law has been extended greatly. In cases where civil war breaks out, or massive riots and disturbances of the peace occur, it is now routine for foreign military forces to be dispatched to that country, usually operating out of the local embassy, to protect their nationals from local strife. The fact that local forces are unable to deal with the incident and protect foreign citizens is seen as sufficient justification for foreign troops to be deployed; active involvement by local military forces in acts against foreign citizens is certainly not viewed as being necessary. The legality of the involvement of foreign military forces is usually only questioned if their operations extend beyond what is necessary to protect foreign nationals from violence; in line with the principle of noninvolvement in the domestic affairs of another state, it has generally been considered illegal for foreign military forces to intervene in a civil war.

But cases like this reveal a significant tension between ethical ideals and the principles of international law. Suppose a civil war has broken out within the borders of the state of Bedania, accompanied by massive riots and disturbances of the peace. As was noted previously, it is considered legally justified for other states around the world to deploy their own military personnel to Bedania to protect their nationals from local strife. But if the state of Aydania is justified in deploying soldiers into Bedania to protect the fundamental rights of Aydanian nationals who are caught up in the conflict, why should it not be justifiable for those troops to also act to protect the fundamental rights of Bedanian nationals who are also caught up in the conflict? This is really the fundamental question that has motivated people to discuss the ethics of armed humanitarian interventions and is the topic to which I will now turn my attention.

JUSTIFICATION FOR HUMANITARIAN INTERVENTION

The modern idea of deploying military personnel on peacekeeping missions arose after the end of World War II and the creation of the UN. When conflicts arose that threatened international peace and stability, the UN was sometimes able to mediate a settlement between the warring parties. Often such situations would require neutral observers to monitor the situation and report on breaches of the conditions of the peace settlement, and so the UN began to organize multinational missions to deploy to such areas and monitor the situation. Such deployments were not limited to international conflicts, since a number of civil wars, especially in Africa and Central America, ended after the UN brokered peace settlements, which often involved the deployment of multinational forces to monitor the domestic security situation in those countries. All of these deployments were organized with the cooperation of the states involved, which resolved any issues in international law since foreign military forces may legally deploy to the territory controlled by other states if they are invited in by the relevant state.

After the end of the Cold War in 1989, the range and number of such deployments began to increase rapidly, and missions began to be organized to deal with other sorts of humanitarian crises, such as famines. Some of these sorts of operations took place in territory controlled by what have come to be known as "failed states"; areas where either no recognizable government existed, or where the government had completely lost its ability to guarantee people's basic rights and to provide services essential to society.

The legal issues in mounting such missions were rather more complicated since in some of these cases there was no recognizable government that could issue an invitation to foreign military forces asking them to intervene. In these cases the authorization of the UNSC was seen as sufficient to resolve such legal questions. The ethical questions in such interventions were considered to be somewhat more straightforward, since the UN-sponsored military forces were not conducting traditional military operations, but rather were present to provide security to the UN civilian workers who were themselves providing food and other aid to local civilian populations. Because the problems that were being dealt with in these missions were essentially natural disasters, and the UN intervention was simply to provide immediate emergency aid, just war theory did not even seem to apply. However, other, more difficult issues arose in cases when the problems that confronted peacekeeping missions were fundamentally caused by human violence.

CASE STUDY 5.5

The Rwandan Genocide

In 1994 there were two main ethnic groups in Rwanda; the Hutus who made up over 80% of the population, and the Tutsis, who made up about 15%. When Rwanda was a Belgian colony, it was dominated by a Tutsi aristocracy; the Belgians supported this arrangement since it would allow them to control the country more easily. During the period of Belgian control people were issued with identification cards that specified their ethnic grouping, and the use of such cards continued until after the genocide of 1994; the existence of these cards made it easy to target people on the basis of their ethnicity.

Rwanda gained independence from Belgium in 1962, and the Hutu majority elected an overwhelmingly Hutu government, which controlled the country until 1994. In the years shortly before independence, there were many clashes between Hutus and Tutsis in Rwanda and also in neighboring Burundi, which had similar ethnic demographics. Due to their control of the army, the Tutsis remained in power in Burundi, which was governed by a military dictatorship. Over the years, tensions grew between the two states; and there were many clashes between the two ethnic groups domestically, with many Tutsis killed or forced to leave their homes in Hutu-dominated Rwanda, with the opposite situation occurring in Burundi, where

Tutsis controlled the military. Tens of thousands of people were killed in this period, especially in Burundi.

Many Tutsis who were driven out of Rwanda settled in Uganda, immediately to the north, and these refugees formed an insurgent army, the Rwandan Patriotic Front (RPF), which invaded Rwanda from the north in 1990. These troops were well-trained and well-equipped; many had been part of the Ugandan army and had combat experience from the Ugandan civil war. They had early success, but were forced to retreat when troops from Zaire and France arrived in Rwanda to support the local government.[28] The RPF began fighting a guerrilla war out of the forests and mountains of northern Rwanda, and this civil war continued until 1993 and the signing of the Arusha Accords, which agreed to a power sharing deal and a peace treaty. A UN peacekeeping force of some 2,500 personnel, largely composed of Belgian troops and under the command of Canadian Major-General Dallaire, was deployed to the country to monitor the cease-fire.

On January 11, 1994, Dallaire received intelligence about four major arms caches in Rwanda and plans by Hutu extremists for a massacre of Tutsis. He informed his superiors of this intelligence and of his intentions to seize the arms caches, but was informed that this would exceed the mandate of the UN forces and was ordered to simply inform the Rwandan government of these possible violations of the Arusha Accords. On April 6, 1994, a plane carrying the Presidents of Rwanda and Burundi was shot down as it approached Kigali airport, killing all on board. Who was actually responsible for this event is still unclear, but the assassination of the Rwandan President started a wave of violence in Kigali and across the country. In this situation, the Arusha Accords gave authority to the Rwandan Prime Minister, Agathe Uwilingiyimanato, a moderate Hutu, but since the Rwandan Army disputed this point, Dallaire decided the Prime Minister would need protection and he committed a group of Belgian and Ghanaian soldiers from the UN force to this task, as well as sending troops to protect other moderates who favored the Arusha Accords. The Prime Minister's house was protected by the Rwandan Presidential guard as well as the UN troops, but in the early hours of April 7, the presidential guard turned their weapons on the UN soldiers and ordered them to surrender. Apparently unsure of what their Rules of Engagement allowed, the soldiers complied with the direction. The Ghanaian soldiers were released but the ten Belgian soldiers were murdered shortly afterward, as was the Prime Minister and most of the other moderates whom the UN troops were trying to protect, along with their families. The murder of the Belgian soldiers was apparently carried out with the explicit intention of encouraging Belgium to end its commitment to the UN force, and it was successful in this regard, for the Belgian contingent was withdrawn from Rwanda almost immediately, leaving Dallaire with only 270 troops and some 200 local authorities under his command. Hutu extremists were now in effective control of the country and the genocide could begin.

Local Hutu radio stations began to broadcast propaganda aimed at inciting the killing of Tutsis and Hutu moderates, and the Rwandan Army and Hutu militias began massacring Tutsis. After UN personnel observed a massacre of Tutsis in Kigali, Dallaire informed the UN that ethnicity was the driving force behind the killings, and he requested an extra 5,000 troops to stop the violence. Instead, he was ordered to leave the country along with the rest of his forces, an order he refused, as he felt he could not abandon the civilians to their fate. Many foreign troops arrived in Rwanda over the next few days, but only to protect their own nationals and evacuate their embassies; none stayed to support Dallaire and his forces. Mass killings of Tutsis began across the country, with most of the victims killed by machetes or small arms fire. The killings were carried out essentially without regard to age or sex, as women and children made up a large number of the victims. In addition, many Tutsi women and girls who were not killed were sexually assaulted, leaving many of them HIV positive; a later investigation by the UN suggested that it was possible that almost all the female Tutsis who survived the genocide had been raped.

The violence in the country ended when the RPF forces, who had renewed their assault after the attacks on Tutsis began, managed to take control of the country in mid-July. Since those who perpetrated the violence made no attempt to document the killings, the exact number of deaths is uncertain; official Rwandan government figures state that more than one million people were killed, about 10% of them Hutus. The UN suggests the death toll was about 800,000, with a somewhat larger percentage of Hutus. About a third of the Tutsis on the planet were exterminated in the 100 days of the Rwandan genocide.

Prompted in large part by the state-sponsored extermination of Jews and other minority groups in German occupied territories in the Holocaust in World War II, the international community adopted the Convention on the Prevention and Punishment of the Crime of Genocide, which came into force in January 1951. This convention defines genocide in legal terms. Various acts including murder, causing serious mental or bodily harm, acting so as to prevent birth, and so on, fall within the definition of genocide if those acts "are committed with intent to destroy, in whole or in part, a national, ethnical, racial or religious group."[29] The existence of such a convention should have made it easier for the member states of the UN to deal with events in Rwanda in 1994, since any party to the convention is theoretically committed to preventing acts of genocide from occurring. However, the legal mechanisms for enforcement of the convention require parties to "call upon the competent organs of the United Nations to take such action under the Charter of the United Nations as they consider appropriate for the prevention and suppression of acts of genocide."[30] In effect, this means that to be legal, any action to prevent a particular instance of genocide must be approved by the UNSC. Rwanda was a member of the UNSC in 1994, and although it did not have a veto, the UNSC's discussions were made more complex by this fact.

Since it was known that a civil war was in progress at the time and at least some of the information coming out of Rwanda about the genocide was unclear, many states apparently felt that it would be inappropriate to intervene in Rwanda, given the long-standing prohibition on interfering in the internal affairs of another state. Thus, foreign states acted only to remove their own nationals from Rwanda, despite Dallaire's clear warnings that ethnicity was the driving force behind the killings and thus genocide was occurring.

The ethical justification for intervening in the Rwandan case is much clearer than the legal situation apparently was at the time. If genocide is occurring then there is really no need for further ethical justification, since an attempt to eliminate an entire national, ethnical, racial, or religious group is perhaps the most heinous crime against humanity it is possible to commit. However, it is also possible to provide a strong ethical justification for intervening in such a situation using just war theory. Most of the six *jus ad bellum* criteria are fairly obviously fulfilled in such a case, with the most problematic ones being just cause and legitimate authority. It may be surprising to many people to hear me suggest that just cause is problematic in such a case. The reason why I suggest this is that the just war tradition has tended to construe just cause fairly narrowly, and ever since the peace of Westphalia, both legal and ethical interpretations of just war have tended to exclude the possibility of interference in the domestic affairs of other states.

With regard to just cause, although many writers claim that defending against aggression is the only possible just cause for war,[31] it can certainly be argued that defending innocent and unprotected people from the aggression of their own state is of no less important than defending one's state from the aggression of another, which would mean that just cause does exist in cases where genocide is occurring, at least in cases where this has the direct or tacit support of the state.[32] After all, if we consider things at their most basic level, then the reason that a state is entitled to engage in war to defend itself against the aggression of another state is because the fundamental human rights of its citizens, things like the right to life, to freedom, to political self-determination, and so on, are threatened by the aggression of the other state. A state is also justified in engaging in warfare to defend citizens of another state, when those same rights are threatened by an aggressor; Case 4.1 (The 1991 Gulf War) is a good example of this. So it is not too much of a stretch to think that a state would also be justified in engaging in warfare if this is the only way of protecting the fundamental human rights of citizens of another state from the aggressive attacks of their own state, or of parties supported by the state, as was the situation in Rwanda in 1994.[33]

With regard to legitimate authority, although the UNSC is the appropriate legal authority to authorize an intervention, in cases where the UNSC is unwilling or unable to act, then ethical authority, as opposed to legal authority, to intervene can be found elsewhere. If defending people from the aggression of their own state is considered to be morally equivalent to defending one state from the aggression of another, then it can be argued that the legitimate authority for such an intervention should also be the same. This would mean that any state could justifiably intervene unilaterally, provided that the correct domestic procedures for the authorization for military action were followed, since this is all that is required when one state takes military action to defend another state from aggression.

Another possibility is that there may be a consensus among a significantly large group of relevant states that action is necessary; although this cannot grant the authority to intervene under international law, it can be taken to provide the ethical authority to intervene. This is essentially what happened in Case 5.2 (The 1999 NATO Intervention in Support of Kosovo), when the NATO member states decided to act to protect the ethnic Albanians of Kosovo from the actions of the Yugoslav government. Although some might argue that the situation on the ground in Kosovo was not as serious as it appeared to outside observers, the consensus among NATO states that action was required, grants ethical authority to the intervention. However, arguing that this consensus granted legal authority to the intervention, despite the lack of authorization from the UNSC, is far more difficult.

In the end, the lack of foreign intervention to prevent the genocide in Rwanda by those states with the power to intervene was probably due more to a lack of political will than any perceived or actual legal or ethical issues. In the United States, for example, having faced a significant domestic political backlash due to the casualties sustained by U.S. troops in the humanitarian intervention in Somalia in 1993,[34] the government was extremely reluctant to become involved in another intervention in central Africa, unless it involved pressing issues of U.S. national security, which was clearly not the case in Rwanda. Even after the United States government privately acknowledged that "acts of genocide" were taking place in Rwanda, government spokespeople avoided using the term in public statements, since doing so would have implied a moral duty to intervene. However, once the full scale of the events in Rwanda became public, there was a significant backlash, particularly in the Western world, against those governments that were seen to be responsible for allowing the genocide to continue. This probably explains, at least partly, why the NATO states were unwilling to allow similar circumstances to develop in Kosovo.

CASE STUDY 5.6

Intervention in East Timor

Originally a Portuguese colony, East Timor was effectively abandoned by Portugal in 1975 as part of the process of decolonization. East Timor briefly declared independence, but was then occupied by Indonesia, and was declared a province of Indonesia the following year. The period of Indonesian occupation, from 1975 to 1999, was marked by violence, including an insurgency campaign by pro-independence forces that continued throughout the occupation. Estimates of the number of East Timorese who died as a result of the occupation vary, but an official report prepared in 2006 estimated a minimum of over 100,000 deaths.[35]

In 1999, the Indonesian government held a UN sponsored referendum in the province to decide its future; voters were given a choice between East Timor becoming an independent state or becoming a Special Autonomous Region within Indonesia. The period before the referendum saw a significant increase in violence, primarily in the form of attacks on pro-independence campaigners by pro-Indonesian militias, allegedly backed by the Indonesian military. This included several massacres of significant numbers of unarmed civilians. The largest, at a Catholic church in a town west of the East Timorese capital, Dili, involved the deaths of at least 61 people. Despite the violence, an estimated 95% of registered voters cast a ballot in the referendum, held on August 30, with 78.5% voting for East Timorese independence.

The announcement of these results on September 4 led to a massive increase in violence and destruction over the next few days. Over a thousand people were killed by pro-Indonesian militia, and 300,000 people, nearly a third of the East Timorese population, were forcibly moved into neighboring (Indonesian) West Timor. In addition the majority of East Timor's infrastructure, including homes, water supply systems, schools, and nearly 100% of the electrical grid, was destroyed. On September 12, under pressure from many states, including the U.S.A.,[36] the Indonesian President announced he would allow UN peacekeepers to enter the province to restore order. On September 15, the UNSC passed Resolution 1264, which authorized action, and the first troops of the Australian-led International Force for East Timor (INTERFET), under the command of Major-General Peter Cosgrove, landed in East Timor on September 20. This show of international force saw a rapid decrease in violence, especially as INTERFET numbers swelled to nearly 10 000, including personnel from 17 different states. Once control was established, international forces remained in place, with one of their functions being to assist the local and UN law enforcement authorities who were investigating the violent crimes committed in the periods prior to, and after, the referendum.

After a period of UN administration, on May 20, 2002, the Democratic Republic of Timor-Leste became the first new sovereign state of the twenty-first century.

The East Timor situation brings together a number of the issues of insurgency and humanitarian intervention. The pro-independence insurgency that operated during the period of Indonesian occupation of East Timor seems to meet the *jus ad bellum* criteria for a justified insurgency. Most notable in this regard is the fact that the Indonesian government did not qualify as a minimally just state with regard to its governance of East Timor. It was not recognized as legitimate by the local population, as evidenced by the massive vote in favor of independence; and, given the number of deaths during the occupation, it can be seen that the Indonesian government also failed to uphold the basic rights of the East Timorese people during this period. The actions of the insurgents appear to be even more ethically justified when it is recognized that they essentially stopped their violent activity when the Indonesian government announced that it would hold the referendum on independence and it became apparent that violence was no longer

necessary to achieve the insurgents' ends. Indeed, when the pro-Indonesian militia began their attacks after the results of the referendum were announced, the
East Timorese insurgents still refrained from violence, as it was apparent to their
leaders that other options were now available; international opinion was clearly
swinging against the Indonesian occupation and might soon lead to independence
without the need for further attacks.

The new international attitude to intervention in such cases was also apparent in the responses, which various states made, to the upswing in violence after
the referendum. Despite the fact that East Timor was under Indonesian control,
the violence in the province was not regarded as simply a domestic matter, especially since the desire of the people for independence had been shown. Though
the massive forcible displacement of the East Timorese population did not constitute an act of genocide under the international convention, such actions had
been a precursor to attempts at genocide in other places, and this gave ethical justification for intervention here. There were still difficulties in international law,
since foreign troops intervening in the situation without the approval of the
Indonesian government could have been seen as an act of war, but once Indonesia
had been pressured into allowing an international intervention, these legal difficulties were resolved. The UNSC resolution was the final step ensuring that the
intervention in East Timor was fully justified under both international law and
the ethical ideals of just war theory.

RESPONSIBILITY TO PROTECT

The concerns that were raised about the failure to prevent genocide in Rwanda
(Case 5.5) and about the justification of other armed humanitarian interventions,
such as in Kosovo (Case 5.2) and East Timor (Case 5.6) led various states and
non-governmental organizations to question some of the fundamental concepts
of international law, particularly with regard to state sovereignty. These concerns
led, in 2001, to the formation of an ad hoc commission of interested states,
known as the International Commission on Intervention and State Sovereignty.
Its purpose was to discuss issues of humanitarian intervention and state sovereignty, and particularly to consider whether it is appropriate for state sovereignty
to remain inviolable if there is evidence that crimes such as genocide and ethnic
cleansing are being carried on inside a state's borders.

The report of this commission argued that state sovereignty was a responsibility, not a privilege, and that each state has an unconditional responsibility to
protect its population from mass atrocities, including genocide, ethnic cleansing,
war crimes, and crimes against humanity. It also argued that all states have a
responsibility to use whatever means are necessary to assist each other in protecting people from these crimes of mass atrocity. Thus, if a state is willing, but

unable, to protect its people from these crimes, other states have a responsibility to assist through mediation and/or capacity building. And if a state fails to protect its citizens from mass atrocities, the international community therefore has a responsibility to intervene, by whichever means are most appropriate: diplomatically in the first instance, more coercively if diplomacy fails, and with the use of military force as a last resort.

The doctrine has become known as "Responsibility to Protect" (RtoP). The basics of the doctrine of RtoP were agreed to by UN member states at the 2005 World Summit and affirmed by a UN General Assembly resolution in 2009. This international consensus certainly reinforces the ethical idea that protecting the citizens of a state from the aggressive attack of their own government is a just cause for launching an armed humanitarian intervention. However, it does not actually alter the situation in international law, since despite these UN resolutions, the UNSC remains the only body which can legally authorize an armed intervention, even on the grounds of RtoP.

NOTES

1. The population density of Gaza City is roughly equivalent to the density of the New York City borough of Queens, with approximately 9,000 people per square kilometer.
2. Specifically under Article 6 of the Fourth Geneva Convention.
3. Large-scale movement of people or goods by air has been essentially impossible since the virtual destruction of Gaza's only airport, Yasser Arafat International Airport, by Israeli forces in 2001.
4. This smuggling passes through a large number of tunnels dug under the border from the Gaza Strip into Egypt.
5. Figures quoted are taken from the counts of ethnicity in official Yugoslavian censuses of 1961 and 1991.
6. Report of the Commission of Experts Established Pursuant to United Nations Security Council Resolution 780, (1992), May 27, 1994, paragraph 130.
7. Quoted in David N. Gibbs, *First Do No Harm: Humanitarian Intervention and the Destruction of Yugoslavia* (Nashville, TN: Vanderbilt University Press, 2009), p. 181.
8. It should be noted, however, that Milosevic's suggested alternative peace plan for Kosovo, presented late in the negotiations, was rejected as unacceptable not only by the delegations from the KLA, the U.S.A., and the Western European countries, but also by the Russian delegation.
9. Under this definition, most, but not all, rebellions will count as insurgencies. The American Civil War, for example, can be categorized as a rebellion, but is not an insurgency under this definition, since the forces of the Confederate Army represented a formally constituted rebelling authority.

10. Chapter 7—Terrorism in *Just Wars: From Cicero to Iraq* (Cambridge U.K.: Polity, 2006), pp. 135–157.

11. "Just War Theory, Law Enforcement and Terrorism: A Reflective Equilibrium." In *War, Morality and Autonomy: An Investigation in Just War Theory* (Aldershot U.K.: Ashgate, 2004), pp.145–160, Epilogue.

12. *War and Ethics: A New Just War Theory* (London: Continuum, 2007).

13. Fotion, *War and Ethics*, p. 89.

14. *Financial Mail*, November 1, 1974. Quoted in Anthea Jeffrey *People's War: New Light on the Struggle for South Africa* (Johannesburg: Jonathan Ball, 2009), p. xxxi.

15. Quoted in Mary Benson, *Nelson Mandela* (Harmondsworth, U.K.: Penguin, 1986), pp. 100–111.

16. This convention branded the policies of apartheid an international crime, not just in South Africa, but wherever similar policies might be practiced.

17. Bellamy, *Just Wars*, p. 138.

18. Bellamy bases his third condition on arguments originally suggested by Janna Thompson in "Terrorism and the Right to Wage War," in Tony Coady & Michael O'Keefe (eds.), *Terrorism and Justice: Moral Argument in a Threatened World* (Melbourne: Melbourne University Press, 2002), pp. 87–96, pp. 92–93.

19. *The Morality of War* (Peterborough, ON: Broadview, 2006), pp. 35–36, p. 83.

20. Given the international attempts to force South Africa to end its policy of apartheid, it could perhaps also be argued that the Nationalist regime was not recognized as legitimate by the international community either. However, although other states did engage in extensive attempts to persuade the Nationalist government to change its policies, I am not aware of any that went so far as to actually withdraw their recognition of the government, something which has occurred on occasion elsewhere, such as when an elected government has been overthrown in a military coup. Perhaps the best way to link this international pressure on the South African government to Orend's conditions is to say that this international pressure demonstrated that other states were aware that the government of South Africa was failing Orend's third condition, in that it was not making a reasonable attempt to satisfy the fundamental human rights of its citizens.

21. South Africa actually also violated Condition 2 in that it launched a number of raids and attacks into neighboring sovereign states where the ANC had camps and other facilities. The aim of these attacks was to disrupt the activities of the ANC.

22. In saying with regard to Case 5.1, I am assuming, in accordance with the official position of the UN, that Israel is still the controlling power in the Gaza Strip.

23. This example comes from Fotion's *War and Ethics*.

24. One interesting issue, beyond the scope of this discussion, is whether the denial of the right to nationalistic self-determination is strong enough to provide just cause for an insurgency against a state that is minimally just in all other respects. For example, if the Serbian government had allowed the continued autonomy of Kosovo but denied it full independence, despite the people of Kosovo wanting to be fully independent, would this provide just cause for an armed insurgency? Of course, even if this did

provide just cause, other conditions like proportionality may not be met, meaning that an armed insurgency still would not be justified.

25. This issue is discussed at some length in Chapter 7 of Bellamy's *Just Wars: From Cicero to Iraq.*

26. In the U.S.A., for example, the Posse Comitatus Act of 1878 prohibits federal forces (Army, Marines, Navy, Air Force, and National Guard units under federal control) from acting in any domestic law enforcement capacity unless specifically authorized by the Constitution or by Congress. The Act does not apply to the U.S. Coast Guard.

27. To be clear here, considerations about whether or not the Gaza Strip is occupied territory only apply to legal questions with regard to the actual launching of an assault. Once a conflict has started, International Humanitarian Law still applies, regardless of whether or not the Gaza Strip is considered to be occupied territory.

28. France claimed that its troops were only present in the country to protect French nationals from the violence, but the French troops took up positions that blocked the RPF advance toward the Rwanda capital of Kigali and its airport.

29. Article 2 of the Convention on the Prevention and Punishment of the Crime of Genocide, http://www.preventgenocide.org/law/convention/text.htm#links (accessed May 6, 2010).

30. Ibid., Article 8.

31. Michael Walzer certainly follows this line. See *Just and Unjust Wars* (New York: Basic, 1977).

32. In cases where genocide is occurring without the support of the state, then that state ought to be attempting to prevent the genocide from occurring. If they are unable to do so, then they ought to be asking for external assistance.

33. Thanks to Ned Dobos for pointing out the need for clarification of this point, as well as for his suggestions about how this clarity might be achieved.

34. These events are famously recounted in Mark Bowden's book, *Black Hawk Down: A Story of Modern War* (New York: Penguin, 1999), which was the basis for the 2001 academy award winning movie of the same name, directed by Ridley Scott.

35. Romesh Silva & Patrick Ball, *The Profile of Human Rights Violations in Timor-Leste, 1974–1999.* Report by the Benetech Human Rights Data Analysis Group to the CAVR, February 9, 2006. The CAVR is the Commission for Reception, Truth and Reconciliation in East Timor, known by its Portuguese initials, CAVR (*A Comissão de Acolhimento, Verdade e Reconciliação*).

36. The United States threatened to suspend military and economic ties with Indonesia, and President Clinton warned Indonesia that if it did not end the violence then it **must** invite the international community to assist in restoring security (emphasis in the original). Clinton also accused the Indonesian military of direct involvement in the violence. See Clinton Fernandes, "East Timor," in C. Fernandes (ed.), *Hot Spot: Asia and Oceania* (Westport, CT: Greenwood Press, 2008), pp. 25–49. President Clinton's remarks are quoted on p. 39, along with comments from the Defense Secretary, the Chairman of the Joint Chiefs of Staff, and the State Department.

FURTHER READING

Coleman, Stephen. "Just War, Irregular War, and Terrorism." In Paolo Tripodi & Jessica Wolfendale (eds.), *New Wars and New Soldiers: Military Ethics in the Contemporary World* (Farnham, U.K.: Ashgate, 2011).

Dobos, Ned. "Is U.N. Security Council Authorisation for Armed Humanitarian Intervention Morally Necessary?" *Philosophia* 38(2010), 499–515.

Dobos, Ned. "Rebellion, Humanitarian Intervention, and the Prudential Constraints on War." *Journal of Military Ethics* 7(2008), 102-115.

Fotion, Nick. *War and Ethics: A New Just War Theory* (London: Continuum, 2008).

Guthrie, Charles & Quinlan, Michael. *Just War: The Just War Tradition: Ethics in Modern Warfare* (London: Bloomsbury, 2007).

Norman, Richard. "War, Humanitarian Intervention and Human Rights." In Richard Sorabji & David Rodin (eds.), *The Ethics of War: Shared Problems in Different Traditions* (Aldershot, U.K.: Ashgate, 2006).

Orend, Brian. *The Morality of War* (Peterborough, ON: Broadview, 2006). Chapter 3: "*Jus ad Bellum* #2: Non-Classical Wars."

Rodin, David. "The Ethics of Asymmetric War." In Richard Sorabji & David Rodin (eds.), *The Ethics of War: Shared Problems in Different Traditions* (Aldershot, U.K.: Ashgate, 2006).

DISCUSSION QUESTIONS

- Is just war theory at all relevant to modern times?
- Can traditional just war theory be applied to modern conflicts such as irregular wars and armed humanitarian interventions? Or can just war theory only be applied to such cases if some modifications to the theory are made? Or is just war theory simply not applicable to these modern types of conflicts?
- When, if ever, is it ethically justified to engage in an armed insurgency against the state? When, if ever, is it ethically justified for a state to engage in counterinsurgency operations?

6

Power and Authority—Issuing and Following Orders

7 CASE STUDY 6.1

Ehren Watada and Iraq

In June 2006, U.S. Army First Lieutenant Ehren Watada refused orders to deploy to Iraq with his unit, becoming the first U.S. commissioned officer to refuse such orders. His refusal was based on the fact that he believed the war was illegal and thus that following such orders would make him party to war crimes. He argued that the war was illegal in several respects, in that it violated the U.S. Constitution and the War Powers Act, as well as the UN Charter, the Geneva Conventions, and the Nuremberg principles banning wars of aggression.

Watada joined the army after the war in Iraq had begun, and was commissioned by the Army's Officer Candidate School in November 2003. He served a year in South Korea before eventually being reassigned to Fort Lewis, Washington. After arriving there Watada became aware that the unit would be deploying to Iraq, and he began to prepare for the deployment by researching the country and the reasons for U.S. involvement in Iraq. It was during this time that he became convinced of the illegality of the war. Watada attempted to resign his commission in January 2006, but the Army refused his request because his period of contracted service had not yet expired.

After his refusal to deploy in Iraq, Watada spoke at a number of public functions and in media interviews to explain his actions. Each time he spoke, he followed the established U.S. Army rules for making public statements in that he notified his commanding officer, wore civilian clothes and not his uniform, and made it clear that he was expressing his personal views and not the views of the U.S. Army or Department of Defense. He stated that he was not a conscientious objector, since he did not object to all wars on principle, but rather that he believed the war in Iraq to be illegal. He has also later claimed that he offered to serve in Afghanistan, where he believed the war was unambiguously legal, but his offer was refused. Watada was

21

apparently offered a desk job in Iraq, without direct combat involvement, an offer which he refused.

Watada was initially charged with seven offences under the Uniform Code of Military Justice, including charges of "missing movement," "conduct unbecoming an officer and a gentleman," and "contempt for officials." Only three charges eventually proceeded to court-martial: one count of "missing movement" for failing to deploy to Iraq, and two counts of "conduct unbecoming an officer and a gentleman" for statements Watada made in speeches and interviews. A hearing determined that there was sufficient evidence against Watada to proceed to a full court-martial. The Judge presiding over the court-martial ruled before its commencement that the issue of whether or not the war was legal was a political question not suitable for judicial consideration. He thus ruled as lawful the order to deploy and prohibited Watada's defense team from presenting any evidence questioning the legality of the war. The prosecution reached a deal with Watada whereby some charges against him were withdrawn in return for his stipulation[1] that he had in fact refused the order to deploy and had made the statements attributed to him.

Watada's term of service ended in December 2006, but the Army kept him on active duty while his case was pending. The initial court-martial began on February 5, 2007. Watada pleaded not guilty to all counts, and the prosecution began to present its evidence against him. The court-martial ended in a mistrial after the Judge ruled that Watada's stipulation, on which the prosecution case was based, amounted to an admission of guilt and was inadmissible. A date was set for a second court-martial, but this was delayed by Watada's legal team launching various appeals against further proceedings on the grounds of double jeopardy, a law that prevents a person being tried twice for the same crime. In October 2008, a ruling was eventually handed down by the U.S. District Court that Watada could not be retried on the three counts that had proceeded to the first court-martial. In announcing the Army's intention to appeal this decision, spokesman Joe Piek made it clear that "The one element that concerns us most is that this case has always been and will forever be about a soldier—in this case, a lieutenant, a commissioned officer—who refused orders to deploy."[2] It was also emphasized that even if the appeal was unsuccessful the Army still had the right to proceed against Watada with the two counts of "conduct unbecoming an officer and a gentleman," which had previously been dropped.

In May 2009, the Army dropped its appeal against the District Court's ruling. On October 2, 2009, Ehren Watada was discharged from the Army.

CASE STUDY 6.2

Marine Advance on Baghdad

A marine company commander was leading his company pushing toward Baghdad in the 2003 invasion of Iraq (Case 4.2), and he was on a tight timeline to join up with other companies in his battalion. He needed to push through a town that was on his route to his rendezvous point. He had received intelligence that the northern sector of that town had been occupied by Republican Guard and Iraqi army enemies of the U.S. forces, who were waiting in ambush. The company commander had been directed to train artillery on that portion of the town that was near the road he had to traverse, since such an attack would clear out any enemy combatants who might threaten his force during their transit through the town. The company commander also had other, less clear, indicators that the enemy may not be there, and he was relatively certain that the section of town that was to be targeted by the artillery was still populated. He was receiving pressure from higher headquarters to speed up his movement to the rendezvous, but, rather than destroy an entire section of the town with an artillery barrage, and against the recommendation of his own staff, he halted his progress to send a reconnaissance element into the town to determine whether the enemy was indeed where it was reported to be. He held back the artillery barrage until receiving reports from his reconnaissance team. It turned out that the enemy had already left the town, and he was therefore able to move his unit through the town without resistance, and without having destroyed a whole section of the town with the likelihood of killing many noncombatants. He made up time elsewhere to make the scheduled rendezvous.

SOURCE: Based on a case written by Captain Bob Schoultz, U.S. Navy (Retired).

DISCUSSION

Every person who serves in uniform in the military must deal with the issuing of orders. Those at the lowest ranks in the military will usually only be following orders, and those at the very highest ranks will most commonly be issuing orders, rather than following them, but for everybody else, issuing and following orders is, in its truest and most literal sense, an everyday occurrence. Ethical issues can easily arise in the process of issuing or following orders, both in combat zones and in peacetime operations, so in this chapter, I will discuss the various issues that may arise and the things that must be considered in dealing with those issues, as well as examining some other topics that arise in this context, such as what makes a person an effective or ineffective leader and why it is important for leaders to set a good moral example. Some readers may question why a discussion about issuing and following orders would include these sorts of comments about leadership. My answer to this question is fairly straightforward; command and leadership are not the same thing, in that people obey commanders, but follow leaders. In the years I have been teaching prospective military officers, I have never come across anyone who was happy simply to command others: All wanted to be leaders. Thus, my discussion about the ethical issues of command, of issuing and following orders, also includes discussion of issues related to leadership as well.

The issuing and following of orders raises inherent issues of power and authority, so before delving into the specific issues raised by military orders, it is worthwhile to take a little time to discuss what we actually mean by the terms "power" and "authority" in this sort of context. The term authority is actually used in a number of different ways, such as to define a relationship between people, or a permission granted to someone, or to recognize someone's expertise in a partic-ular field of knowledge. Thus the meaning of the term "authority" will differ depending on the context in which it is used. For example, when saying that a platoon leader has authority over the soldiers in their platoon, the term is being used to define the relationship between the leader and the soldiers. On the other hand, saying that the officer presiding over a court-martial has the authority to decide on the severity of any punishment issued by the court is to recognize that the presiding officer has been given the permission to decide on punishment, whereas making the claim that the same presiding officer is an authority on the law that applies to this case is to make a claim about the presiding officer's exper-tise in that area. When discussing the issues raised by the issuing and following of orders, it is obviously the first of these, the authority relationship, which is the most important, but the others should not be ignored.

The term "power" can also be used in different ways, such as to define the ability that a person or group has, or to refer to a permission that has been given to do specific things. So if an officer was to claim that they had the power to eliminate all enemy forces in a particular area, they would be using the term to refer to the ability of the forces they commanded, but if they were to say that they had been given the power to accept the enemy's surrender, then they would actu-ally be talking about a permission that had been granted to them. Strictly speak-ing, when talking about the power to accept the enemy's surrender, the officer is actually talking about having the authority to do so. To avoid these sorts of confu-sions, for the purposes of this discussion, which focuses on dealings between peo-ple, I will use the term authority when talking about a right or permission and the term power when talking about what a person or group actually has the ability to do. It should be noted that when the terms are used in this way, power and authority do not always go together; a person might have the authority to do something, but not the power, or they might have the power to do something, but not the authority. For example, in Case 4.6 (The Falklands War) it is clear that the commander of the Argentine Air Force had the authority to sink all the ships of the British naval force sent to recapture the Falkland Islands, but lacked the power to do so. On the other hand, the commander of the coalition forces in Case 4.1 (The 1991 Gulf War) apparently had the power to advance on Baghdad and topple the regime of Saddam Hussein, but clearly lacked the authority to do so since UNSC Resolution 678 only authorized the use of force to expel Iraqi forces from Kuwait.

Even in cases where a person has authority, this authority will always be lim-ited in scope. In particular, there will always be limits on the specific people that a person has authority over, or is considered an authority by, and in what area that authority applies. So to take the previously mentioned example of the officer presiding over a court-martial, this officer will have authority over the conduct of the trial and the people involved with it, such as the accused, the various lawyers dealing with the case, witnesses, and so on. However, this officer would not have authority over those same people at a different time and place, such as at a local restaurant. The scope of a person's expertise will also be limited in similar ways, so while the officer presiding over a court-martial might be an authority on the law that applies to such proceedings, it is unlikely that the same officer is also an authority on constitutional law, even though this an another topic within the same general field, that of law.

In considering the authority of military commanders, the limits on the scope of that authority must always be taken into account. Such authority usually has some strict legal limits: a commander cannot order someone to perform an illegal action, for example, but usually has other limits as well, which may be defined explicitly by regulations or orders from a higher authority, or may simply be defined by tradition. If we are considering the limits on authority in terms of the people someone has authority over, it is clear that even relatively senior officers, who have a great deal of authority over those under their command, will have substantially less authority over other personnel who are not under their direct command, and may well have no authority at all over military personnel from another state who are part of the same multinational force. Even in dealing with the personnel directly under their command, the same officer will also have limits with regard to the areas in which they can legitimately apply that authority. So although it might be perfectly acceptable for them to order a subordinate to wash a particular military vehicle, it would not be acceptable for them to order that same subordinate to wash the commander's civilian car.

CONSIDERING AUTHORITY

In examining the ethical issues raised by the exercise of authority in the military, particularly with regard to the issuing and following of orders, there are certain factors that must be considered. These include (1) the source of the authority that is being discussed and (2) the steps that may be taken to support and enforce that authority if it proves to be ineffective in a particular situation. This second point has often not been well understood, so I will briefly address it before coming back to discuss the importance of understanding the source of a person's authority.

Effectiveness: If some person A has authority to control the actions of another person B, and B does what they have been told to do simply because they respect the authority held by A, then we can say that A holds effective authority in that situation. However, if B does not do what they have been told to do, then A does not have effective authority in that situation. In the military, the most obvious evidence of authority is the rank structure and the issuing of orders, and since orders are usually followed, it might seem, at least within the military, that authority is almost always effective. But the situation is not as simple as it first appears, for even when orders are followed there may be other factors at play beyond the simple authority of the person issuing those orders.

CASE STUDY 6.3

Wearing Body Armor In Afghanistan

British troops operating in certain areas in Afghanistan after 2001 were periodically subjected to mortar attacks by forces sympathetic to the Taliban. The accommodation areas were mortar-proof, but the separate toilet area, a relatively flimsy plywood structure, was not. Higher command therefore issued an order that all personnel were to wear their body armor whenever they visited the toilet. This order was not popular with the troops, since the body armor was uncomfortable in the sweltering heat and quick trips to the toilet without body armor seemed to be of relatively low risk, especially in cases where the base hadn't been mortared in months.

SOURCE: Based on a case by Patrick Bury, a former infantry Captain in the Royal Irish Regiment, who served in Afghanistan.

Case 6.3 is a concrete example of this sort of problem. If the soldiers in this case obeyed the order they had been issued simply because the order had been issued by their commanding officer, then the authority was effective. If they disobeyed the order and did not wear their body armor for trips to the toilet, or even if they removed it while in the toilet where no one could see them, then the authority was ineffective. In a case like this there may be various other factors involved that tend to either support or undermine the authority of the commanding officer. One obvious point is the fact that these soldiers could be punished in various ways if they are found to be disobeying the order. The threat of possible punishment for disobeying the order supports the commanding officer's authority in this case. However, if the soldiers continually disobey the order and are continually being punished, then the authority is obviously ineffective in this situation. In a case like this, if a soldier who actually obeys the order does so simply because they fear being caught doing the wrong thing and punished for it, then they are being motivated not by the authority itself, but rather by the fear of punishment, and thus it can be argued that the authority itself is actually ineffective. The desired result, of getting the soldiers to wear their body armor on trips to the toilet, is being achieved, but it is being brought about, not by respect for the authority of the commanding officer, but rather by the threat of force. Though this distinction might seem unimportant, it does have important implications in terms of the leadership of the officer involved, a point discussed a little later in this chapter.

Source: The authority that people have to direct the actions of others comes from two main sources: It either comes from within a particular institution, or it is what might be termed "personal" authority and is derived independent from any institution. If the authority comes from an institution it can either be an "original" authority or a "delegated" authority.

An original authority arises directly as a result of the relationship that the person has with the institution. This can be either because the authority is given to every member of that institution, or because this particular person has the ultimate authority within that institution. A police officer possesses original authority in the first sense, in that every police officer, simply by virtue of being a police officer, has the authority to enforce the law within their area of jurisdiction. The owner of a business has original authority in the second sense, for the owner will be the ultimate authority within that business.

A delegated authority on the other hand, arises as a result of a person's relationship to others within a particular institution, rather than their relationship with the institution itself, in that the authority a person holds has been granted to them by another person. To delegate such authority, that other person must hold a higher level of authority than the person to whom they are granting delegated authority. Any chain of command is a system of delegated authority; each person in the chain has been granted a level of delegated authority by the person who is superior to them in the chain. It is important to note that any chain of command or other system of delegated authority will ultimately end, and at the very top of the system there must be a holder of original authority. Any delegated authority that a person has, no matter how far down the chain of command they are, is ultimately granted by this holder of original authority.

The difference between original and delegated authority is perhaps most clearly illustrated by considering a relatively simple decision, such as the decision by a small food retailer to purchase food from a particular supplier, and comparing the avenues of appeal open to someone within the institution who disagreed with the decision the person in authority had made. If the decision was made by someone who possesses original authority, such as the owner of the company, then a person within the institution (i.e., an employee) who disagreed with the decision could attempt to convince the owner that the decision was not a good one. If the company owner cannot be convinced in this way, then there is no higher authority the employee could appeal to. However, if the decision was made by a store manager, rather than by the owner of the company, the situation is rather different. The store manager holds delegated authority, so an employee who disagreed with the decision could seek to appeal the decision by talking to the next higher level of management, perhaps an area manager, and then to the level above that, and so on all the way up to the owner of the company.

I have claimed that any rank structure, including that of the military, is a system of delegated authority where the authority that any individual has is effectively granted to them by someone with a higher level of authority. However, since we are not accustomed to thinking about authority in these terms (i.e., thinking about the authority wielded by a particular military officer as being something that is granted to them by another person), the fact that the military command structure is actually a system of delegated authority is usually not obvious at first glance. There are various other reasons why this is the case, including the numerous and complex levels of command that often exist within the military; the fact that the military forces of a particular state will usually consist of a number of different branches (e.g., Army, Navy, Air Force); and the fact that there are usually a considerable number of laws and other regulations that lay out a system of control for the exercise of authority within the military. Nevertheless, the military chain of command is ultimately a system of delegated authority, and this is clear from the fact that any decision that is made by a person in a position of authority in the military can be overruled by someone with a higher level of authority, that is, by a person who is superior to them in the direct chain of command.

I mentioned another type of authority, personal authority, which does not arise out of any institution or have any legal basis. People will follow the directions of an individual with a large degree of personal authority simply because they feel, for whatever reason, that they ought to do so. There are various factors that may contribute to someone having a high level of personal authority. Some people are exceptionally charismatic, or have an air of confidence that makes other people trust their judgment.[3] Sometimes particular people within a group are known to be knowledgeable about particular situations, or have previous experience with similar problems, and thus others tend to follow their lead in those sorts of situations. Some people have a significant level of personal authority simply because they are famous.[4]

Personal authority is extremely important in military contexts, despite its noninstitutional nature. Those who are perceived to have a high level of personal authority are likely to be followed, whether or not they are the people who are actually supposed to be in charge. This is particularly the case in combat situations, especially in ground combat, where experienced and confident personnel can sometimes end up in effective command of groups of soldiers despite being outranked by other soldiers who are present.[5] To retain effective authority in such situations, those in positions of command in the military need to be able to rely on personal authority as well as the institutional authority provided by their rank. They need to be seen to be competent, confident, and in control of the situation. They need to set a clear example and be both respected and trusted by those under their command; they also need to be clear about what their mission is and how to achieve it. In short, they need to develop those attributes that military forces tend to recognize under the heading of leadership. To command, they need to be leaders and not simply be commanders.

In the same way that possessing the attributes of leadership will tend to make an officer's authority effective, there are various ways in which an officer can act, and things an officer can do, which will tend to make their authority ineffective.

Consider Case 6.3 (Wearing Body Armor in Afghanistan), for example. If an officer in command of troops at this post in Afghanistan sets a poor example by ignoring the order to wear body armor on visits to the toilet, then it can be expected that those under that officer's command will do the same thing. Such actions are likely to immediately undermine the authority of that officer, since by their own actions they have suggested to their troops that the orders of superior officers do not have to be followed. If this officer ignores orders issued to them by their commander, then why should they expect the troops under their command to do any differently? Of course, there are other ways in which a person can undermine their own authority as well. Consider the following case.

CASE STUDY 6.4

The Logistics Officer's Problem

Major Stock had been posted to the Persian Gulf region as a logistics officer, and several months into the deployment was given the crucial task of negotiating a major local supply contract, worth millions of dollars to the successful supplier. Given the situation, there were of course quite a few people who were keen to get the business, but he knew that there were only a few companies that were actually equipped to handle a contract of that size, so in fairly short order he had cut the list of potential suppliers down to three possibilities.

In most Middle-Eastern states, business negotiations are really about relationships, not contracts, and to get a decent deal on a contract like this Major Stock had to spend quite a lot of time getting to know the relevant people in these companies, a process that also involved being offered quite a few gifts, which are a recognized part of the relationship-building process in that part of the world. Since a contract like this was going to be extremely important for these companies, Major Stock also knew that some of the gifts he was going to be offered would be pretty special, and he would have to handle things carefully; while he needed to keep the Defence Force policy on accepting gifts in mind, he also needed to avoid giving offence to the people he was negotiating with.

Major Stock was meeting with the representative of one of the companies, Mr. al-Yasir, for the fourth or fifth time, when he was informed of the latest gift which was being offered. Mr. al-Yasir told Major Stock that he was arranging for the Major and the other officers in his unit to have the use of a "special" suite at a top hotel, which would be well equipped with good food, alcoholic beverages, and a bunch of lovely young women who would be only too pleased to "make you all comfortable." In short, all the comforts of home these officers had been missing would be provided, at no cost at all, thanks to the generosity of Mr. al-Yasir's company. He even brought into the meeting a couple of the young women who would be "providing hospitality" there in the room, and Major Stock had to admit that they were among the most beautiful women he had seen in his time in the Middle-East. Not wanting to offend Mr. al-Yasir by refusing outright, Major Stock made some of the polite, but noncommittal, comments he had learned so well while dealing with these situations. The women soon left the room and discussions continued for some time afterward, as is common in that part of the world, until Major Stock was eventually able to politely wind up the meeting and return to base.

During a routine meeting with his immediate superior officer later that day to report on the state of negotiations for the contract, Major Stock made passing mention of Mr. al-Yasir's offer, and to his surprise his married superior took an immediate interest. He ordered Major Stock to contact Mr. al-Yasir and get him to organize the "recreation room" as soon as possible. "We might not give the company the contract," the officer said. "It really all depends on who can give us the best deal, but we can certainly enjoy Mr. al-Yasir's hospitality in the meantime."

Major Stock was rather shocked at what his superior had ordered, and he was far from certain about how to proceed. He wasn't certain about the legality of the situation, and given the circumstances he was unsure about the advisability of discussing it with one of the lawyers in his section. He was certainly uncomfortable about arranging a situation in which his apparently happily married boss could break his wedding vows. In the end, Major Stock decided to simply ignore the order and when his superior asked about it later, Major Stock informed him that Mr. al-Yasir had been unable to deliver on his promise.

There are several problematic aspects to the order that has been issued to Major Stock in this case. The first problem is that the order may well have been an order to act illegally. While a member of the military is required to obey all lawful orders, no member of the military is duty bound to follow an illegal order. In fact, the opposite situation usually applies, as in most countries military personnel are thought to have a positive duty **not** to follow illegal orders. Such a principle is firmly established in military law. Since the Nuremburg trials of German war criminals in the aftermath of World War II, it has been an accepted principle of military conduct that the claim that one was merely following orders is not a valid legal defense against a charge of having engaged in war crimes. While Major Stock was obviously not being ordered to commit a war crime in this case, if the order is not a lawful one then it should not be followed.

There are a number of ways in which the order issued to Major Stock might not be lawful. The first problem is that the "gift" being offered by Mr. al-Yasir might be a violation of local law. Prostitution is illegal in all Middle-Eastern states, and this being the case, any officers "being made comfortable" by the women in Mr. al-Yasir's employ might be engaging in illegal behavior. However, this might not actually be classified as prostitution, depending on such factors as how the women are being paid, what they are actually being paid for, and so on. It might also be an offense to possess or consume alcohol in this country, although in a number of Persian Gulf states, top hotels are legally allowed to supply alcohol to foreign guests under certain circumstances, so that aspect of this situation might be acceptable.

Another problem with Mr. al-Yasir's offer is that accepting it might breach military regulations. Most Western states have fairly stringent regulations regarding the acceptance of gifts from possible suppliers, which military personnel acting on behalf of those states are required to follow, and taking advantage of Mr. al-Yasir's hospitality might well contravene those regulations. However, Major Stock was aware that it was considered appropriate to accept certain gifts while negotiating a contract such as this in the Middle-East, even in cases where it would not be appropriate to accept those same gifts at home. Such regulations are almost inevitably tied to the monetary value of what is being offered, and since the actual cash value of what Mr. al-Yasir was offering was probably not wildly at odds with what might reasonably be accepted as a gift in these sorts of negotiations, it may not be illegal to accept such hospitality under the government's regulations.

Whether Major Stock is being asked to something illegal or not may be questionable, especially for someone without legal training. However, it is quite obvious that what he is being asked to do is unethical, quite apart from the issue of whether this would be helping his superior to break his wedding vows. As I have mentioned, law and ethics are intimately related, though they are not the same thing. The fact that there are so many legal questions about this case immediately suggests that there will be ethical problems as well. It is usually the case that there is a significant difference between the legal standards of behavior required of military personnel, which in some circumstances can be quite low, and the standards of behavior that are seen to be ethically required of such personnel, which are usually considerably higher than the legal standards. When questioning whether accepting this offer from Mr. al-Yasir would fall within the regulations that apply to acceptance of gifts from possible suppliers, it is worthwhile to consider not merely the letter of the law, but also its spirit, which is probably a better guide to the ethics of the situation. One reason why such regulations exist is obviously to ensure that military personnel who engage in corrupt practices while negotiating with suppliers can be charged and punished for those actions. However, at a broader level the aim of such regulations is to try to ensure that the process of awarding such contracts is (1) fair and unbiased and (2) seen to be fair and unbiased by outside observers. Accepting Mr. al-Yasir's offer in this case may not, in fact, influence the outcome of the contract, since it might be, as Major Stock's superior suggests, that the contract will simply go to whichever company can provide the best deal. However, accepting an offer like this one would almost certainly be **seen** to be influencing the awarding of the contract, which is one of the things that gift acceptance regulations are aiming to prevent.

Another principle that is usually thought to apply to the actions of military personnel, and indeed to government officials generally, is that they should not become involved in situations where they may be acquiring personal benefit at government expense, or even in situations where this might appear to be the case to an impartial observer. Accepting Mr. al-Yasir's offer is certainly a situation like that, since there is no benefit at all for either the state or the military as a whole, but there could be seen to be considerable benefit for the individual officers who take advantage of this particular offer. This would be especially problematic if the situation were to become public, since the reputation of the military as a whole is likely to be damaged by allegations that individual officers accepted the sort of hospitality that was being offered here. When issues of ethics are discussed in short military professional development courses, it is common for presenters to refer to what is known in general terms as the "media test": How would these actions be perceived if they were to appear tomorrow on the front page of a major newspaper or on an evening news bulletin back home; and, could you defend your actions? This sort of test of ethical behavior is better suited to dealing with tests of integrity than ethical dilemmas, but can be illustrative in both. Accepting Mr. al-Yasir's offer would clearly fail the media test.

Having said all this, Major Stock's response to the situation, ignoring the order and then lying to his superior and claiming Mr. al-Yasir was unable to deliver on his promise, which may seem like a fairly graceful solution to the problems he faced, was also less than ideal in at least some respects. In effect, Major Stock is denigrating Mr. al-Yasir and his company, so Major Stock's superior may now be dubious about the ability of the company to deliver on the final contract if they do indeed make the best offer. This may lead to the contract being awarded to someone else. While this obviously harms Mr. al-Yasir's company it also harms the military, since the contract will be awarded to another company that may charge more and/or be less equipped to provide what is required. Although it is obviously somewhat more confrontational, perhaps the best way to deal with the situation would be for Major Stock to gently remind his superior that accepting an offer like this would clearly fail the "media test," and since the military likes to avoid that sort of publicity, politely refusing Mr. al-Yasir's offer would be a much better option.

It is also instructive to think about what effect a situation like this is likely to have in the future, especially with regard to the authority of Major Stock's superior. By ordering Major Stock to do something that is clearly unethical as well as being, at best, legally problematic, his superior will obviously have undermined his personal authority with regard to Major Stock. It is obvious this is the case, since Major Stock chose to ignore the order rather than following it, demonstrating that the superior's authority was ineffective in this situation. However, there is more going on in this case as well. To exercise leadership, commanders need to set a good example for those under their command, not only with regard to following the orders of their superiors, as was noted in the discussion of Case 6.3 (Wearing Body Armor in Afghanistan), but also in moral terms. Setting a poor moral example will tend to undermine an officer's personal authority, and given the close relationship between law and ethics, this will tend to undermine their legal authority as well. This will make it more likely that an officer's overall authority will be ineffective, despite the legal requirement to follow orders issued by a superior officer.

THE ETHICAL PROBLEMS OF ORDERS

In examining the ethical problems involved with the issuing and following of orders, I think there are several fundamental questions that need to be grappled with. While it is obviously the case that a commander should never be issuing illegal orders, a further, and perhaps more difficult, question is whether there are in fact legal orders that ought not to be issued as well. A second important question is what a commander ought to do in cases where they are issued two or more sets of orders that come into conflict with each other. A third important issue is whether it is wrong for members of the military to question, or perhaps even to refuse to obey, a lawful order that has been issued to them.

When discussing ethical issues with those who are training to be military officers, I have often had them give voice to the idea that the most important duty of a military officer is to make sure that everyone under their command gets home alive. I am not sure where this idea comes from, although it is perhaps not coincidental that this is also a view that is often expressed in films and television programs, especially those which are shot from the point of view of junior officers. However, this idea is seriously flawed and the flaw is quite obvious on closer examination. All military deployments involve risk, even deployments to provide humanitarian assistance after natural disasters, so if the most important duty of commanders was to ensure that all military personnel survived, then these personnel would never be deployed at all. Indeed, since even training military personnel involves risk, if the primary duty of those in command was to ensure the safety of all military personnel, then it would be better to not have a military at all.[6]

In fact, the most important duty of a military commander is to fulfill the mission with which they have been entrusted. However, as was mentioned in Chapter 3 during the discussion of the triangular balance of command responsibilities, the duty to fulfill the mission needs to be balanced against an understanding of exactly how important that mission is, and thus (1) how many military lives and how much military property can legitimately be risked in undertaking that mission, and (2) how many civilian lives can legitimately be risked and how much civilian property legitimately damaged or destroyed to achieve that mission. Given the importance of fulfilling the mission with which they have been entrusted, a military commander may well be faced with serious ethical problems when issuing and following orders, since those orders can have an immediate and serious effect on both the people under that person's command and other people, particularly noncombatants, who may be in the area.

CASE STUDY 6.5

Orders to HMS *Alacrity*

BACKGROUND HMS *Alacrity* was a 3,000 ton Type 21 frigate in the Royal Navy. She served as part of the British taskforce sent to the South Atlantic to retake the Falkland Islands after the Argentine invasion of those islands in 1982 (see Case 4.6). The Falklands consist of two main islands, East Falkland and West Falkland, and over seven hundred smaller islands. The two main islands are separated by a large strait, known as Falkland Sound.

To retake the islands the British needed to find a suitable site for an amphibious landing. The best possible site was at Carlos Water, in Falkland Sound on the western side of East Falkland. However, since an Argentine ship had been observed laying mines in the approaches to the main harbor at Port Stanley, the island's capital, the taskforce commander, Rear Admiral Sandy Woodward, was concerned about the possibility that the Argentines might also have mined the northern end of Falkland Sound, and indeed the southern end as well. The particular problem for him in this case was that none of the ships in the taskforce was equipped for minesweeping, so the only way to find out if there were any mines in Falkland Sound was to "search" for them with the hull of a ship. Since large mines of this type would almost inevitably sink any ship that ran into them, the mission would have to be given to an "expendable" ship, like HMS *Alacrity*. When writing about the situation, Admiral Woodward states that he didn't like the idea of telling Commander Christopher Craig, the captain of the *Alacrity*, to go and try to get himself blown up by a mine, but he also couldn't afford to ignore the possibility of mines that might sink one or more of the amphibious landing vessels filled with troops as they approached the landing beaches.

In his book Woodward described the situation in the following manner:

I phoned Commander Craig on the voice-encrypted network and said "Er...Christopher, I would like you to do a circumnavigation of East Falkland tonight. All the way around to the south, then north up Falkland Sound and out past Fanning Head to rendezvous with *Arrow*." I also told him to come up the Sound very noisily, exploding a few star-shells and generally frightening the life out of the Args. I added, "If you see anything move, sink it, but be out of there and home by dawn, so you're clear of the land before they can fly."

He was silent for a few moments and then he said, "Umm, I expect you would like me to go in and out of the north entrance a few times, Admiral. Do a bit of zig-zagging."

"Oh," I said, feigning surprise and feeling about two inches high. "Why do you ask that?"

"I expect you would like me to find out whether there are any mines there," he said quietly.

I cannot remember what I said. But I remember how I felt. I think I just mentioned that I thought that would be quite useful.

He replied, with immense dignity, "Very well, sir." Then he went off to pre-pare for the possible loss of his ship and people the best way he could. I shall remember him as one of the bravest men I ever met. This was Victoria Cross material but, strangely, only if it went wrong.

I personally felt awful not to have had the guts to be honest with him and wondered what the devil he was going to tell his ship's company about their task tonight and about my pitiful performance, which, for a sea-going admiral to one of his commanders, beggared description.

SOURCE: From Admiral Sandy Woodward (with Patrick Robinson), *One Hundred Days: The Memoirs of the Falkland Battle Group Commander* (Annapolis, MD: Naval Institute Press, 1992), p. 203.

Issuing orders that will put lives at risk is always going to be a serious business. Even in the absence of essentially unexpected accidents, such as those mentioned in note 6, military commanders can be faced with such situations in peacetime operations, as was the case in Cases 3.1 (HMAS *Westralia* Fire) and 3.2 (Leave No One Behind). However, in combat situations the problems that orders raise can be even more acute, such as in the HMS *Alacrity* case. In ordering *Alacrity's* commander to use his ship to "search" for any mines in Falkland Sound, Admiral Woodward was issuing orders that he knew could result in the loss of the ship and everyone aboard, but in the context of the attempt to retake the Falkland Islands such orders were a military necessity; Admiral Woodward needed to be prepared to sacrifice an expendable resource, in this case HMS *Alacrity* and her crew, to protect the amphibious landing vessels and the troops they contained, a military resource that was indispensable to the overall mission he needed to achieve. In actually following the orders, on the other hand, Commander Craig knew that he was risking his ship, his own life, and the lives of his entire crew in fulfilling a specific mission that he recognized was in fact vital to the overall task.

Lower ranking military leaders are obviously extremely unlikely to have to make decisions on the same scale as the *Alacrity* case, but they certainly do have to make decisions that will risk the lives of some of those under their command, either to save other people, or to fulfill the mission with which they have been entrusted. The effect that these sorts of decisions can have is perhaps most obvi-ous in ground operations in combat zones or other hostile areas. When a small unit is assigned a particular task within a hostile area, it is almost inevitable that some of the individuals within the unit will need to be assigned to tasks that are more difficult or more dangerous than others. In a situation such as that discussed in Case 6.2 (Marine Advance on Baghdad), for example, the reconnaissance ele-ment that is sent into town will be likely to be in more danger than the main force elements that follow. In sending the recon element ahead to determine what the situation on the ground actually was, rather than simply laying down artillery fire as he had been directed to, the company commander was risking the lives of the men in the recon element to protect noncombatants. Since the company probably contained marines who had special training in these sorts of recon missions the decision about who to send may have been relatively straightforward in this case. However, repetitive and dangerous missions might well raise different questions.

Military forces that have been deployed to help maintain stability in post-conflict areas, such as those deployed to Afghanistan after 2001 and to Iraq after 2003, are often required to conduct combat patrols of various localities within their area of operations. Although most of the tasks with which these units are engaged in have a significant degree of risk attached to them, some specific duties will entail a higher degree of risk than others, including some tasks that have to be repeated on a regular basis. What sort of considerations should the commanders of such units take into account when deciding which soldiers will be allocated to these higher risk tasks? One obvious factor that could be taken into account is the level of training the individual soldiers had completed. Since the level of training often varies across the unit, perhaps the more highly trained soldiers ought to be allocated to the more dangerous tasks, since the higher level of training they have received might make those tasks somewhat less risky for them than for other soldiers who have been trained to a somewhat lower level.[7] However, if the same soldiers are to be continually allocated to higher risk tasks, this may well lead to resentment among those soldiers. Of course, the fact that some soldiers have undertaken a higher level of training is not a guarantee that those soldiers actually possess a higher level of competence in undertaking such tasks, so another factor the commander could take into account would be the perceived level of competence of the soldiers under their command. But this carries with it the same problem as relying on the more highly trained soldiers, that the more competent soldiers may resent being continually allocated to higher risk tasks. As one officer I spoke to put it, you don't want to reward competence with danger, and incompetence with safety.[8]

Another possible way to deal with the problem would be to attempt to ensure that the more risky tasks were shared relatively equally among the soldiers in the unit, despite any differences in competence or training. But then the question arises as to whether it is justifiable to expose the less highly trained or less competent soldiers to risky tasks given that those tasks will, as a result of the lower levels of training or competence of these soldiers, be more dangerous for those soldiers than they would be for others within the unit. Any commander in a similar situation will have to work out how to balance the relative levels of danger faced by members of the unit, while at the same time dealing with any problems of resentment among those under their command. It is important to remember that the question at issue here cannot be addressed by simply examining what legal requirements are placed on a commander in a situation such as this, since none of the problems which I have mentioned here are legal ones. It would be perfectly legal for the commanders of such units to have allocated the most dangerous tasks of their deployment in basically any way they saw fit. It is only when the ethics of the situation are considered that these sorts of problems ever arise in the first place.

The distinction between what is legal and what is ethical can be important in other respects as well. It may be perfectly legal for someone in command of others in a combat situation to order those under their command to act in certain ways or to complete particular tasks. However, although it may be legal to order those under your command to complete a particular task, whether it is always ethical to do so is sometimes a completely different question.

CASE STUDY 6.6

Placing the Strobe

BACKGROUND The film *Black Hawk Down*, based on the book of the same name by Mark Bowden, is a somewhat fictionalized depiction of the events that unfolded during a U.S. Special Forces mission in Somalia in 1993. The mission struck trouble when one of the supporting Black Hawk Helicopters was shot down and crashed in the city, and the U.S. troops had to rush to the scene of the crash to secure the site and render aid to the survivors, while defending themselves against hundreds of angry Somalis, armed with AK-47s and Rocket-Propelled Grenades. As night fell, several dozen U.S. soldiers were trapped in the city defending the site of the crashed helicopter with its wounded occupants. The overall commander of the operation, Major General Garrison, ordered his MH-6 Little Bird helicopters to make strafing runs to support the encircled troops.

Staff Sergeant Matt Eversmann is in charge of one of the units that is defending the helicopter, having been placed in command of the "chalk"[9] shortly before the commencement of the operation after his Lieutenant suffered an epileptic seizure. He is in radio communication with the Little Bird overhead, and tries to inform the pilot of his position, but the Little Bird pilot is unable to identify his target in the darkness and confusion. Eversmann throws an infrared strobe, which will be visible to the pilot through his night-vision equipment, across the street to mark the building that the Little Birds ought to attack, but the strobe lands in some debris under an overhang and can't be seen from overhead. Under covering fire from the rest of the chalk, Eversmann runs across the street amidst a hail of bullets from the Somalis, retrieves the strobe, and throws it onto the roof where it can be seen by the Little Bird pilots, who immediately commence their attack run.

In the situation that is described in this case, it would obviously be legal for Eversmann to order another soldier to run across the street to retrieve the infrared strobe and throw it onto the roof.[10] In fact there are reasons for thinking that this would actually be a good idea. As was noted in the case this chalk would normally have been commanded by a Lieutenant, but is now being commanded by Eversmann who is "acting up" one level for this mission. If Eversmann was to be seriously injured or killed, the chalk will not only be deprived of his leadership, it will also now be under the command of a lower ranked noncommissioned officer who would be "acting up" two levels of command, a task which may well be quite difficult for him.[11] It may also be that another soldier is actually more competent to complete this task than Eversmann is. Another soldier might be a faster and more agile runner, for example. However, there are also some bad reasons why Eversmann might want to order someone else to do this job, such as if Eversmann was simply too scared to do the job himself.[12] While it would clearly be legal for Eversmann to order another soldier to plant the strobe, if his only reason for doing so was because he was too scared to do the job himself, then while this would be a legal order it would also be an unethical order.

Students that I have spoken to have often suggested to me that one of the fundamental principles of leadership is that you should never order anyone to do something that you would not do. This is clearly something of an ideal that will not always apply in practice, since there are many times when a leader might order others to do things that the leader would not do, and perhaps even **could** not do. An officer in command of a group of technical specialists, for example, might often order individuals under their command to do things that the officer simply is not capable of doing. However, ordering another person to do something that you are capable of doing but are too scared to do is something which clearly fits into this category. If it is clear that fear is the main reason why a leader is ordering someone else to undertake a dangerous task, then this will tend to undermine the authority that leader possesses, and he or she might well find their subordinates refusing to obey the order. The immorality of ordering someone into danger to save your own skin will undermine the moral authority of the leader, which will of course tend to make their overall authority ineffective.

At this point it seems that we are coming to an answer to the first of the questions I asked in this section, whether there are legal orders that ought not be issued. Orders that risk the lives of some to save others might seem at first glance to be orders of this type, but in fact they are a necessary, albeit difficult, part of military operations. On the other hand, ordering someone else to do something that you could do, but for some reason refuse to do, does seem to be problematic, and issuing such orders will almost inevitably undermine the authority of the person involved.

What of the second question which I posed, about what to do when orders come into conflict with each other?

CASE STUDY 6.7

Come Right!

I was a LTJG (Lieutenant Junior Grade) on my first ship, and had just qualified for Officer of the Deck (OOD). I had qualified OOD ahead of my peers, so was anxious to prove myself to my Captain. I was Officer of the Deck and Conning Officer while steaming in formation with an Aircraft Carrier (CVN).

We were 250 yards off the carrier's port bow (much too close for safety). When a tactical signal is executed, the C.O. always wants to smartly shift the rudder to come to the new station. (The Admiral is watching from the Carrier, we want to look professional.)

When the signal was executed, "Standby, execute!" the Captain orders me to: "Come Right."

It was apparent to me that if we came right, we would almost certainly collide with the CVN as we went across her bow. (A maneuvering board solution later proved that to be true.)

So I said to the Captain, "I can't, Sir."

He again ordered to me to "Come Right!"

I repeated a second time, "I can't, Sir."

Then he took two quick steps toward me, and with his face right in mine, yelled "DAMN IT, COME RIGHT!"

What would you do if you were me?

SOURCE: Case written by U.S. Navy CAPT (Ret.) W. Rick Rubel and reprinted from W. Rick Rubel & George Lucas (eds.), *Case Studies in Military Ethics* (Boston: Pearson Education, 2004).

There are a number of ways in which this situation could be characterized, but perhaps the simplest is to think of it as a case of conflicting orders. The first responsibility of the OOD is to ensure the safe navigation of the ship and thus to avoid running aground or colliding with any other vessels. This is the first set of orders that the OOD has been issued. The second and apparently conflicting order the OOD has been issued in this case is the repeated direction from the Captain of the ship, his Commanding Officer, to "Come Right." The Captain has many years of seagoing command experience, far more than the OOD, but the order issued will apparently put the ship in immediate danger so the question remains, what should the OOD do?

One option would be to clarify the order, and perhaps to make clear what your concerns about carrying it out are. In this case that might involve pointing to the carrier and reminding the captain that coming right will put the ship right across, and probably under, the aircraft carrier's bow. Another option would be to surrender command of the ship to the Captain,[13] but the question then arises as to what ought to be done if the Captain actually persists in turning the ship across the carrier's bow.

The question of what to do when orders come into conflict probably merges, at least to some degree, with whether it is ever reasonable to question, or even refuse to obey, an order. While it might be claimed that a member of the military should never question their orders, in fact I would argue that, at least for an officer and probably for any person in the military who is in command of others, the reverse is in fact true, and that these people should **always** question their orders. What I am suggesting here is not that such people ought to be arguing with their superiors about the right course of action every time they are ordered to do something. But military personnel who are being ordered to do something, particularly those in positions of leadership such as officers or senior noncommissioned officers, ought to be thinking about what they are being ordered to do, and why, even if in the majority of cases they only "question" the order that they have been issued inside their own heads. There are (at least) two reasons why it is important for military personnel to think about the orders they are being issued: (1) it is part of the duties of all military personnel to refuse orders which are manifestly illegal, so it is obviously problematic for military personnel to unthinkingly follow orders, since this may lead them into following illegal orders without question; and (2) if a military leader, at any level, is going to properly carry out an order, it is necessary for them to understand the commander's intent in issuing that order. So perhaps, in this context, it might be suggested that military personnel should not question their orders, but that they should question the plan behind the order, especially if this is necessary for them to understand the commander's intent.[14] Understanding the commander's intent allows a military leader to recognize when their orders have become unworkable or out of date, a situation which may well arise in a combat situation, and thus to form a new plan to accomplish the mission if and when this becomes necessary.[15]

Since the consequences for refusing to obey orders can be severe, choosing not to obey orders is always an extremely significant decision. All members of the military should, of course, refuse to obey illegal orders, and officers have in fact been prosecuted for obeying orders that they should have known to be illegal. However refusing to obey legal orders is another matter. This brings me back to the two cases at the beginning of this chapter, Case 6.1 (Ehren Watada and Iraq) and Case 6.2 (Marine Advance on Baghdad). Ehren Watada disobeyed what he believed to be an illegal order, and accepted the consequences of his refusal to obey by facing a court-martial. The intricacies of the trial and appeal process in the end meant that the legality of those orders was never actually determined, but any possible future that Watada might have had within the Army was clearly at an end.[16]

The Marine company commander faced a somewhat different situation. His intelligence suggested that enemy units were occupying a section of the town that he needed to pass through, and it appears that it would have been legal for him to launch an attack using the artillery that had been made available to him. However, other indicators suggested the initial intelligence may have been incorrect, so he utilized other resources at his command to reconnoiter and ascertain the current situation on the ground. I believe that the truly significant factor in this case is that the Marine Captain in charge of this company understood his commander's intent, which was to ensure a safe and rapid passage of the company through the town. Given the indications that the enemy had already left, the company commander felt it would be unethical to destroy a large section of the town without reason, and through his actions he was able to fulfill his orders to rendezvous with the other units of his battalion without causing significant, and as it turned out, unnecessary collateral damage in the town.

However, officers can face situations that are even more problematic, such as in the following case.

CASE STUDY 6.8

Reinterpreting Orders

BACKGROUND Australian Defence Force personnel were deployed to Afghanistan as part of the Reconstruction Taskforce working in Oruzgan province. Their job was not to engage in direct attacks on the insurgent forces in the area, but rather to provide expert assistance to the rebuilding and modernization work taking place there. Lieutenant (LT) Matthew Deane was in command of one of the three platoons that together comprised the taskforce's security company, which had responsibility for ensuring that the work of the engineering units in the area could proceed safely. Each platoon consisted of three sections, nine men under the command of a Corporal and mounted in armored personnel carriers, plus a small command unit; just over 30 men all told. Each platoon in the security company had a designated patrol area, and the platoons came to know these areas very well. Just inside the northern edge of LT Deane's patrol area was an Afghan village that was believed to be something of a Taliban stronghold. The Army intelligence reports suggested that the number of armed Taliban fighters in the village could swell to over two hundred within an hour in response to any incident. Armed with these intelligence reports, LT Deane spoke to his superiors, and it was agreed that his platoon would not venture too near; a line which the platoon would not cross was drawn across the map a mile or so south of the village.

LT Deane's platoon returned to base mid-afternoon, and he immediately reported to his Company Commander (OC)[17]. Brief engagements with the enemy did occur sporadically, but the engagement today had lasted for several hours and had taken place at the limit of the patrol area, almost exactly at the "no go" line a mile south of the troublesome village. In another unusual event for this part of the province, the platoon had returned to base bearing the dead body of an enemy fighter, whose clothes and equipment would be closely examined by the intelligence specialists. The OC was pleased with LT Deane's report, but wanted to push the enemy forces in the area a bit harder.

"Matt, we've got them on the run here, and I want to keep them off balance," the OC began. "I want your platoon to go back out and sweep through the village so they can't regroup there."

LT Deane was surprised at the order. "Sir, the streets are very narrow, so the vehicles can't get through. If we make a sweep through the village we'll be on foot and badly outgunned if the intelligence reports about Taliban numbers are at all accurate. We had agreed that the patrols would stop a mile south of the village."

"We are the thin red line here in Oruzgan," the OC responded. "And right now Matty, you are the thinnest part of it. Get your men rearmed, mount up, and get out there."

LT Deane argued with him for 15 minutes behind closed doors, but the OC could not be moved. The base was somewhat isolated, and Deane had no immediate way to contact higher command to question these orders, so he gathered together his section leaders and told them what they had been ordered to do. As he expected, the men were not at all happy about it.

"Always said he was a gong chaser," said one of the corporals. "He just wants a medal, and doesn't give a shit about what happens to the rest of us."

LT Deane suspected that this was true, and while the OC's orders to sweep through the village had been very clear, Deane believed this was a serious mistake. In any case, he had already decided what to do before he met with his section heads. "Re-arm and mount up," he said to them. "You know those two tall hills a couple of hundred metres south of the village?" The men nodded. "We're going to set up an OP (observation post) on each one. We'll be able to see clearly if anything is going on in the village but we'll still have the protection and firepower of the vehicles, and can get out quick if we need to. We'll stay there til it's nearly dark, then come back and report on anything suspicious." The OPs were duly established, and the soldiers observed events in the village for several hours. They didn't see anything untoward that afternoon, and returned to base at nightfall.

After the incident, the OC made no direct comment on the way LT Deane had reinterpreted his orders, and Deane was not subsequently charged with the offence of "failure to obey a lawful order" as he had feared he might be. However, the OC was later heard to say, on more than one occasion, that he thought LT Deane was a coward, and his end of deployment report on LT Deane's performance was less than complimentary.

The situation in this case is quite unlike that in Case 6.2 (Marine Advance on Baghdad). There is no difficulty at all in understanding the intent of the OC, since that has been made perfectly clear to LT Deane, as have his orders. Nor is this an issue of conflicting orders, as was the situation in Case 6.7, since the OC was the officer who had issued the earlier order to stop patrols short of the village, and now he has issued a new order that supersedes the previous one. Having "questioned" his OC at length about the plan behind the orders, Deane can be in no doubt about what he has been ordered to do and why; however, his problem is that he thinks that the order is a stupid one, as well as suspecting that the order was issued by the OC out of selfish motives, in this case the OC's desire to be rewarded with a medal. Military law quite obviously requires Deane to follow these orders, since the law only distinguishes between legal and illegal orders, and makes no mention of stupid or selfish orders.[18] The two big, and interrelated, issues Deane has to wrestle with when deciding if and how to follow the orders that he has been issued are (1) that in his opinion the orders he has been issued and the intent of the OC are at odds with the overall mission of the taskforce in Afghanistan; and (2) that the specific task he has been given within the overall mission is not important enough to justify the level of risk that will be borne by his men and himself.

Apart from simply following his orders or reinterpreting them in the way he did, there are a number of other courses of action that Deane could have pursued here. He could, for example, attempt to delay the patrol through the village by agreeing with the OC about the course of action, but insisting that to maximize the possibility of success more time was needed for planning, coordination of fire support from other units and services, and so on, in the hope that this might buy enough time for the orders issued by the OC to be overtaken by other events. Another possibility would be to follow the order but do so by carefully establishing defensive positions near the village and then commencing a recon-by-fire and feint attack, being ready to withdraw to the prepared defensive positions in the event that the expected Taliban forces did emerge. This would expose his troops to less risk than simply entering the village, but may be problematic in other respects, since opening fire in this way may breach the rules of engagement that have been issued, and may also result in unintended civilian casualties. Such civilian casualties are particularly problematic when we take into account the triangular balance of command responsibilities, which was mentioned both earlier in this chapter and in Chapter 3. LT Deane has a responsibility to protect those under his command and to achieve his mission, but this also has to be balanced with his responsibility to protect noncombatants and their property. He is certainly not entitled to protect his subordinates at the expense of local civilians, especially if the mission he has been given is as controversial as this one was. Another possibility would be for Deane to demand orders in writing from his OC and then to protest those orders in writing himself. Such a move would obviously breach the trust that usually exists between a superior and their subordinate, however it would send a clear message that Deane believed this order to be a mistake but had been overruled by his OC. To take this course of action would be an extremely serious move, since Deane would essentially be going on the record as saying that he believed his commander was incompetent, which may well kill his career if those involved in later examinations of the incident were to disagree with him.

Relatively junior military leaders have always had to deal with superiors issuing orders that either appear to be not well thought out, selfishly motivated, or even simply stupid. A junior officer might, for example, be correct in thinking that their superior has planned a particular operation poorly, and that this will lead to a unnecessary level of risk being borne by those under the junior officer's command. However, it may also be the case that the junior officer is simply wrong in their judgment of the orders they have been issued, since these orders may be based on more information than is available to the junior officer, be part of a wider plan to which the junior officer is not privy, and so on. Sometimes the superior officer is simply smarter than their subordinates might believe!

In Case 6.8 (Reinterpreting Orders), LT Deane knew that there was no larger plan, and he took the opportunity available to him to protest the order he was issued, and to clarify his OC's intent. Thus, he was well informed when making his decision not to follow the orders he had been issued, a situation which may not apply to other junior military leaders who are issued orders that appear to be problematic. While the action Deane actually took in this case did protect his men, it certainly left Deane himself open to various forms of retribution from his OC, as well as leaving the OC in position to issue similar orders to others in the future. This is rather problematic if Deane really does believe his OC is issuing orders that are not in the best interests of the overall mission. Some people, of course, would argue that Deane's duty in this case was simply to follow the orders he had been issued.

Some of the issues raised by problematic orders involve issues of integrity. If you issue an order, then you ought to take responsibility for it, including taking responsibility for the consequences of that order. If you question either an order or the plan behind it, then you ought to do it appropriately, by being respectful to those issuing the orders, but at the same time making your concerns clear. If you choose to disobey an order, as Ehren Watada did (Case 6.1: Ehren Watada and Iraq), then you need to be prepared to defend your actions, and the integrity to accept the consequences if you are found to have done the wrong thing. Whether you agree with Watada's actions or not, it has to be accepted that he was more than willing to stand up for his convictions, even stipulating in court that he had, in fact, refused the order to deploy to Iraq and had made the statements which were attributed to him.

If you obey an illegal order, you have to take responsibility for that action, as well as living with the consequences of obeying an order that you should have refused. The case of Hugh Thompson and the My Lai massacre was mentioned in Chapter 1. According to several accounts, Thompson was directly ordered to leave the area and ignore the actions of the U.S. soldiers, who were killing civilians, an order which Thompson rightly refused. On the other hand, LT Calley, the officer in command on the ground in My Lai, defended his actions on the grounds that he was simply following orders. The court-martial rejected this defense, and Calley was convicted on 22 counts of premeditated murder and sentenced to life in prison. Though his sentence was later commuted on several occasions, Calley has also had to live with his actions.

NOTES

1. A stipulation is an agreement that certain facts are true, and thus there is no requirement to prove them in court.
2. Quoted in "The Trials of Ehren Watada" by Jeremy Brecher and Brendan Smith, *The Nation*, June 1, 2009.
3. Military personnel, for example, often talk about certain officers having "command presence," which is essentially the type of authority I am discussing here. It is not tied to rank, but seems to be a feature that some, and only some, officers naturally possess.
4. A significant amount of advertising is based on straightforward appeals to the personal authority of famous individuals, along the lines of "I'm famous and I use this product, so you ought to use it too!" Such appeals obviously work, at least to some extent, since if they did not then advertisers would not waste time and money having celebrities endorse their products.
5. This issue is discussed in *Black Hawk Down: A Story of Modern War* by Mark Bowden (New York: Penguin, 1999). Of special interest in this regard is the section on pp. 172–174. U.S. Army Ranger Captain Mike Steele noted that when his unit was moving through the streets of Mogadishu under heavy fire, in company with members of the elite Delta Force, the less experienced Rangers tended to follow the Delta Force operators, a unit many Rangers aspired to join later in their careers, rather than staying in their teams. This resulted in a rapid breakdown of unit integrity.
6. An indication of the risks of both training missions and humanitarian assistance deployments can be found in the fact that the two individual incidents that have caused the largest number of casualties among Australian Defence Force personnel since the end of the Vietnam War both occurred outside combat zones. On the night of June 12, 1996, two Australian Army Black Hawk helicopters collided and crashed during a training exercise, killing eighteen men and injuring another ten. On April 2, 2005, an Australian Navy Sea King helicopter crashed on the island of Nias, off the west coast of Indonesian Sumatra, while engaged in humanitarian relief operations in the aftermath of the 2005 Sumatran earthquake. Nine Australian Defence Force personnel, seven men and two women, were killed and two others were injured.
7. One clear indication of the way in which levels of training may differ greatly among members of the same unit is evident in the experiences of the U.S. 69th Infantry Regiment, a National Guard unit based in New York City. During their operations in Iraq in 2004 and 2005, many members of the unit were involved in incidents where the combat infantryman badge (CIB) would normally be awarded, but a lot of the

soldiers in the unit could not be awarded the CIB since they had not attended infantry school and thus had not undertaken the training required to make them eligible to receive the award. This is discussed in Sean Michael Flynn's book, *The Fighting 69th: From Ground Zero to Baghdad* (New York: Penguin, 2007), p. 218. It was apparently in recognition of this situation that the U.S. Army approved a new award, the Combat Action Badge (CAB), which would be awarded to such personnel.

8. Thanks to Marine Lieutenant Colonel Dan Healey for this point.

9. In U.S. military terms a chalk is a group of soldiers deployed from a single aircraft. In this film, Eversmann's "Chalk Four" was a squad of Rangers who deployed from Black Hawk Super Six-One, which was the first helicopter to be shot down.

10. In the actual battle as recorded in the book by Mark Bowden, one of the Rangers, Specialist Lance Twombley, was in fact ordered by his Sergeant to place a marker out on the road to help the Little Bird pilots identify their targets. See *Black Hawk Down*, p. 218.

11. This sort of eventuality is something that soldiers train for; the ideal is that any officer, commissioned or noncommissioned, ought to be able to do the job not only of their immediate superior, but also of the superior two rungs up the command ladder. Whether this ideal always applies in practice is, of course, another matter.

12. Just to make it perfectly clear, the comments I am making here, while hypothetical in any case, are referring to the character of Matt Eversmann as portrayed by Josh Hartnett in the film Black Hawk Down, and in no way refer to the actual Staff Sergeant (Later First Sergeant) Matt Eversmann on whom that character is based.

13. In fact this was the course of action the OOD took: see W. Rick Rubel, "Come Right: The Sequel," in W. Rick Rubel & George Lucas (eds.), *Case Studies in Military Ethics* (Boston: Pearson Education, 2004).

14. My thanks to Joe Thomas, the U.S. Naval Academy's Distinguished Military Professor of Leadership, for his thoughtful comments on this issue.

15. It is fairly obvious that some of the things I am saying here seem to conflict with a lot of military training, particularly basic training, which is apparently designed to get military personnel to follow orders immediately and without question. There is certainly something problematic about training people to obey orders without question while simultaneously demanding that these same people refuse to obey orders that are manifestly illegal.

16. In a similar British case, however, Flight Lieutenant Malcolm Kendall-Smith, a Royal Air Force doctor, was found guilty of refusing orders to deploy to Iraq and was sentenced to eight months imprisonment as well as having to pay a substantial sum toward his legal costs. His defence, that the Iraq war was illegal, was ruled irrelevant since the orders he refused to follow were issued after the invasion had finished, and at a time when British forces were in Iraq at the invitation of the democratically elected government. See "RAF Doctor Jailed Over Iraq Refusal," *The Guardian*, April 13, 2006.

17. In the British Army, Australian Army, and many other Commonwealth countries, the term "CO" (Commanding Officer) is used only to refer to the Battalion Commander, since that officer (who will usually be a Lieutenant Colonel) is in overall command

of the unit. An army company is considered to be a subunit of the Battalion, so a Company Commander (usually a Major, occasionally a Captain) is referred to as the OC (Officer Commanding).

18. My thanks to retired U.S. Navy SEAL Captain Bob Schoultz for recognizing the importance of this point, and for his other comments on this case, including his suggestions about the various courses of action that were open to LT Deane.

FURTHER READING

May, Larry. "Superior Orders, Duress, and Moral Perception." In Larry May, Eric Rovie, & Steve Viner (eds.), *The Morality of War: Classical and Contemporary Readings* (Upper Saddle River, NJ: Pearson Education, 2006), pp. 430–439.

Smith, Hugh. "Conscientious Objection to Particular Wars." *War and Society* 8(1990), 118–34.

Tripodi, Paolo. "Deconstructing the Evil Zone: How Ordinary Individuals Can Commit Atrocities." In Paolo Tripodi and Jessica Wolfendale (eds.), *New Wars and New Soldiers: Military Ethics in the Contemporary World* (Farnham, U.K.: Ashgate, 2011).

Wolfendale, Jessica. *Torture and the Military Profession* (New York: Palgrave MacMillan, 2007). Chapter 4: "Obedience in the Military."

DISCUSSION QUESTIONS

- What is more important for a military commander, to have power over their subordinates or for those subordinates to have respect for the commander's authority?
- Are there orders that a military commander should not issue?
- Are there legal orders that members of the military should not follow?

7

≁○

Discrimination and Proportionality I
Traditional Issues of Jus In Bello

┌─────────────────── CASE STUDY 7.1 ═══════════════════┐

Airpower and Marine Assault

INTRODUCTION During the fall of 2005, units of the I Marine Expeditionary Force (I MEF) were assigned responsibility for stability operations in Iraq's al-Anbar province and the Euphrates River Valley towns of Ramadi, Fallujah, Hit, and Haditha. The I MEF Marines were there to protect the Iraqi citizens against a complex mix of insurgent groups consisting of Saddam Hussein's former regime elements, foreign fighters travelling the Euphrates River Valley from Syria, and the Jordanian-born Al Qaeda in Iraq (AQI) leader Abu Musab al-Zarqawi. A Rifle Company from Camp Pendleton operated from a Forward Operating Base (FOB) together with the other companies from their parent battalion.

A Marine Battalion was conducting combat operations in the provincial capital. Insurgents were fighting from well-established positions in houses and from rooftops. Despite the MEF's best efforts to encourage the noncombatants to depart and avoid heavy fighting, many of the buildings in the Area of Operations were still inhabited. Compounding the difficulty for the MEF, the terrorized inhabitants hid from Marines so their presence was difficult to detect. A Company from the Battalion was engaged in heavy combat, clearing insurgents from their zone, using a combination of infantry attacks, tanks, and armored bulldozers to reduce enemy positions.

The Company made steady progress, moving building by building down both sides of a street. At the end of the street was a "T" intersection. At the "T" was a large, concrete, two-story house that the enemy had turned into a fortified position. Windows and firing ports in the front of the house provided the insurgents with excellent fields of fire as the Marines worked their way down the street. The insurgents concealed their position until the Marines had worked their way to

148

within 25 meters. Then they initiated mass, well-aimed, surprise fires on the Marines in the street. Several Marines were wounded.

Marines quickly established a base of fire and attempted to suppress the enemy fire. One group of Marines moved into position to assault the house. They conducted a dynamic breach of the garden gate and rushed into the front yard in preparation of assaulting the house itself. As they neared the front door, the insurgents command detonated an Improvised Explosive Device (IED) buried in the yard, killing or wounding six Marines.

The Company Commander ordered his Marines back into covered positions where they continued suppressive fire into the façade of the building. The Commander was determined to get to his casualties and extract them to safety. Every attempt resulted in withering fire from the insurgents in the house, preventing the Marines from reaching the injured. The Company Commander called forward a tank to assist in suppressing the enemy fire. Using the tank's smoke, main gun, and the coaxial machine gun, the Company finally reached the injured Marines and moved them to safety, but the enemy continued to resist.

The Company Commander, furious at the enemy tactics and frustrated with his inability to reduce the enemy position, called the Forward Air Controller (FAC) forward. The Company Commander and the FAC coordinated close air support to destroy the enemy position.

The FAC coordinated with on-station Marine F-18 Hornets and conducted a laser-designated air strike. A Hornet dropped a single 1,000-pound bomb through the roof of the fortified house, leveling it. Enemy fire immediately ceased.

The Marine Company moved quickly through rubble of the target house and confirmed eight insurgents Killed In Action (KIA). At the rear of the house, in a small building crushed by the collapsed home, the Marines also found four bodies presumed to be the residents who were apparently forced into the building by the insurgents. The bodies included a man, a woman, and two young children.

SOURCE: From *Discussion Material for Small Unit Leaders: Issues of Battlefield Ethics and Leadership*, written and published by the Lejeune Leadership Institute, Marine Corps University, Quantico, VA, 2008. Published as Case 1.2 in that material.

DISCUSSION

Having examined the ethical issues involved in the decision to go to war, that is, *jus ad bellum*, it is time to turn to the ethical issues involved in the actual conduct of a war, that is, *jus in bello*. Some realists have argued that such ideas are ridiculous, and that the only thing that matters in war is winning, in other words that "all is fair in love and war." There are several famous quotations that are often offered in support of this view, such as General William Sherman's "War is hell," and "War is cruelty and you cannot refine it"[1]; or the Prussian Chief of Staff, General von Moltke's, suggestion that "the greatest kindness in war, is to bring it to a speedy conclusion. It should be allowable, with that view, to employ all means."[2] Yet even von Moltke conceded that there were in fact some limits which ought to be applied to warfare, for the full version of the second sentence of the quotation reads, "It should be allowable, with that view, to employ all means save those that are absolutely objectionable." Since a great number of the ideas of *jus in bello* have been codified into international law, perhaps it can be concluded that these laws specify what von Moltke did not; those things which **are** absolutely objectionable in war.

The two most fundamental concepts of *jus in bello* are those of discrimination and proportionality. Although there are a number of other ideas that are often discussed under the heading of *jus in bello*, such as a ban on the use of prohibited weapons, or the use of methods which are *mala in se* (i.e., evil in themselves), these can be seen to be derived, at least in substantial part, from the principles of discrimination and proportionality. Thus, this discussion will focus only on those two principles, drawing in other issues as they become relevant. Given the intricate link between ethics and law, it is unsurprising that the principles of discrimination and proportionality should be found in those sections of international law that deal with the conduct of war. Although the focus of the discussion here is on ethics rather than law, I will make note of these points of international law at times, since the fact that an ethical principle has come to be established as a point of law serves to demonstrate the importance of that ethical principle.

At their core, the principles of discrimination and proportionality represent an attempt to limit the inevitable destruction of war and to try to ensure that those people engaged in what modern military personnel often refer to as "killing people and breaking stuff" actually kill the right people and break the right stuff, at least as far as this is possible. The principle of discrimination asserts that the only appropriate targets are those concerned with the enemy's war effort, and the principle of proportionality claims that the damage that is done in prosecuting such targets needs to be in line with the actual military value of the target itself. Case Study 7.1 (Airpower and Marine Assault) is an illustration of these problems in a modern context. While the Marines in this case were fighting against insurgent forces rather than the military forces of a state power, the battle described in this case follows fairly traditional lines. In traditional conflicts, as is the case in modern irregular conflicts, issues of collateral damage commonly arise. The question that could well be asked in relation to Case 7.1 is whether the Company Commander acted properly in handling this incident and whether the civilian deaths which resulted from his actions in dealing with these insurgents can be considered to be legitimate collateral damage, or whether he should have acted differently in this situation. To answer a question like this, the issues of discrimination and proportionality must be explored in some depth; this will be the topic of Chapters 7 through 11. Although there will be areas of overlap in the discussion in these chapters, the main focus of this particular chapter will be the way in which the principles of discrimination and proportionality play out in traditional conflicts. In Chapter 8, I will examine the way in which these principles apply to irregular conflicts, such as counterinsurgency operations and conflicts involving irregular forces, whereas in Chapter 9, I will examine similar issues in peacekeeping and peace enforcement operations, and in armed humanitarian interventions. Issues related to the treatment of those who have been taken into custody will be examined in Chapter 10, and Chapter 11 will extend this discussion into consideration of the ethics of terrorism and torture.

DISCRIMINATION

Fundamentally, the principle of discrimination requires those charged with carrying out military operations to distinguish between legitimate and illegitimate targets. The principle is usually laid out as a series of rules of warfare, which, in the words of the famous just war theorist Michael Walzer, are designed to "set certain classes of people outside the permissible range of warfare, so that killing any of their members is not a legitimate act of war but a crime."[3] In fact there is more to discrimination than this, since the principle requires that military personnel distinguish between legitimate and illegitimate attacks not only on people but also on structures, equipment, materials, and so on. However, it is true that the most well-known and generally well-recognized aspect of the principle of discrimination is the idea of noncombatant immunity. It is this aspect of the principle that most frequently finds its way into the international law of armed conflict, and where breaches of the principle of discrimination are generally considered to be the most serious within those same laws.

At its most basic, the principle of noncombatant immunity claims that the only people who may legitimately be subjected to direct attacks are enemy combatants, and that noncombatants are never legitimate targets for direct attacks. However, the immunity that noncombatants have is only a qualified one, in that although they may have immunity from direct attack, they do not have immunity from harm. Thus, although it is illegitimate to directly target noncombatants, this certainly does not mean that every attack which causes harm to noncombatants is an illegitimate one, for noncombatants may be harmed, even killed, as a result of an attack against a legitimate military target. Equally important, noncombatants only retain their immunity from direct attack as long as they retain their status as noncombatants, so if a noncombatant actively engages in any form of combatant activity, then they will lose their immunity and may be directly targeted. I will discuss what this actually means in practice later in this chapter, but first I want to consider a somewhat different question: Why is it actually ethically permissible to attack any and all enemy combatants during a time of war?

The Ethical Permissibility of Targeting Combatants

It is quite clear that international law allows any and all enemy combatants to be attacked at any time during an armed conflict. However, as was noted in Chapter 1, law and ethics do not always coincide and the mere fact that it is legal to attack enemy combatants does not in itself mean that it is ethical to do so. If it is true, as Walzer asserts, that "a legitimate act of war is one that does not violate the rights of the people against whom it is directed,"[4] then, if it is legitimate to target enemy combatants, this must mean that doing so does not actually violate their rights. In particular, given that targeting combatants may well kill them, it must be that attacking combatants and killing them does not violate their right to life. As I briefly mentioned in Chapter 2 during my discussion of deontological theories of ethics, one way to understand how such a claim can coherently be made is to suggest that through some action that they have taken, combatants have in fact forfeited their claim to certain rights, including, in at least some circumstances, their right to life. But if this is the case, then what action have combatants taken, which noncombatants have not, which leads to this forfeiture?

In ordinary circumstances, we think that someone must have done something wrong to forfeit their rights. When someone commits a crime and is later arrested and imprisoned for that crime, then this appears to violate their right to liberty, but by their actions in committing that crime this person has forfeited their right to liberty and thus imprisoning them does not actually violate their rights. In committing a crime for which they may be imprisoned, the criminal must have violated the rights of another person, since if they have stolen from someone then they have violated that person's right to own property, if they have kidnapped someone then they have violated that person's right to liberty, and so on. Consider a very simple case, in which a person (Andrew) is walking along the street and is attacked by another person (Bill). If Bill engages in an unprovoked attack on Andrew then it is quite clear that Andrew has the moral right to defend himself. However, that right certainly has limits, so if Bill is obviously seriously intoxicated and takes a wild drunken swing at Andrew, for example, then we wouldn't think that Andrew is justified in pulling out a gun and shooting Bill in the head. So while Bill may have forfeited some moral rights by attacking Andrew, he certainly hasn't forfeited **all** of his rights and thus Andrew's response to this attack, if it is to be justified, will need to be a reasonable and proportionate one.[5] If a police officer were to intervene in this case and attempt to take Bill into custody, then the police officer may use reasonable force in effecting an arrest. This shows, in accordance with the principle of rights forfeiture, that Bill has forfeited the right not to have reasonable force used against him. However, Bill may not use any force to resist the police officer's attempt to arrest him; if Bill does resist the arrest then doing this will violate the moral rights of the police officer.[6]

This "domestic analogy"[7] has obvious similarities with cases of international armed conflict; however, there are also significant differences between a domestic case, like the one I have just described, and a similar international case. One difference is with regard to how the concept of necessary force applies in each case. In domestic situations the concept of necessity continues to apply throughout the period in which force is used, so if, for example, the police officer continued to strike Bill after arresting him, despite Bill being handcuffed and helpless, then this would clearly be an unnecessary use of force and would violate Bill's rights. However, in the international case, the principle of necessity only applies to *jus ad bellum* determinations. Thus once a war has commenced, a state which has legitimately engaged in this war may, if it wishes, continue to fight until a final victory has been achieved. As David Rodin notes,

> An example of this was the Allies' campaign against Japan and Germany in the Second World War. Once the war had commenced, the Allies were legally permitted to, and did, seek the unconditional surrender of their enemies, even after they had liberated all the territories subject to the initial acts of aggression.[8]

A second difference between the individual domestic case and situations of international armed conflict is even more important as far as the current discussion of issues of *jus in bello* goes. At the individual level, as I have already noted, if Bill engages in an aggressive attack on Andrew, then Bill has forfeited some of his rights, while Andrew has not. If Bill's attack is a murderous one and the only way that Andrew can defend himself is to kill Bill, then this would be considered a justifiable act of self-defense. Thus, if Andrew was to kill Bill, this would be morally justified, but if Bill was to kill Andrew, this would be murder. At the international level, however, the situation is quite different, since there is a level of reciprocity involved that is not found in ordinary domestic cases of rights forfeiture, in that combatants on both sides of a conflict are thought to be morally legitimate in targeting each other.

If Aydania and Bedania are at war with each other, then as far as the military personnel who are actually fighting the war goes, it doesn't matter if Aydania launched an aggressive attack against Bedania or if it was the other way around. Regardless of which side of the conflict they are on, combatants are considered to be justified in killing enemy combatants, provided they do so within the constraints of the laws of armed conflict. Despite being in stark contrast to the analogous domestic situation, this concept, which is commonly referred to as "the moral equality of combatants,"[9] is enshrined in international law, as well as being widely accepted by writers in the philosophical literature and just war tradition.[10] The leaders of a state that launches an aggressive attack, that is, an attack which violates the conditions of *jus ad bellum*, may be considered to be both legally and morally culpable for their actions and thus after the war they may be charged with war crimes or crimes against peace. But the military personnel who actually carry out the conflict are essentially considered to be mere tools of the state and are thus considered neither morally nor legally responsible for the aggressive actions entailed by the war itself. As Walzer puts it, "We draw a line between the war itself, for which soldiers are not responsible, and the conduct of the war, for which they are responsible, at least within their own sphere of activity. Generals may well straddle the line, but that only suggests that we know pretty well where it should be drawn."[11]

For all that it is widely accepted, the idea that military personnel are mere tools of their political masters is problematic in a number of respects. There have been times in the past when those serving in the military have been forced to march off to war without any real idea of what they were fighting for and no way of finding out, but that is certainly not always the case today. When states engage in armed conflict in the twentieth-first century the basic information required to make a judgment about the ethics of engaging in such a conflict is often available to the average person on the street, including those who are actually being called on to serve. Of course, in some cases it may be that certain vital information about the justification for a conflict is only available to a select few. Highly classified intelligence about the plans and capabilities of a potential enemy might fall into this category, for example. However, even in such cases, democratic governments of modern times are forced to explain their actions to the people and thus at the very least, the fact that such intelligence exists will be known, which in itself might allow people to make at least basic judgments about whether or not war is justified. The 2003 Invasion of Iraq (Case 4.2) is perhaps an example of such a situation. The governments of those states favoring war with Iraq claimed to have detailed and highly classified intelligence which proved that a war was necessary. Yet many people, despite knowing this intelligence existed, still felt that war could not be justified and in many cases expressed this view by attending protests.[12]

If those fighting a war are able to assess the ethical justification for an armed conflict, at least to a certain degree, then it is difficult to see why they should not be thought to be at least partially morally responsible for the harms caused if they are fighting on behalf of a state that has launched an aggressive war. The fact that the claim that one was "merely following orders" is no defense for illegal conduct within a war also seems relevant here; if a person is still considered responsible for their actions if they follow illegal orders within a war, then why should they not also be considered to be responsible for their actions if they follow an illegal order to go to war in the first place? To a large degree this was the claim made by Ehren Watada (see Case 6.1: Ehren Watada and Iraq). While technically it may not always be illegal to launch an aggressive war, it will still be morally wrong. Thus, it seems reasonable to conclude that those who follow orders to engage in an aggressive war must bear at least some of the moral blame for that war.

It could be argued that military personnel ought not to be held responsible for their actions if they are **forced** to fight in a war that they believe is unjust. Thus, if soldiers have been conscripted to fight and/or are being forced into conflict against their will, then they should only be held responsible for actions that are within their control; that is, they are responsible for violations of *jus in bello* but not for violations of *jus ad bellum*. But once again such a claim is not really analogous to the situation in domestic cases, where if someone engages in actions which would normally be considered to be seriously wrong, but asserts that they performed those actions under coercion or duress, then this is considered an excuse, but not a justification, for those actions. In other words the fact that a person was being coerced is seen as an explanation for that person's behavior and as a mitigating factor in determining what punishment ought to be levied against that person, but the mere fact that this person was acting under duress does not mean that whatever they did was ethically acceptable. In the case of military personnel who are fighting on behalf of a state that has launched an aggressive war, although these people may be forced into battle against their will, they are still involved in actions that have extremely serious consequences, in that they are attempting to cause death and injury to others, and it is hard to see why they should not be held at least partly responsible for those consequences. After all, as Brian Orend points out, troops forced into battle against their will, such as conscripted soldiers, usually do have an alternative to fighting, in that they can surrender to their opponents at the first opportunity.[13] Indeed, this was an option that was exercised by thousands of the Iraqi soldiers who were forced to fight in the 1991 Gulf War (Case 4.1).

Thus, in cases where military personnel are being ordered to fight in what they believe to be an aggressive and unjustified war, such personnel have two main options: to refuse to go to war in the first place, like Ehren Watada (Case 6.1), or to surrender at the first non-life-threatening opportunity. Of these options, the first is clearly preferable to the second, since this may actually stop the unjust war from taking place. While such an option may be available to those serving in the military forces of a truly democratic state, those serving in the military forces of a totalitarian state might literally be forced into combat, in an aggressive war, at the point of a gun. Thus, the option of surrender may be the only one available to such military personnel.[14]

Although there is a strict separation between *jus ad bellum* and *jus in bello* in terms of international law, it is difficult to sustain this same separation when assessing the situation in purely ethical terms. As I noted in Chapters 4 and 5, it is logically impossible for both sides in a conflict to be in compliance with the principles of *jus ad bellum*, so whereas military personnel who are on the "just" side in a conflict (assuming there is one) will clearly be ethically justified in attacking opposing combatants, it is difficult to see how military personnel who are engaged in fighting an unjust war can be totally excused from responsibility for fighting in such a war. As Orend suggests, we may consider such persons to be like minor accomplices to a major crime;[15] certainly not fully responsible for the *jus ad bellum* violations involved in engaging in the war, but nonetheless still not totally blameless.

Having said all this, there does still seem to be a further problem that needs to be addressed. Although we might not think that military personnel on the "unjust" side of a war are totally justified in killing enemy combatants, we do intuitively think that there is a significant difference between deliberately killing combatants and deliberately killing noncombatants, and that this distinction applies to those on both sides of the conflict. Thus, whereas those on the "unjust" side of the conflict may not always be thought to be fully justified in killing enemy combatants, neither side's combatants will be justified in deliberately killing noncombatants.

So once again we return to the question asked earlier in the chapter. What action have combatants taken that noncombatants have not, which leads to the idea that combatants have forfeited some right that allows them to legitimately be targeted? Ultimately, the basis for a claim such as this has to be that combatants, whichever side of a conflict they are on, are potentially dangerous people who are involved in an attempt to kill or injure opposing combatants. Since combatants on both sides of the conflict face a serious threat of being harmed by combatants on the other side of the conflict, they are thus legitimately able to target anyone who is involved in this process. As Orend suggests, a "legitimate target in wartime is anyone or anything engaged in harming"[16] and thus that any attack on a person or institution not engaged in harming is a legally and ethically illegitimate attack. But, for a claim such as this to be intelligible to those making decisions on the battlefield, the idea of what it means to be "engaged in harming" has to be teased out. Orend does not mean that a combatant may only legitimately target those enemies who are actually firing on "friendly" forces at the time. The idea here is rather that legitimate targets are those persons or institutions intrinsically connected to the enemy's overall attempt to harm. In the end this idea does play out somewhat differently in traditional wars, where discrimination is perhaps more simple, than it does in modern "irregular" wars, where discrimination is often more difficult.

The Principle of Noncombatant Immunity

The idea of noncombatant immunity, that combatants may be attacked and noncombatant may not, seems simple on the surface. However, in warfare such distinctions are not always easy to make, even in "traditional" conflicts, for the line between combatant and noncombatant does not simply equate to whether or not a person is wearing an enemy uniform. The difficulties of making such a distinction can easily be seen by examining relevant norms of international law on this issue, remembering that such norms indicate important ethical principles, and thus examining the law highlights not merely the legal, but also the ethical, principles involved.

The law of armed conflict generally allows attacks at any time on any and all uniformed members of the enemy military, be they soldiers on the frontline of the battle, command personnel directing operations, ground crew maintaining and re-arming aircraft, or sailors on a navy vessel. All have equal status as combatants and thus are liable to attack at any time. However, some uniformed members of the enemy military, such as medical personnel and religious personnel (i.e., chaplains), enjoy official protected status under the Geneva Conventions and may not be attacked as long as they do not directly engage in combat operations. Yet even those members of the enemy military who can routinely be engaged may enjoy protected status under certain circumstances. Those who are making a genuine attempt to surrender may not be legitimately attacked, for example, nor may enemy personnel who are unable to fight due to injury, the shipwrecked at sea, or aircrew parachuting from a disabled aircraft.[17] The law of armed conflict also allows attacks on certain civilians whose work is intimately connected to the war effort, such as those engaged in the supply or manufacture of weapons to the enemy's armed forces. However, these civilians are not considered combatants, and so are not subject to attack at any time. Rather, they may only be attacked while engaged in those activities that directly relate to the war effort. Thus, a civilian employed at a weapons plant can only be legitimately attacked while he or she is actually working at that weapons plant.

In modern wars, which are often fought among the people and also often involve guerrilla forces, irregular forces, or insurgents, the situation is even more complex. When enemy forces do not wear uniforms and tend to hide amongst the civilian population, it can be difficult to distinguish legitimate targets from illegitimate ones, especially in cases where the local population appears to be supporting the enemy. For military personnel involved in a conflict like this, it can seem like every member of the population is a legitimate target, since all of them seem to be involved in the conflict in one way or another. Yet military forces are still legally and ethically required to apply the principle of discrimination, and only engage in attacks on legitimate targets, so a determination of who and/or what counts as a legitimate target will still have to be made.

Perhaps the best way to get a proper understanding of who might legitimately be targeted in nontraditional conflicts is to look at who may and may not be targeted in traditional conflicts. Doing this helps to highlight what it means to be involved in the "attempt to harm" enemy combatants, an idea which can then be transferred to nontraditional conflicts. In traditional conflicts, any uniformed member of the enemy's armed forces, apart from those with protected status such as medical personnel, can legitimately be included as a part of the enemy's attempt to harm, and thus can legitimately be targeted in an attack. However, if a uniformed member of the enemy's forces makes it clear that they are no longer a part of the attempt to harm, for example by throwing down their arms and surrendering, then they may no longer legitimately be targeted. Thus, in a traditional conflict, any uniformed member of the enemy's forces is presumed "guilty" and thus is a legitimate target for attack unless there is evidence to the contrary, such as a symbol which proclaims that person's protected status, for example, an armband marked with the Red Cross. The same logic allows for attacks on the enemy's military facilities or equipment except in cases where they are marked to identify protected status, for example, Red Crosses on the deck and sides of a naval vessel identifying it as a hospital ship.

Unlike uniformed members of the armed forces, civilians are basically presumed to be "innocent," and thus not subject to direct attack, unless there is evidence which demonstrates otherwise. Civilians who support the enemy's attempt to harm through direct action, and by this I mean by such things as supplying weapons to the armed forces, rather than simply by voting for a government that engages in aggressive warfare, may be targeted, but only while engaging in that action. However, not all those who are supporting the enemy are legitimate targets, for some of the things the enemy forces require will be things that are required for everyday life, rather than for making war. As Walzer points out, "the relevant distinction is not between those who work for the war effort and those who do not, but between those who make what soldiers need to fight and those who make what they need to live, like the rest of us."[18] So the factories that produce and supply the enemy with rifles and ammunition can legitimately be targeted, but the ones supplying them with all the other things they might require for everyday life, such as food, water, blankets, medical supplies, and so on, may not be legitimately attacked.

This same sort of distinction also applies to irregular wars, but in these sorts of conflicts it will generally be more difficult to determine who is part of the "attempt to harm" and thus who may actually be targeted, since enemy forces in such conflicts generally do not wear uniforms and usually look just like the civilian members of the population. Thus, in such cases the presumption of "guilt" tends to be turned around somewhat, in that all persons who look like civilians will be presumed to be "innocent" unless there is evidence to the contrary. Thus, only those who have positively identified themselves as being members of the enemy forces, such as by engaging in a direct attack on friendly forces, would be legitimate targets for military action. In irregular wars, it is also more important than ever to keep in mind Walzer's distinction between those supplying what soldiers need to fight and what they need to live. Although it is legitimate to directly attack those supplying arms to the enemy's irregular forces, it is not legitimate to directly attack those who supply the enemy's irregular forces with food, clothing, or even temporary shelter. These issues will be discussed in more depth in the next chapter.

Issues of discrimination can obviously be very difficult to deal with in some circumstances, especially given the fact that a particular individual may be a legitimate target in some situations but not in others. In fact, even if that individual is actually serving in the opposition's armed forces, it may not always be legitimate to target that person with military force.

CASE STUDY 7.2

The Incident at the Fallujah Mosque

On November 12, 2004, U.S. Marines from the 3rd Battalion, First Marine Regiment who were involved in operations in southern Fallujah, Iraq, were attacked by insurgents armed with AK-47 assault rifles and rocket-propelled grenades (RPGs).

After taking several casualties from the enemy fire, the Marines launched an attack on those buildings that had been identified as the source of the incoming fire; a mosque and a building adjacent to it. Ten insurgents were killed and five others were wounded in the mosque. The Marines, who were accompanied at the time by Kevin Sites, an embedded journalist, examined the five wounded Iraqis, none of whose injuries appeared to be life-threatening, and began preparations to evacuate them to a military hospital for treatment. However, the unit was immediately ordered to support other ongoing combat operations, and the wounded Iraqis were left in the mosque, under the belief that another Marine unit would come and evacuate them in the near future.

The following day, Saturday November 13, U.S. forces received reports that various buildings, including the mosque which had been stormed the day before, had been reoccupied by insurgents during the night. Two Marine units that had not been involved in the attack on the mosque the day before were ordered to the scene. One unit moved to approach the mosque from the rear, the second, which Sites was now accompanying, approached from the front. Gunfire could be heard inside.

Sites was present when a Lieutenant from one of the units asked a Marine what had happened inside the mosque. The Marine replied that there were people inside. "Did you shoot them?" the lieutenant asked. "Roger that, sir," the second Marine replied. "Were they armed?" the lieutenant asked. The second Marine shrugged in reply.[19]

When he entered the mosque, with his camera rolling, Sites saw that the only occupants were the five wounded men who had been left behind the day before.[20] Four of them had been shot again, apparently by members of the Marine squad who had entered the mosque moments earlier. One of the men appeared to be dead, and the three others were severely wounded. The fifth man was lying under a blanket, apparently not having been shot a second time.

In the video footage, as Sites approaches two of the men, who are lying on the floor of the mosque, a Marine who is standing over another man can be heard calling out "He's fucking faking he's dead—he's faking his fucking dead." Sites' camera pans up in time to see the Marine raise his rifle and fire into the man's head from point-blank range.[21] Another Marine can be heard to say, "Well, he's dead now."

When told that the man he shot was a wounded prisoner, the Marine, who himself had been shot in the face the day before but had already returned to duty, told Sites: "I didn't know, sir. I didn't know."[22]

An investigation of the incident commenced immediately, with the aim of determining whether the Marine involved had breached either the Law of Armed Conflict or the Rules of Engagement (ROE). On May 6, 2005, it was announced that the Marine, who had apparently also shot two of the other wounded Iraqis before Sites entered the mosque, would not face a court-martial. The U.S. Marine Corps announced the decision in a press release:

> The evidence supports the conclusion that the shooting of all three AIF (anti-Iraqi forces) by the corporal during the assault on the mosque was consistent with the ROE. The evidence indicates that based on the actions of those AIF, the corporal reasonably believed that they posed a hostile threat to him and his fellow Marines and justifiably fired in self-defense. The enhanced videotape of

the shooting supports the corporal's claim that the wounded AIF was concealing his left arm behind his head. While it is not clear whether the AIF in the video-tape made any overtly threatening gestures, it is clear that the Marines of 3/1, to include [sic] the corporal, were aware that feigning death was a common enemy TTP (tactics, techniques & procedures). Accordingly, it was reasonable to believe that the corporal fired on the AIF after reasonably believing that the individual was committing a hostile act by exhibiting a known enemy TTP (i.e., feigning death and subsequently moving his concealed arm). Based on all the evidence in the case, and the rules of engagement that were in effect at the time, it is clear that the corporal could have reasonably believed that the AIF shown in the videotape posed a hostile threat, justifying his use of deadly force.[23]

Obviously this case does not come from a fully traditional war, in that the forces who the Marines were facing did not wear uniforms. However, the discrimination issues in this case are of a more traditional variety, in that they revolve around the issues of when a combatant ceases to be a combatant, and what level of risk combatants ought to take on to avoid causing harm to those who may be noncombatants. The investigation into the incident determined that the Corporal involved had acted in compliance with the Law of Armed Conflict and with the ROE that were in place, but of course the fact that his actions were legal does not necessarily mean that they were also ethical. If the Marine Corporal in question had known that the men in the mosque had been captured, then left there, the day before, he may well have acted differently in this case; indeed his lack of knowledge of this fact is obviously relevant to the determination of the legality of the Corporal's actions. But to determine whether the Corporal acted ethically here, there is a further question which must be answered. Given that the men in the mosque were all injured and were making no direct and obvious attempts to harm the Marines, should they now be treated as noncombatants unless they were to demonstrate some hostile intent?

One of Walzer's suggestions in this regard is that military personnel are morally required to take "due care" to respect the rights of noncombatants, and that this can, and does, mean that military personnel will be required to take on an additional level of risk in some circumstances if this is what is required to protect those rights.[24] However, exactly what level of risk is actually required is a very open question.

The Corporal in Case 7.2 (The Incident at the Fallujah Mosque) was aware that feigning death while hiding a weapon was a known tactic of those he was fighting against, and it was this, coupled with his ignorance of the fact that the men in the mosque had been captured and disarmed the day before, that apparently made it legally acceptable for him to use deadly force in dealing with these men. With regard to the specific case of the man whose death was captured by Kevin Sites' camera, although it was legally acceptable for the Corporal to use deadly force and shoot the man in the head, this was clearly not the only option available to him. He could, for example, have kept the man covered with his rifle while calling for other Marines to search the man for weapons. However, shooting the man was obviously the option that carried the least risk for the Corporal and his fellow Marines. Exactly how much riskier it would have been for this Corporal to pursue another option is perhaps the most important question here, since any determination about whether the actions of the Corporal were ethical or not will revolve around the question of what level of risk ought to be borne by those who face such situations. One criticism that can be directed against some ROE which have been instituted in various modern conflicts, is that these ROE do not go far enough in terms of the "due care" that is required to protect the rights of noncombatants, including enemy personnel who have been rendered *hors de combat*. This is another issue I will consider in greater depth in the next chapter.

Of course, it has to be recognized that in warfare, perfect discrimination is not always possible, for military and civilian facilities often exist side by side and enemy military personnel may be in close proximity to civilians. So though a soldier might be attacking a legitimate military target, they can foresee that there will be civilian casualties as well. Causing the death or wounding of noncombatants in such attacks is commonly described in military circles as collateral damage. Collateral damage is acceptable in an attack as long as certain conditions are met, conditions which basically coincide with those required by the doctrine of double effect (DDE) which was discussed in Chapter 2. In general terms, the DDE states that if a person is acting with the aim of achieving a good effect, but foresees that their action will also produce bad consequences, it is permitted for the person to take this action as long as (1) the action that is being taken is otherwise morally permissible; (2) the agent involved is aiming to achieve the good effect and not the bad effect; (3) the bad effect is not the means by which the good effect will be achieved; and (4) the good that will be achieved is proportionate to the bad effect that will occur. In military terms, what this means is that if a soldier is doing something that is ordinarily permissible in war, for example, attacking a legitimate target, and is doing so with a legitimate aim, for example, intending to kill enemy troops and not kill enemy civilians, and if the good which will be achieved is, in military terms, proportional to the damage that will be done, then the attack may be launched, despite the foreseen collateral damage. Obviously, one essential part of this that must be discussed in more depth is the idea of proportionality. Since proportionality is itself one of the fundamental principles of *jus in bello*, that is the topic I will now discuss.

PROPORTIONALITY

The essential idea of proportionality is that the destruction being brought about by military operations must not be out of line with the good end being sought through those operations. So, as military personnel go about their business of "killing people and breaking stuff," they ought to ensure that they don't kill more people, even enemy military personnel, or break more stuff, even enemy military equipment and installations, than is necessary to achieve their objective. While this may seem an odd claim, especially to those who are currently involved in fighting a war, it makes more sense when it is considered in greater depth.

The first thing to consider with regard to discussions of the importance of proportionality is the fairly obvious fact that people rarely, if ever, go to war simply for the sake of going to war. It is usual that there is some particular objective being sought. Few wars result in utter military defeat and occupation for one of the belligerents—the defeats of Germany and Japan in World War II are exceptional in this regard—and so it has to be recognized from the time a war begins that at some point diplomatic negotiations will probably take place. Although people would obviously prefer to negotiate from a position of strength, which means conducting a successful military campaign, this is not the same thing as leveling undue destruction on your enemy. Engaging in excessive destruction, that is, using means which are not proportional, is likely to make your enemy resentful and thus less likely to want to negotiate a lasting peace, not to mention the fact that a resentful enemy is likely to resist for longer, thus prolonging the war. As John Rawls puts it, "the means employed must not destroy the possibility of peace or encourage a contempt for human life that puts the safety of ourselves or of mankind in jeopardy."[25]

To illustrate the point Rawls is making here, consider the following fictional, but historically realistic, example. Imagine two states who have engaged in a war that involved deliberately disproportionate tactics such as massacres of enemy civilians, rape as a weapon of war, the deliberate destruction of buildings of religious or cultural value to the other side, and so on. Any negotiated peace between these two states will face enormous difficulties, since the use of such tactics will inevitably leave lasting resentment and hatred, and either side is likely to need little provocation to resume such a war in the future. However, if disproportionate tactics had not been used in the first place, then negotiating a lasting peace between these states is likely to be much easier, since those lasting hatreds are much less likely to have been created in such a war.

The second thing to consider about proportionality is that the damage being wrought in a particular military engagement can be considered on two levels: the tactical level, that is, the individual battle; and the strategic level, that is, the whole campaign. It is perfectly possible for a particular act of war to seem disproportionate at the tactical level but fully proportionate at the strategic level. The following case is a commonly cited example of such a situation.

CASE STUDY 7.3

Sinking of the *General Belgrano*

The U.K. and Argentina have been engaged in an extremely long-running dispute over the Falkland Islands in the South Atlantic (see Case 4.6). In April 1982,

Argentina attempted to secure its claim to sovereignty by invading the Falkland Islands and other British possessions in the South Atlantic. The invasion was condemned by the UNSC, which passed a resolution urging the two states to seek a diplomatic resolution to the dispute. However, diplomatic attempts at a resolution failed, and the U.K. dispatched a task force to retake the islands by amphibious assault.

The British faced considerable difficulty in launching a successful assault, since the islands were located less than 500 km (300 miles) from the Argentine coast on the South American mainland, but more than 12,000 kilometers (7,400 miles) away from Great Britain. This gave theoretical air superiority to the Argentine air force. Argentine naval forces in the area also possessed virtual parity with the British naval forces assigned to the task force, and in the cruiser ARA *General Belgrano*, the Argentines had a warship that outgunned any single ship available to the British.

As British naval forces approached the Falklands in late April, Argentine naval forces had left port, apparently to take up positions around the islands, thus threatening the British amphibious landings. British submarines were dispatched to locate the most important elements of the Argentine fleet, namely, the aircraft carrier ARA *Veinticinco de Mayo* and the cruiser *General Belgrano*. The *Belgrano* was duly located by the nuclear submarine HMS *Conquerer* on April 30, which shadowed the cruiser and its accompanying destroyers for more than a day. The British had declared a 200 nautical mile (370 kilometer) exclusion zone around the Falklands, and the *Belgrano* was currently outside that zone, yet Admiral Woodward, the British naval commander, considered the *Belgrano* a threat to the fleet and thus to the invasion, and requested permission to attack. The situation was discussed at cabinet level, and on May 2, the British Prime Minister, Margaret Thatcher, issued orders for the *Conquerer* to engage the *Belgrano*.

At 1557 on May 2, the *Conquerer* fired three torpedoes at the *General Belgrano*; two of these torpedoes hit their target. The first torpedo blew the bows off the ship, but although forward compartments began to flood, the bulkheads held. The second torpedo struck much further aft, exploding in the aft machine room, knocking out all the electrical power on this ship, and blasting up through two messes and a recreation area before blowing a large hole in the deck. The loss of electrical power was a critical issue, since it meant that the pumps could not be used to get rid of the water pouring in through the damaged bow, nor could the *Belgrano* send out a distress call to alert its escorts to the attack. Twenty minutes after the attack, the Captain was forced to give the order to abandon ship. The escorting destroyers, unaware of the attack, but apparently having detected an enemy submarine, continued on course and began dropping depth charges, and it was not until after dark, when the life rafts from the *Belgrano* had scattered, that they returned to the scene of the sinking and attempted to rescue survivors. Argentine and Chilean ships rescued 770 men over the next few days, but 323 men were killed in the sinking of the *Belgrano*.

The sinking of the *Belgrano* was probably the most controversial aspect in the conduct of the Falklands War, and was much discussed in Britain after the war had ended. The problematic issue here is not a legal one: Britain and Argentina were at war, and thus the *Belgrano* was certainly a legitimate military target. The problematic issue is whether the damage done in the attack, that is, the sinking of the ship and the death of hundreds of Argentine sailors, was justified in light of the amount of direct military advantage the attack achieved. Most controversy existed around the fact that the cruiser was outside the 200 nautical mile total exclusion zone when it was sunk, which meant that at the time it was fired on it was not a direct tactical threat to British operations. The controversy was heightened in Britain when it was discovered that the *Belgrano* was actually sailing away from the Falklands when it was attacked, and that a Peruvian brokered peace proposal, which might have averted the war, was on its way to Britain at the time the attack was launched, though the British cabinet claims that this proposal was not received until after the *Belgrano* had been sunk.

In tactical terms, the attack on the *Belgrano* does seem to be disproportionate, for the reasons mentioned previously. However, the strategic situation seems quite different; the ships of the Argentine navy represented a threat to the British amphibious assault on the Falklands, and waiting until the *Belgrano* actually attacked one of the British warships could have been disastrous to the campaign. Given the power balance between the two adversaries, the loss of a British aircraft carrier or troop transport may well have been decisive. The sinking of the *Belgrano* also revealed to the Argentine navy how vulnerable their ships were to British submarines; their ships returned to port and essentially took no further part in the war. Thus, while the attack might seem disproportionate at a tactical level, it does seem to be proportionate at a strategic level.

The sinking of the *General Belgrano* is an easy case for proportionality in one respect, however, as an enemy naval vessel at sea in a time of war is a purely military target and doesn't usually involve discussion of noncombatant casualties.[26] A much more common situation, which is also rather more difficult to assess, is when directing an attack against a military target is likely to have other nonmilitary effects, such as the destruction of civilian structures or causing significant casualties among the civilian population. In some cases, making an assessment of proportionality may be reasonably straightforward, such as in the case of an attack that will kill a large number of enemy troops but may also cause some damage to various surrounding civilian structures. However, in other cases, assessment of proportionality may be extremely difficult, such as when an attack may cause significant civilian casualties but will probably cause severe disruption to the movements of enemy forces. Determining proportionality in such cases may be particularly difficult because this may require comparison of what are essentially incommensurate values. So although it may be relatively easy to determine whether an attack is proportional when this calculation simply involves balancing casualties amongst combatants with casualties amongst noncombatants, it will be much harder to determine what is and is not a proportional attack in cases where an attack is expected to cause significant disruption to an enemy's military apparatus but where this attack will also cause significant noncombatant casualties. Lives versus lives is a relatively easy comparison; disruption versus lives is certainly not as straightforward. Consider the following case.

CASE STUDY 7.4

The Dam Busters Raid

In 1939, at the beginning of World War II, a British engineer and aircraft designer named Barnes Wallis started to investigate ways of making aerial strategic bombing more effective. Since he had been involved in the design of bombers for the Royal Air Force, he had a good working knowledge of current theories of aerial bombing, which, due to inaccuracies in bomb aiming, relied on dropping large numbers of small bombs onto a target in the hopes of achieving significant damage. Wallis began to think about where and how bombing could hurt the German war effort the most, and he quickly recognized that it would be impossible for aerial bombing to destroy a significant number of armament factories, given the number of German factories and the fact that these factories were dispersed all over Germany. Thus, he focused on a new idea, which was to destroy the sources of power that could not be hidden or dispersed, such as coal mines, oil fields, and the dams which produced hydroelectricity. Coal mines were, he concluded, too far underground to damage, and the main oil fields in Romania were too far away, so he concentrated his attention on dams. The dams that caught his attention were located in the Ruhr, the heartland of German military production. These dams were significant producers of hydroelectricity and also accounted for nearly all the water supply to the Ruhr.

As Wallis researched what the effects of breaching these dams would be, he became convinced that the destruction of these dams would deal a severe blow to the German war effort. Not only would breaching the dams deprive German industry of the hydroelectric power they provided, but it would also disrupt war industries in many other ways. Current German production methods required 8 tons of water to produce 1 ton of steel, but water would be in short supply if the dams were destroyed and this was likely to cause critical bottlenecks in the production of a number of important pieces of military hardware, including tanks, aircraft, guns, and locomotives. In addition, breaching the dams would send massive floods down the lower river valleys, destroying vital roads, railway lines, bridges and factories. But damaging the dams would require both precision bomb aiming and bombs far bigger than anything that was currently available.

Wallis was not the only person thinking about an operation such as this, and after lengthy planning the attack on the dams went ahead on the night of May 16–17, 1943, using a 5-ton bomb specially designed by Wallis for the attack. The attack succeeded in breaching the Möhne and Eder dams, and the Sorpe dam was damaged. Of the 19 Lancaster bombers involved in the raid, 11 returned safely to England; the other 8 were shot down. Due to the low flying required by the raid, only three of the crew survived the downing of their planes; all were captured as prisoners of war.

Estimates of the damage caused by the raid vary. At the time, Allied sources suggested the raid had severely damaged the German war machine, though some German sources apparently viewed the damage as being much less significant. Some support for the British position can be found in the writings of the German Minister of Armaments and War Production, Albert Speer, who thought the dams so vital that he diverted massive resources to rebuilding and protecting them, at the expense of other projects. It is certain that a large number of roads, railways, and bridges were washed away, and that a significant number of factories and power stations were inundated with water, as was one of the area's largest military airfields. In addition, thousands of workers had to be diverted to deal with the after effects of the raid, including rebuilding communication links and industry devastated by the flooding and reconstruction of the dams, which also included building improved defenses to protect these dams against future raids. One unexpected effect was in terms of loss of food production; large swathes of farmland were devastated, and several thousand animals, mostly cattle and pigs, were drowned. In terms of the human cost of the raid, in addition to the allied airmen who lost their lives, at least 1,350 people were killed in the raid, mostly drowned by the floods. Few of these were German military personnel; in fact the majority of those killed caused by the raid were not German at all, but rather were foreign citizens, since over half of those killed were interned in prisoners of war or forced labor camps which had been located in the river valleys below the dams.

In 1977, Protocol I Additional to the Geneva Conventions made it illegal, under international law, to engage in attacks on installations such as dams, dykes, or nuclear power stations if such attacks would cause the release of dangerous forces that would cause severe losses amongst the civilian population, even in cases where such installations are themselves viable military targets.

SOURCES: Paul Brickhill, *The Dam Busters* (London: Evans, 1952); John Sweetman, *The Dambusters Raid* (London: Cassell, 2002).

An attack such as this one inevitably brings into play the ideas of DDE, which was discussed earlier in this chapter as well as in Chapter 2. The attack in Case 7.4 (The Dam Busters Raid) was being launched to achieve specific military objectives; the destruction of the source of electrical power for many German military factories and the disruption of the production of the steel that was required for a lot of military hardware. However, it was also recognized that breaching these dams would have other nonmilitary effects, including large numbers of civilian casualties and the destruction of civilian farms and housing. To determine whether such an attack would be ethically permissible, an assessment needed to be made about whether the attack would comply with the four conditions of the DDE.

The first condition seems to be met, since the dams which were being attacked could be considered to be valid military targets because the electricity the dams produced was important for the German war effort. The second condition also seems to be met, since the primary aim of the attack was to achieve the military aims, that is, the disruption of military production, and not to achieve the other nonmilitary effects. The third condition is perhaps a little more problematic, since this condition requires that the good effect be achieved directly and not as a result of the bad effect, and it could be argued that the damage that would be caused by the floods that would be released after the dams had been breached was also an intended effect of the attack. However, it does seem likely that the dams would have been attacked even if it had been clear that the ensuing floods would not do any damage to German military production. In any case, the dams themselves were the target of the attack, so condition three of the DDE does seem to be met in this case. However, not all attacks on dams could actually meet this condition of the DDE. If the main aim of an attack like this was to use the massive floods which would be released by breaching the dams as a means of destroying some militarily vital bridges that crossed the river below the dam, then such an attack would fail to meet this condition of the DDE, since the good effect, that is, the destruction of the important bridges, would be brought about by means of the bad effect, the breaching of the dam.[27]

The most problematic aspect of the DDE with regard to Case 7.4 (The Dam Busters Raid) is the fourth condition regarding the proportionality of the attack. Breaching the dams was obviously going to involve a significant amount of collateral damage in the form of noncombatant casualties, as well as a lot of other damage to nonmilitary installations such as shops, farms, and houses. To make an assessment of proportionality in this case, those planning the raid needed to work out how severe the damage to German military production would be, as well as assess the strategic value of the raid in terms of increased morale among the population of Britain and her allies, and then balance that against the collateral damage that would be done to those German and foreign noncombatants as well as to nonmilitary industries. This sort of calculation would be much easier to accomplish in the present day than it was in 1943; the British planners had to rely on pre-war data to try to determine what the actual effect of breaching the dams would be on the German armament industry, information which was rather outdated even at the beginning of the war in 1939. In addition, the planners faced considerable difficulties in determining what the collateral damage was likely to be, since overall intelligence about the area downstream of the dams was based on high-altitude surveillance photos, and these photos could not be taken with any greatly regularity, since the resources required to engage in such reconnaissance were in great demand for the planning of a great number of other raids as well.

From the "total war" perspective of World War II, the military value of this raid was seen to be worth the collateral cost, but later international protocols do suggest that other thinkers after the war did not agree with this assessment. It is notable that the conditions established in Protocol I are not simply an attempt to ensure that condition three of the DDE is complied with, since the articles in question do not only forbid the destruction of installations like dams and dikes in cases where the intention is to produce the military effect through the subsequent flooding. The fact that these articles forbid destroying installations that control dangerous forces, even in cases where these installations are themselves valid military targets, demonstrates that the concern here is the collateral damage that would result from the destruction of such installations.[28]

MODERN ASSESSMENT OF COLLATERAL DAMAGE

Modern day assessments of what counts as acceptable collateral damage rely on both discrimination and proportionality. Military personnel are expected to make a clear attempt to discriminate between legitimate and illegitimate targets, and even to take on a level of additional risk, both to themselves and to those under their command, to ensure that collateral damage is either eliminated or, in cases where that is not reasonable, kept to the lowest possible levels. In cases where military action is likely to cause collateral damage, it is the responsibility of the commander to ensure that any collateral damage that is caused is strictly in proportion to the actual military value of the target. Thus an attack against a truly high value military target might proceed if there is the likelihood of significant collateral damage, but the same amount of collateral damage would not be justified in an attack on a lower value target. A military commander who is directing attacks that may result in collateral damage is in a serious position; they must be able to assess the means by which such an attack might be carried out to see if a more discriminate attack is feasible, as well as being able to make a good judgment about the actual military value of the target to decide whether the target is valuable enough to justify the collateral damage likely to be incurred in an attack.

Having examined various issues relating to discrimination and proportionality, it is now possible to return the case that began this entire discussion and make some reasonable assessment about the actions of the officer involved in that case. Case Study 7.1 (Airpower and Marine Assault) is a good example of the problem of assessing collateral damage. In this case, the Company Commander is faced with a determined and apparently well-resourced enemy who are defending a fortified position from a Marine assault. The Commander attempts the most discriminate form of attack, a direct assault on the door, but his troops are wounded by the enemy's prepared explosive defenses. He then uses the next most discriminate form of attack available, in the form of a tank, and only when this fails does he resort to an air strike that levels the building. However, even when resorting to an air strike, it is a precision strike, guided by laser and using a single bomb, thus reducing the possibility of excessive collateral damage. The attack is as discriminate as possible in all its aspects, and the final strike is a proportionate response, required to secure a specific military objective. Although this strike apparently did cause collateral damage in the form of civilian deaths, the commander had acted appropriately by making every attempt to avoid such damage if possible.

Of additional interest here is the fact that the insurgents who the U.S. Marines faced also obeyed the rules of *jus in bello* to a large degree. Their fire was discriminate in that they fired only on the Marines approaching their position. The weak point in their position, the front door, was protected by an explosive that was command detonated, thus allowing discrimination in its use as well, and they had placed the civilians in a separate area rather than leaving them exposed to direct fire from the incoming Marines, though obviously they could have gone further in this regard by allowing the civilians to leave the location entirely.

Even in cases where the target of an attack is a legitimate military objective, if an attack is indiscriminate, then any collateral damage caused by that attack is almost certainly going to be considered to be excessive, and those in charge of ordering the attack may well find themselves charged with war crimes, as happened in the following case.

CASE STUDY 7.5

Conviction of Milan Martic´

On June 12, 2007, Milan Martić, the former president of the now defunct Serbian Republic of Krajina, was convicted of war crimes and crimes against humanity by the International Criminal Tribunal for the Former Yugoslavia. Among the acts for which he was held responsible were cluster bomb rocket attacks on Zagreb on May 2 and 3, 1995, attacks which were apparently launched in response to Croatian attacks on territory in the region of Krajina. In passing judgment, the court made note of the following relevant facts:

> 462.[29] The M-87 Orkan is a non-guided projectile, the primary military use of which is to target soldiers and armoured vehicles. Each rocket may contain either a cluster warhead with 288 so-called bomblets or 24 anti-tank shells. The evidence shows that rockets with cluster warheads containing bomblets were launched in the attacks on Zagreb on 2 and 3 May 1995. Each bomblet contains 420 pellets of 3mm in diameter. The bomblets are ejected from the rocket at a height of 800-1,000m above the targeted area and explode upon impact, releasing the pellets. The maximum firing range of the M-87 Orkan is 50 kilometres. The dispersion error of the rocket at 800-1,000m in the air increases with the firing range. Fired from the maximum range, this error is about 1,000m in any direction. The area of dispersion of the bomblets on the ground is about two hectares. Each pellet has a lethal range of ten metres.

> 463. The evidence shows that the M-87 Orkan was fired on 2 and 3 May 1995 from the Vojnić area, near Slavsko Polje, between 47 and 51 kilometres from Zagreb. However, the Trial Chamber notes in this respect that the weapon was fired from the extreme of its range. Moreover, the Trial Chamber notes the characteristics of the weapon, it being a non-guided high dispersion weapon. The Trial Chamber therefore concludes that the M-87 Orkan, by virtue of its

characteristics and the firing range in this specific instance, was incapable of hitting specific targets. For these reasons the Trial Chamber also finds that the M-87 Orkan is an indiscriminate weapon, the use of which in densely populated civilian areas, such as Zagreb, will result in the infliction of severe casualties. By 2 May 1995, the effects of firing the M-87 Orkan on Zagreb were known to those involved. Furthermore, before the decision was made to once again use this weapon on Zagreb on 3 May 1995, the full impact of using such an indiscriminate weapon was known beyond doubt as a result of the extensive media coverage on 2 May 1995 of the effects of the attack on Zagreb.

469....due to the characteristics of the M-87 Orkan and due to the large-scale nature of the attack, the Trial Chamber finds that the shelling constituted a widespread attack directed against the civilian population of Zagreb....

Having ordered this indiscriminate attack, Milan Martić was found to be individually criminally responsible for the death of 7 civilians and the wounding of 207 civilians and 7 military personnel. He was also found guilty of other offences and was sentenced to 35 years in prison.

There are a number of weapons, or types of weapons, which have been banned by international convention, either because they are seen to inflict unnecessary suffering, that is, they are disproportionate, or because they are seen to be indiscriminate. For example, chemical and biological weapons and antipersonnel landmines have all been banned by international treaties on the grounds that they are indiscriminate, and permanently blinding laser weapons and weapons designed to produce fragments undetectable by x-rays have been banned as being disproportionate. The use of incendiary weapons has not been banned, but certain uses of these weapons are seen as violations of *jus in bello*, such as the use of incendiaries on civilians or near concentrations of civilians.

Even if it is considered reasonable to use a weapon in some circumstances, this does not mean that its use in other circumstances will not violate the conditions of *jus in bello*. The weapon used in Case Study 7.5 (Conviction of Milan Martić) was a multiple rocket launcher firing cluster bombs, a weapon which can be used in a proportionate and discriminate manner.[30] However, in this case the court found that the weapon had been used in an indiscriminate manner, since those ordering its use knew that it was not capable of hitting a discrete military target within an urban environment like the city of Zagreb, but ordered its use regardless of the likely civilian casualties.

SUMMARY

The principles of discrimination and proportionality are fundamental to the idea of *jus in bello*. The principle of discrimination asserts that the only appropriate targets are those concerned with the enemy's war effort, that is, with those directly involved in the enemy's attempt to cause harm. This leads to the most common expression of the idea of discrimination, the principle of noncombatant immunity, which states that noncombatants may never be directly targeted for attack. In traditional conflicts, it is relatively easy to determine who is and is not a combatant, despite the fact that this distinction does not simply equate to whether or not a person is wearing an enemy uniform. Although noncombatants may not be directly targeted, this does not mean that they cannot legitimately be harmed, since noncombatants may well be killed or injured as part of the collateral damage of an attack on a legitimate military target. However, to be legitimate, any collateral damage must also be in accordance with the principle of proportionality. This principle asserts that the damage that is done in prosecuting valid military targets needs to be in line with the actual military value of the target itself. Thus, an attack against a truly high value military target might proceed if there is the likelihood of significant collateral damage, but the same amount of collateral damage would not be justified in an attack on a lower value target.

These two fundamental principles of *jus in bello* are considered so important that they have been incorporated into the law of armed conflict in various ways. Thus a commander who directs an attack that breaches either one of these principles, that is, an attack which is indiscriminate or an attack which deals disproportionate damage, may find themselves charged with a war crime. Consideration of discrimination and proportionality is thus extremely important in all conflicts, but the issues that are raised in relation to these principles tend to vary depending on the type of conflict being considered. More traditional conflicts against state forces tend to raise different issues from those that are important in modern conflicts, such as counterinsurgency operations and conflicts against non-state forces, or armed humanitarian interventions and peacekeeping or peace enforcement operations. Discussion of the issues of discrimination and proportionality in the context of these modern conflicts is the focus of the next two chapters.

NOTES

1. The "War is Hell" quote is usually attributed to a speech which Sherman gave to the graduating class of the Michigan Military Academy in 1879, "War is Cruelty" from Sherman's *Memoirs* (1875) cited in Michael Walzer, *Just and Unjust Wars* (New York: Basic, 1977), p. 32.
2. Cited in Walzer, *Just and Unjust Wars*, p. 47.
3. Walzer, *Just and Unjust Wars*, p. 42.
4. Ibid., p. 135.
5. David Rodin argues that there are in fact three conditions that must be met for violent self-defense to be justified: an attack must be imminent, rather than merely expected at some stage in the future; a violent response must be necessary, that is, the

defendant could not avoid being harmed by the attack in some other manner, such as by running away; and the violent response must be proportionate. See *War and Self-Defense* (New York: Oxford University Press, 2003), pp. 40–43.

6. While I am explicitly talking about moral rights in this discussion, there is an obvious overlap in such case between moral and legal rights. Whereas the legal rights a person may have will vary somewhat depending on the jurisdiction being considered, in a simple assault case like I have described here the moral rights I am discussing will actually equate to the legal rights that the various parties have, at least in every legal jurisdiction that I am aware of.

7. This term comes from Walzer. See *Just and Unjust Wars*, pp. 58–59.

8. *War and Self-Defense*, p. 112. The example is perhaps overdrawn, since both Germany and Japan were still occupying significant foreign territories at the time of their respective surrenders.

9. See Walzer, *Just and Unjust Wars*, pp. 34–40.

10. David Rodin explicitly rejects this idea because of its disanalogy to the domestic situation. See *War and Self-Defense*, especially Chapter 8.

11. *Just and Unjust Wars*, pp. 38–39.

12. An international day of protest against the proposed war was organized, with rallies against the war held around the world on February 15, 2003. According to the BBC, between six and ten million people around the world attended antiwar protests on February 15, http://news.bbc.co.uk/2/hi/europe/2765215.stm (accessed September 15, 2011). These protests are also listed in *Guinness World Records, 2004*, as the largest antiwar protests in history.

13. Brian Orend, *The Morality of War* (Peterborough ON: Broadview, 2006), p. 109.

14. One possible objection to what I have said here is that for some military forces, surrender may simply be considered a totally unacceptable option. For example, Article Two of the Code of Conduct of the Armed Forces of the United States says "I will never surrender of my own free will. If in command, I will never surrender the members of my command while they still have the means to resist." As I hope I have made clear, what I am discussing in this section are the possible avenues of protest that are available to members of the armed forces in the event that they are being forced to fight in a war they believe is clearly unjust. Since refusal to deploy to an unjust war is an option open to the military personnel of democratic states, like the U.S.A., it is highly unlikely that members of the armed forces of the U.S. would be forced to resort to mass surrender as their only means of protest at being forced into combat in an obviously unjust war, though surrender may be the only form of protest available to those forced to fight in the armed forces of a dictatorship. To be clear, I am not advocating mass surrender of U.S. personnel in other circumstances. My thanks to Lt. Col. Arnold Piper, U.S. Army (Ret.), for pointing out the need for clarification of this issue.

15. *The Morality of War*, p. 109.

16. Ibid, p. 107.

17. The French term *hors de combat*, which literally means "outside the fight," is often used in international law, and sometimes in other contexts, to describe those who are

incapable of performing their military function. In a legal context the term may be used to describe those who: (1) have been captured; (2) have expressed a clear intention to surrender; and/or (3) are unable to defend themselves due to unconsciousness, wounds, or sickness. See Article 41 of Protocol I Additional to the Geneva Conventions (1977). Although the legal definition only addresses people, any object or piece of military equipment that can no longer perform its military function could be referred to as *hors de combat*.

18. Walzer, *Just and Unjust Wars* p. 146.

19. Kevin Sites, "Open Letter to Marines: What Happened in the Fallujah Mosque," http://www.msnbc.msn.com/id/6556034/ns/world_news-mideast/n_africa/ (accessed May 2, 2011).

20. Edited footage of the incident, including commentary by Sites, is available at http://www.wired.com/video/security/security/9525752001/kevin-sites-fallujah-shooting/1813573885 (accessed May 2, 2011). Raw footage is available at http://www.spike.com/video-clips/dsg5hc/kevin-sites-fallujah-shooting-video (accessed May 2, 2011).

21. When watching the video of the incident, the range can be estimated through measurements of the length of the Marine's rifle and the height of the Marine himself. The distance between the muzzle of the rifle and the head of the man he shoots is certainly no more than 1.5 meters (5 feet).

22. Sites, "Open Letter to Marines."

23. Parenthesized explanation of abbreviations added. USMC Press Release, "Marine Involved in Mosque Shooting Will Not Face a Court-Martial," quoted in "U.S. Navy Finds Soldier Shot Wounded Iraqi at Fallujah in Self Defense," http://en.wikinews.org/wiki/U.S._Navy_finds_soldier_shot_wounded_Iraqi_at_Fallujah_in_self_defense (accessed May 2, 2011).

24. *Just and Unjust Wars*, pp. 151–159.

25. John Rawls, *A Theory of Justice* (New York: Oxford University Press, 1971), p. 379.

26. In fact, the sinking of the *Belgrano* did involve some civilian casualties; two of the journalists who were on board the ship at the time of the attack were killed.

27. Such a situation has occurred in fiction, though I am unaware of a factual case like this. For example, the heroes of Alastair MacLean's *Force Ten From Navarone* (London: Fontana, 1994) breach a dam in Yugoslavia during World War II to destroy a vital bridge located below the dam.

28. See Article 56 of the Protocol Additional to the Geneva Conventions of August 12, 1949, and relating to the Protection of Victims of International Armed Conflicts (Protocol I), June 8, 1977. Some special exceptions are recognized within the Protocol itself.

29. Numbered paragraphs quoted from Prosecutor *v.* Martić, No. IT-95-11-T, Judgement (International Criminal Tribunal for the Former Yugoslavia, June 12, 2007).

30. There is now an international treaty, the Convention on Cluster Munitions, which came into force on August 1, 2010, and would apply to the use of a weapon like the M-87 Orkan. State parties to this treaty agree that they will not use, produce, or stockpile various types of cluster munitions. Several major producers and users

of cluster munitions did not sign the treaty, including the U.S.A., Russia, China, and India. It should be noted that the treaty does not ban various types of cluster munitions that are seen to not have indiscriminate effects.

FURTHER READING

Coppieters, Bruno & Fotion, Nick (eds.). *Moral Constraints on War: Principles and Cases* (Lanham, MD: Lexington, 2002).
Orend, Brian. *The Morality of War* (Peterborough, ON: Broadview, 2006). Chapter 4: "Just Conduct in War."
Walzer, Michael. *Just and Unjust Wars* (New York: Basic, 1977).

DISCUSSION QUESTIONS

- Should military personnel on the "unjust" side in a conflict be held responsible for the actions that they have taken during that conflict, or should only the political leaders who decided to engage in an "unjust" war be held responsible for such things?
- Are the criteria of discrimination and proportionality equally important, or is one more important than the other in terms of the ethical ideas of *jus in bello*?
- Is it reasonable to apply an idea like the doctrine of double effect when discussing the ethical permissibility of causing collateral damage during armed conflict?

8

⇦⚬

Discrimination and Proportionality II
Jus In Bello *in Irregular Wars*

=== CASE STUDY 8.1 ===

Casualties in the 2008–2009 Gaza War

In 2005, Israel undertook a unilateral withdrawal from the Gaza Strip, which it had controlled since the Six Day War of 1967, with the Israeli cabinet formally declaring an end to Israeli military rule in the territory on September 12 (see Case 5.1). The West Bank and Gaza Strip territories were both theoretically under the control of the Palestinian Authority, but fighting between the two main Palestinian factions, Fatah and Hamas, which occurred in 2007, resulted in an effective split in Palestine, with Fatah establishing a government in the West Bank and Hamas retaining control in the Gaza Strip. This result caused Israel to close the border entry points into the Gaza Strip to all goods except immediate humanitarian aid. Between 2005 and 2007, Palestinian groups in Gaza fired about 2,700 locally made Qassam rockets into Israel, killing 4 Israeli civilians and injuring 75 others. Egypt brokered a truce between Hamas and Israel in 2008, but negotiations to extend the truce broke down following an Israeli military incursion into Gaza in November 2008, and a subsequent increase in Palestinian rocket attacks on Israel.

On December 27, 2008, Israel commenced "Operation Cast Lead" against Hamas. It began with two waves of air-strikes; in the first, 100 preplanned targets were hit in less than 4 minutes, in the second, 30 minutes later, another 60 targets were hit. These strikes hit Hamas headquarters, government offices, and 24 police stations; Israel claimed that since Hamas was a terrorist organization, anyone associated with Hamas was a legitimate military target, especially those carrying arms in the name of Hamas, such as police officers. Air strikes continued over the following days, often targeting the homes of Hamas commanders, which Israel claimed were equivalent to military control centers in the Gaza Strip. Israel adopted a number of measures in these strikes that were intended to reduce civilian casualties. These measures included dropping millions of leaflets urging the population to evacuate, and making tens of thousands of telephone calls to buildings likely to be targeted within the next 10 to 15 minutes, warning people to leave the area. In places where large numbers of civilians gathered on rooftops, thus preventing attacks on those buildings, Israeli planes often dropped small non-explosive devices onto open areas of the roof, with the aim of scaring civilians into leaving the area.

Israeli ground forces entered the Gaza Strip on January 3. These forces were apparently attempting to achieve several interrelated objectives: to seize control of areas from which rockets had been fired into Israel, thus preventing further attacks; to destroy all the arms and ammunition dumps they could locate, thus disarming radical militants; and to destroy the military command and control apparatus of Hamas.

Hamas had apparently been preparing for an Israeli attack for several years, and had stockpiled weapons at strategic sites, as well as creating a maze of tunnels under the buildings in Gaza City and creating a range of sophisticated booby traps. One example of such a booby trap was apparently observed by Ron Ben-Yishai, an Israeli journalist embedded with the Israeli troops. He said that Hamas had placed a manne-quin in a hallway off the main entrance of a building in northern Gaza; the mannequin was rigged to explode and bring down the building if fired on.[1] To avoid booby traps the Israeli soldiers tended to enter buildings by breaking through side walls, rather than using doors, and then moving from room to room inside the building by batter-ing holes in interior walls, thus avoiding exposure to snipers and suicide bombers.

Most important, Israel treated the engagement as a war, not a police opera-tion. So while they made attempts to warn civilians to leave battle areas, the Israeli soldiers were ordered to "go in heavy," using air attacks, artillery, and tank fire to deal with any resistance before moving forward, and advancing behind tanks and armored bulldozers or riding in armored personnel carriers, so as to ensure they spent as little time in the open as possible.[2] Such tactics served to protect the sol-diers, but it could be claimed this came at the expense of civilian casualties. In one widely reported incident, dozens of people were killed or injured when the Israelis shelled the street adjacent to a UN school where refugees were taking shelter.[3] The Israelis said they returned fire in response to mortar shells fired at Israeli troops; however, the UN personnel claimed that no militants were in the school.

Israeli ground forces eventually penetrated deep into Gaza City in engage-ments with Hamas fighters; though they encountered many booby traps and impro-vised explosive devices, the Israeli troops generally suffered few casualties while inflicting heavy losses on Hamas. Israel announced a unilateral ceasefire on January 17, and completed the withdrawal of troops from the Gaza Strip on January 21.

It is certain that 13 Israelis were killed during the conflict, including three non-combatants and four Israeli soldiers killed in friendly fire incidents. Casualty figures on the Palestinian side are much less certain. Estimates of the total number of Palestinians killed range from the Israeli figure of 1,166[4] through to the Palestinian Ministry of Health figure of 1,440.[5] Israeli figures claim that over 700 of the dead were combatants, but this figure is under serious dispute since it includes at least 248 police officers killed in air strikes on police stations, as well as many other people whose status as combatants is questionable. By way of contrast, the Israeli Human Rights organization, B'Tselem, claims the total Palestinian death toll was 1,385, including 248 police officers and 762 noncombatants.[6]

DISCUSSION

Having discussed the way in which the ideas of discrimination and proportionality apply to traditional conflicts, it is now possible to look at how these same principles apply to modern irregular conflicts. As I noted in Chapter 7, the principle of discrimination asserts that the only appropriate targets are those concerned with the enemy's war effort, and the principle of proportionality claims that the damage that is done in prosecuting such targets needs to be in line with the actual military value of the target itself. Although the ideas are quite simple, actually applying these principles in practice, even in traditional wars, is quite difficult. Applying these principles across the range of modern conflicts is even more difficult, especially given the range of different types of operations in which modern militaries are engaged, which might include counterinsurgency operations, open conflict against irregular forces, armed interventions aimed at preventing humanitarian crises, peacekeeping and peace enforcement operations, and so on. Fortunately, the types of *jus in bello* problems that are encountered in such operations tend to cluster around some central themes, which means that for the purposes of considering those problems, this wide range of operations can be divided into two general categories: (1) counterinsurgency/counterterrorism operations and combat against irregular forces, which I will collectively refer to as irregular wars; and (2) armed humanitarian interventions, peacekeeping, and peace enforcement operations, which I will collectively refer to as humanitarian operations and which will be discussed in the next chapter.

Case study 8.1 (Casualties in the 2008–2009 Gaza War) provides a good example of some of the problems of discrimination and proportionality that can arise in a modern context in irregular wars, in this case in a battle between the forces of a state and an irregular opponent. After the war, and indeed during it, Israel was accused of engaging in indiscriminate and at times disproportionate attacks during its assault on Hamas fighters in the Gaza strip. Israel responded by arguing that the civilian casualties were legitimate collateral damage, foreseen but unintended results of legitimate attacks on military targets. The Israeli military also claimed that it had taken all the reasonable steps that it could to warn civilians about impending attacks. In addition, Israel claimed that many, if not most, of the civilian casualties were a direct result of the tactics of Hamas who, they claimed, tended to hide amongst the civilian population, effectively using civilians as shields against Israeli attacks.[7] There were certainly allegations after the war that fighters on both sides had committed war crimes; the investigations of the UN Human Rights Council suggested that both sides had, at least at some times during the conflict, ignored the requirements of discrimination, and suggested that some Israeli attacks may also have ignored the requirements of proportionality.[8]

These claims and counterclaims highlight the main issues of *jus in bello* that arise for the armed forces of a state when engaged in a conflict against an irregular enemy. The first problem is that of discrimination. How do you know who your enemy is and who you may and may not legitimately target? The second problem is that of proportionality. If you are engaging a legitimate target, then of course there can be legitimate collateral damage in the form of civilian deaths and injuries and the destruction of civilian buildings and other objects. But what actually counts as a proportionate attack in these sorts of circumstances, and what level of collateral damage is reasonable? As will become clear during the discussion of these issues, some writers have argued, in essentially the same manner as Israel did, that it is reasonable to expect a somewhat higher level of collateral damage when fighting against an irregular enemy than when engaged in a traditional war, and even that the armed forces of the state are not responsible for collateral damage that is caused in fighting an irregular enemy if that enemy chooses to hide amongst the civilian population or fight in areas where there are large numbers of civilians.

DISCRIMINATION IN IRREGULAR WARS

Obviously, the biggest difficulty in dealing with the forces of an irregular opponent is the issue of discrimination. When fighting against the armed forces of another state discrimination is relatively simple, since enemy combatants wear uniforms and are thus relatively easily distinguished from civilians. What this means, as was mentioned in the last chapter, is that uniformed military personnel are assumed to be part of the enemy's attempt to harm and are always legitimate targets unless they are specifically identified as protected persons, (i.e. medical personnel and chaplains) or are *hors de combat*. But irregular forces are a different matter, since those who are not in uniform are usually assumed to not be part of the enemy's attempt to harm and thus they may not be attacked unless, to use Brian Orend's term, they are actively engaged in an attempt to harm.[9]

This idea is reflected in the definitions that can be found in those international laws which are related to the principle of discrimination, such as the Geneva Conventions of 1949 and the Additional Protocols of 1977. These laws define combatants by what they do, but define civilians, that is, noncombatants,[10] by what they **don't** do. Article 4 of the Third Geneva Convention provides a series of clauses that define those various groups who are classified as "lawful combatants" and who thus are entitled to prisoner of war status. Anyone who does not fit into one of these categories is considered a noncombatant and will remain so as long as they **don't** wear a uniform and **don't** directly participate in hostilities. If a person does directly engage in hostilities, then they lose their noncombatant status and may be directly targeted.

Of course, there is a problem that immediately arises, whether one is concerned with the legal situation or, as is the case in this discussion, with the underlying ethical situation. The problem is that it can be very difficult to determine what counts as direct participation in hostilities when dealing with irregular forces, especially since many people seem to think that this category does not simply map across to the equivalent roles within a conventional army. This is particularly obvious when examining the sorts of arguments that have been presented about who may and may not be legitimately targeted when the military forces of a state are engaged in conflict with an organization that espouses the use of terrorist tactics, a point to which I will return shortly.

However, even in irregular wars, sometimes issues of discrimination will be straightforward. Someone who is firing any sort of weapon at uniformed military forces is obviously directly participating in hostilities. It makes no difference whether this person is firing a one-person weapon, such as a pistol, a rifle or a rocket-propelled grenade, or if they are helping to fire a weapon that requires more than one person to operate, such as a mortar, a rocket, or an artillery piece; engaging in such an action obviously counts as direct participation in hostilities. However, there are a range of other actions a person might engage in, which are not so obviously a type of direct participation.

CASE STUDY 8.2

Defending the Crashed Helicopter

BACKGROUND The following incidents occurred in Somalia in October 1993, during Operation Gothic Serpent. About 100 elite U.S. soldiers—comprised of U.S. Army Rangers and members of the top secret Delta Force, commonly known as D-boys—were dropped into the market area of the city of Mogadishu on a mission to capture two top lieutenants of a Somali warlord. The mission struck trouble when one of the supporting Black Hawk Helicopters, call sign *Super Six One*, was shot down and crashed in the city, and the U.S. troops had to rush to the site of the crash to secure the area and render aid to the survivors, while defending themselves against hundreds of angry Somalis, armed with AK-47s and Rocket-Propelled Grenades (RPGs).

Closer to the wrecked helicopter, a woman kept running out into the alley, screaming and pointing toward the house at the southeast corner of the intersection where many of the wounded had been moved. No one shot at her. She was unarmed. But every time she stepped back behind cover a wicked torrent of fire would be unleashed where she pointed. After she'd done this twice, one of the D-boys behind the tail of *Super Six One* said, "If that bitch comes back, I'm going to shoot her."

Captain Coultrop nodded his approval. She did, and the D-boy shot her down on the street.

Then there was the woman in a blue turban, a powerful woman with thick arms and legs who came sprinting across the road carrying a heavy basket in both arms. She was wearing a bright blue-and-white dress that billowed behind her as she ran. Every Ranger at the intersection blasted her. Twombly, Nelson,

Yurek, and Stebbins all opened up. Howe fired on her from further up the hill. First she stumbled, but kept on going. Then, as more rounds hit her, she fell and RPGs spilled out of her basket onto the street.

SOURCE: From *Black Hawk Down: A Story of Modern War,* by Mark Bowden (New York: Penguin, 1999), p. 217.

This case study is an interesting example of discrimination in an irregular conflict. The U.S. and UN forces that had been deployed to Somalia were not fighting against a uniformed enemy, and the American troops involved in the incidents described in Case 8.2 (Defending the Crashed Helicopter) knew that although there were a lot of armed Somalis in the area who were intent on doing them harm, there were also a lot of innocent civilians present as well. The first woman mentioned in the case was unarmed, and the U.S. troops initially presumed her to be an innocent civilian and did not shoot at her. However, the actions that she took demonstrated that she was a combatant and thus a legitimate target, for she was providing direct military support to the forces engaging the U.S. troops by directing their fire against the U.S. position. The second woman, in the blue turban, was also providing direct military support to the Somali forces by transporting ammunition, in this case RPG rounds. Since she was directly participating in hostilities in this manner, she could be legitimately targeted by the U.S. soldiers. In telling the story of this incident, Mark Bowden does not make it clear whether the soldiers actually knew what she was carrying when they shot at her; given the restraint these soldiers demonstrated in other situations, it seems there must have been some sign of what she was carrying, otherwise it is difficult to explain why so many of the soldiers fired at her. Even though it was proven after the fact that the woman was a legitimate target, given that they had the opportunity to assess the situation before they had to act, these soldiers could be criticized for shooting at her if they had no clue that she was actually directly participating in hostilities at the time they opened fire.

Rules of Engagement and Civilian Casualties in Irregular Wars

The issue of collateral damage, specifically civilian casualties, tends to be a much bigger problem in irregular wars than it is in traditional wars. There are a number of reasons for this. Perhaps the most important is the fact that irregular wars, unlike traditional ones, tend to be intermittent affairs without clearly defined "front lines" of combat. In traditional wars, civilians usually have some awareness of where combat is likely to take place and therefore tend to make attempts to remove themselves from those areas. This is one reason why traditional wars often create large refugee populations. But in irregular wars, where lines of combat are not clearly defined, civilians often have little opportunity to remove themselves from the battle space and thus they can easily be trapped in dangerous situations when combat begins. Another reason why civilian casualties are often a problem in irregular wars is that insurgent groups, who are usually going to be significantly outgunned by state military forces, rely on being able to hide themselves amongst the local civilian population; in the words of Chairman Mao, "The guerrilla must move amongst the people as a fish swims in the sea."[11] Therefore, it will usually be the case in irregular wars that conflict occurs in civilian areas, and thus that there will be a significant likelihood of civilian casualties as a result of that conflict. In at least some cases, insurgent groups may even welcome civilian casualties, especially if those casualties are caused by actions of counterinsurgency forces, since if the counterinsurgent forces demonstrate an apparent lack of regard for the welfare of local civilians, then this may push those civilians to provide greater support for the insurgent group's cause.

Most modern theories of counterinsurgency war suggest that the only way to actually win such a war is to adopt a "population-centric" approach; to try to separate an insurgent group from their support base in as many ways as possible and to try to ensure that assisting the insurgent forces will actually be contrary to the overall interests of the civilian population. Since the level of support for the insurgency is likely to be increased if the actions of counterinsurgency forces tend to cause a large number of casualties among the civilian population, reducing the number of civilian casualties can actually be seen to have significant strategic importance in many irregular wars. However, the perceived need to reduce the number of civilian casualties that are caused by counterinsurgency operations often raises another significant issue, both for those who are actually engaged in fighting against irregular forces in counterinsurgency operations and those who direct and plan such operations. Since it will usually be the case that to reduce the number of civilian casualties military personnel will have to take on an increased level of risk, how can the need to protect civilians best be balanced against the need, indeed the right, of military personnel to protect themselves?

In his book on modern just war theory, Nick Fotion argues quite extensively that the *jus in bello* principle of discrimination **does** apply to non-state entities engaged in irregular warfare against states. However, he also claims that it is impossible for national forces to uphold the principle of discrimination to a high standard when engaged in irregular wars.[12] The interesting part about this second claim is that he really does not argue for it at all, but rather seems to think that everyone will take it for granted that this claim is true. In fact, his discussion of this particular issue lasts exactly four sentences.

> However, in a struggle falling under (irregular just war theory) national military forces face certain obvious difficulties: they often cannot identify their enemies; the rebels hide in rural and/or urban areas and do not wear uniforms; they look like innocent civilians; they often choose to fight in places where real innocents are found in large numbers. These difficulties make it impossible for the

national forces to honour the discrimination principle to a high standard. This does not mean that they can attack innocents intentionally, but it does mean that the amount of collateral damage allowed by the Rules of Engagement will be greater—inevitably so. The choice is either to allow more such damage or demand that nations simply not resist rebel groups and, in effect, let these groups win because they have placed themselves in the midst of the general population.[13]

Clearly the sorts of irregular conflicts that Fotion has in mind here are ones like the conflict between the Israeli Defence Forces and Palestinian insurgent groups in the occupied territories, or the conflict between U.S. troops and insurgent groups in Iraq, or between international forces and the Taliban in Afghanistan. Obviously, such conflicts are extremely significant in the modern world, but there are many other types of irregular conflicts where the types of conditions that Fotion is gesturing to here either do not apply at all, or only apply in a limited way. Full-scale armed rebellions against the forces of the state, such as occurred in Libya in 2011, are a good example to consider in this context. Given this, it is dangerous to generalize in the way that Fotion has done here.

Of particular concern is the implied claim that the deaths of innocents as collateral damage in attacks by the state forces are not the fault of those state forces themselves but rather are the fault of the rebels who chose to fight in a location that placed those innocents in harm's way. There are several reasons why this particular claim is dangerous. If the state military feels that they do not hold any moral responsibility for collateral damage incurred in clashes with the rebel group(s), then they are less likely to take steps to limit that collateral damage.[14] It is also the case that the location of clashes is not always chosen by the rebel group. If the state military forces gain intelligence about the location of a group of insurgents and decide to launch an attack, then in such situations if the clash takes place in a heavily populated area it is because the state military forces, and not the rebel group, have chosen to bring the battle there. Finally, and of particular importance in cases where battles occur away from the home of the state military forces, for example, U.S. military forces in Iraq, Fotion's claim encourages those state military forces to see civilians in the vicinity of the battle as mere obstacles in the way of fulfilling the military objective, rather than as innocents who have a right to be protected from the conflict.

It is fairly obvious that the country of operation tends to make an enormous difference to what counts as acceptable collateral damage. During the Allied aerial bombing campaign in World War II, it was recognized that many attacks on military targets would be likely to cause extensive collateral damage. Such attacks went ahead against sites inside Germany, but generally were not considered against similar sites in occupied France. Michael Walzer reports that when attacking these sorts of targets in occupied France, pilots of the Free French air force were willing to take on a much higher level of risk to themselves to try to reduce the amount of collateral damage these raids caused, leading them to specialize in precision bombing at a very low altitude.[15] In a modern situation, it would seem highly unlikely that U.S. military decision makers would think that the sorts of collateral damage caused by a missile strike against a high-value target in Iraq would be acceptable if the same target happened to be located in Atlanta, Georgia. But since noncombatants are still noncombatants no matter what country they come from or where they are living, there doesn't seem to be any legitimate ethical reason for drawing such distinctions, unless you take the view that some noncombatants are, for one reason or another, less innocent than other noncombatants are. I will discuss this idea again later in this chapter, as well as in Chapter 11 during the discussion of terrorism.

Some counterinsurgency theorists might go even further in criticizing Fotion's ideas than I have done here, since they would claim that it is ridiculous to think of civilians in the vicinity of the battle as obstacles in the way of fulfilling the military objective; winning the support of the local population actually **is** the military objective in a counterinsurgency campaign.[16] If this is the case, then in terms of the success of the overall campaign, it may be more important to reduce, or even eliminate, civilian casualties among the local population than it is to kill or capture insurgents.

So how should military commanders on the ground attempt to draw a balance between the risk to civilians and the need to protect their own troops? Such commanders will almost inevitably fall back on the rules of engagement (ROE) that they have been issued. In effect, the ROE are the "grunt's eye view" of the overall strategy of the war. The leaked ROE for U.S. operations in Iraq in the years after the fall of Saddam Hussein's regime make it clear that although all reasonable attempts should be made to avoid collateral damage, the usual (i.e., conventional war) criteria of discrimination and proportionality apply, and thus significant collateral damage is acceptable if this is seen by the on ground commander as necessary to protect his troops.[17] In fact, these ROE specifically state that "Commanders have the inherent authority and **obligation** to use all necessary means available and to take all appropriate action in self-defense of their units and other U.S. Forces and Coalition Forces."[18] Thus, although attempts should be made to avoid civilian casualties if this is possible, such casualties are certainly not ruled out by the ROE, and the section quoted previously suggests that commanders are actually obliged to protect their troops by any means necessary, even if this will cause significant collateral damage. However, this is certainly not the only approach that can be taken to such matters.

CASE STUDY 8.3

Assault on a Taliban Compound

Intelligence reports indicated that the Taliban was using a series of compounds in Oruzgan Province, Afghanistan, as a staging base and as a facility for the manufacture of Improvised Explosive Devices (IEDs). An assault on these compounds was given a high priority by the Australian Special Operations Task Group, and the operation commenced on November 23, 2007.

Commandos of the 4th Battalion, Royal Australian Regiment, began their assault on the compound in the early hours of the morning. Aided by night-vision goggles, the commandos were easily able to identify the mud-brick buildings in the cool autumn night. As they neared the first of the buildings, they observed a sentry climbing off a roof. The sentry was ordered to surrender and lie down; instead he raised his weapon, and was immediately shot dead by the approaching Australian forces. Another man armed with an AK-47 appeared about 25 meters (80 feet) away in an aqueduct. He too was shot.

Private Luke Worsley was one of the first soldiers to go through a window into one of the inner rooms. He knew that the noise from the shooting that had already occurred would have alerted anyone inside, but delaying the entry would have given the Taliban fighters more time to prepare, thus risking more Australian deaths. Worsley found himself confronted with a man holding a heavy machine gun. Worsley managed to warn his colleagues and fire several shots before being shot in the head and killed.

An intense close-quarter battle began within the compound, involving high volumes of small arms fire. Australian troops were at a decided disadvantage, since they were largely exposed to heavy hostile fire from several covered positions that were located in the eastern rooms of the compound. At this point, a dazed child, a toddler about 2 years old, wandered into the field of fire, apparently seeking shelter in a room on the other side of the compound. The Australian commander called for his forces to cease fire; once the toddler was safely out of the way, the Australians resumed the battle.

Soldiers managed to identify the source of a large amount of enemy fire; a room that appeared to contain at least two enemy fighters who were shooting out of the window at the Commandos. Several grenades were thrown into this window by the Australian soldiers and shooting from this location ceased. The Commandos were still under fire from other locations, and other sources of enemy fire were successively identified and neutralized, by small arms fire or the use of grenades.

After all enemy firing had ceased, Australian forces performed clearance drills, moving through the rooms of the compound to check for any remaining Taliban fighters. In one room, the first against which grenades had been used, soldiers found the bodies of two Taliban fighters, a man and a woman, as well as a crying baby, less than 6 months old. One of the soldiers picked the baby up and checked it for injuries, but there was no evidence of a wound or blood on the baby or its clothing, so he placed the baby in a corner of the room, out of harm's way, while the rest of the rooms in the compound were cleared. Soldiers investigating another source of heavy enemy fire, found another dead Taliban fighter, as well as the body of a teenage girl, aged between 13 and 16, who had apparently been killed by Australian fire during the battle. Several suspected Taliban members were taken into custody. The toddler who had walked across the compound during the fire fight was found safely with other civilians. However, when the Australian soldiers returned to the room where the baby had been found, they discovered that the baby had now died. It was suspected that the baby may have been killed by internal injuries caused by a grenade blast, but this could not be confirmed, as both the baby and the teenage girl were immediately taken away for burial, in accordance with local customs.

SOURCE: Compiled from articles by David McLennan published in *The Canberra Times*, May 13, 2008.

The approach taken by the Australian forces in Case 8.3 seems to represent something of a contrast to the approach of the Israeli troops in Case 8.1 (Casualties in the 2008–2009 Gaza War), in a number of respects. The Israeli approach was apparently to warn civilians that an attack was imminent, thus giving them the opportunity to leave the area, but then to use air attacks, artillery, and tank fire to deal with any resistance once an attack was underway and therefore providing the maximum possible level of protection for the ground forces involved in the attack. Perhaps the approach taken by the U.S. forces in Case 3.4 (Military Dispute over Casualties in Afghanistan) could be considered a step further along that path, with ground forces not risked at all during the attack on the alleged Taliban stronghold. The approach taken by the Australian Commandos did not involve any warning for the civilians in the area, but did seem to involve the ground forces taking on a significantly increased level of risk to attempt to minimize civilian casualties, even to the extent of ceasing fire when the toddler walked across the compound, despite the fact that the Commandos were in exposed positions and at a tactical disadvantage, and even after they had already suffered a fatality among their own forces.

Of course, in the end the exact manner in which the balance between protecting civilians and protecting military personnel will be drawn in a particular conflict is not going to be decided by junior military commanders. But if junior commanders do not understand why they and their troops are being put at greater risk to protect local civilians, particularly if they feel that those local civilians are actually supporters of the insurgency, then there will inevitably be problems with the implementation of the ROE when they are applied at ground level in a conflict.

The situation facing U.S. troops in Iraq in the years following the 2003 invasion is a good example to consider here. Quite a lot of people, both military and civilian, wrote at the time about the situation the U.S. forces in Iraq faced and argued that the ROE were too restrictive and thus threatened the lives of U.S. personnel.[19] Some certainly argued that protection of military personnel is the first priority of a commander, and thus strenuously argued against ROE that they thought placed troops in unnecessary danger. However, there are some important problems with this view.

In the first place, it should be obvious that the highest duty of a military commander is not to protect his or her troops; although this is important, it is certainly less important than other things, like the duty to serve the state. More important in this context is the fact that achievement of the mission is more important than the protection of the lives of the military personnel involved in the operation; if this were not the case, then military personnel would never be sent on missions where there was a danger of death, a point which was raised in Chapter 6, in connection with the ethical issues raised by orders that risk the lives of military personnel.[20] In the context of irregular war, if the mission of the personnel involved in a particular operation is to protect the lives of civilians, even at the cost of the lives of some of those military personnel, then this simply has to be accepted as part of the cost of being involved in a counterinsurgency war. This is where ideas about the importance of force protection may start to become very problematic. It was once suggested to me, by an extremely distinguished retired British General,[21] that force protection is idiocy in disguise. If the mission is important enough for troops to be sent on in the first place, then it should be important enough for troops to die for. If the mission is not important enough for troops to die for, then they should never be sent out in the first place, since the best force protection is to stay at home.

Difficult Cases of Discrimination in Irregular Wars

Generally speaking, traditional wars tend to be relatively short, consist of a series of essentially continuous conflicts, involve large battles between armies of a significant size, usually cause a sizable number of casualties per day and have fairly definite start and end points. The Six Day War of 1967 (Case 4.4) is a perfect example of this type of conflict. Some irregular conflicts may follow a similar pattern; whereas Operation Cast Lead (Case 5.1) did not involve engagements between large groups of troops, in most other respects it largely followed a traditional war pattern. However, other types of irregular conflicts, particularly counterinsurgency operations, may last a lot longer, often involve intermittent conflicts between small groups of combatants on an irregular basis, usually cause a relatively small number of casualties per day, and often have rather indefinite start and end points. There are a number of modern examples of these sorts of situations, including the U.S. and allied operations in Iraq after the conclusion of major combat operations post-invasion in 2003, the NATO and allied states operations in Afghanistan since 2001, and the conflict between Israeli forces and Palestinian militants, which has continued for decades, despite varying periods of relative peace.

These long-term, low-intensity conflicts tend to create significant levels of fear and unrest. State armed forces who attempt to take direct action against these irregular forces, particularly if they attempt to take preemptive military action, often face extremely difficult problems in attempting to discriminate between those who can reasonably be considered to be combatants and those who cannot. This is obviously an important distinction when military action is contemplated, since combatants can be directly targeted, but noncombatants cannot. Situations where the opposing irregular forces are engaged in terrorist tactics, such as suicide bombings, can be particularly difficult to deal with in this respect. Consider the following list, compiled by Asa Kasher and Amos Yadlin,[22] of various ways in which someone might be involved in terrorist activity. Although the list is focused on the problems Israel faced in dealing with Palestinian militants in the early years of the twenty-first century and is slanted toward the issues created by Islamic suicide bombers, it has general relevance nonetheless.

1. Persons posing an immediate danger (e.g., a bearer of an explosive belt).[23]
2. Persons providing immediate support to persons posing an immediate danger (e.g., a driver, a guide).
3. Persons dispatching other persons to pose an immediate danger.
4. Persons preparing devices for acts or activities of terror (e.g., an "engineer" producing explosive belts, or the director of a "laboratory" of such production).
5. Persons providing essential ingredients of devices of terror (e.g., a "pharmacist" deliberately supplying major ingredients of explosives, or a person who lends crucial funds).
6. Persons planning an act or activity of terror, whether its operational idea or its practical details.
7. Persons recruiting certain other persons to carry out acts or activities of terror.
8. Persons making operational decisions to carry out a planned act or activity of terror.
9. Persons making general operational decisions related to acts or activities of terror (e.g., a decision to adopt a policy of making attempts to carry out acts or activities of terror, or granting permission for certain women to participate in an activity of terror and bear explosive belts).
10. Developing and operating funding channels that are not crucial to acts or activities of terror.
11. Preaching in a mosque in general praise of past suicide bombers.
12. Making payments to families of past suicide bombers, when and where such payments are not crucial for acts or activities of terror.
13. Issuing posters in praise of past suicide bombers.
14. Being involved in political, social, or religious leadership of an organization that has a terrorist arm without having any personal involvement in decision making processes directly related to acts or activities of terror.

The order in which the various activities are ranked on this list is intended to show how directly those activities relate to a particular act of terrorism. Thus, the closer to the top of the list a particular activity is, the more immediate the threat that someone undertaking that particular activity poses and the more reasonable it is for direct military action to be taken against the person undertaking that activity. Kasher and Yadlin suggest that anyone involved in one of the first nine activities on this list can be considered directly involved in terrorism and thus would be a combatant and a legitimate target for a military attack. Those people who are indirectly involved in terrorism (i.e., engaged in Activities 10–14 on the list) may not be directly targeted. These distinctions formed the basis of the Israeli doctrine of responses to terrorist activity in the early part of the twenty-first century.

CASE STUDY 8.4

Israel and Targeted Killing

The Second Intifada[24] commenced in late September 2000, and began a period of markedly increased violence between Israelis and Palestinians. Palestinian tactics during the Intifada included nonviolent general strikes and protests, as well as attacks on Israeli soldiers, police, security personnel, Jewish settlers, and civilians. One of the Israeli government responses to the Intifada was to begin an open policy of targeted killing (sometimes referred to as "targeted foiling"). The essence of the policy was simple; those engaged in ongoing violence against Israeli civilians would be killed if and when the opportunity arose. Originally, the only targets were the bombers themselves, but as time went on the list expanded to include bomb makers and those who planned attacks on Israel. According to Lieutenant General Moshe Ya'alon, the Israeli Military Chief of Staff from 2002 to 2005, there were 300 to 1,000 wanted men on the list of possible targets.[25]

Israeli lawyers and military analysts had concluded that the policy was legal if carried out according to six specific conditions: that arrest is impossible; that targets are combatants; that senior cabinet members approve each attack; that civilian casualties are minimized; that operations are limited to areas not under Israeli control; and that targets are identified as a future threat.[26] Implementing the policy required cooperation from a number of different organizations within the Israeli government, including Israel's internal security agency Shin Bet, the Israeli Defence Force, (in particular the Israeli Air Force (IAF), who carried out many of the attacks), Military Intelligence, the Defence Ministry, and the Prime Minister's office.

Exact figures on the number of Palestinians killed during these operations are impossible to obtain, but the Israeli human rights organization B'Tselem estimated that 339 Palestinians were killed by these operations between 2000 and 2006, of whom 210 people were targets and the rest were bystanders.[27] According to the same organization, 295 Gazans were killed by Israeli security forces in 2007, more than half of them from the air, and 323 Gazans were killed in the first 4 months of 2008, over 70% of them in air strikes.[28]

Some very high profile Palestinian figures were killed under the Israeli policy. In August 2001, Abu Ali Mustafa, the leader of the Popular Front for the Liberation of Palestine, was killed while sitting at his desk in a first floor office; Israeli Apache Helicopter gunships had fired two rockets through his office window.[29] On July 23, 2002, the leader of the military wing of Hamas, Salah Shehade, was killed when an IAF F-16 dropped a 1-ton laser guided bomb on the two story house where he was staying. Those planning the strike apparently knew that Shehade's wife would also be killed in the attack, but did not expect the level of collateral damage that occurred.[30] Apart from Shehade and his wife, 13 other people were killed in the attack, including 9 children, while 50 more people were injured.[31]

Perhaps the most high-profile person killed was the founder and spiritual leader of Hamas, Sheikh Ahmed Yassin. Yassin was 67 years old, a nearly blind quadriplegic, who was confined to a wheelchair. Nonetheless, the Israeli government argued that he was directly involved in the planning of terrorist attacks on Israel and thus they made a number of attempts to kill him. On March 22, 2004, they succeeded. As Yassin was being wheeled out of a mosque toward a waiting car after morning prayers, he was hit by Hellfire missiles fired by an Apache helicopter. Yassin's two bodyguards were also killed, as were nine bystanders.[32] A total of 200,000 people attended Yassin's funeral.[33] Abdel Aziz al-Rantisi, who co-founded Hamas with Yassin and succeeded him as the political head of Hamas in Gaza, died a few weeks later, on April 17, 2004. He was killed when Israeli Apache helicopters fired two Hellfire missiles at his car, killing him, his bodyguard, his 27-year-old son, and two civilians.[34] After the death of al-Rantisi, Hamas announced that it would no longer publicize the identity of its leaders.

The Israeli program of targeted killing was not trying to kill people who were actually engaged in a terrorist attack at that particular moment, but rather aimed to kill people who were believed, on the basis of reliable intelligence, to be involved in ongoing terrorist activities. In other words, it aimed to kill those who were going to be involved in a terrorist attack in the future, and the whole point of the targeted killing program was to prevent those future attacks from actually happening. One of the six conditions Israel applied when engaging in these attacks was that the target must be a combatant. Essentially, what this meant was that the person had to be engaged in one of the first nine activities on Kasher and Yadlin's list, mentioned earlier in this chapter. But the various activities that are included on that list are problematic in at least one respect, in that they do not obviously equate to combatant positions in the armed forces of a state. Consider, for example, the particular case of Hamas, a number of whose leaders were killed in the Israeli campaign. As well as a military wing that has been engaged in attacks on Israel for many years, Hamas also has a political wing and a social welfare wing, which builds schools and hospitals, as well as running many relief and education programs, orphanages, mosques, health care clinics, and soup kitchens. According to Israeli intelligence estimates, 80–85% of Hamas' budget is spent on political and social welfare activities, with the remaining devoted to military operations.[35]

In claiming that all those who were targeted were "directly involved in hostilities" and were thus combatants, Israel was claiming that those in the military arm of Hamas occupied positions that were equivalent to the armed forces of state, despite the fact that these people were not in uniform. This being the case, members of the military arm of Hamas could legitimately be targeted at any time, in the same way that those in uniform can legitimately be targeted at any time during a war. Thus Role 1 on Kasher and Yadlin's list obviously equates to ordinary soldiers who fight on the front line, Role 3 to the junior commanders who dispatch those soldiers on their missions, Role 6 to the middle ranking officers who balance tactical and strategic concerns, Role 8 to the generals who decide how the war will be conducted, Role 7 to the military recruiters, and so on.

As far as a lot of positions within the military arm of Hamas go this may be quite a reasonable claim, but in a conventional military force several of the roles that are included on Kasher and Yadlin's list would actually be filled by civilians. While those civilians are legitimate targets when they are actually fulfilling a military role, they, unlike those in uniform, may not be attacked at any time. Consider Role 4, for example. Those who manufacture weapons for a conventional military force are not uniformed personnel, they are civilians. In wartime, they may be attacked while they are fulfilling their military function, but they may not be attacked at any time. Thus, in a conventional war it is legitimate to attack someone in weapons manufacturing while they are actually building weapons, but they cannot legitimately be attacked while driving home from work. Of course, there will be some uniformed personnel who do work directly on weapons, such as those who are engaged in weapons repair, those who load bombs onto planes and arm them, and so forth. Although these people are subject to attack at any time, they are a very small percentage of the people who actually build weapons. Role 5 is even more problematic, since in a conventional military force those who supply the raw materials for weapons manufacture will certainly be civilians.

One significant difference between the work done by civilians who are manufacturing weapons for a conventional army, and the work done by those who fit into Role 4 on Kasher and Yadlin's listing, is that building weapons for a conventional army is legal, while building weapons that will be used in terrorist attacks is not. Therefore, a person who is building weapons that will be used in terrorist attacks can clearly be arrested at any time and charged with a criminal offence, but this is a very different thing from saying that they can be attacked and killed by military forces at any time. I suspect that it is because of this particular distinction that a number of European states refer to the Israeli targeting killing program as a system of extrajudicial execution, that is, state execution of alleged criminals without the oversight of judicial proceedings or the usual legal processes. One point that could be made in defense of the Israeli targeted killing program at this point is that the first condition that needed to be met for a person's name to be placed on the list of possible targets (as noted in Case 8.4: Israel and Targeted Killing) was that it had to be impossible to arrest that person.

So in theory, the only possible alternatives in dealing with that person are either to kill them in a targeted attack or let them continue with their involvement in terrorist activities. But difficulty in arresting a criminal, even one involved in mass murder, is not usually taken as justification for allowing that person to be killed on sight, particularly not in a manner that risks collateral damage.[36]

If Role 8 equates to the generals who are planning how the war will be conducted, then Role 9 seems to be the cabinet of the civilian government. Whereas some members of an ordinary civilian cabinet might be legitimate targets in time of war, such as the defense minister, for example, it is extremely difficult to claim that other members of the cabinet are combatants, despite the fact that they may well have agreed to war within the confines of a cabinet meeting. The same sort of claim would seem to apply to members of a broad-ranging organization like Hamas; although it may be that the organizing group as a whole agrees to a particular strategy in the fight against Israel, it would be a stretch to say that those in charge of the social welfare arm of Hamas ought to be classified as combatants simply on this basis.[37]

As can be seen from these examples, determining what counts as "direct participation in hostilities" in an irregular conflict is far from simple. Indeed, there are other examples of tasks that might be seen as direct participation in an irregular conflict but where an equivalent task is not seen in the same light in a traditional conflict. Even Kasher and Yadlin's Role 2 is not entirely unproblematic, given that they suggest that being a driver for a person who poses an immediate danger is sufficient to count as direct involvement in a conflict. Many of the Unmanned Aerial Vehicles (UAVs) operated by the United States are flown by pilots who work at Air Force bases just outside Las Vegas; the planes are operated remotely by these pilots half a world away. The spouse of one of these pilots might well drive them to the base at the start of their shift, knowing full well that the pilot they are driving will be engaging in offensive operations, via the UAV, in a few minutes time. This is functionally equivalent to Role 2, driving a militant to a location from which they will launch an attack, yet it seems perfectly clear that although the UAV pilot is a combatant, the person driving them to the Air Base from which they operate is not. To be clear, my point here is not that anyone acting in Role 2 in an irregular war is not a combatant; it is simply to suggest that a note of caution is appropriate when determining the combatant status of people in the vicinity of an irregular war.

To be considered a combatant, a person must, as Orend notes, "be engaged in harming."[38] Providing insurgents with food or temporary shelter is not sufficient, since as Walzer points out "the relevant distinction is not between those who work for the war effort and those who do not, but between those who make what soldiers need to fight and those who make what they need to live, like the rest of us."[39] Being engaged in harming will mean more than simply being a member of an organization like Hamas, which has political and social welfare arms as well as a military arm. Although it could be argued that the military arm of Hamas is fundamental to its overall existence, other members of the organization who are not part of the military arm cannot be considered to be engaged in harm simply because of their membership in this organization.[40] When Israel launched its attack on Gaza in 2008 (Case 8.1: Casualties in the 2008–2009 Gaza War), the target list for the initial air strikes included police stations, on the basis that Hamas was a terrorist organization and thus anyone who carried arms in the name of Hamas, as police officers did, was a legitimate target. One problem with this argument is that Hamas was also the democratically elected government of the Gaza Strip, and police officers help to maintain law and order, which is an essential social good. Given this fact, police officers ought to be seen as part of what is necessary to live, rather than what is necessary to fight, and thus ought to be considered to be noncombatants unless they prove their status as combatants through direct involvement in hostilities. Israel's decision to attack these police stations was criticized by international groups such as Human Rights Watch and the United Nations Human Rights Commission.

Merely speaking out in support of the actions of a particular insurgent group is also not sufficient to make a person a combatant; if it was, then it would logically follow that a civilian who spoke publicly in favor of a traditional war would also be a combatant. Kasher and Yadlin suggest that a person who lends vital funds to a terrorist organization is also directly involved in terrorism, under Role 5, and thus is a combatant.[41] As I have noted, this is certainly open to dispute at best, since such a person does not seem to be directly participating in hostilities.[42] What does seem clear is that a person could not be considered a combatant simply because they had made a donation to an organization such as Hamas, which spends the majority of its money on its political and social welfare arms. To suggest that such a person is a combatant would be to follow the argument of Osama bin Laden, who claimed that since taxes fund military operations, everyone who pays tax is therefore a combatant and a legitimate target.

PROPORTIONALITY IN IRREGULAR WARS

When the principles of *jus in bello* are applied to irregular warfare, most of the specific difficulties that arise in this context are with regard to discrimination. While the principle of proportionality is still important, the problems that arise in irregular wars with regard to proportionality are very similar to the ones that arise in traditional wars. The fact the something is a legitimate military target means that it can be directly targeted, but an attack will only be justified if it is also proportionate. Thus, if a particular military target has been identified and a commander has to make a decision about whether that target will be attacked, and if so, how it will be attacked, the considerations will be essentially the same whether the conflict is an irregular conflict or a traditional one. The commander will need to determine what the military value of the target is, what collateral damage is likely to be caused by an attack of a particular type, and whether the target is of sufficient military value to justify the level of collateral damage that will be caused.

In the wake of allegations of war crimes committed by both Israel and Hamas during the Gaza War (Case 8.1: Casualties in the 2008–2009 Gaza War), the UN Fact Finding Mission on the Gaza Conflict (UNFFMGC) was sent to investigate.[43] The report of that mission criticized the Israeli attacks on police facilities on the first day of the conflict, as did a report issued by Human Rights watch. However, while Human Rights Watch criticized the attacks as being indiscriminate, in that the attacks were not directed against a military target,[44] the report of the UNFFMGC report did so primarily on the grounds that those attacks were disproportionate:

> The attacks against the police facilities on the first day of the armed operations failed to strike an acceptable balance between the direct military advantage anticipated (i.e. the killing of those policemen who may have been members of Palestinian armed groups) and the loss of civilian life (i.e. the other policemen killed and members of the public who would inevitably have been present or in the vicinity), and therefore violated international humanitarian law.[45]

While civilian casualties are obviously extremely important, they are not the only factor that needs to be considered when making determinations about the proportionality of an attack. It is clear that during the Gaza War, Israel attempted, in various ways, to reduce civilian loss of life, such as by warning civilians of impending attacks and encouraging them to evacuate. Groups such as Human Rights Watch have questioned whether such warnings gave civilians sufficient time to clear the area, and thus whether these warnings were adequate in terms of fulfilling Israel's obligation to prevent civilian casualties. However, even if the warnings do give enough time for civilians to evacuate themselves, and thus allow the buildings to be targeted without causing civilian casualties, the proportionality of such attacks can still be questioned if they are directed against buildings that are not primarily military in nature.

Some civilian structures, like hospitals, are entitled to special protection but lose that special protection if they are being used for military purposes. However, proportionality still applies, so if it is determined that such structures are being used for military purposes, and if attack is contemplated, then the special status of these structures needs to be taken into account when determining that proportionality. For example, it was alleged that the war room for the leadership of Hamas was located in a bunker beneath Gaza's largest hospital.[46] If this report had been confirmed, then the hospital could have been directly targeted, since it was being used for a military purpose. However, attacking the hospital would have been disproportionate given the civilian casualties and other damage that would have occurred; given how important medical facilities are in a war zone, an attack on the hospital would probably still have been disproportionate even if it had been possible to ensure that all the civilians had been evacuated prior to the attack.

During the attack on Gaza, Israel also deliberately targeted the homes of Hamas commanders, arguing that the nature of the Hamas command structure mean that the homes of the commanders were equivalent to military control centers. Even if this claim is true, the direct military benefit gained by such attacks still needs to be balanced against the collateral damage such an attack will cause. Suppose that a relatively minor Hamas commander lives in a multistory apartment block and let us grant, for the sake of argument, that his home is considered to be a military command center and thus a valid target for a direct attack. If Israel was to launch an air strike against his home, although they would be destroying a military command center, they would also be destroying the home of the commander and his family, plus the homes of his neighbors, and in all likelihood also destroying all the worldly goods of those families as well. Even if there are no civilian casualties in the attack, leaving a large number of people homeless and depriving them of most of their possessions is a significant cost that has to be balanced by direct military gain for this attack to be justified.

In the Gaza War, Israeli soldiers were ordered to "go in heavy" and used air strikes, artillery, and tank fire to suppress any Hamas resistance before soldiers on the ground advanced.[47] Quite apart from the civilian casualties these tactics may have caused, acting in this way inevitably meant that a lot of damage would be caused to civilian structures, since a single gunman firing at the Israeli forces from a building could well lead to that building being virtually destroyed. Such destruction is a significant cost of such operations, especially given the fact that the Israeli blockade around Gaza restricted the flow of all goods into Gaza, and that construction materials were essentially prohibited, since Israel feared they could be used for military purposes. A satellite-based assessment of the damage in the Gaza Strip, conducted immediately after the end of hostilities, estimated that over 2,500 buildings had been destroyed or severely damaged, over 160 kilometers of road had been badly damaged by shelling, as had more than 2,000 hectares of cultivated land, including 28 hectares of greenhouses. In addition, more than 2,000 hectares of land had been targeted for demolition by IDF bulldozers, tanks, and (apparently) incendiary shelling operations.[48] More than 50,000 Gazans were left homeless after the conflict.[49] These sorts of costs need to be considered when examining both the proportionality of the war as a whole and the proportionality of individual operations within it. Even when a military response is justified within an irregular war, if it is going to be an ethical response, it must be both discriminate and proportionate.

NOTES

1. Quoted in Steven Erlanger, "A Gaza War Full of Traps and Trickery," *New York Times,* January 11, 2009.
2. Ibid.

3. John Ging, "Press Conference By Director Of Gaza Operations, United Nations Relief And Works Agency For Palestine Refugees In The Near East," United Nations Department of Public Information, News and Media Division, New York, January 6, 2009. Retrieved from http://www.webcitation.org/5dkw6ASwn

4. "IDF Releases Cast Lead Casualty Numbers," *Jerusalem Post*, March 28, 2009, http://fr.jpost.com/servlet/Satellite?cid=1237727552054&pagename=JPArticle%2F ShowFull (accessed April 12, 2010).

5. Figures from the Palestinian Ministry of Health reported by the United Nations Office for the Coordination of Humanitarian Affairs, http://unispal.un.org/unispal. nsf/85255db800470aa485255d8b004e349a/50a7789ce959e0c285257554006d3e56? OpenDocument (accessed April 12, 2010).

6. See http://www.btselem.org/english/Gaza_Strip/Castlead_Operation.asp (accessed April 12, 2010).

7. Erlanger, "A Gaza War Full of Traps and Trickery."

8. Details of the investigation, including the full text of the report, can be found at http://www2.ohchr.org/english/bodies/hrcouncil/specialsession/9/FactFinding Mission.htm

9. Brian Orend, *The Morality of War* (Peterborough, ON: Broadview, 2006), p. 107.

10. In these conventions, the term civilian is synonymous with noncombatant.

11. Mao Tse-tung, *On Guerrilla Warfare*, trans. Samuel B. Griffith II (Chicago: University of Illinois Press, 2000), quoted in Christopher Paul, "As a Fish Swims in the Sea: Relationships Between Factors Contributing to Support for Terrorist or Insurgent Groups," *Studies in Conflict & Terrorism* 33(2010), 488–510, p.488.

12. *War and Ethics: A New Just War Theory* (London: Continuum, 2007).

13. Ibid., p. 122.

14. David Rodin has argued that military forces equipped with sophisticated modern weaponry are actually more liable for collateral damage incurred in operations, rather than less liable, as Fotion claims. See "The Ethics of Asymmetric War," in Richard Sorabji & David Rodin (eds.), *The Ethics of War: Shared Problems in Different Traditions* (Aldershot, U.K.: Ashgate, 2006), pp. 153–168.

15. See *Just and Unjust Wars* (New York: Basic, 1977), p. 157.

16. See, for example, David Kilcullen, "Twenty-Eight Articles: Fundamentals of Company-level Counterinsurgency," written for the U.S. Department of Defense, March 2006 (http://usacac.army.mil/cac2/coin/repository/28_Articles_of_COIN-Kilcullen%28Mar06%29.pdf).

17. ROE taken from http://wikileaks.org/wiki/US_Rules_of_Engagement_for_Iraq (accessed January 14, 2009).

18. Ibid., p. E-1-6, emphasis added.

19. Since almost all of this discussion was conducted online, it has become more difficult to find as time has gone on. However, there are still a large number of such articles archived at sites such as http://www.captainsjournal.com and other blogs and articles can also be found from the links on that site.

20. What I have called the triangular balance of command responsibilities, which was mentioned in chapter three and again in chapter six, is also of clear importance here.

That in every operation, military commanders always have to balance: (1) the responsibility to achieve the mission; (2) the responsibility to protect their own forces; and (3) the responsibility to protect other persons.

21. Personal discussion with General Sir Rupert Smith (Ret.), Australian Defence Force Academy, May 2006.

22. See "Military Ethics of Fighting Terror: An Israeli Perspective," *Journal of Military Ethics* 4(2005), 3–32, pp. 13-14. Kasher and Yadlin also authored the Israeli Defence Force's official doctrine on the war against terror.

23. Obviously there are many other ways in which someone could pose a direct threat, such as firing a weapon (rifle, mortar, RPG, etc.) at military personnel or noncombatants.

24. An Arabic word meaning "uprising."

25. Quoted in Laura Blumenfeld, "In Israel, a Divisive Struggle Over Targeted Killing," *Washington Post*, August 27, 2006.

26. Daniel Reisner, quoted in Blumenfeld, Ibid.

27. Quoted in Mark Lavie, "Israeli Supreme Court Votes to Uphold Military's Policy of Targeted Killings," *New York Sun*, December 15, 2006.

28. Quoted in Barbara Opall-Rome, "Israel: Airstrike Accuracy Doubled in 2 Years," *Defense News*, May 26, 2008.

29. Peter Cave, "Israel Assassinates Ali Abu Mustafa," *ABC News—AM*, August 28, 2001, http://www.abc.net.au/am/stories/s353525.htm (accessed May 15, 2011).

30. Blumenfeld, "In Israel, a Divisive Struggle Over Targeted Killing."

31. Max Boot, "Retaliation for Me, But Not for Thee," *The Weekly Standard*, November 18, 2002.

32. Al-Jazeera, "The Life and Death of Shaikh Yasin" *Al-Jazeera.net* March 25, 2004.

33. Ilene R. Prusher & Ben Lynfield, "Killing of Yassin a Turning Point," *Christian Science Monitor*, March 23, 2004.

34. Greg Myre, "In Loss of Leaders, Hamas Discovers a Renewed Strength," *New York Times*, April 25, 2004.

35. Matthew Levitt, *Hamas: Politics, Charity, and Terrorism in the Service of Jihad* (New Haven, CT: Yale University Press, 2006), p. 237. It should be noted that Levitt's somewhat controversial conclusion is that the political and social services are essential to maintaining Hamas' military operations, and thus he argues that the entire organization, including the social welfare wing, is a terrorist group and should be treated as such.

36. My thanks to Deane-Peter Baker for pointing out the importance of these distinctions in this particular debate.

37. If those directing the social welfare arm were also involved in military actions in a more direct manner, then they may well be classified as combatants on the basis of that other involvement. My point here is that **merely** being a member of the organizing committee of such a group seems insufficient to classify one as a combatant.

38. *The Morality of War*, p. 107.

39. *Just and Unjust Wars*, p. 146.

40. Membership of an organization that does not have such extensive social and political wings **may** be another matter. If the organization only has a military arm, then, and

only then, might mere membership of the organization be considered to equate to being engaged in harm.

41. "Military Ethics of Fighting Terror," p. 13.

42. It is important to note at this point that although a person cannot be considered a combatant simply because they have directly funded a terrorist attack, this does not mean that (1) they have done nothing wrong, or (2) that no action at all can be taken against this person. The fact that this person is a noncombatant means that they cannot be directly targeted by military personnel. However, providing direct funding for a terrorist attack is an offense and thus this person could be taken into custody and criminally charged for their actions.

43. The fact finding mission was heading by Richard Goldstone; thus the report of the mission is commonly known as the Goldstone Report. Goldstone himself later backtracked on many of the war crimes allegations made against Israel in the report (http://www.washingtonpost.com/opinions/reconsidering-the-goldstone-report-on-israel-and-war-crimes/2011/04/01/AFg111JC_story.html).

44. http://www.hrw.org/en/news/2008/12/30/israelgaza-civilians-must-not-be-targets (accessed May 30, 2011).

45. "Human Rights in Palestine and Other Occupied Territories: Report of the United Nations Fact Finding Mission on the Gaza Conflict" (Goldstone Report), p. 12.

46. Erlanger, "A Gaza War Full of Traps and Trickery."

47. Ibid.

48. Data provided through analysis of images taken by UNOSAT, a program of the United Nations Institute for Training and Research (http://www.unitar.org/unosat/).

49. "Gaza Looks Like Earthquake Zone," *BBC News*, January 20, 2009. Retrieved June 1, 2011, from http://news.bbc.co.uk/2/hi/middle_east/7838618.stm

FURTHER READING

Amidror, Yaakov. "Winning Counterinsurgency War: The Israeli Experience." Paper in the *Strategic Perspectives* series, Jerusalem Center for Public Affairs, 2008.

Coleman, Stephen. "Just War, Irregular War, and Terrorism." In Paolo Tripodi & Jessica Wolfendale (eds.), *New Wars and New Soldiers: Military Ethics in the Contemporary World* (Farnham, U.K.: Ashgate, 2011).

Fotion, Nick. *War and Ethics: A New Just War Theory* (London: Continuum, 2007).

Gross, Michael L. *Moral Dilemmas of Modern War: Torture, Assassination and Blackmail in an Age of Asymmetric Conflict* (New York: Cambridge University Press, 2010). Chapter 5: "Murder, Self-Defense or Execution? The Dilemma of Assassination."

Kasher, Asa & Yadlin, Amos. "Military Ethics of Fighting Terror: An Israeli Perspective." *Journal of Military Ethics* 4(2005), 3–32. Also of note are the various papers responding to Kasher and Yadlin within the same volume of the *Journal of Military Ethics*.

Shue, Henry. "Civilian Protection and Force Protection." In David Whetham (ed.), *Ethics, Law and Military Operations* (Basingstoke, U.K.: Palgrave Macmillan, 2011).

DISCUSSION QUESTIONS

- Is the combatant/noncombatant distinction still relevant to conflicts in the twenty-first century?
- Does the concept of "direct participation in hostilities" provide any real guidance to military personnel when dealing with irregular forces in modern conflicts?
- If insurgent forces deliberately hide themselves among the civilian population, does this mean that those insurgents, rather than the counterinsurgency forces, ought to be held responsible for any civilian deaths that occur in clashes between insurgents and counterinsurgent forces?

9

+○

Discrimination and Proportionality III

Jus In Bello *in Humanitarian Operations*

CASE STUDY 9.1

NATO Attacks and Dual-Use Targets

On March 24, 1999, the North Atlantic Treaty Organization (NATO) launched an air campaign against the Federal Republic of Yugoslavia (FRY, now known as Serbia). Several NATO member states were adamantly opposed to putting troops on the ground before a peace agreement had been reached, so those in command of the operation were only able to engage in air and missile attacks during the campaign. The campaign was apparently expected to swiftly achieve its objectives, but eventually lasted for 78 days before an agreement was reached that allowed the deployment of a UN mandated international peacekeeping force into the region (see Case 5.2).

To keep pressure on the FRY and its President, Slobodan Milošević, NATO needed to continue to mount attacks against targets within the borders of the FRY. Unfortunately, the number of purely military targets that could be attacked was relatively small and thus the NATO commanders were forced to find other legitimate targets to attack. Therefore, as the campaign wore on and the number of strikes increased, NATO came to attack a wide range of more strategic targets, including various facilities involved in the production, refining, or storage of petroleum, oil, and lubricants; railway lines and marshalling yards; road and railway bridges, particularly those crossing major rivers like the Danube; electrical power generation and transmission facilities; and a range of command and control facilities. Virtually all of these strategic targets were dual-use structures, in that although they obviously had a military function, which was what made them legitimate targets for attack, they also had a significant civilian function.

Some attacks on these dual-use targets were conducted in a manner designed to produce little to no collateral damage and to have relatively short-term effects; the initial attacks on the power plants in the vicinity of Belgrade are a good example of this. Planes attacking the power plants released graphite bombs (also known as "soft bombs"), which dispersed clouds of very fine carbon filaments that drifted down onto the uninsulated components below, causing a massive number of short circuits and shutting off the electrical output. While about 70% of the country was blacked out by these initial attacks, Serbian engineers were able to restore the power supply in less than a day. Graphite bombs were also deployed in later attacks, but conventional explosives were also used to knock down power lines and destroy transformer stations.

Whereas some attacks on dual-use targets were intended to have temporary effects, other attacks were obviously going to continue to have an impact long after the conflict was over. The destruction of the bridges over the Danube River is a good example here; as well as being wide and difficult to cross, the river is itself also a major shipping and transportation corridor. The bridges NATO destroyed could not be rebuilt quickly, in part because any reconstruction efforts would need to be managed in a way that continued to allow the substantial volume of river traffic to continue to use the waterway. Illustrative of the problems that were faced in this regard is the fact that the Liberty Bridge, which crosses the Danube in Novi Sad, Serbia's second largest city, was not reopened until 2005.

DISCUSSION

The last chapter examined the sorts of issues that can arise with regard to *jus in bello* in irregular wars, particularly in counterinsurgency operations and in conflicts where the armed forces of a state battle against the irregular forces of a non-state group. However, these types of conflicts are not the only sort of nontraditional wars that arise in the modern context. In the last few decades another type of non-traditional conflict has become of increasing importance, what might be termed armed humanitarian operations. The sorts of operations that will be discussed in this chapter are not military operations that are launched to provide humanitarian assistance in response to a natural disaster, such as earthquake relief in Haiti or flood relief in Pakistan. Rather, the focus here is on *jus in bello* issues that arise in the course of armed military missions that have been launched to deal with problems caused by human violence of one sort or another. There are various different types of operations that fall into this general category, but the very nature of such operations means that they share some common features, which by and large are not shared with irregular wars of the type discussed in the previous chapter.

Peacekeeping and peacemaking operations organized by the UN or other organizations are a good example of this type of intervention. Peacekeeping operations are situations where peace has been established and the formerly warring parties consent to the deployment of independent peacekeeping forces; these military personnel move into the area to monitor cease-fire or peace agreements, aid with reconstruction, monitor elections, and so on. Peacemaking operations, sometimes referred to as peace enforcement operations, are carried out in situations where there is an existing conflict of some sort, and independent external forces move into the area to separate the warring parties and/or force them to negotiate with each other. As will be discussed later in this chapter, it is not always easy to draw a clear line between these peacekeeping and peacemaking operations, and thus people might well argue about whether the situation that military personnel are dealing with in a particular deployment is essentially a peacekeeping operation or peacemaking one.

The NATO operation in the Balkans in 1999 (Case 5.2: The 1999 NATO Intervention in Support of Kosovo and Case 9.1: NATO Attacks and Dual-Use Targets) is an example of a different type of humanitarian armed intervention: a military campaign directed against the forces of a state, in this case the Federal Republic of Yugoslavia (now known as Serbia), to protect an ethnic minority within that state (the Albanian Kosovars) from threats of violence and ethnic cleansing. Of course, there are no absolute distinctions between these various types of conflict since the focus of an operation might change. Indeed, the ideal outcome of most peacemaking operations is for them to eventually become peacekeeping operations. It can also be the case that one type of intervention ends so that another can begin, as was the case when the NATO operations in support of Kosovo ended and a UN mandated peacekeeping mission began in the province. Even though some of the same troops were involved in the later operation it was clearly of a different character than the bombing campaign that preceded it.

Although the various types of humanitarian operations may shade into each other in some circumstances, they do all share some features that mark them out as rather different types of conflict to the irregular wars, which were discussed in the previous chapter. The most important difference is that in all these types of operations the aim of the intervening military forces is to protect people within **other** states from violence and/or the ravages of war, rather than to directly advance the interests of their own state.[1] Since the very aim of the operation is to protect people, usually civilians, within these other states, the methods that are utilized in the course of a humanitarian operation will need to reflect this aim. Thus the Rules of Engagement (ROE) which are issued to the military personnel who are engaged in such operations, will, at least in most circumstances, need to be very different from the ones that would be issued to the same personnel if they were involved in an irregular war, rather than a humanitarian operation. Specifically, if the ROE are going to be ethically appropriate for such operations, then they will need to be very restrictive with regard to the circumstances when it is justifiable for the intervening forces to inflict significant amounts of collateral damage, in the form of civilian casualties, among the people the intervention is aiming to protect.[2] A concrete example of this can be found in the 1999 NATO Intervention in Support of Kosovo (Case 5.2), since one of the significant criticisms of this intervention was the fact that the NATO bombings inflicted a significant number of collateral casualties amongst Albanian Kosovars, the very ethnic group the intervention was launched to protect.

Humanitarian operations of the sort I am discussing here are a relatively recent phenomenon. The first official UN peacekeeping operation saw international troops deployed to the Middle East to monitor the cease-fire that came into force at the end of the Arab-Israeli war in 1948. This force was designated the United Nations Truce Supervision Organization (UNTSO) and although its role has changed from time to time as a result of renewed hostilities in the region (notably in 1956, 1967, and 1973), it has remained active ever since, acting as a go-between for the hostile parties in the area, and attempting to ensure that isolated hostile incidents do not escalate into major conflicts. Armed military interventions launched for purely humanitarian purposes are an even more recent concept, with the first operation of this sort probably being the operations in Somalia in 1992.[3] Ethnically motivated violence against civilians during the breakup of the former Yugoslavia, as well as condemnation of the international failure to deal with events in Rwanda (Case 5.5: The Rwandan Genocide) led to an increased commitment to such operations in several parts of the world, including the previously mentioned operations in support of Kosovo and in East Timor (Case 5.6: Intervention in East Timor).

JUS IN BELLO IN ARMED HUMANITARIAN OPERATIONS

The problems of *jus in bello* which arise in the context of armed humanitarian interventions mounted to stop wide-ranging human rights abuses, such as the 1999 NATO operation in support of Kosovo (Case 9.1: NATO Attacks and Dual-Use Targets), are somewhat different from those that tend to arise in both traditional wars and in modern irregular conflicts. One issue that arises in the context of such operations is the question of whether traditional ideals of discrimination are actually appropriate when addressing who and what ought to be targeted in such campaigns. This is particularly the case when most of the risk in the war appears to fall only on one side of the conflict, as occurred in the 1999 NATO air campaign. Another issue is the question of whether it is appropriate to launch attacks on dual-use targets, since such attacks can be considered problematic in terms of both discrimination and proportionality.

One of the criticisms of the 1999 NATO campaign was that the states involved in the attacks on what was then known as the Federal Republic of Yugoslavia (which for the sake of brevity and simplicity I will refer to simply as Serbia) were not willing to commit ground forces to the conflict, which meant that the entire campaign had to be conducted using airpower alone. Even then, the NATO states were so unwilling to risk casualties among their pilots and aircrew that the planes were generally required to fly at a minimum altitude of 15,000 feet (approximately 5,000 meters), which would place them above the effective range of virtually all of the Serbian ground-based air defenses; essentially NATO seemed willing to kill but not be killed. This combination of a reliance on airpower and a minimum altitude had a number of significant effects, of which the most commonly discussed is the perception, sometimes disputed, that this led to an increase in collateral damage during the campaign.

There are essentially two opposing views in the dispute about whether the policy of enforcing a minimum altitude on NATO pilots resulted in increased levels of collateral damage during the campaign. Those who assert that this policy did result in increased collateral damage claim that flying at higher altitudes makes it more difficult for pilots to pick out their targets accurately and thus that there will inevitably be more attacks which fail to hit the intended target. Since these bombs and missiles must therefore have hit something else, the resulting destruction caused by these misses is, by definition, collateral damage. Those who assert that the policy did not result in more collateral damage generally point out that "smart" weapons are actually more accurate if they are delivered from a greater altitude, since this gives the weapon a greater opportunity to self-correct its trajectory. If the target has been selected as a result of faulty intelligence, as was apparently the case when the Chinese embassy in Belgrade was bombed on May 7, then the height at which the planes were flying is immaterial since the same target would have been hit in any case. Unfortunately, there is no conclusive way of knowing whether or not this policy did result in more collateral damage since there is no other similar operation to which this one can be directly compared. However, it does seem that some targeting errors were made as a result of the minimum altitude policy, such as the occasion when NATO pilots fired on what was apparently believed to be a military convoy, but turned out to be vehicles carrying Albanian Kosovar refugees; more than 70 civilians were killed in the attack.[4]

Another significant, and perhaps under-discussed aspect of this campaign, is the fact that NATO's reliance on airpower alone, coupled with the minimum altitude policy, meant that this was the only armed conflict in modern history, possibly the only war ever, where all the combat losses were borne by one side. Although several NATO planes were shot down and two U.S. service members were killed in a helicopter crash during a training flight, no NATO personnel were killed in combat. The lack of risk to NATO forces that resulted from conducting the campaign in this manner raises questions about whether the traditional idea of discrimination still ought to apply to a campaign that is being fought in such a way that all, or almost all, of the risk seems to fall on one side of the conflict. International law on the issue makes it quite clear that combatants may legitimately be targeted at any time, and there is no reason to think that the legal situation might change simply because all the risk in a particular conflict seems to fall on one side. However, it is plausible to suggest that the ethical situation might change in such circumstances. During the discussion in Chapter 7 about why it is ethically permissible to target combatants, I noted that "since combatants on both sides of the conflict face a serious threat of being harmed by combatants on the other side of the conflict they are thus legitimately able to target anyone who is involved in this process".[5] So it does seem reasonable to question whether it is still ethically legitimate to target any and all enemy combatants, if the manner in which the war is being conducted means that those combatants have no realistic prospect of actually causing harm to any of the personnel opposing them.[6]

Since it is easier to discuss an issue like this in specific terms rather than general ones, consider the situation during the 1999 NATO campaign. Since NATO was relying solely on airpower and flying at a significant altitude, only a few small sections of the Serbian military had any realistic prospect of causing harm to the NATO forces, these being the Air Force and the fixed or vehicle mounted surface-to-air missile systems.[7] NATO attacks on these units were obviously ethically appropriate, since such actions are clearly self-defensive in nature. However, attacks on other Serbian units are much more problematic. Although it was obviously legal for NATO to target Serbian ground forces, such as infantry and tanks, these attacks can no longer be justified as straightforward cases of self-defense or defense of other friendly combatants. These Serbian forces cannot be thought to pose a threat to NATO ground forces since no NATO ground forces were ever involved in the conflict. If this argument is pursued to its logical conclusion, then it would seem that there would be only a few targets that it would have been ethically appropriate for NATO to attack. The aforementioned Air Force and antiaircraft missile systems would still be legitimate targets for attack and so would the senior military personnel who were in the chain of command above them and who issued orders to these units. Plausibly the only other ethically legitimate targets would be those people who actually bore some form of moral guilt with regard to the war, in other words those senior military and political figures who must take responsibility for the violation of *jus ad bellum* that is implicit in starting an unjust war.

However, there is another path that can be taken toward providing an ethical justification for attacks on Serbian ground forces during the NATO campaign. Although these ground forces were not a threat to NATO forces, they were a direct threat to NATO's "allies" in the conflict, being the irregular forces of the Kosovo Liberation Army (KLA), and it was this fact which made the Serbian ground forces ethically legitimate targets for NATO attacks. It is also possible to argue that the war was launched to prevent ethnic cleansing in Kosovo, and the Serbian forces were legitimate targets due to their involvement in that ethnic cleansing. This certainly gives some ethical justification for attacking Serbian military forces within and around Kosovo, but it would be a bit of a stretch to say that this provides ethical justification for attacking a squad of conscripted Serbian infantry who were sitting in some foxhole on Serbia's northern border.

Having said all this, although all the specific examples which arise out of the 1999 NATO air campaign might be able to be dealt with, it is certainly still possible that in some future "riskless" war it may be difficult, if not impossible, to provide an ethical justification for attacking any and all enemy combatants, despite the fact that such attacks are legally permissible. In such a war, the only ethically permissible targets would be those enemy personnel who actually pose a direct threat to friendly personnel and the few people who could be held ethically responsible for starting an unjust war.

Dual-Use Targets

One major point of contention, both during the NATO air campaign and after it, was with regard to the appropriateness of the targets that had been selected for attack. All the targets NATO attacked in the early stages of the campaign were clearly military ones, or more accurately, given the cases of mistaken identity, were believed to be clear military targets. However, as the campaign wore on and the list of targets had to be extended, many more strategic targets came to be included. Many of these strategic targets were what are known as dual-use targets; dual-use in that they have a military function but also a civilian function. Many different types of objects and facilities can have a dual function: a bridge across a river can allow military personnel and equipment to cross that river and get to the scene of a battle, but it can also allow a civilian to cross the river to get from their home to their place of work; a power plant can provide electricity to a military base or a surface-to-air missile system, but can also provide electricity to houses and hospitals; a railway line can be used to move troops but can also provide public transport; an oil refinery can provide fuel for both tanks and tractors; and so on.

Attacks on dual-use targets can be problematic in terms of both discrimination and proportionality. If a dual-use target has relatively little military value, then attacks on that target may be considered to lack the relevant level of discrimination, especially if this target is highly valuable for civilian life. Even if a target has significant military value, if the overall level of harm done to civilians by destroying it is great, then the attack may be considered disproportionate. Since in actual conflicts, like the NATO campaign, the focus has tended to be on what is legal, rather than what is ethical, in practice both these criteria have probably been ignored to a greater or lesser extent.

Under international law, a military objective is defined in the provisions of Protocol I of the Geneva Conventions. Article 52(2) states that

> Attacks shall be limited strictly to military objectives. In so far as objects are concerned, military objectives are limited to those objects which by their nature, location, purpose, or use make an effective contribution to military action and whose total or partial destruction, capture or neutralization, in the circumstances ruling at the time, offers a definite military advantage.

It is important to note that this is actually a two part definition, in that to qualify as a military objective an object must (1) make an effective contribution to military action; **and** (2) be such that its destruction, capture, or neutralization offers a definite military advantage in the circumstances ruling at the time. Thus, under the law, to qualify as a legitimate military target, it must be the case that destroying that object would provide a definite military advantage right now, based on a reasonable expectation about what the military forces on both sides of the conflict might be expected to do in the future. Suppose, for example, that there was a major bridge and a secondary bridge across a river, both of which could be used by the enemy to get their soldiers to the front line. There was also a third bridge, which the enemy, could, in theory, also use to get their soldiers across this river, but this third bridge was an ancient rope and wooden bridge, high up in the mountains, accessible only to determined hikers after a 3-day trek, normally only used by monks on a pilgrimage to a tiny cave which...well, you get the idea. There is a definite military advantage to be gained by destroying both the major bridge and the secondary bridge and it would be perfectly legal to destroy both of those bridges at the same time, since if only one was destroyed then the enemy could be expected to use the other. Even though the bridge high up in the mountains theoretically represents "the one remaining river crossing," there would be no military advantage in destroying it and thus, that third bridge would not be a valid military target.[8]

Although this definition does place some limits on what qualifies as a military target, it is rather problematic when examining the ethics of attacks on dual-use targets. Any object will qualify as a military objective if it makes an effective contribution to military action and if its destruction offers a definite military advantage at the time, but such a definition entirely excludes any consideration of the object's value to civilian life. Consider a power plant that delivers 5% of its output for military purposes and 95% of its output for civilian purposes, including supplying power to houses, shops, and hospitals. Since this power plant makes an effective contribution to military action, by supplying power to some military facilities, it will legally qualify as a legitimate military objective, provided that destroying it offers some definite military advantage. In legal terms, the civilian function of the power plant is totally irrelevant when deciding whether an attack on it is discriminate, unless it is an object that has special protected status under law, like a hospital or a building of special cultural significance. To ignore its civilian function is certainly problematic in ethical terms.

When considering the proportionality of an attack, the tendency has been to focus merely on the immediate damage that will be done in the course of attacking a particular target and not on the long-term indirect harm that may be caused by an attack on a particular object. Thus, an attack on a military headquarters in the middle of a city might be considered disproportionate if that attack is likely to cause a large amount of collateral damage in the form of civilian casualties or damage to surrounding civilian structures. However, during the 1999 NATO campaign, attacks on bridges across the Danube were not considered to be disproportionate, despite the certain knowledge that the destruction of these bridges would continue to harm the local civilians long after the conflict had ended (see Case 9.1: NATO Attacks and Dual-Use Targets).

In fact, the long-term indirect effects of the destruction of some types of dual-use facilities can be catastrophic. In the early stages of the 1991 Gulf War, the Iraq electrical system was extensively targeted through air and missile attacks. This was considered legitimate since the Iraq military required electricity to power many of its weapons systems. However, this electricity also supplied power to water purification and pumping systems, to sewage treatment plants, to hospitals, to food refrigeration facilities, and to irrigation systems for farmers. Such effects can hardly be considered inconsequential in a hot and generally arid country like Iraq. Several reports published after the war estimated that the number of civilian deaths that could be directly attributed to the destruction of the power supply were orders of magnitude higher than the number of civilians killed by direct effects of the war, and numbered in the tens of thousands.[9] In modern times, when such effects are so well recognized, they simply cannot be ignored when calculating the proportionality of an attack on dual-use facilities such as power generating facilities and transmission systems.

Attacks on dual-use facilities can obviously provide significant military benefits in some circumstances. However, when considering whether such attacks are justified in terms of *jus in bello*, it is obvious that such attacks can be extremely problematic with regard to the principles of both discrimination and proportionality. If such attacks are to be ethically justified, then the value of the potential target to civilian life needs to be carefully evaluated, as do the long-term effects of depriving the civilian community of its benefits.

PEACEKEEPING OR PEACEMAKING?

As was mentioned earlier, peacekeeping operations have traditionally been undertaken in situations where the formerly warring parties have reached some sort of cease-fire or peace agreement, and that agreement involves those parties consenting to the deployment of independent peacekeeping forces, who will move into the area to monitor those agreements and engage in other operations, such as aiding with reconstruction, where this is appropriate. UNTSO is a classic example of this sort of deployment; during its history, the military personnel attached to this force have monitored cease-fire agreements between Israel and all its neighbors, Egypt, Jordan, Syria, and Lebanon. UNTSO has also monitored more substantial agreements that have been established between these different parties at various times, most notably with regard to the peace agreement between Israel and Egypt in the Sinai Peninsula, the cease-fire agreement between Israel and Syria in the Golan Heights, and the peace agreement between Israel and Lebanon along their mutual border. Many other UN peacekeeping operations along similar lines have been mounted in other parts of the world.

Importantly, in all of these deployments, the role of the UN forces has been to act strictly as impartial observers; the personnel attached to these operations are empowered by their ROE to use lethal force if this is necessary to protect themselves, but their role in these deployments is to observe and report on violations of the peace agreements, rather than to intervene to prevent problems from arising in the first place. Their strict impartiality has also been important in these sorts of circumstances, since if the UN peacekeepers are seen to favor one side of the dispute over the other, then their reports on any violations of the peace agreement may be seen to be biased, which is likely to lead to a loss of trust in the role of the peacekeepers and thus be more likely to lead to future problems with that peace agreement.

Since somewhat different situations are expected to arise in peacekeeping operations compared to peacemaking operations, it can be argued that the ROE that are established for each type of operation ought to be somewhat different from each other. However, in actual fact this has often not been the case, and the ROE that have been issued for both peacekeeping and peacemaking operations have tended to be very similar. This problem has perhaps been exacerbated to some extent by the fact that the history of peacekeeping operations extends back much further than that of peacemaking operations, and thus the ROE for early peacemaking operations were based on the established ROE for peacekeeping operations, despite the fact that these ROE may not have been fully applicable to the somewhat different situation faced by troops involved in peacemaking. Thus, one problem that can arise in humanitarian operations is when the ROE that have been established for a particular operation are not really suited to the various different types of situations that may arise on the ground.

CASE STUDY 9.2

Protecting Civilians by Endangering Troops

The United Nations Protection Force (UNPROFOR) was the UN peacekeeping force in Croatia and in Bosnia and Herzegovina during the Yugoslav wars and was created upon the first UN involvement in February 1992. At its height, UNPROFOR consisted of nearly 40,000 troops, drawn from the armed forces of 40 different states.

Part of the mandate of UNPROFOR was to ensure that certain regions within Croatia (United Nations Protected Areas or UNPAs) were demilitarized and that any people residing in those areas were protected. However, the Rules of Engagement (ROE) for the mission were considered problematic, to say the least, by the soldiers who made up UNPROFOR, as they were not well defined and subject to a range of differing interpretations. One officer who had to deal with such problems was Canadian Colonel George Oehring, who was faced with the problem of local Serbian troops stealing food and other supplies from the few Croats who remained in the village of Matasi, southwest of Knin. These Croats had remained in the village despite earlier attempts at ethnic cleansing, but Oehring was worried that they were now likely to starve if these thefts continued; he also felt that he needed to take some tangible steps to fulfill his responsibilities to these civilians, given that the UNPROFOR mandate required that minorities be protected from the fear of armed attack.

The ROE did not contain clauses that allowed the use of force to protect the lives and property of these Croatian civilians within the UNPAs, but did allow the UN peacekeepers to use force, up to and including deadly force, to protect themselves. Thus, Oehring decided that he would need to ensure that any threat to the Croatian civilians would constitute a threat to the UN peacekeepers, so he literally camped armed UN troops at the doorsteps of the few remaining Croatian houses. To make sure that the Kenyan soldiers who were to undertake these missions clearly understood his intentions, he also spent a lot of time discussing the situation with the Kenyan CO and his officers to make sure that they all understood both their responsibility to protect these civilians and what their rights to use force were in the event that they were threatened in any way by the Serbian forces.

Writing about the situation later, Oehring noted some of the problems with what he had done in this case:

> I don't know what the lawyers would say about all this, but I didn't care then as I don't care now. I felt confident in succeeding on any witness stand. Deliberately endangering soldier's lives in order that they are forced to defend themselves and thereby achieve another aim may be of dubious legality at best, granted. But when such "endangerment" is in fact the only way our legitimate military mission could be accomplished—as surely it was here—then the legal focus must change. How can it be otherwise? And surely this philosophy is and always was at the root of the whole Peacekeeping idea—the philosophy of deliberate endangerment.[10]

As time passed it became clear that the tactic Oehring had adopted was working; the Kenyan soldiers under his command protected the Croatian civilians in Matasi very effectively, and similar tactics were adopted by other UN peacekeepers during their attempts to protect civilians in other villages in the UNPAs. But while effective, this tactic was also resource intensive, and UNPROFOR simply did not have enough soldiers on the ground to be able to protect all the threatened civilians within the UNPAs in this manner.

SOURCE: Based on the situation described in Colonel George J. Oehring (Ret.), "Rights to Engagement," *The Bulletin* (A publication of The Army Lessons Learned Centre, Canada) 7(2)(October 2000), pp.11–13.

As was mentioned earlier, the traditional role of UN troops involved in peace-keeping operations was to observe and report any violations of cease-fire agreements, but not to become actively involved in any conflict, except when necessary for their own self-defense. This may be reasonable in a deployment like UNTSO in the Middle East, where there is some form of existing peace agreement between the belligerent parties and when the belligerents are state forces who violate this agreement by targeting each other. However, such an idea is obviously much more problematic when any of these conditions are not met: if there is no existing peace agreement; if some of the belligerents in the area are not state forces but rather are irregulars or paramilitary groups; and if cease-fire agreements, if and when they do exist, are violated by forces who are not targeting enemy combatants, but instead are targeting civilians. If UN forces are only allowed to act in direct self-defense, then they will be placed in the position which apparently confronted members of UNPROFOR on a number of occasions, and may thus be forced to simply watch as atrocities were carried out by state or semi-state forces in the area.[11]

It was this problem which Colonel Oehring was trying to combat in Case 9.2 (Protecting Civilians by Endangering Troops). His solution was to deliberately put troops in his command in harm's way by stationing them outside the homes of the Croatian families who were being threatened. While his solution did actually work, his task would obviously have been much simpler if the ROE had allowed UN forces to get involved in situations in a wider range of circumstances and to use a much wider range of levels of force, rather than simply allowing them to use deadly force if necessary for self-defense. In short, what is really necessary in situations like this is for the UN troops to not act simply as impartial observers, but rather to act like police officers. Police, or at least good police, are impartial, in that they treat everyone with equal respect no matter what their nationality or ethnic background, but they are not mere observers, since they are permitted, and indeed are required, to become involved in situations where people's fundamental human rights are being threatened.

Of course the big difficulty with expecting soldiers to act like police officers, as was mentioned in the context of discussion of Case 3.5 (Esequiel Hernandez Shooting) is that police are trained and equipped very differently from military personnel. Soldiers who are expected to act like police officers are likely to run into difficulties in situations where their military training does not adequately prepare them for the tasks they are likely to face. One of the reasons why this difficulty arises is that the usual principles of discrimination and proportionality still apply in situations where military personnel are effectively being asked to act as police officers. But the standard military equipment and the resources backing up the military personnel are such that these principles may actually be very difficult to apply appropriately, in that it can be very hard for such personnel to know who they ought to take action against and what sort of action they can take that will actually be proportionate.

One specific example Oehring actually mentions in his original paper, from which Case 9.2 is derived, is of a soldier stealing chickens from a Croatian civilian. As he notes, "An unarmed Serb soldier entering a chicken coop and walking away with its residents...couldn't be engaged with deadly force."[12]

Oehring's solution was to position the Kenyan troops under his command so that they would always become targets in such a situation, which would thus allow them to take action in response. But consider the situation that would apply here if the ROE for UNPROFOR had been framed so as to allow the UN troops to act more like police officers. In particular, consider, in terms of discrimination and proportionality, the options that would be available to one of these Kenyan soldiers when compared to an ordinary police officer who has the authority to act in that region.

The first problem is the issue of discrimination. If a local civilian was to allege that a particular person had stolen from them, the Kenyan soldier has neither the necessary expertise nor the necessary authority to investigate the matter. Thus, if Kenyan soldiers were to take action against the alleged thief, they cannot be sure that they are actually "aiming" at the correct target. The local police officer, on the other hand, has the training and the authority to investigate the matter further and thus to determine what action, if any, ought to be taken against the alleged thief. However, this sort of "discrimination" is not always going to be a problem, since if the Kenyan soldier actually sees the Serb soldier entering the chicken coop and walking off with the chickens, it is clear that it is legitimate to take action against that Serb soldier; in analogous military terms, the Kenyan soldier knows he is aiming at the right target in such a case. But proportionality is going to be much more problematic for the Kenyan soldier than it would be for the police officer in such a case. The soldier has very few options available to him in the form of direct actions that he could take; essentially little more than shouting, hitting, or shooting. Of these, shouting is unlikely to be effective in such a situation, and shooting would obviously be disproportionate, which essentially means that the Kenyan soldier would have no proportionate option other than trying to tackle the Serb soldier hand to hand. In contrast, the average police officer in a modern Western democracy usually has a range of nonlethal weapons which would be available and proportionate for use in such a situation: a baton or nightstick; probably an incapacitant spray;[13] and quite possibly an electroshock muscular incapacitation weapon such as a TASER.[14]

These differences in equipment between soldiers and police officers could be reduced, if it were thought necessary, by issuing UN personnel who are deployed for peacemaking missions with some of these nonlethal weapons and thoroughly training them in their use. It also may well have been the case that an ordinary police officer who had jurisdiction within the village of Matasi at that time might not have had access to any more nonlethal weapons than the Kenyan soldier did. However, what is even more important than the proportionality of the direct actions the Kenyan soldier and a local police officer could take at the time of the theft, is the proportionality of the actions the two would be able to take **after** the event. Even if the Kenyan soldier was able to stop the Serb soldier from taking the chickens, neither he nor anyone else within the hierarchy of the UNPROFOR mission actually had the authority to level any punishment against the Serb soldier, and this would in fact have been the case even for much more serious crimes than are being discussed here. Thus, while the theft may have been prevented and the presence of the UN soldiers may act as a deterrent to future thefts, there is no genuine possibility of punishing the guilty party.

A police officer within the village of Matasi, on the other hand, would have had the authority to charge the Serb soldier, allowing the matter to be taken to court and with the possibility of the soldier being punished for his actions. Admittedly such an outcome would require a functional criminal justice system, an impartial court, and an impartial police officer, probably a highly unlikely state of affairs in that part of the world at the time. Still, the fundamental point remains the same in any case: there are essential differences between military personnel and police officers, and even if the ROE the military operate under allow them to act like police officers in certain respects, there will still be limits to the extent to which it is even possible for military personnel to act like police officers, particularly in the context of a peacemaking operation.

There can also be other difficulties that can arise for military personnel who are being asked to act in a role more familiar to police officers. These difficulties are particularly obvious when the task these military personnel have been given involves them dealing extensively, or perhaps even exclusively, with noncombatants. Once again this is a situation police officers are well prepared for, but which is entirely outside the usual range of military activities.

CASE STUDY 9.3

The Baby Ram

SITUATION In an Eastern European country racked by ethnic violence, U.S. Army units, part of a larger UN force, are attempting to prevent confrontations between two hostile ethnic groups. A program of ethnic cleansing led to a massive exodus of refugees who are now returning to their homes. Until the recent conflict, the two groups had lived in integrated towns and villages. A carefully orchestrated plan is in place for the gradual movement of small groups of the Andolosians back into their homes where they formerly lived side by side with the other ethnic group, the Zandals. The current mission of the U.S. Army force is to prevent the arrival of Andolosians ahead of the agreed upon schedule, especially the arrival of large, unruly groups that would spark violent confrontations. People on each side seek revenge for recent atrocities.

Captain Tan has set up four roadblocks at choke points on the road that refugees must take to return to a town that has been a flashpoint. His orders are to prevent any Andolosians from returning to the town until the following Monday. When Monday comes, he is to let only families or groups of three or fewer people through the roadblocks. They are to be spaced so that no large groups suddenly appear in the town. The Zandals suffered badly at the hands of the Andolosians during the conflict and even small incidents could spark rioting as the Andolosians return.

At his command post at the second roadblock Captain Tan receives a report that a large group of Andolosians has broken through the first roadblock. The lieutenant rendering the report states that three Andolosian men aggressively approached the roadblock carrying babies in front of them at chest height. When they reached the line of U.S. troops blocking the road, they strode forward thrusting the babies at the soldiers. The lieutenant reported that he let the Andolosians through rather than endanger the infants and that the rest of the people surged through the roadblock behind the "baby ram."

As he receives the report, Captain Tan sees a mass of people—thirty to forty—marching swiftly toward his second picket line. Several men in the vanguard are indeed carrying babies. It appears they plan to repeat their ramming tactic.

SOURCE: Case written by Anthony E. Hartle and reprinted from *Moral Issues in Military Decision Making*, 2nd ed., Revised (Lawrence: University Press of Kansas, 2004), pp. 186–187.

The situation described in Case 9.3 (The Baby Ram) is obviously going to be difficult for the soldiers involved to deal with. Basic military training is about preparing military personnel for combat. In blunt terms it is about killing people, in particular examining who it is legally appropriate to kill and when, how, and why it is appropriate to kill them. The basic equipment that military personnel are issued with is also focused on this task. All the fighting equipment issued to an ordinary soldier is designed for one of two purposes: either to help the soldier kill enemy personnel, or to protect the soldier from the enemy's attacks. Thus, one of the reasons why peacekeeping operations can be so difficult for the personnel involved is that many situations those personnel will have to deal with are ones where it is clearly not appropriate to kill **anyone**, yet where some forceful action must still be taken. It is this problem that Captain Tan must deal with in Case 9.3.

There is no explicit mention in the case of the ROE that these U.S. forces have been issued, but given the background material that is provided, it is obvious that although these soldiers could use lethal force in self-defense, they would not be justified in using lethal force in any other circumstances. This is essentially the same situation that Colonel Oehring faced in Case 9.2 (Protecting Civilians by Endangering Troops). The large group of Andolosians who are approaching the U.S. roadblocks are obviously not a threat to the lives of the American soldiers, they are simply threatening the mission that Captain Tan and his troops have been entrusted with. The basic dilemma for Captain Tan and his troops is that the general mission for which they have been deployed, that is, to keep peace in the country and attempt to ensure that civilians are protected from harm, seems to be at odds with what is required to achieve the specific mission they are currently tasked with, that is, to prevent large groups of Andolosians from returning to the town. The reason these two things appear to be at odds with each other is that the primary means that military personnel are trained to use to achieve their objectives, that is, the application of lethal force, is obviously inappropriate for the task at hand. Using lethal force would almost certainly stop this large group of civilians from re-entering the town ahead of schedule, but the resultant civilian casualties would certainly undermine the goals of the overall mission, not to mention the fact that using lethal force against this group of unarmed civilians would clearly be a breach of international law.

In this case it is clear that the Andolosian civilians are reasonably well informed about the sort of ROE the UN peacekeepers will have been issued and thus they know that the Americans, or indeed any other UN peacekeeping forces placed in the same sort of situation, will not shoot unarmed civilians except under extraordinary circumstances. They also know that the Americans will be extremely reluctant to cause any civilian casualties and will be especially wary of causing injury to babies or small children. It is this very reluctance the Andolosians are exploiting through their "baby-ram" tactic.

As Hartle points out in his analysis of this case,[15] although it might seem at first glance that the only options open to Captain Tan are either to allow the Andolosians through the roadblock or to take direct action, which will risk harming the babies in the group, there are other options available. It may be possible to separate the men who are carrying babies from the rest of the group, for example, or for the soldiers to slowly fall back in front of the group, thus delaying the Andolosians sufficiently to allow the American soldiers enough time to modify the later roadblocks in such a way as to make the baby-ram tactic ineffective.

Case 9.3 (The Baby Ram) highlights, once again, the sorts of problems that can arise when military personnel are asked to perform tasks that would ordinarily be performed by police officers. Given that dealing with civilians, including unruly civilians, is a fundamental part of a police officer's job, modern police officers will usually be both better trained and better equipped to deal with this sort of situation than Captain Tan and his troops were. This is certainly not intended as a criticism of the job that military personnel have done in peacekeeping and peacemaking operations; my point is simply that such operations are quite different from those that military personnel are fundamentally trained to undertake and thus problems ought to be expected when military personnel are required to act in the role of police officers, just as they would be if police officers were required to fight a war. The differences between police and military personnel have been recognized, at least to some extent, by the UN; this is obvious from the fact that many UN peacekeeping, as opposed to peacemaking, operations, now include a significant number of international police officers among their personnel.

Even in more traditional peacekeeping situations, such as deployments like UNTSO in the Middle East, military personnel can still be faced with difficult decisions, particularly with regard to when it is or is not appropriate for them to open fire on those who appear to pose a threat.

CASE STUDY 9.4

The Child Soldier

The Australian troops had been posted to the Middle East to serve as part of a multinational peace-building and peacekeeping operation, intended to keep a zone of separation between the hostile parties in the area. As well as maintaining observation posts and checkpoints, the operation also involved regular mounted patrols through the separation zone. To maintain high visibility for the international peacekeeping force it was decided that these patrols would be conducted by troops travelling in open-backed trucks. The operation had begun well, but in recent times there had been a number of incidents in which the patrolling troops had been engaged with small arms fire and rocket propelled grenades, and several soldiers had been seriously wounded. In light of this, the Rules of Engagement (ROE) had been relaxed somewhat, allowing troops to fire on anyone who was seen to be carrying a weapon and who appeared to pose a direct threat to the safety of the peacekeepers.

Lieutenant Kathryn Williams was in charge of the patrol that moved through the separation zone that afternoon. She felt quite exposed crouched in the back of the open truck and she was sure the other soldiers around her felt the same. As the truck moved through the open space in the center of town, she spotted a boy, probably 10 or 12 years old, holding an AK-47 and standing by a house on the far side of the space. He was probably about 100 meters away, and as she watched him she saw the boy bring the weapon up and point it at the truck.

She instantly aimed her Austeyr rifle at him, calling out a warning to the other troops in the truck, but even as she did so she realized it was unnecessary, for she could see out of the corner of her eye that at least two other soldiers had the boy in their sights as well. Through the sights of her weapon she could see the boy quite clearly, and she watched as he brought one hand up and appeared to cock his gun. She held her sights on him, watching, waiting, until the truck drove around a corner and the boy passed from her sight.

During the debriefing that evening, one of the Corporals from her squad mentioned the incident. It transpired that everyone on that side of the truck had seen the boy, and all had kept their weapons trained on him, yet none had fired, even though the ROE clearly allowed them to do so. While several soldiers said they would have had no hesitation in firing if they had seen an adult acting in the same manner, none had wanted to fire in this case without being certain the boy was a genuine threat, and not simply a child playing a game. However, many of the soldiers were now worried about whether their actions that day had increased the risk, both to themselves and to future patrols through the area.

SOURCE: Stephen Coleman, "The Child Soldier," *Journal of Military Ethics* 10(2011) p. 316.

In the modern world it is not uncommon for personnel involved in peacekeeping or peacemaking operations to be confronted with children who appear to pose a threat, either directly, as is the case with child soldiers, or indirectly where children may act as lookouts or as a relay for information. Such situations can obviously be difficult for the personnel involved, since most people have a natural inclination to protect children and are thus often unwilling to take action against children who pose a threat to the peacekeepers, even in cases where they would take action against an adult in the same situation, as was the situation in Case 9.4 (The Child Soldier). What has happened in Case 9.4 is that Lieutenant Williams and the other soldiers on the truck have decided to treat this person differently simply because of his age, or more accurately, because of their perception of his age. The central question here is whether or not the soldiers involved acted correctly in this matter and whether the boy's age is relevant when determining what actions are appropriate in this situation. This is a point where reasonable people might disagree. It can certainly be argued that the age of the boy is a relevant consideration in determining whether or not it is reasonable to engage him; on the other hand, it can also be argued that his age is not really relevant and insist that the only questions that ought to be considered are whether his actions "pose a direct threat to the safety of the peacekeepers" and what effect engaging this boy would have on the overall success of the mission for which these soldiers have been deployed.

It is notable that there is both a legal question and an ethical question that need to be answered here. The legal question is whether or not the ROE did in fact allow the soldiers to open fire on this child. If the answer to that question is "yes," then the further ethical question that needs to be answered is whether it is actually justifiable to open fire. Although the exact ROE for the operation were obviously somewhat more detailed than is stated in the case, some might be tempted to argue that whereas the soldiers were allowed to open fire on "anyone who was seen to be carrying a weapon and who appeared to pose a direct threat to the safety of the peacekeepers," this still did not legally allow them to fire on this child, because as a child, and not an adult, it was questionable whether he actually **did** appear to be a threat. Anyone who makes such a claim will almost certainly feel that the age of the boy involved is ethically relevant when one is deciding whether or not he **ought** to be engaged. In the end, the answer to the legal question is clear, since it is stated in the final paragraph of Case 9.4 (The Child Soldier) that the ROE did allow the soldiers to open fire on this boy. However, the answer to the ethical question is of course more open to argument.

There seem to be three possible positions that could reasonably be taken with regard to what ought to be done in a case like 9.4. They are

1. to engage the boy because he was a threat to the soldiers in the truck;
2. to not engage the boy unless he actually opens fire, even though a man would be engaged under the same circumstances; and

3. to not engage either the boy in this case or a man in the same circumstances, unless that person actually opened fire on the truck.

It is clear that the main concern of someone who would recommend Option 1 is the safety of those under their command. The main concern of someone who would recommend Option 3 is probably the fact that the overall mission is a peace-building and peacekeeping operation; thus, their argument is that a higher level of restraint is required than would be the case in other types of operations. In effect, this is suggesting that the peacekeeping forces need to model the behavior they would like to see the locals display during their interactions with each other.

Many people instinctively lean toward Option 2 in a situation like this, though if they are anything like a lot of the students who I have discussed this case with, they may struggle to explain why. A cultural norm of protecting children might be mentioned, or wanting to be able to meet one's own eyes in the mirror the next day. In fact, the strongest argument in favor of Option 2 is probably the fact that children are not considered to be fully morally responsible for their actions, nor fully cognizant of the consequences of those actions, whereas adults are. So a child may not realize the likely consequences of pointing a gun at soldiers, and probably has not chosen to do so entirely of their own accord. An adult, on the other hand, does know the consequences, and if the adult fires at those soldiers, then this adult can be considered to be fully morally responsible for that action.

One other issue that may be relevant to decisions about whether it is ethically appropriate to open fire on this particular child soldier is the past history of incidents in this area. Given that the case actually mentions that the ROE were changed in response to recent incidents, then any pattern evident in those incidents ought to be considered in this situation. If the recent attacks on patrolling peacekeepers actually involved child soldiers, for example, then that is clearly a relevant consideration here. Similarly, if guns are uncommon in this area, then the mere fact that this child is carrying one is cause for concern. On the other hand, if guns are very common in the area, and/or if child soldiers have not been involved in previous attacks, then that might be taken as an indication that restraint is called for in this case.

The decision about whether or not it is appropriate to open fire on the child soldier in Case 9.4 (The Child Soldier) is essentially an issue of discrimination. The fact that these sorts of problems have become so common in the context of peacekeeping and peacemaking operations, as well as the fact that the military personnel who are engaged in such operations are so often called on to act like police officers, has led some people to suggest that military personnel ought to be equipped with some of the weaponry that modern police officers are. In particular, the claim is that military personnel ought to be equipped with various types of nonlethal weaponry that could be used in such situations.[16] However, equipping military personnel in this way might actually introduce a new range of problems.

CASE STUDY 9.5

Moscow Theatre Siege

On October 23, 2002, 40 to 50 armed Chechens, claiming allegiance to the militant Islamic separatist movement in Chechnya, seized control of a crowded theatre in the Dubrovka district in Moscow, about 4 kilometers southeast of the Kremlin. While some of those in the theatre managed to escape, the Chechens succeeded in securing some 850 to 900 hostages, threatening to kill these hostages unless Russian military forces immediately withdrew from Chechnya. Surreptitious phone calls between hostages and those outside the theatre suggested that the hostage takers were in possession of small arms, such as assault rifles and grenades, as well as mines and other explosives, which had apparently been deployed to many places within the theatre building after the Chechens seized control.

During negotiations over the next few days, the Chechens released approximately 200 hostages, including children, pregnant women, foreigners, and those requiring medical care, but the Chechens repeated their threat to start executing other hostages if their demands were not met.

Early in the morning on October 26, special forces (Spetsnaz) from the Russian Federal Security Service surrounded and stormed the building. For those inside the building, the first indication that an assault was taking place was when gas began to appear in the main auditorium where all the hostages were being held. The gas, a still unidentified aerosol anesthetic, rendered many hostages, and some of the Chechens, unconscious. The hostage takers did not detonate any explosives in response to the gas, but instead began to fire at Russian positions. After a fierce gun battle, which lasted more than an hour, the Spetsnaz blew open the front door and entered the auditorium, directly engaging those Chechens who remained conscious, and apparently executing any who had succumbed to the gas.

After regaining control of the theatre, the Spetsnaz began bringing out the dead and unconscious bodies of hostages who had been overcome by the gas. Almost all the hostages required medical care due to their inhalation of the gas, but those treating the hostages were never told what sort of gas had been used in the assault, and apparently were not told that gas was even used until after the event, and were thus completely unprepared for the mass casualties they had to treat. Two days after the siege ended, some 118 hostages had been confirmed dead, and of the 646 former hostages who remained hospitalized, 150 were still in intensive care and 45 were in critical condition. At least 33 of the hostage takers and 129 hostages died during the raid or over the following days. Despite official Russian government claims that none of the hostages died due to poisoning, it appears that almost all of the hostages died as a result of exposure to the gas, rather than from injuries sustained during the exchange of gunfire between the Chechen hostage takers and the Spetsnaz.

An official investigation into the incident by the Moscow Prosecutor's office was suspended in 2007. The investigation provided no positive information about what gas was used, whether an antidote had been available, how many hostage takers were involved in the siege, how many hostages were released by the operation, or who had decided on the manner of the assault and ordered its implementation.

Although those involved in the Moscow theatre action were not military personnel in the strict sense, and this was not an incident in any sort of conventional war, this case does illustrate some of the possible problems with issuing nonlethal weapons to military personnel. The forces engaged in the recapture of the Moscow theatre used a tranquilizing gas, which was intended to have an indiscriminate effect. If this was to occur in warfare, then it would seem to violate one of the fundamental principles of both the law of armed conflict and *jus in bello*. However, this indiscriminate effect was intended to be both nonlethal, in which respect it was obviously less than fully successful, and for the benefit of the noncombatants involved in the incident. This raises some important questions that need to be discussed. Should the use of nonlethal weapons be preferred as a means of warfare, since using such weapons has the potential, not well realized in this case, to reduce noncombatant deaths? And does the use of an indiscriminate weapon such as this actually violate the principles of *jus in bello* if it is being used only to reduce noncombatant deaths?

One problem for military use of nonlethal weapons is that this use may violate current international law in some circumstances. The 1993 Chemical Weapons Convention, for example, bans the use of Riot Control Agents (RCAs) as weapons of war,[17] though not for use in law enforcement, including domestic riot control situations.[18] This situation was actually commented on by then Secretary of Defense, Donald Rumsfeld, who complained in testimony to the House Armed Services Committee that "in many instances our forces are allowed to shoot somebody and kill them, but they're not allowed to use a non-lethal riot control agent."[19] However, it could perhaps be argued that the use of RCAs is actually permitted in military operations short of war, such as operations launched for humanitarian purposes, or peacekeeping, peacemaking, and peace enforcement operations.

The reason that the Chemical Weapons Convention actually bans the use of RCAs as a weapon of war is almost certainly due to another concern with the military use of nonlethal weapons: that these weapons may be used as lethal force multipliers rather than lethal force avoiders and thus that they may be used in combination with the use of lethal force, thereby increasing, rather than decreasing, the lethality of the military operations in which such weapons are used. In fact this appears to have been what happened in Case 9.5 (Moscow Theatre Siege). When the Russian Special Forces stormed the theatre, none of the Chechens were taken alive, despite the fact that some of the hostage takers were rendered unconscious by the gas in the same way in which many of the hostages were. It appears that rather than taking these people into custody, the Russian Special Forces simply executed them while they were unconscious. In the context of military operations this would again be a violation of the law of armed conflict, since acting in this manner equates to targeting enemy personnel while they are *hors de combat*.

There are also issues for military use of nonlethal weapons with regard to the *jus in bello* considerations of discrimination and proportionality. Consider the issue of proportionality. Donald Rumsfeld noted that it seems odd that military personnel might be allowed to shoot someone, but not use a nonlethal agent, and this certainly does seem counterintuitive, to say the least. So intuitively it might seem to be the case that if it is considered proportional to shoot someone, then it must also be proportional to use any nonlethal agent; if it is proportional to kill someone, then it must also be proportional to use a weapon that is not intended to kill. However, the mere fact that a weapon is not intended to kill its target does not mean that the weapon does no harm, and some weapons that are intended to have nonlethal effects have been banned by other international conventions on the grounds that the use of these weapons does actually cause disproportionate harm. The use of permanently blinding laser weapons, for example, has been banned under Protocol IV of the Convention on Certain Conventional Weapons;[20] these weapons are considered to cause disproportionate harm despite the fact that the effects of such weapons are nonlethal. Thus, problems related to the proportionality of nonlethal weapons cannot simply be ignored; it cannot simply be assumed that all nonlethal weapons will meet the requirements of proportionality in any case where the use of lethal force would be considered to be proportional.

Even more serious with regard to the use of nonlethal weapons by military personnel are the problems with regard to discrimination. When the principle of discrimination is applied to the use of lethal force, it is always applied before the use of that force; military personnel are simply not permitted to deliberately target noncombatants. However, many advocates of nonlethal weapons seem to advocate their use in a manner that applies the principle of discrimination **after** the use of force rather than before. The following quotation from Michael Gross is a good example of this:

> Unlike the use of ordinary weapons, non-lethal weapons deliberately target civilian noncombatants so that the harm they suffer is no longer incidental but intentional. Targeting civilians in this way requires that one subject the principle of noncombatant immunity to a "lesser evils" test that compares a small amount of intentional harm with a greater level of non-intentional harm that comes from using high explosives. If the former is significantly less than the latter, then there are moral grounds to targeting civilian noncombatants with non-lethal weapons.[21]

The Russian Special Forces in Case 9.5 (Moscow Theatre Siege) used nonlethal weapons in almost exactly the manner that Michael Gross has advocated. The Russian forces could have simply relied on conventional weapons when they decided to storm the theatre, and if they had done so, it is highly likely that a number, possibly a very large number, of the hostages would have died, either directly killed by the hostage takers or by being caught in the cross fire. If the Russian forces had engaged in a conventional assault and if such an assault is considered in purely military terms, then it would appear to follow the principle of discrimination, since even if the Russian forces killed some of the hostages in the process of assaulting the theatre, they would only have been directly targeting the Chechen hostage takers. What actually happened, of course, was that the Russian forces used a nonlethal weapon, in the form of the anesthetic gas, which they pumped into the theatre's ventilation system. If the actual assault is considered in purely military terms, then it seems to fail the principle of discrimination; since an anesthetizing gas is an indiscriminate weapon, the best way to characterize the situation seems to be to say that all the occupants of the theatre were targeted by this nonlethal weapon.

Of course not all the nonlethal weapons that might be used by military personnel are likely to cause the same level of problems as occurred in the Moscow theatre siege. The issues of discrimination that would arise out of the use of nonlethal weapons that target an individual, like pepper sprays or TASERs, for example, are essentially the same as arise out of the use of lethal weapons, in that the main issue is whether it is appropriate to fire at this particular individual or not. Thus, if it is indeed legal for military personnel to use these types of weapons in at least some circumstances, the problems of using such nonlethal weapons might be considered to be a reasonable cost, if they can solve some of the other problems that arise for military personnel in peacekeeping and peacemaking operations.[22]

NOTES

1. Of course their state's interests may be indirectly advanced in some way and this will in many, if not most cases, be a significant consideration in the minds of the political leaders who decide to commit troops to these operations in the first place.
2. It should be noted that this claim is not universally supported. For example, Gerhard Øverland claims that soldiers who are involved in humanitarian interventions are actually ethically justified in inflicting **higher** than normal levels of collateral damage, in the form of casualties amongst the civilians they are trying to defend, if this reduces the level of risk faced by the intervening military personnel. See "High-Fliers: Who Should Bear the Risk of Humanitarian Intervention," in Paolo Tripodi & Jessica Wolfendale (eds.), *New Wars and New Soldiers: Military Ethics in the Contemporary World* (Farnham, U.K.: Ashgate, 2011), pp. 69–86.
3. This was the intervention that ultimately led to the events of *Black Hawk Down*. See Cases 6.6 (Placing the Strobe) and 8.2 (Defending the Crashed Helicopter).
4. See the report of Human Rights Watch, "Civilian Deaths in the NATO Air Campaign," Volume 12, no. 1, February 2000, http://www.hrw.org/legacy/reports/2000/nato/ (accessed June 23, 2011).
5. See p. 156.
6. It is important to remember that since a conflict such as this is one between states, rather than an irregular conflict, all uniformed members of the enemy's armed forces are assumed to be part of the enemy's attempt to harm, and thus can be legally targeted. It is this assumption that seems problematic when all of the risk is falling on

one side of the conflict. Thanks to Deane-Peter Baker for pointing out the need for clarification on this point.

7. It is technically possible for shoulder mounted surface-to-air missile systems to hit targets flying at these altitudes, but this would be considered to be extreme range for such missiles and as such they were highly unlikely to be effective.

8. I think the main idea of this two part definition is to rule out the sort of attacks that might be mounted along the lines of, "If we do A, and the enemy does B, and then we do C, and the enemy does D…and then we do W, if the enemy does X, then it might be important to destroy Y and Z, so we had better attack and destroy Y and Z straight away."

9. See, for example, the report of Human Rights Watch, "Needless Deaths in the Gulf War: Civilian Casualties During the Air Campaign and Violations of the Laws of War" (New York: Human Rights Watch, 1991), and J. W. Crawford III, "The Law of Noncombatant Immunity and the Targeting of National Electrical Power Systems," *Fletcher Forum of World Affairs* 21(1997), 101–119.

10. Colonel George J. Oehring (Ret.), "Rights to Engagement," *The Bulletin* (A publication of The Army Lessons Learned Centre, Canada) 7(2)(October 2000), pp.11–13, p.13.

11. This problem is certainly not exclusive to UNPROFOR; many other UN peace-keeping deployments have faced similar situations, including the UN forces who remained in Rwanda while the genocide was occurring in that country (see Case 5.5: The Rwandan Genocide).

12. "Rights to Engagement," p. 13.

13. Police in different jurisdictions use different types of incapacitant sprays, such as pepper sprays (OC or PAVA spray) or some form of tear gas (CS spray), but all have similar incapacitating effects.

14. TASER is actually the brand name for a device that uses an electric current to disrupt the brain's ability to control the muscles of the body.

15. Anthony E. Hartle, *Moral Issues in Military Decision Making*, 2nd ed., Revised (Lawrence: University Press of Kansas, 2004) pp. 187–188.

16. The term "nonlethal" is somewhat controversial since virtually any weapon can have lethal effects in some situations. This has led people to seek other terminology that could be used to describe them. Examples include, "soft-kill weapons," "less-than-lethal weapons," "sub-lethal weapons," and so on. See David A. Koplow, *Non-Lethal Weapons: The Law and Policy of Revolutionary Technologies for the Military and Law Enforcement* (Cambridge: Cambridge University Press, 2006), pp. 9–10 and Neil Davison, *"Non-Lethal" Weapons* (Basingstoke, U.K.: Palgrave Macmillan, 2009).

17. *Convention on the Prohibition of the Development, Production, Stockpiling and Use of Chemical Weapons and on their Destruction* (1993). Article I, Point 5: "Each State Party undertakes not to use riot control agents as a method of warfare."

18. Ibid., Article II, Point 9(d).

19. Quoted in Brad Knickerbocker, "The Fuzzy Ethics of Nonlethal Weapons," *Christian Science Monitor*, February 14, 2003.

20. The full name of this treaty is the *Convention on Prohibitions or Restrictions on the Use of Certain Conventional Weapons Which May Be Deemed to Be Excessively Injurious or to Have Indiscriminate Effects*. Since permanently blinding laser weapons are not by their nature indiscriminate, it is obvious that the reason for the inclusion of such weapons in this treaty is that they may be deemed to be "excessively injurious," that is, that they cause disproportionate harm to their targets. Protocol IV, regarding permanently blinding laser weapons, was adopted in October 1995.

21. Michael L. Gross, "The Second Lebanon War: The Question of Proportionality and the Prospect of Non-Lethal Warfare," *Journal of Military Ethics* 7(2008), 1–22, pp. 15–16.

22. For further discussion of some of the issues raised by military use of nonlethal weapons, see Stephen Coleman, "Discrimination and Non-Lethal Weapons: Issues for the Future Military," in David Lovell & Igor Primoratz (eds.), *Protecting Civilians in Violent Conflict: Theoretical and Practical Issues for the 21st Century* (Farnham, U.K.: Ashgate, 2012).

FURTHER READING

Ceulemans, Carl. "The NATO Intervention in the Kosovo Crisis: March–June 1999." In Bruno Coppieters & Nick Fotion (eds.), *Moral Constraints on War: Principles and Cases* (Lanham, MD: Lexington, 2002).

Coleman, Stephen. "Discrimination and Non-Lethal Weapons: Issues for the Future Military." In David Lovell & Igor Primoratz (eds.), *Protecting Civilians in Violent Conflict: Theoretical and Practical Issues for the 21st Century* (Farnham, U.K.: Ashgate, 2012).

Gross, Michael L. *Moral Dilemmas of Modern War: Torture, Assassination and Blackmail in an Age of Asymmetric Conflict* (New York: Cambridge University Press, 2010). Chapter 9: "Risking Our Lives to Save Others: Puzzles of Humanitarian Intervention."

Gross, Michael L. "The Second Lebanon War: The Question of Proportionality and the Prospect of Non-Lethal Warfare." *Journal of Military Ethics* 7(2008), 1–22.

Kashnikov, Boris. "The NATO Intervention in the Kosovo Crisis: Whose Justice?." In Bruno Coppieters & Nick Fotion (eds.), *Moral Constraints on War: Principles and Cases* (Lanham, MD: Lexington, 2002).

Øverland, Gerhard. "High-Fliers: Who Should Bear the Risk of Humanitarian Intervention." In Paolo Tripodi & Jessica Wolfendale (eds.), *New Wars and New Soldiers: Military Ethics in the Contemporary World* (Farnham, U.K.: Ashgate, 2011), pp. 69–86.

DISCUSSION QUESTIONS

- Do the standard conditions of *jus in bello* apply to armed humanitarian interventions, or must these criteria be modified in some way to be relevant to such operations?

- Can the use of airpower alone be an ethically legitimate means to pursue a war that has been launched for purely humanitarian purposes?
- If military personnel were to be issued nonlethal weapons in some circumstances, should they generally be required to use such weapons before resorting to the use of lethal force, or would it be justifiable for them to use lethal force without even attempting to use nonlethal weapons first?

Issues of Surrender and Detention

┌─────────────── CASE STUDY 10.1 ═══════════════┐

Operation Red Wings

Operation Red Wings (sometimes referred to as Operation Redwing) was a mission to kill or capture Ahmad Shah, leader of a group of anti-coalition militia in a mountainous region in Kunar Province, in the far east of Afghanistan. A four-man group from SEAL Team 10, led by Lieutenant Michael Murphy and consisting of Petty Officers Matthew Axelson, Danny Dietz, and Marcus Luttrell, was to be inserted at night, by helicopter, to a location several miles from the village where Ahmad Shah was suspected to be operating. Their mission was to observe the village, make a positive identification of Shah, and then, depending on the force that Shah was seen to have available to him, either capture or kill Shah themselves, or call in a larger force for an assault. Reviewing the pre-mission maps and photographs of the area, the team was concerned about the lack of adequate cover in the area surrounding the village, which would make it difficult for them to stay concealed. Late in the night on June 27, 2005, the team was inserted. They moved, under cover of darkness and rain, to a preplanned observation point above the village to wait for daylight. However, once it became light they realized that their position had a less than ideal view of the village, so they moved to a new, but less defensible, position, which allowed significantly better observation.

As the morning of June 28 wore on, three local goat herders stumbled upon the SEAL team's hiding place. While the goat herders were unarmed and insisted they were not members of the Taliban, they stared at the SEALs with obvious dislike. Dietz attempted to contact HQ via radio, but was unable to get an answer from anyone. The SEALs had no rope or other means of securing the goat herders, and the goats themselves threatened to give away the team's position. Unable to get any higher level guidance, LT Murphy laid out the team's options: (1) kill the goat herders and throw their bodies off the cliff; (2) kill the goat herders and try to cover up their bodies where they were; or (3) let the goat herders go and leave the area as quickly as possible in case the Taliban showed up. Murphy was also clear that if the goat herders were killed, the bodies would be found and that the Taliban would use the killings for political purposes, which would mean that the SEAL team would probably end up being charged with murder.

According to Luttrell, Murphy put the decision of what was to be done to a vote. Axelson voted to kill the Afghans, insisting that "We're not murderers. No matter what we do. We're on active duty behind enemy lines, sent here by our senior commanders. We have the right to do everything we can to save our own lives. The military decision is obvious. To turn them loose would be wrong."[1] Dietz abstained, and Murphy allowed Luttrell the deciding vote, but warned him that the killings would have to be reported, that they would be attacked by the "U.S. liberal media" and would almost certainly face murder charges. Luttrell voted to release the herders. He would later state, "It was the stupidest, most southern-fried, lame brained decision I ever made in my life. I must have been out of my mind. I had actually cast a vote which I knew could sign our death warrant. I'd turned into a fucking liberal, a half-assed, no-logic nitwit, all heart, no brain, and the judgment of a jackrabbit."[2]

After letting the goat herders go, the team moved to their first observation point so as to throw off anyone attempting to intercept them at their old location. Here, Dietz continued his attempts to reach HQ via radio to request an immediate extraction, but he was again unsuccessful. Approximately 2 hours after the goat herders had been released, the SEALs were confronted by a force of Afghan fighters; estimates of their number ranged from 8 to 200.[3] The relatively short period of time that elapsed between when the goat herders were released and when the militia arrived led Luttrell to conclude that the goat herders must have notified Shah and his men of the SEAL team's presence.

Shah's men set up a well organized attack, coming at the SEALs from three sides. This forced the SEALs to begin a frantic half running, half falling descent of the mountain slope behind them. All of them sustained injuries during the descent, having either been hit by gunfire, injured by the fall itself, or both. Several times they stopped at new defensive positions, but each time they were again forced to retreat, fighting continually and hoping to inflict enough casualties on the Afghan militia that they would be forced to withdraw. After some 45 minutes of fighting, knowing that the team's radio was still unable to get proper reception in the mountainous terrain, Murphy moved into an open space to give himself sufficient reception to make an emergency call for support using his mobile phone. He was shot in the abdomen during the conversation, but nevertheless returned to his cover after the call and continued the battle.

After 2 hours of fighting, only Luttrell remained alive, the other members of his team having succumbed to multiple gunshot wounds. Badly injured, Luttrell managed to escape after apparently being blown off the mountain ridge by a rocket-propelled grenade, which knocked him unconscious. He was later found and protected by local villagers before finally being rescued by U.S. forces on July 3. However, by then the American Special Forces had suffered even more casualties. A quick response force had been launched in response to Murphy's phone call and several helicopters carrying SEALs and Marines were dispatched to the scene of the battle. The first one to arrive on the scene was a Chinook helicopter, carrying eight SEALs and crewed by eight members of the 160th Special Operations Aviation Regiment. Just after the rear ramp had been lowered to allow the SEALs to fast-rope to the ground, a rocket-propelled grenade flew in through the open ramp and exploded inside the helicopter. All 16 men on board were killed.

Murphy was later awarded the Medal of Honor for his part in the battle, while Luttrell, Axelson, and Dietz were all awarded the Navy Cross.

DISCUSSION

The main focus of the last few chapters has been a discussion of the people who military personnel can legitimately aim to injure and kill in the course of the different types of conflict that are likely to occur in the modern era. But in any conflict it is likely that military personnel will also being taking people into custody, so the main aim of this chapter is to examine the different types of people whom military personnel might take into custody and discuss how they ought to be treated. This is not as straightforward as it may seem, since in fact different types of people who might be detained during the course of a conflict actually ought to be treated differently, and the divisions between these groups are not always clear. A lot of the discussion in this chapter, perhaps more than any other, will be about particular issues of international law, and particularly the law of armed conflict (LOAC).[4] This is because many of the ethical issues that will be discussed in this chapter have been considered to be so important by so many people for such a long period of time that those ethical principles have come to be codified into international law. Thus, although the focus of the discussion is on the ethical issues, in this area at least, some lengthy discussion of LOAC is simply inevitable.

Although there are a range of ways in which a particular individual might come to be detained by the military, most of them require at least some degree of consent from that person; if that person is fighting, they will usually need to stop fighting; if they are taken by surprise, they will need to decide not to fight. In simple terms, most people taken into custody by the military will need to have surrendered, at least in some form. So some examination of the basic issues of what it means to surrender seems like a good place to start the discussion in this chapter.

SURRENDER

In simple terms, surrender is an agreement to stop fighting. However, in some circumstances, which will be discussed shortly, it is actually quite an unusual agreement. Surrender can be undertaken by an individual combatant, by units of various sizes, by entire armies, and even by states. When surrender involves these larger groups, such as states or armies, it is usual for there to be some negotiations to be involved and for certain conditions to be agreed on.[5] Thus, when a war ends in a negotiated surrender of one side, it may be the case that the victor agrees to allow the withdrawal of the defeated party's troops to behind particular borders, that both parties agree that control of particular territories pass from one side to the other, and so on. Unconditional surrender, of the kind which was demanded of Germany and Japan at the end of World War II, means, as its name implies, that no guarantees are given to the surrendering party and that the victor is able to impose whatever terms it wishes, limited only by the victor's own sense of morality. In treaties and other legal documents, such surrender is often referred to as "surrender at discretion"; that the future treatment of those who have surrendered will be at the discretion of those who have captured them. When individuals or small units surrender, in effect this is always an unconditional surrender. Thus, while uniformed combatants who are surrendering might expect that they will be treated in accordance with the provisions of international law, they have no means of actually ensuring that this will happen and are reliant on the integrity of those taking them into custody.

It is an accepted part of LOAC that an enemy who wishes to surrender must manifest an unconditional and unambiguous intent to do so. Customary indications that a person wishes to surrender include such things as laying down their weapons, raising their hands above their head, or waving a white flag. However, in international law there is no universally accepted procedure for conveying the message that one wishes to surrender. This means that if you search a book about LOAC, it is actually quite common to find discussion of things like who qualifies to be treated as a prisoner of war (POW), what the rights of a POW are, how POWs ought to be treated, and so on, but to not even find an entry on the term "surrender" in the book's index. Use of a white flag is a part of LOAC, since the white flag is a recognized symbol of truce and displaying one indicates a desire to communicate with the opposing forces. Since what will be discussed is usually the surrender of the forces displaying it, the white flag is commonly thought of solely in those terms, but it can in fact be used for other purposes. On some occasions during the trench warfare of World War I, for example, white flags were used to organize a temporary cease-fire, during which the dead in the no-man's-land between the trenches could be collected and buried.

Given that the white flag is a recognized emblem in LOAC, it is not surprising that there are clauses in international law that discuss the use and misuse of the white flag. Article 37 of Additional Protocol I, for example,[6] states that "It is prohibited to kill, injure or capture an adversary by resort to perfidy." In simple terms, perfidy in armed conflict means acting in a way that deceives your adversary into believing that you are entitled to special protection under LOAC while intending to use that deception for military advantage. This law does draw a distinction between ruses and perfidy; ruses are allowed but perfidy is not. The distinction here is that ruses are intended to mislead an enemy or encourage that enemy to act recklessly but do not do so by undermining the ideas of special protection, which form part of LOAC. Thus camouflage, decoys, dummy attacks, misinformation, and so on are all ruses and are a legitimate part of war, whereas attacking someone while you are waving a white flag is an example of perfidy.

One of the problems that can arise with regard to surrender in modern conflicts relates fairly directly to the fact that surrender is not an explicit part of international law. What this means, in effect, is that the specific ideas and traditions related to who may surrender and how they may do it may vary in some significant respects depending on where the conflict occurs and who is actually involved in that conflict. Of particular significance in this respect is the fact that the traditions about the process of surrender vary significantly between land, sea, and air forces.

CASE STUDY 10.2

White Flags in Desert Storm

The following events occurred during the 1991 Gulf War (Case 4.1).

Ground: "There were few examples of perfidious practices during the Persian Gulf War. The most publicized were those associated with the battle of Ras Al-Khafji, which began on 29 January. As that battle began, Iraqi tanks entered Ras Al-Khafji with their turrets reversed, turning their guns forward only at the moment action began between Iraqi and Coalition forces. While there was some media speculation that this was an act of perfidy, it was not; a reversed turret is not a recognized indication of surrender per se....However, individual acts of perfidy did occur. On one occasion, Iraqi soldiers waved a white flag and laid down their weapons. When a Saudi Arabian patrol advanced to accept their surrender, it was fired upon by Iraqi forces hidden in buildings on either side of the street. During the same battle, an Iraqi officer approached Coalition forces with his hands in the air, indicating his intention to surrender. When near his would-be captors, he drew a concealed pistol from his boot, fired, and was killed during the combat that followed."

Sea: The Commanding Officer (CO) of a United States guided missile frigate, the USS *Nicholas* (FFG 47) was in charge of a surface action group (SAG) that consisted of the *Nicholas* and several Kuwaiti Navy ships. They were dispatched to a position amid offshore oil platforms in the northern Gulf and ordered to conduct offensive operations against any Iraqi units that may be in vicinity. The CO received information that suggested that some of the oil platforms, which had been abandoned during the war, may have been occupied by Iraqi troops, and he sent helicopters to investigate.

Approaching the platforms to as close as a hundred yards at a 150-foot altitude, the helicopters were not fired upon and their crews were able to observe 23mm anti-aircraft batteries on the top decks of several platforms, ammunition cases next to the guns, personnel in green fatigues standing around on the platforms, sandbagged bunkers and wooden personnel shelters, Zodiac (rubber) boats, diving gear and communications antennas. They also observed two persons on two separate platforms waving white cloths. These observations were reported to the ship, where they were reported to the CO and logged in the Tactical Action Officer's (TAO) log. The log entries included the reports that the helicopter personnel had observed personnel waving "white flags" on two platforms. At no time did the helicopters observe any hostile acts, the manning or training of any weapons, or receive any fire, even though they were very close to the Iraqis and clearly visible, and thus extremely vulnerable.[7]

The CO later testified that he did not believe that the white flags indicated a general intention to surrender being expressed by all personnel on board the oil platforms. He also stated that he had been informed by the Kuwait personnel that Iraqi forces had used white flags as a ruse during the Iran-Iraq war (1980–1988). After dark, the SAG launched a 3-hour-long attack on the platforms using missiles, rockets, and gunfire. After the engagement, helicopters from the *Nicholas* conducted a battle damage assessment, during which they observed survivors in a rubber boat. This boat was located by the *Nicholas* and taken on board, and the Iraqi personnel were taken into custody. During processing, one of the Iraqis asked, through an interpreter, why the ship had fired on them when they had tried to surrender. Subsequent investigation of the platforms by Navy special operations teams encountered no resistance, but did uncover large stocks of weapons and communications equipment. Five Iraqi soldiers had been killed in the previous day's attacks, and 23 were taken prisoner.

Air: A large Iraqi convoy (of 2–4 miles in length) was attacked while retreating at night along the road from Kuwait City to Basra. F-15E Strike Eagles bottled up the convoy by destroying large vehicles at the front and back of the convoy as they passed through specific choke points, and general attacks on the convoy were ordered as day broke. A large number of Air Force, Marine, and Navy aircraft of different types attacked and strafed this "target rich environment" of stopped and slow moving trucks, tanks, and civilian vehicles. Reports indicated that some Iraqis were waving white flags along the highway, but some pilots reported coming under antiaircraft fire, apparently directed and coordinated from within the convoy. White flags were thus ignored and attacks continued throughout the day.

SOURCES: *Ground:* U.S. Department of Defense, "Final Report to Congress: Conduct of the Persian Gulf War," Appendix O, The Role of the Law of War, April 10, 1992, p. 632. *Sea:* Based on the description of events in Rear Admiral Horace B Robertson, Jr., "The Obligation to Accept Surrender," *Naval War College Review* 46(Spring 1993), pp. 103–115. *Air:* Based on Martin L. Cook & Phillip A. Hamann, "The Road to Basra" in W. Rick Rubel & George R. Lucas (eds.), *Case Studies in Ethics for Military Leaders*, 3rd ed. (New York: Pearson Custom Publishing, 2009), pp. 83–92.

A person waving a white flag is entitled to special protection, as is a person or a vehicle that displays one of the symbols used by medical or religious personnel, that is, the Red Cross, Red Crescent, or Red Crystal. While displaying any of these symbols when you are not entitled to use them is a violation of international law; Article 37 discusses the specific offence (which is considered a grave breach of LOAC) of using them to gain a military advantage and kill, injure, or capture enemy personnel in the process. The reason that perfidy is seen to be so serious is that it undermines the protection of those who are legitimately entitled to that protection. In Case 10.2 (White Flags in Desert Storm), the CO of the *Nicholas* said that he had been told by the Kuwaiti officers under his command that Iraqi troops had used white flags as a ruse during the Iran-Iraq war. In fact, as is also noted in Case 10.2, similar Iraqi attacks allegedly occurred in this conflict as well, this time involving the Saudi Arabian forces. If Iraqi forces had acted in this manner, then opposing forces would be much less likely to believe that the display of a white flag represented a legitimate desire to negotiate and/or surrender, which means that Iraqi troops who were expressing a genuine desire to surrender were less likely to be taken seriously and thus they could have been killed, despite their desire to stop fighting and give themselves up.

A similar allegation, of misuse of the internationally recognized symbols of protection, was made by Israel, during investigations of alleged war crimes committed in the Gaza War (Cases 5.1: Operation Cast Lead and 8.1: Casualties in the 2008–2009 Gaza War). Israel claimed that Hamas had used ambulances to transport fighters, and even had some fighters dressed in medical clothing to drive those ambulances.[8] If this did indeed occur, then it would make it more likely that attacks would be launched against medical personnel and vehicles that were involved in legitimate medical operations and therefore ought to be protected.

One particular example in Case 10.2 (White Flags in Desert Storm), which has been much discussed, is that of the Iraqi tanks entering the battle of Ras Al-Khafji with their turrets reversed, then turning them at the last moment and opening fire. Such a situation probably illustrates one of the limits of language inherent in LOAC. As I mentioned earlier, perfidy is prohibited according to Article 37 of Additional Protocol I. That article provides several examples of perfidy, the first of which is "The feigning of an intent to negotiate under a flag of truce or of a surrender." Since a "flag of truce" (i.e., a white flag) is defined in LOAC, misuse of such a flag is easily recognized. However, as was also mentioned earlier, there is no official and internationally recognized means of conveying the message that one wishes to surrender. So if a person is apparently trying to surrender, and then engages in an attack while doing so, it can be very difficult to prove that this action actually counts as perfidy unless that person has misused a white flag in the process. There are various actions a person can take that have been generally accepted as indications of a desire to surrender, but such actions aren't actually defined in LOAC as signs of surrender. Since approaching the enemy with reversed turrets was a traditionally accepted sign of surrender, we can certainly say that it is ethically wrong for Iraqi tanks to enter a battle with turrets reversed and then for them to turn their turrets and open fire at the last moment, but it is much more difficult to claim that this is actually an example of perfidy.

In fact, the same can probably be said about another example in the "ground" section of Case 10.2 (White Flags in Desert Storm). It is claimed that the Iraqi officer who approached Coalition forces with his hands in the air and then drew a concealed weapon and opened fire had engaged in perfidy. Granted, approaching the enemy with your hands in the air is a traditional method of indicating a desire to surrender, much more widely accepted than tanks entering a battle with their turrets reversed (probably because surrendering soldiers have been a part of conflict for a lot longer than surrendering tanks have). But since LOAC doesn't actually say that this action **always** represents surrender, what the Iraqi officer did in this case is obviously ethically wrong, but still may not actually constitute perfidy.

In the "sea" section of Case 10.2, although the CO of the *Nicholas* may have been told that Iraqi troops had used white flags inappropriately in the past—and to be clear, in terms of international law, if Iraqi troops used white flags in the manner the Kuwaiti officers seemed to be suggesting, then this would have been perfidy, not a ruse—when this incident came before a U.S. Naval Board of Inquiry, it became clear that this was only one reason why he had chosen to ignore the white flags that were being waved by some individuals on board the oil platforms.[9] In land warfare, individual surrender is a possibility, so if it is apparent that some individuals in an enemy unit are making a genuine attempt to surrender while others in the same unit wish to continue fighting, then those who are engaged in combat with that unit have a legal and ethical obligation to treat the two groups differently. Thus, although it is perfectly reasonable to continue firing at those who are continuing to fight, it would be wrong to target the soldiers who are making a genuine attempt to surrender.

In combat at sea the circumstances are rather different. At sea, the traditional signal that a ship wishes to surrender is the striking of the colors, though raising a white flag could clearly serve as an alternative to this. However, in the context of any normal naval battle, it is clearly impractical to accept the surrender of some members of an opposing ship's company, but to continue fighting against others. Therefore, the tradition at sea has been that the entire vessel must surrender and thus that an offer of surrender can only be accepted if it carries the authority of the commander of the vessel. Thus, in the situation faced by the *Nicholas* in Case 10.2 (White Flags in Desert Storm), under the laws of naval warfare the CO was not legally obliged to accept the surrender of individual Iraqi soldiers, even though he would have been if the engagement had been occurring on land. Whether the CO's actions were ethically appropriate or not is another matter, a point to which I will return shortly.

In aerial warfare the situation is different again. Given the obvious practical difficulties involved with one aircraft accepting the surrender of another in midair, in traditional aerial dogfights surrender was essentially a non-issue. In such cases it was common for attacks against a particular aircraft, even an extensively damaged one, to continue until either it became clear that the aircraft was too badly damaged to stay aloft, or the pilot and crew bailed out. However, as was noted in connection with Case 2.4 (Shooting the Downed Pilot), those parachuting from an aircraft in distress are not considered legitimate targets and in modern times such people are considered to be *hors de combat* under LOAC. In terms of modern air-to-air combat, surrender is probably even less of an issue, since these days enemy aircraft are usually engaged from beyond visual range and thus, once combat has commenced, surrender is virtually impossible. But the situation described in the latter part of Case 10.2 (White Flags in Desert Storm) does demonstrate that issues of surrender can arise when aircraft engage opposing ground forces and thus illustrates one of the other problems that can arise with regard to surrender.

In modern warfare combat at a distance is obviously extremely common; aerial and/or long-range bombardment of targets is routine in such conflicts and forces that are attacked in this way, like the Iraqi forces on the road to Basra in Case 10.2, might well have had enough of the conflict and express a desire to surrender. In some respects this situation represents the general case of land warfare, where some opposing forces wish to surrender and others wish to keep on fighting, since while some Iraqi soldiers were waving white flags, the U.S. aircraft were apparently also being attacked by antiaircraft fire from other Iraqi personnel in the convoy. Thus, the standard response would be to direct attacks against the enemy personnel who were continuing to fight and not targeting those attempting to surrender.

But there is a further problem here in terms of international law, since legally, surrender is only a practical proposition if there is someone to surrender to. The Iraqi soldiers who wished to surrender waved white flags at the aircraft attacking the convoy, but for the surrender to be completed these personnel needed to hand over their weapons and be taken into custody by U.S. or allied personnel. Since the attack on the convoy was exclusively an air attack and there were no U.S. or allied ground forces involved, there was no way that these Iraqi soldiers could be taken into custody. In such circumstances it was seen to be legal to allow the attacks on the convoy to continue, despite the white flags that were being waved. Again, whether this is ethical is another matter. By this standard, as long as there were no ground forces nearby who could formally accept the surrender of these Iraqi troops, it would apparently be legal to continue attacks on the convoy even if **all** the enemy personnel in the convoy were waving white flags. But even if this would be legal, it certainly would not be ethical to continue to attack enemy forces who have clearly indicated their desire to surrender, and thus are no longer part of the enemy's attempt to harm.

Attacking enemy forces who are simply in retreat is both legal and ethical, since such forces might well be retreating to better defensive positions where they can regroup and continue the battle. But the situation on the road from Kuwait City to Basra does seem to represent a rather different sort of situation from launching attacks against enemy military forces retreating to better defensive positions. Admittedly, there was some antiaircraft fire coming from within the convoy, but it seems that most of the Iraqi military personnel here had no desire to continue fighting. Thus, the first problem here is one of discrimination. Although pilots attacking this convoy could attempt to direct attacks away from those personnel waving white flags, given the speed at which the planes would be travelling when attacking the convoy and the difficulties of making out details on the ground at those speeds, continuing to attack in this case will inevitably mean that some, perhaps many, Iraqi personnel will be killed while trying to express their desire to surrender. In this particular case, an additional ethical question that can be raised is whether the attacks made against this convoy were actually proportionate, as is ethically required by *jus in bello*. Destroying the tanks and larger pieces of military equipment certainly seems reasonable. However, the overall proportionality of the attacks on the convoy is rather more problematic, given the huge number of aerial attacks made over the course of the day, coupled with the fact that many of these attacks were directed not against tanks and artillery pieces, but against largely defenseless Iraqi military personnel either on the ground or in civilian vehicles. Overall, the legality of the attacks is really not an issue, but the ethical questions remain.

CASE STUDY 10.3

After the Battle

Perhaps one of the most dangerous tasks in modern warfare is conducting "battlefield clearances": checking over enemy dead and wounded after the engagement. In a number of conflicts, those engaged in such tasks have found themselves in peril as a result of the actions of the enemy. Injured enemy combatants may still be armed and willing to defend themselves, and uninjured enemy personnel may be hiding among the dead and injured, waiting to shoot once their attackers have exposed themselves, by leaving cover to move forward and conduct clearances. In some cases, dead bodies may even be booby trapped.

The dangers posed to those conducting battlefield clearances have led to a number of responses. In the Vietnam War, for example, after all the shooting had finished at the end of a fire fight, some American units would toss grenades at enemy positions and at groups of enemy bodies before conducting battlefield clearances to protect themselves from Vietnamese fighters, wounded or not, who might be waiting to open fire again as soon as the American troops broke cover.

Some coalition units in Iraq in 2003, after having on several occasions taken fire from Iraqi troops who were feigning death, almost routinely engaged, that is, shot, any visible enemy bodies with coaxial machine gun fire. Ground units in the same campaign, after dealing with a number of similar cases, as well as booby-trapped bodies, apparently sometimes adopted a "shoot first, examine later" policy, whereby any enemy combatant who appeared to be feigning death was likely to be shot without warning. This may or may not be what happened in the famous television footage, shot by embedded journalist Kevin Sites, which shows a U.S. Marine shooting an apparently unarmed and injured enemy combatant in November, 2004 (Case 7.2: The Incident at the Fallujah Mosque).

Situations such as those in Case 10.3 do reveal some tensions in the laws of war. From the perspective of the "defender," it is clearly deceptive to encourage your enemy to break cover by acting in a manner that suggests that you are injured or dead and thus unable to continue the fight, but whether it is illegal or not depends on how it is actually done. Simply ceasing fire and allowing your enemy to assume from this that you are dead is certainly legal and is considered to be a legitimate military ruse, but it is considered to be perfidy to kill or injure an enemy by actively feigning a severe wound and then attacking again when your enemy approaches. The situation with regard to booby traps is similar, for although the use of booby traps is legal under international law, attaching such devices to dead bodies is a war crime.From the perspective of the "attacker," knowing that the enemy may well engage in deceptive conduct to encourage you to lower your guard means that you are quite justified in taking legitimate steps to protect yourself against the effects of such deceptive actions. However, it is clear that international law requires that those who are *hors de combat* (i.e., incapable of performing their military function), such as those who are wounded to the point where they are unable to continue the fight, be protected from harm, and it is a serious offense under international law to engage in violence against such persons.

One of the main concerns of LOAC is to limit the death and destruction of war to what is actually necessary from a military perspective. It is this idea that has led to things like bans on weapons that cause superfluous injury; indiscriminate attacks; attacks against those who do not pose a threat, such as civilians; and attacks directed against those who were formerly considered combatants, but are now considered noncombatants because they no longer pose a threat. This includes people who are already in custody; making a genuine attempt to surrender; parachuting from an aircraft in distress; adrift in lifeboats having been shipwrecked; and unable to defend themselves from attack because of sickness, injury, or unconsciousness.

Some of the actions taken by the military personnel in Case 10.2 (White Flags in Desert Storm) are somewhat problematic with regard to this ban on attacks against those who are no longer a threat. The attack by the *Nicholas* against Iraqi-held oil platforms may have been legal under the law of naval warfare, but also appears to be an attack against those who were making a genuine attempt to surrender. The air attacks against the Iraqis on the road to Basra in the same war might also be thought to fit into the same category. While a lawyer might perhaps argue that the Iraqis were not making a "genuine attempt to surrender" given that they were waving a white flag at aircraft that could not possibly take them into custody, at the same time it could be argued that this attempt to surrender really can't be considered to be a false attempt, unless the Iraqis actually knew there were no allied ground forces in the area who could accept their surrender.

One thing the various situations discussed in Case 10.2 (White Flags in Desert Storm) do illustrate is the way questions of law can become divorced from questions of ethics. Consider the "sea" section of the case, for example. The CO of the *Nicholas* may well have been correct in asserting that the law of naval warfare did not require him to accept the surrender of the Iraqi forces on the oil platforms, but it is also clear that the situation was not a run-of-the-mill naval battle. While the CO of the *Nicholas* had been warned that Iraqi forces had used white flags inappropriately in the past, there was no evidence to suggest that was also happening in this case; the Iraqis did not, for example, wave a white flag to encourage the U.S. helicopters to approach and then open fire on those helicopters, despite the helicopters being only a hundred yards away at a 150-foot altitude. The information provided to the CO by those helicopter crews also stated that the Iraqi military personnel who were manning the oil platforms were wearing green fatigues, which suggests that these Iraqis may have been Army, rather than Navy, personnel and thus may have been unaware of the requirements of naval law with regard to surrender. After all, waving a white flag at an approaching helicopter would be a perfectly normal means for land forces to indicate that they wished to surrender.

Given these various factors, although the CO of the *Nicholas* might have no legal obligation to accept this offer of surrender, it does seem that he at least has an ethical obligation to investigate whether or not this is actually a genuine offer of surrender. It could be argued that there is no way of doing this without exposing those under his command to some risk, but a "no risk" standard is simply not a reasonable one to apply here. The appropriate question to ask is whether this offer of surrender can be explored in more depth without exposing U.S. and allied military personnel to undue risk. There do seem to be several ways in which that could be done, the simplest of which would probably be to send one of the helicopters back to the oil platforms with one of Kuwaiti officers on board, equipped with a load-hailer. If, for example, the Iraqi personnel obeyed an instruction to drop their weapons into the ocean and take to the water in the Zodiac rubber boats, then it would be reasonable to assume that this was a genuine attempt to surrender. As was mentioned earlier, after the conclusion of hostilities in the Gulf War, the CO of the *Nicholas* faced a board of inquiry about his handling of the incident. Although the purpose of the investigation was to determine whether or not the CO's actions were legal, the findings of the board clearly articulate some of the ethical concerns I have raised here:

> The board concluded that the CO's decision, made in the fog of battle and under difficult conditions at the beginning of combat operations when the attitude of enemy forces toward surrender was unknown, was tactically sound and did not violate the law of armed conflict. It found further, however, that he should have investigated further and discussed his evaluation of the white flags with the XO and key officers, that he should have reported this significant event to his superiors, and that his failure to take these actions represented a serious lapse of judgment. An endorsing senior also faulted other officers of the command who had direct knowledge of the display of white flags for failing to come forward with their advice and concerns.[10]

There is no general requirement, either in military law or even in military ethics, that enemy personnel be given specific opportunity to surrender before they are attacked. But when those personnel have apparently taken some steps in the direction of surrendering, then there does seem to be an ethical requirement to investigate those attempts and give those persons a genuine opportunity to surrender, even if there is no legal requirement to do so in some cases.

At least some of the actions taken by military personnel in Case 10.3 (After the Battle) are also rather questionable. The actions of the American units in Vietnam can plausibly be defended through the doctrine of double effect.[11] Their intention in throwing grenades at enemy positions and groups of enemy bodies at the conclusion of a fire fight was to protect themselves from Vietnamese soldiers who were still able to fight, yet it was clearly foreseeable that this would result in the deaths of some enemy soldiers who were legitimately *hors de combat* and who were thus entitled to special protection under LOAC. This same defense is not so readily available to the troops who engaged enemy bodies with coaxial machine gun fire in Iraq in 2003, since the intention here was not to deal with Iraqi soldiers who might be concealed near the dead bodies but rather to make sure that all the apparently dead bodies were indeed dead. Acting in this way inevitably meant that they would be shooting and killing some Iraqis who had been wounded and were now unable to defend themselves.

Although many things may be breaches of LOAC, not all of them are considered to be equally serious. The most serious offenses are "grave breaches of LOAC," commonly known as war crimes, and are those offenses committed against people who do not represent a threat to military personnel. Thus killing, torturing, or otherwise causing suffering to POWs, civilians, or the sick and wounded are all considered grave breaches of LOAC, and so is "denial of quarter": killing or wounding an enemy who is unable to fight due to sickness or wounds or one who is making a genuine offer of surrender. People involved in any of these types of war crimes are considered to be personally responsible for their actions in such cases. The idea that people are personally responsible for their actions if they are involved in war crimes is in marked contrast to the situation of those who are involved in legitimate acts of war. This is reflected in LOAC, which makes it clear that as long as military personnel fight in accordance with the laws of war they are not to be held personally responsible for their actions, no matter who many enemy combatants they may have killed. The section of LOAC that most obviously reflects this idea is that dealing with what happens to combatants who fall into the hands of the enemy.

PRISONERS OF WAR

A POW is a combatant who has been captured by an enemy power during or immediately after an armed conflict and is thereby entitled to certain protections under LOAC, specifically through Geneva Convention III (GCIII). Only legitimate combatants, plus a few other specific categories of people, are actually entitled to be classified as POWs; all other people are classified as civilians and thus fall under the coverage of Geneva Convention IV (GCIV). The designation of someone as a POW is important for various reasons. It is important for those who qualify as POWs because of the protections to which they are entitled by virtue of the designation, but more than that, it is important in principle because the protections that are accorded to POWs make it clear that such people are not considered to be criminals and thus are not personally responsible for the actions they have taken during the conflict.

Article 4 of GC III specifies who is entitled to be treated as a POW. The list of such people is quite lengthy and includes members of the armed forces of parties to the conflict; members of militia or resistance movements; civilians in noncombat support roles who carry military identification cards; inhabitants of invaded territories who take up arms upon approach of the enemy; members of the merchant marine of parties to the conflict; and so on. Importantly, to qualify for POW status, people who are members of some of these less well-defined groups, such as militia or resistance movements or inhabitants of invaded territories, must carry their arms openly and act in accordance with the principles of LOAC. Whether a person is a POW or not, once they are taken into military custody they are considered to be a protected person, thus any person in military custody may be not be attacked unless they engage in a hostile act or attempt to escape.

The articles of GCIII contain an exhaustive list of the rights held by those designated as POWs and of the protections to which they are entitled. Among the less well-known parts of the convention are discussions of the work that POWs may and may not do; differences in the treatment of commissioned and noncommissioned officers; the payment and allowances that the detaining power ought to give to POWs; the amount that POWs must be paid for any labor they undertake outside a POW camp; the amount of rest that POWs who labor outside a POW camp are entitled to each day; and so on. In fact, the list of rights and protections enumerated in GCIII is so voluminous, that it apparently leads some people, including many of my former students, to wonder whether the whole convention is ridiculous.

However, the fundamental ethical idea that is expressed in the convention is that those who qualify for POW status must be humanely treated and protected from harm. Specifically, POWs must be adequately fed and accommodated, may not be tortured for information, may refuse to answer any questions beyond those required for basic identification, and will be repatriated as soon as is practicable after the end of hostilities. What this makes clear is that someone who qualifies as a POW is being detained, not because they have done anything criminally wrong, but simply so that they cannot resume fighting in the conflict. This distinction is clearest when considering the differences in the way in which a soldier and a murderer are treated after being taken into custody.

```
┌──────────════════════        CASE STUDY 10.4      ════════════──────────┐
```

The Sniper and the Murderer

The states of Aydania and Bedania are at war. Albert is a trained sniper in the Aydanian army whose unit is defending a vital bridge that Bedanian troops are attempting to capture. The rest of the members of Albert's unit are killed, but Albert continues to fight, killing three Bedanian soldiers and wounding five others before he is finally captured after being knocked unconscious by the explosion of a rocket-propelled grenade. After his capture, Albert is interned as a POW until the conflict ends. He is then repatriated back to Aydania as part of an end of war POW exchange, which also sees Bedanian POWs returned to Bedania.

Charlie is an Aydanian citizen who has recently moved to take up residence in the capital city of Bedania. When the war breaks out, Charlie arms himself with a rifle, takes up a position at the window of his flat, and starts to shoot at Bedanian men walking past in the street. Charlie kills three men and wounds five others before running out of ammunition, at which point Bedanian police officers storm into his flat and arrest him. Charlie is charged with three counts of murder and five of attempted murder, found guilty, and sentenced to life imprisonment.

```
└─────────════════════════════════════════════════════════════─────────┘
```

Albert and Charlie have killed and wounded exactly the same number of people. How can the differences in their treatment be ethically justified? The essential difference between the two situations is that Albert has engaged in a legitimate act of war and Charlie has not. Charlie has acted on his own initiative and not on behalf of the state of Aydania, and has targeted people who not only pose no threat to him, but are also unable to defend themselves. Albert, on the other hand, has only targeted enemy combatants, who are, in the terms used in Chapter 7, part of the enemy's attempt to harm; they are also able to defend themselves against Albert's attack. Bearing in mind the distinction between *jus ad bellum* and *jus in bello*, whether Aydania's war on Bedania is just or not, as a legitimate combatant in that war, Albert is not considered to be personally responsible for his actions, even though he has killed exactly the same number of Bedanian men as Charlie.

It can certainly be the case, particularly in the middle of an ongoing conflict, that people question why POWs ought to be treated in such a manner and why the principles outlined in GCIII ought to be followed. There are two main arguments for treating POWs in a special manner, the first simply being the argument I have already outlined, that since legitimate combatants are not personally responsible for their actions, once they are no longer a threat and have been taken into custody they should simply be interned in a manner that respects their fundamental human rights but does not allow them to return to combat. The second argument for according special treatment to POWs is a consequentialist one. This argument suggests that enemy POWs ought to be treated in accordance with the provisions of GCIII because this increases the likelihood that the enemy will do the same with POWs they capture, and there are historical examples which tend to bear this out. In World War II, for example, German and Italian POWs captured by the British Commonwealth and the United States were generally treated in accordance with the provisions of the Geneva Convention of 1929,[12] and POWs from the British Commonwealth, the United States, and France were treated similarly by their German and Italian captors; the vast majority of these POWs were repatriated back to their home countries at the end of the war. In contrast, German POWs captured by the Soviet Union were treated poorly, as were Soviet POWs captured by the Germans, and the death rate among these POWs was massively higher than among the POWs captured in the course of combat in other parts of the European Theatre in World War II. In fact, as the end of the war approached, and it became obvious to everyone that Germany was going to be utterly defeated, many German units attempted to maneuver themselves away from the approaching armies of the Soviet Union and into the path of advancing U.S. and British forces, with entire German divisions surrendering to the British and Americans. Yet at the same time, German units that still faced Soviet forces tended to fight fiercely, since they knew how they would be treated if captured by the U.S.S.R..

While enemy combatants who are entitled to POW status are commonly captured by military personnel during combat operations, they are certainly not the only people who might be taken into custody. Dealing with those who are not POWs, and in many cases are not even combatants, brings a range of other ethical problems for military personnel. Depending on the circumstances, those taken into custody might be combatants whose entitlement to POW status is questionable, such as insurgents; noncombatants who are hostile, or potentially hostile, to the military personnel; noncombatants who need to be taken into custody for their own protection; noncombatants requiring medical care; and so on. The issue that the Navy SEALs in Case 10.1 (Operation Red Wings) had to deal with was that the people they took into custody were clearly noncombatants; the three goat herders were simply going about their daily lives when they stumbled on the SEAL team's position. Given the firepower that was apparently available to Ahmad Shah, merely possessing the information that the SEALs were in the area meant that the goat herders were a potential threat to the lives of the SEALs. So how could they deal appropriately with the noncombatants they had taken into custody?

When discussing what ought to be done with the goat herders, Axelson claimed that "We're not murderers. No matter what we do. We're on active duty behind enemy lines, sent here by our senior commanders. We have the right to do everything we can to save our own lives."[13] In terms of LOAC, this claim is clearly false, for a number of reasons. The goat herders who they had taken into custody were clearly civilians and civilians are always entitled to protection under GCIV. Even if the goat herders were combatants, it would still be illegal to execute them once they had been taken into custody and had ceased to be a direct threat. This applies even in the unusual circumstances faced by the SEALs. Article 41(3) of Additional Protocol I notes that

> When persons entitled to protection as prisoners of war have fallen into the power of an adverse Party under unusual conditions of combat which prevent their evacuation as provided for in Part III, Section I, of the Third Convention, they shall be released and all feasible precautions shall be taken to ensure their safety.

It is true that the United States has not ratified Protocol I, but this clause is still part of customary international law. Indeed, if there was any doubt about whether U.S. personnel are bound by that clause, such doubt ought to be dispelled by the following statement, found in the U.S. Army Field Manual on the Law of Land Warfare:

> A commander may not put his prisoners to death because their presence retards his movements or diminishes his power of resistance by necessitating a large guard, or by reason of their consuming supplies, or because it appears certain that they will regain their liberty through the impending success of their forces. It is likewise unlawful for a commander to kill his prisoners on grounds of self-preservation, **even in the case of airborne or commando operations**, although the circumstances of the operation may make necessary rigorous supervision of and restraint upon the movement of prisoners of war.[14]

In ordinary circumstances enemy combatants can be killed, but once an enemy combatant has been taken into custody that person is no longer a direct threat and thus they can no longer be targeted unless they engage in a hostile act or attempt to escape. Since noncombatants are not a threat they can never be directly targeted. Once military personnel have taken someone into custody they are responsible for the welfare of that person, thus it will never be acceptable to simply kill someone who has been taken into military custody. The goat herders in Case 10.1 (Operation Red Wings), being both noncombatants and persons in military custody, can to some degree be thought of as doubly protected. They certainly could not be killed by the SEALs because of something they might do if they were released.

But perhaps a person might argue that this is a situation where law and ethics do not coincide and it is actually ethically appropriate to break the law. I have noted earlier in the book that such situations can occur, but it is very difficult to argue that this is one of them. The first thing to recognize is that it is essentially impossible to argue that it is appropriate to violate LOAC on the grounds of military necessity, because such considerations have already been incorporated into LOAC. The principle of military necessity is one of things taken into account when the treaties that make up LOAC are drafted, and any clauses which need to be modified due to this principle will be re-drafted long before a treaty gets to the stage of being signed, let alone ratified. So to argue that a given situation is one where it is appropriate to violate the law, it would either need to be the case that the particular situation being discussed was one that was not considered when the law was being written, or that the circumstances were so unusual that the law could not take them into account. It is fairly clear that neither of these things apply in Case 10.1. The U.S. Army Field Manual clearly says that "It is likewise unlawful for a commander to kill his prisoners on grounds of self-preservation, even in the case of airborne or commando operations."[15] If the law already specifies what cannot be done in a situation identical to that in Case 10.1, then the SEALs in that case clearly could not argue that the situation they faced was so unusual that it had not been considered when the law was written, or that the circumstances they faced were so unusual that the law did not apply. In a case like this, law and ethics quite obviously **do** coincide. In a situation like this, killing the goat herders is murder, whether or not this is necessary to save the lives of the SEALs.

The status of the goat herders could be seen by some as somewhat problematic, because despite being noncombatants who did not pose a direct threat, if released they could take actions that could potentially threaten the lives of the SEALs. Yet the legal status of these goat herders was really never in doubt. However, in some cases the legal status of people taken into military custody can be much more questionable. For example, after the attacks on September 11, 2001, the United States government claimed that those who were engaged in military or military-like activities against the United States and who did not fall into the category of POWs, should be defined as "illegal enemy combatants" who are thus entitled to neither the protections given to POWs or to the protections given to common criminals. This definition of unlawful combatants is extremely controversial and is at odds with claims such as that expressed by the International Committee of the Red Cross (ICRC):

> Every person in enemy hands must have some status under international law: he is either a prisoner of war and, as such, covered by the Third Convention, a civilian covered by the Fourth Convention, [or] a member of the medical personnel of the armed forces who is covered by the First Convention. **There is** no intermediate status; nobody in enemy hands can fall outside the law.[16]

To be clear, the claim being expressed in the preceding quotation from the ICRC's commentary on GCIV is not that civilians cannot commit offenses in wartime. Rather the claim is that a person must either be entitled to POW status, in which case merely participating in the war is not an offense, or they must be a civilian. If the person is a civilian who is not entitled to participate in the war, then that person will be held to be personally liable for their actions. If they kill an opposing combatant in combat, then they can be criminally charged for that action in a way in which a combatant who is entitled to POW status cannot. Thus, the view that is expressed in the ICRC's commentary is that a person who kills an enemy combatant in combat and then is later captured by that enemy is either (a) entitled to POW status or (b) is a criminal who can thus be charged and dealt with through the courts, but who must be granted the usual rights held by a criminal while going through this process. This is very different from the idea expressed by the U.S. definition of "illegal enemy combatants," since part of the claim within that definition is that such person do not even have the rights that are granted to common criminals. Thus, unlawful combatants, according to the U.S. definition, could be held without trial more or less indefinitely. Of course, the reason why there was, and is, a desire to categorize some people in this way is because of the fact that such people are either considered to be terrorists themselves or associate with terrorists. Thus, to understand whether categorizing these people in this way is at all reasonable, it is necessary to examine what terrorism actually is and when, if ever, it might be thought to be justified.

NOTES

1. Marcus Luttrell with Patrick Robinson, *Lone Survivor: The Eyewitness Account of Operation Redwing and the Lost Heroes of SEAL Team 10* (London: Sphere, 2008), p. 203.
2. Ibid., p. 204.
3. The enormous range in the estimate of the number of fighters the SEALs faced is because of the huge discrepancies between the various sources that describe the battle. In *Lone Survivor* (p. 209), when describing his first sighting of the force that had come to attack them, Luttrell says that when he looked up the hill "Lined along the top were between eighty and a hundred heavily armed Taliban warriors, each one of them with an AK-47 pointing downward. Some were carrying rocket-propelled grenades." He later states that "the two hundred estimate was a lot closer than the eighty minimum we had been advised" (p. 215). However, in "Operation Red Wings: What Really Happened?" *Marine Corps Gazette* 95(2010), 62–67, Ed Darack notes "Shortly after RED WINGS, a number of Marines of 2/3 carefully reviewed Luttrell's after-action report [AAR] and the R&S [reconnaissance and surveillance] team's gear manifest to learn of any recent changes in enemy tactics, techniques, and procedures and, more importantly, to ascertain what additional threats they might face during operations and patrols due to Shah acquiring the SEAL team's gear. In the AAR Luttrell stated that the team was attacked by 20 to 35 ACM [anti-coalition militia]. (Analysis of 2 videos made by Shah, as well as other intelligence, indicated 8 to 10 total, a common ACM team size for this area.) Twenty was the number initially released by CJTF-76 public affairs" (p. 66, explanation of abbreviations added). Other sources also quote differing numbers; the citation for the Medal of Honor awarded to LT Mike Murphy states that he faced 30 to 40 enemies, yet the "summary of action" related to the same decoration states that Murphy and his men faced an "enemy force of more than 50 anti-coalition militia." Darack's estimate seems most reasonable, based as it is on a large amount of intelligence, including aerial and eye witness studies of the battlefield after the fact, some from the men sent in to rescue Luttrell and/or to retrieve the bodies of the American personnel killed

in the action. However, Luttrell was the only person actually involved in the battle to make a report.

4. There are a significant number of international conventions that are taken to be a part of LOAC. Of these the most important are the four Geneva Conventions (GC I–IV; I covers the treatment of sick and wounded on land, II covers the treatment of sick and wounded at sea, III covers the treatment of Prisoners of War, and IV covers the treatment of civilians in time of war). Other conventions considered to be part of LOAC include the three Additional Protocols to the Geneva Conventions and various conventions that prohibit or regulate the use of certain weapons.

5. In some cases, larger groups may actually refuse to surrender unless certain guarantees are given, such as a guarantee the surrendering personnel will be treated according to the requirements of the Geneva Conventions.

6. Protocol Additional to the Geneva Conventions of August 12, 1949, and relating to the Protection of Victims of International Armed Conflicts (Protocol I), June 8, 1977. While some states, such as the United States, Iran, Israel, Pakistan, and Turkey have not ratified Protocol I, the clauses discussed here are accepted to be part of customary international law and thus binding even on those who are not party to this convention.

7. Rear Admiral Horace B Robertson, Jr., "The Obligation to Accept Surrender," *Naval War College Review* 46(Spring 1993), pp. 103–115.pp. 103–104.

8. See Steven Erlanger, "Weighing Crimes and Ethics in the Fog of Urban Warfare," *New York Times,* January 16, 2009.

9. See Robertson, "The Obligation to Accept Surrender," p. 105.

10. Ibid.

11. The doctrine of double effect was examined in Chapter 2, during the discussion of deontological theories of ethics, and also in Chapter 7, in relation to considerations of discrimination and proportionality in terms of collateral damage.

12. This was the convention in force at the time of World War II. It was updated in 1949 along with the earlier conventions, and has been known as GCIII since that time.

13. Luttrell, *Lone Survivor,* p. 203.

14. Clause 85, *United States Army Field Manual 27-10, The Law of Land Warfare,* U.S. Department of the Army, July 18, 1956, as modified by Change No. 1, July 15, 1976. Emphasis added.

15. Ibid.

16. *Commentary on the Geneva Conventions of 12 August 1949: Volume IV, Relative to the Protection of Civilian Persons in Time of War* (Geneva: ICRC 1958), p. 51 (emphasis in original). The International Criminal Tribunal for the Former Yugoslavia explicitly affirmed this principle in its judgment in the 1998 "Celebici" case.

FURTHER READING

Luttrell, Marcus (with Robinson, Patrick). *Lone Survivor: The Eyewitness Account of Operation Redwing and the Lost Heroes of SEAL Team 10* (London: Sphere, 2008).

Robertson, Horace B., Jr. "The Obligation to Accept Surrender." *Naval War College Review* 46(Spring 1993), 103–115.

Walzer, Michael. *Just and Unjust Wars* (New York: Basic, 1977). Chapter 19: "War Crimes: Soldiers and Their Officers."

DISCUSSION QUESTIONS

- Are the Geneva Convention requirements on the treatment of Prisoners of War still relevant to modern conflicts?
- Is it justifiable to claim, as the U.S. government has done, that some prisoners captured in the War on Terror ought to be classified as unlawful combatants, and for people in such a classification to be entitled to neither the protections given to POWs nor to the protections given to common criminals?
- Would it have been ethically appropriate for the SEALs in Operation Red Wings (Case 10.1) to have killed the Afghan goat herders, if they had been certain that the goat herders would inform the local Taliban fighters of the presence of the SEALs if they were released?

11

❧

Supreme Emergency,
Terrorism, and Torture

┌══════════════ CASE STUDY 11.1 ══════════════┐

The Petraeus Letter to the Troops

BACKGROUND In early May 2007, newspapers around the world ran stories reporting the results of a study conducted by the U.S. Mental Health Advisory Team (MHAT) in Iraq in 2006. Between August and October of that year, the MHAT had surveyed 1,320 soldiers and 447 marines involved in Operation Iraqi Freedom, asking questions not only about mental health, but also about character and ethics. The following were some of the results (figures in brackets show the percentage of soldiers [S] and marines [M] who agreed or strongly agreed with the statement).

- All non-combatants should be treated with dignity and respect (S = 47%, M = 38%).
- Torture should be allowed if it will save the life of a Soldier/Marine (S = 41%, M = 44%).
- Torture should be allowed in order to gather important information about insurgents (S = 36%, M = 39%).
- I would risk my own safety to help a non-combatant in danger (S = 25%, M = 24%).
- (I have) insulted/cursed at non-combatants in their presence (S = 28%, M = 30%).
- (I have) damaged/destroyed Iraqi property when it was not necessary (S = 9%, M = 12%).
- (I have) received training that made it clear how I should behave towards non-combatants (S = 86%, M = 87%).
- NCOs and Officers in my unit made it clear not to mistreat non-combatants (S = 71%, M = 67%).
- (I have) encountered ethical situations in Iraq in which I did not know how to respond (S = 28%, M = 31%).

I would report a unit member for:

- Injuring or killing an innocent non-combatant (S = 55%, M = 40%).
- Stealing from a non-combatant (S = 50%, M = 33%).
- Mistreatment of a non-combatant (S = 46%, M = 32%).
- Not following general orders (S = 46%, M = 35%).
- Violating ROEs (S = 47%, M = 34%)
- Unnecessarily destroying private property (S = 43%, M = 30%).

Concerned at the results that had been uncovered, General David Petraeus, the Commander of Multi-National Force-Iraq, sent the following letter to all military personnel under his command:

10 May 2007

Soldiers, Sailors, Airmen, Marines, and Coast Guardsmen serving in Multi-National Force-Iraq:

Our values and the laws governing warfare teach us to respect human dignity, maintain our integrity, and do what is right. Adherence to our values distinguishes us from our enemy. This fight depends on securing the population, which must understand that we—not our enemies—occupy the moral high ground. This strategy has shown results in recent months. Al Qaeda's indiscriminate attacks, for example, have finally started to turn a substantial proportion of the Iraqi population against it. In view of this, I was concerned by the results of a recently released survey conducted last fall in Iraq that revealed an apparent unwillingness on the part of some US personnel to report illegal actions taken by fellow members of their units. The study also indicated that a small percentage of those surveyed may have mistreated noncombatants. This survey should spur reflection on our conduct in combat.

I fully appreciate the emotions that one experiences in Iraq. I also know firsthand the bonds between members of the "brotherhood of the close fight." Seeing a fellow trooper killed by a barbaric enemy can spark frustration, anger, and a desire for immediate revenge. As hard as it might be, however, we must not let these emotions lead us—or our comrades in arms—to commit hasty, illegal actions. In the event that we witness or hear of such actions, we must not let our bonds prevent us from speaking up. Some may argue that we would be more effective if we sanctioned torture or other expedient methods to obtain information from the enemy. They would be wrong. Beyond the basic fact that such actions are illegal, history shows that they also are frequently neither useful nor necessary. Certainly, extreme physical action can make someone "talk;" however, what the individual says may be of questionable value. In fact, our experience in applying the interrogation standards laid out in the Army Field Manual (2-22.3) on *Human Intelligence Collector Operations* that was published last year shows that the techniques in the manual work effectively and humanely in eliciting information from detainees.

We are, indeed, warriors. We train to kill our enemies. We are engaged in combat, we must pursue the enemy relentlessly, and we must be violent at times. What sets us apart from our enemies in this fight, however, is how we behave. In everything we do, we must observe the standards and values that dictate that we treat noncombatants and detainees with dignity and respect. While we are warriors, we are also all human beings. Stress caused by lengthy deployments and combat is not a sign of weakness; it is a sign that we are human. If you feel such stress, do not hesitate to talk to your chain of command, your chaplain, or a medical expert. We should use the survey results to renew our commitment to the values and standards that make us who we are and to spur re-examination of these issues. Leaders, in particular, need to discuss these issues with their troopers—and, as always, they need to set the right example and strive to ensure proper conduct. We should never underestimate the importance of good leadership and the difference it can make.

   Thanks for what you continue to do. It is an honor to serve with each of you.
   David H. Petraeus
   General, United States Army
   Commanding

DISCUSSION

Violence and the fear of violence have been used as tools of politics for a very long time. Many rulers across the world have held power through the use of violence, fear, and intimidation. But although historically such things were weapons used by the strong to maintain order among the masses, in more recent times fear has often been used as a weapon of the weak against the strong. Over the last few decades, things such as plane hijackings, assassinations, hostage taking, rocket attacks, and conventional and suicide bombings have occurred all over the world, often used as a political tactic by members of a relatively powerless group seeking to draw attention to their cause. The rise of mass media, then of the Internet, has brought with it an almost insatiable desire for news stories, particularly in the Western world. This has meant that terrorist attacks directed either against these Western countries, or against their citizens or agencies in other countries, usually garner large amounts of publicity. In many, if not most cases, the resultant publicity is an integral part of the plans of those responsible for the attack, since the publicity aids in spreading the fear of an attack throughout the target population.

   In many states around the world, military personnel are either the targets of terrorist attacks or are an integral part of the counterterrorism measures their governments have put into place to deal with such attacks. Thus a book on military ethics can hardly be considered complete without some discussion of the problems raised by both terrorism and the responses to it.

   Perhaps the most basic issue that must be faced when examining terrorism is in defining what the term means. The actual definition of terrorism has been one of the major stumbling blocks during UN attempts to create a Comprehensive Convention on International Terrorism, with the major area of disagreement between UN member states not about what ought to be included in such a definition but rather about what ought to be **excluded**. One definitional problem area is whether such a convention ought to cover the actions of the armed forces of a state. Some states want to ensure that the actions of armed forces in conflict zones are excluded from such a convention, since such actions are already governed by other conventions, while other states appear keen to ensure that an international convention on terrorism could be used as a further constraint on the actions of a state's armed forces. A second problem area with regard to the coverage of an international convention is with regard to the activities of liberation movements. Some states want to ensure that the actions of national liberation movements would **not** be included in these conventions, particularly in cases where such territory is under foreign occupation.

In the modern world there are literally hundreds of definitions of terrorism, most of which have been deliberately created to include certain types of action and exclude others. For example, consider the following definition, formulated by Asa Kasher and Amos Yadlin:

> An act, carried out by individuals or organizations, not on behalf of any state, for the purpose of killing or otherwise injuring persons, insofar as they are members of a particular population, in order to instil fear among the members of that population ("terrorize" them), so as to cause them to change the nature of the related regime or of the related government or of policies implemented by related institutions, whether for political or ideological (including religious) reasons.[1]

This definition is used by the authors in the context of their discussion on the ethics of military action against terrorism, which I examined in Chapter 8. Kasher and Yadlin clarify two specific points in this definition. In noting that their definition is restricted to individuals or organizations not acting on behalf of a state, they suggest that state-sponsored acts of terror properly fall under the auspices of LOAC and traditional just war theory, and since this type of conflict is not the focus of their paper they deliberately exclude state-sponsored terrorism from their definition.[2] In addition they are quite clear about the fact that according to their definition the targets of acts of terror are persons in general, and not necessarily noncombatants, so it is possible under this definition for all the victims of an act of terror to be combatants, for example, members of a frontline army platoon, and even combatants engaged in direct military activities, such as a combat patrol.

One questionable aspect of this definition, given the insistence that the victims of a terrorist act can be combatants, is the difficulty in drawing any sort of distinction between terrorism, which is almost always deemed to be morally wrong, and guerrilla warfare, which is usually seen to be acceptable. Many of the attacks carried out by resistance fighters in Europe during World War II would seem to fit this definition of terrorism, for these attacks were carried out by members of a non-state organization, directed against members of a particular population, that is, members of the German military and those seen to be collaborating with them, with the clear political aim of disrupting German control and, at least with regard to actions against collaborators, instilling fear. The objectives of guerrilla war can also be the same as the objectives of terrorist activity; indeed it could be argued that the aim of Palestinian activities is to end foreign occupation of their territory, which is the same as the aim of resistance activities in Europe in World War II. The authors claim that there are significant differences between guerrilla warfare and terrorist activity. For example, they suggest that guerrilla warfare is conducted primarily for the purpose of disrupting military activity, and that guerrilla warfare is directed against military targets and military infrastructure. Although they do not make the claim explicitly, it can be presumed that they believe that terrorist acts are not conducted for the same purposes or against the same targets. Thus, they conclude that guerrilla acts are very similar to military acts and so fall under the scope of traditional just war theory, whereas terrorist acts are very different from military acts. However, these differences certainly do not seem to be captured by their definition of a terrorist act.

A rather different approach is taken by Alex Bellamy,[3] who notes that the terms "terrorism" and "terrorist" are not merely descriptive, but have a negative moral connotation. The famous claim that "one man's terrorist is another man's freedom fighter"[4] arises out of the fact that the term "terrorist" has this negative moral connotation; if it did not then no one would object to being called a terrorist. Bellamy thus begins by assuming that terrorism is immoral and then attempts to determine what specific characteristic of terrorism makes it immoral, for if such a feature can be isolated, then this would seem to be a defining feature of terrorism. Bellamy lists four characteristics common to most definitions of terrorism, and notes that most authors will point to one or more of these characteristics when trying to explain why such an action is wrong. The four characteristics are that (1) terrorism is politically motivated violence; (2) terrorism is conducted by non-state actors; (3) terrorism intentionally targets noncombatants; and (4) terrorism achieves its aims by creating fear within societies.[5] Bellamy concludes that it must be the fact that terrorism intentionally targets noncombatants that makes it immoral, since all the other listed factors can be a part of legitimate military activities. Defining terrorism in this way does fit in neatly with just war theory, which would claim that terrorism is wrong because it violates the principle of discrimination. Many other definitions of terrorism also rely on the targeting of noncombatants as a defining factor,[6] so for the rest of this discussion I will use the term in that manner; so in this discussion, "terrorism" can simply be taken as a shorthand term for "the intentional targeting of noncombatants." However, this very definition of terrorism raises one possible problem. It was assumed at the start that terrorism is always immoral, which seems to rule out the possibility of arguing that terrorism might be morally justified in some circumstances. Yet Michael Walzer[7] and writers following in his footsteps, have argued that in cases of supreme emergency it can be legitimate to deliberately target noncombatants.

SUPREME EMERGENCY

The essential idea at the heart of what Walzer calls the supreme emergency doctrine, or as Brian Orend refers to it, the supreme emergency exemption,[8] is that desperate times call for desperate measures. If the situation is dire enough, and the consequences faced are serious enough, then it will be justifiable to act in ways that would normally be prohibited. In concrete terms, what this means is that a state, or perhaps a state-like entity, can ignore the usual standards of *jus in bello* if, and only if, three specific conditions are met. The first condition, and one which can easily be overlooked, is that the state must be the victim of aggression, not the aggressor. The second condition is that the victimized state must be about to be militarily defeated. The third condition is that the consequences of the victim state being defeated are so catastrophic that it is justified to use any means possible to avoid that defeat.[9] In just war terms what this means is that a state with *jus ad bellum* on its side can, in extreme circumstances, ignore at least some of the usual restrictions of *jus in bello*. As Orend notes,[10] this is an idea that pushes the relationship between *jus ad bellum* and *jus in bello* to its limit, and it is certainly not a part of international law.

Although states can, and do, resort to supreme emergency reasoning very easily, the conditions that must be met for this to be ethically justified are actually very stringent. The first condition makes it clear that only a victim of aggression, and not a state that has launched an aggressive war, can ever reasonably claim to be facing a supreme emergency. The second condition, that military defeat must be very near, makes it clear that discarding the *jus in bello* restrictions is an absolute last resort. Thus, it will not be sufficient to have merely suffered some military setbacks or to have lost the initiative in the war. The third condition is the one that is especially important, however. In saying that supreme emergency can only be resorted to if the consequences of losing will be catastrophic, the idea is to limit supreme emergency to cases where it is clear that defeat will lead to enslavement of the population, or widespread massacres of innocent people, or even ethnic cleansing and genocide. If defeat in the war will simply mean that the defeated party will have to make humiliating political concessions, or be forced to pay large reparations (even if these reparations are unjustified), or even if it will result in the loss of political sovereignty for the people of the defeated state, this is not sufficient for supreme emergency to apply. Given the stringency of these conditions it is perhaps not surprising that the only possible example of supreme emergency that Walzer provides is from World War II, when Britain was at war with Nazi Germany.

CASE STUDY 11.2

The Decision to Bomb German Cities

The situation that faced the British Prime Minister, Winston Churchill, in 1940, was extremely serious. Britain stood alone against Germany.[11] In September 1939, Germany had invaded and occupied Poland with support from the USSR, who thus appeared to be a German ally. Denmark and Norway had been conquered in a swift campaign in the spring of 1940, and then France, one of the world's great powers, had been invaded and conquered in only 6 weeks. An invasion of the British Isles was clearly the next German objective, and air attacks aimed at softening up Britain for an invasion had already begun. Importantly, Britain did not merely face the possibility of military defeat, for as Churchill noted, a German victory "would be fatal, not only to ourselves, but to the independent life of every small country in Europe."[12] Walzer is quite clear about how serious such a situation would be:

> Nazism was an ultimate threat to everything decent in our lives, an ideology and a practice of domination so murderous, so degrading even to those who might survive, that the consequences of its final victory were literally beyond calculation, immeasurably awful. We see it—and I don't use the phrase lightly—as evil objectified in the world, and in a form so potent and apparent that there could never have been anything to do but fight against it.[13]

Faced with this situation late in 1940, Churchill authorized the Royal Air Force (RAF) to begin indiscriminate bombing raids on German cities, apparently in the belief that the only way to pursue victory in the war was to take the fight to Germany using the only means at his disposal; RAF Bomber Command. The deliberate targeting of noncombatants, which had previously been forbidden, was now required, and terror bombing became the order of the day.

A situation such as this, according to Walzer, meets the requirements of supreme emergency, for not only was Britain faced with the very real possibility of defeat, but such a defeat would potentially leave all of mainland Europe in the hands of the Nazis. This example has been much discussed and various aspects of it have been criticized. However, it is important to note that although Walzer argues Britain faced a situation of supreme emergency in 1940 and that indiscriminate bombing of German cities was justified, he also makes it quite clear that such a policy can only be justified as long as a supreme emergency exists. Once the U.S.S.R. and the U.S.A. had been drawn into the war against Germany in 1941, and particularly once the Allied powers began to win some victories against the Germans in 1942 and 1943, it is clear that the conditions of supreme emergency no longer hold, and thus the continuation of terror bombing throughout the rest of the war cannot be ethically justified.[14] Both Walzer[15] and Orend[16] are also very clear that the supreme emergency argument cannot be used to justify dropping nuclear weapons on Japan (see Case 2.3: First Use of the Atomic Bomb). The war in Europe was over and Japan, while still resisting the Allies, was certainly not about to win the war. Even if it is true that using nuclear weapons on Japan actually saved lives in the long run, in itself a fairly problematic calculation, it is quite obvious that arguments about supreme emergency have no place in such a discussion.

Orend grapples with the problem of supreme emergencies at length and tries to come up with some coherent strategy for dealing with the problems that such situations raise.[17] He considers whether such situations actually exist in the real world, and, pointing to relatively recent historical examples of groups targeted with genocide, such as the Rwandan Tutsis (see Case 5.5: The Rwandan Genocide), suggests that such situations demonstrate that genuine supreme emergencies can arise.[18] He eventually concludes that those faced with a case of supreme emergency are stuck in a situation where every possible option will involve the violation of an important moral principle. Thus, whatever option is eventually chosen in such a case will require moral wrongdoing. However, he does suggest some rules that ought to be followed to make sure that the situation actually is a supreme emergency, and that resorting to deliberate violations of the rules of *jus in bello* is in fact the best of the bad options available. The rules Orend suggests, which he calls "rules of prudence," are essentially the principles of *jus ad bellum*, but applied in a slightly different context. This should not be surprising; if such rules are required before resorting to a large scale rights-violating activity like war, then it is logical that they should also apply to abandoning the principles of *jus in bello*, which are a limitation on the scale of rights violations within war.

Though he does not couch his discussion in exactly the same terms as are used in *jus ad bellum*, Orend suggests that before abandoning the principles of *jus in bello*, those considering such an action should (a) consider whether this really is a last resort; (b) publicly declare what they intend to do, knowing that this will also serve to; (c) make an appeal to the international community for help; (d) ensure they have the right intention in acting in this manner; and (e) have a reasonable probability of success.[19] As a reminder, the three conditions that need to apply for anyone to be faced with a supreme emergency in the first place are (1) they must be the victim of aggression, (2) facing imminent defeat, and (3) the consequences of that defeat must be catastrophic. If Orend's rules of prudence are combined with these three conditions, it can be seen that they are equivalent to the principles of *jus ad bellum*.

The six principles of *jus ad bellum* and their supreme emergency equivalents are

1. Just cause, equivalent to (1) victim of aggression;
2. right intention, equivalent (obviously) to (d) right intention;
3. last resort, equivalent (obviously) to (a) last resort;
4. public declaration by a legitimate authority, equivalent to (b) public declaration and (c) appeal to the international community;
5. probability of success, equivalent (obviously) to (e) probability of success; and
6. proportionality, equivalent to (3) catastrophic consequences of defeat.

To be clear, if a state is engaged in a just war, then all the conditions of *jus ad bellum* must have been met before the war commenced. So it might seem that the same conditions will inevitably be met when considering the supreme emergency situation. However, there are a number of reasons why this is not actually the case. Some points are the same, certainly, but other principles are being applied to a somewhat different type of situation than when the decision was being made about whether or not to go to war, and further information may well have come to light since the war commenced as well. Consider just a few of these points in relation to the decision Churchill faced in 1940, for example.

With regard to right intention, when the war commenced in 1939 the intention that needed to be considered was about why Britain was going to war. In 1940, when considering whether it is right to order the RAF to engage in indiscriminate bombing of German cities, one thing that needs to be considered, which did not need to be considered in 1939, is whether the intention in giving such an order is simply to exact revenge on the Germans for their terror attacks on British cities. The consideration of last resort is also very different, since in 1939 the issue was whether war was the last reasonable option to prevent Germany's aggressive territorial expansion; but in 1940, the question is whether there are any other options within the context of war, apart from engaging in indiscriminate attacks on German cities, which would aid in the defeat of Germany. The proportionality issue also seems to have changed in a significant way, as the aggressiveness of the German regime has become more apparent, the probability of success that needed to be considered in 1939 was about achieving something by going to war, whereas now it is about whether engaging in terror bombing of German cities will actually help to win the war, or at least stave off defeat, and so on.

If an attack that violates the principles of *jus in bello* meets all these conditions then, and only then, can it be said to be justified under the doctrine of supreme emergency. Thinking in this way about supreme emergency allows a clear analysis of such situations, and probably reveals other options that might be pursued in such cases. Even if the principles of *jus in bello* are to be set aside, there are different ways in which this might be done. For example, Orend points out that rather than engaging in terrorism by deliberately targeting noncombatants, it is possible to set aside other *jus in bello* rules, such as the ban on prohibited weapons, while still aiming at legitimate military targets.[20]

Even in cases where a violation of the principles of *jus in bello* is thought to be justified, if the action which will be taken is not a one-off attack but rather is an ongoing campaign, like in Case 11.2 (The Decision to Bomb German Cities), then it is important that the situation be re-examined at regular, and frequent, intervals. If the conditions of supreme emergency no longer apply, then violations of the principles of *jus in bello* can no longer be justified. Although some aspects of the decision to bomb German cities are ethically problematic even under supreme emergency, what is most ethically abhorrent about the situation is that this terror bombing campaign continued long after the state of supreme emergency had ended.

At this point, some readers are no doubt wondering what all this discussion of supreme emergency has to do with the modern world. Although discussion of supreme emergency may seem to be quite removed from ordinary circumstances, in fact this is not so, since the ideas central to the supreme emergency argument have been used to justify both the use of terrorism by non-state groups and a range of state responses to such terrorism.

SUPREME EMERGENCY AND TERRORISM IN THE MODERN WORLD

Perhaps the clearest argument that has been presented in defense of at least some terrorist activity in the modern world was written by James Sterba, who argued in papers published in 2003[21] and 2005[22] that Palestinian terrorist attacks on Israel can be justified using the supreme emergency argument. The overall argument is much longer than can be presented here, but the main points are reasonably simple.

During 1967, Israel seized control of the Palestinian West Bank from Jordan (see Case 4.4: The Six Day War),[23] and has been illegally occupying that land ever since, in violation of a number of UN resolutions. Since the 1993 Oslo Peace Accords, the number of Israeli settlements in the Occupied Territories has doubled and though Sterba doesn't mention it as part of his argument, the establishment of extensive Jewish settlements in the West Bank since 1967 is also almost universally condemned as a violation of international law. In the West Bank, although Israelis make up only 15% of the population, they control 40% of the land, and 37% of the water. Israel failed to abide by a range of commitments made in the Oslo Peace Accords, such as redeploying of a third of its military forces, and releasing certain Palestinian prisoners. Recent Israeli peace proposals do not discuss either a right of return for Palestinians forced off their land by Israeli expansion, or compensation in lieu of return for such people. Given this evidence, Sterba concludes that the Palestinian cause is a just one, but also notes that the Palestinians do not have the military resources to resist the occupation or fight the Israeli military forces directly, especially given the fact that Israel has access to the most advanced U.S. weapons and receives $4 billion dollars a year from the U.S. to buy them.[24] Sterba's ultimate conclusion is clear:

> Given that the Palestinians lack any effective means to try to end the Israeli occupation or to stop Israel's further expansion into Palestinian territories other than by using suicide bombers against Israeli civilians, why would this use of suicide bombers not be justified in much the same way that Walzer justifies the British terror bombing in the early stages of World War II? If the Israelis have the ultimate goal of confining most Palestinians to a number of economically nonviable and disconnected reservations…then surely the Palestinians have a right to resist that conquest as best they can.[25]

One practical problem with the recourse to supreme emergency reasoning is that it is very easy to assume that since some of the conditions of supreme emergency are met in a particular case, they must all have been. Once a decision to violate the principles of *jus in bello* has been made, it is also very easy to allow that violation to continue long after it is really necessary, as was illustrated by the way in which Britain continued to engage in terror bombing of German cities until virtually the end of World War II. Sterba's argument seems to fall foul of both of these problems.

One possible problem with Sterba's argument is his claim that the Palestinians lacked any effective means to fight against Israel other than engaging in suicide bombings against Israeli civilians. If this claim fails then the whole supreme emergency argument in favor of the use of terrorism by the Palestinians collapses, since even if the Palestinians were being victimized by Israel and the Israeli intention was to limit the Palestinians to "economically nonviable and disconnected reservations," the use of terrorism can only be justified if it actually is a last resort. If Palestinian groups restricted themselves to attacks on Israeli military targets they would still be respecting the principles of *jus in bello*, even if suicide bombings were the mechanism by which such attacks were carried out. This is one point where the importance of one's definition of terrorism become obvious; since they respect the principle of discrimination, suicide attacks against Israeli military targets are not terrorism by the definition I am using in this discussion but such attacks are terrorism according to the definition of Kasher and Yadlin, which was quoted near the beginning of this chapter.[26]

Even if Sterba is correct in concluding that the Palestinian people faced a situation of supreme emergency and thus were justified in engaging in suicide bombings against Israeli civilians, this argument clearly does not apply to the entire period of Israeli occupation. When Israel was negotiating the Oslo Peace Accords with the Palestinians, for example, it is clear that violating the principles of *jus in bello* was not the **only** possible way forward at that time. The situation has been similar at other times during the occupation as well, such as when Israel withdrew from the Gaza Strip. In fact, the refusal of certain Palestinian groups to renounce the use of terrorism has been cited as a barrier to peace in the region by a large number of parties.

SUPREME EMERGENCY AND COUNTERTERRORISM IN THE MODERN WORLD

Counterterrorism is a general term that is used to describe a wide range of activities aimed at the prevention of terrorism, minimization of the effects of a terrorist act, and the prosecution of those involved in terrorist activities. Thus counterterrorist activities may involve law enforcement personnel, military personnel, law makers, experts in international law and finance, medical personnel, espionage services, private military companies, businesses;...the list is virtually endless. Given the range of activities that are thought to fall under the general heading of counterterrorism it is unsurprising that the ethical status of such activities ranges from being totally unproblematic to being extremely dubious. Providing training to medical teams so that they are prepared to deal with the mass casualties resulting from a terrorist attack is an example of a fairly unproblematic activity, whereas widespread torture obviously sits at the other end of the ethical spectrum.

Counterterrorism strategies are generally understood to be more ethically problematic when they infringe on people's moral rights, particularly when they do so in a manner which does not allow for any freedom of choice. Infringements on more fundamental rights are obviously also more problematic than infringements on less fundamental rights. Consider airline security as an example. The rise in hijackings and bombings aboard planes in the 1970s and 1980s led to an increase in the levels of security on commercial aircraft. In many countries this led to the requirement that all baggage be scanned for explosives and/or other dangerous items. Having your baggage scanned is a violation of your privacy, but it is not a particularly serious one, and it does still allow for some freedom of choice; if there are things you don't want scanned then you can either leave them at home, not put them into your bags, or simply not fly at all. A somewhat more serious violation of privacy was the requirement, which many countries established some time later, that all passengers pass through a metal detector. As security has tightened, more and more restrictions have been placed on those who wish to fly, particularly in the United States, both in terms of the intensity of the searches people must undergo before they are permitted to board a plane (including requirements that people must remove their shoes, coats, and jackets prior to scanning and then, later, the requirement that all passengers either undergo a full-body image scan or an extensive and intrusive pat-down search, possibly both) and the items that they are allowed to take on board with them (which has included bans on firearms; all types of knives; metal cutlery; items of sporting equipment such as cricket bats, baseball bats, and hockey sticks; knitting needles; aerosol containers; handcuffs; cable ties; and all liquids above a certain volume).

Modern aviation security requirements clearly infringe on individual rights to a much greater degree than those that were practiced in the 1960s, and such practices can be ethically objectionable, particularly if a certain passenger is subjected to additional searches simply because of perceptions about his or her ethnicity, or for the gratification of those performing the searches. However, although the modern regulations are clearly intrusive and rights infringing, this is still something that has an element of choice to it, albeit a small one, since a person who really objects to the modern requirements might be able to avoid flying. Counterterrorism strategies that remove even this level of freedom, such as measures to monitor all electronic communication within a particular country, are even more ethically problematic.[27] So are strategies that infringe on rights which are more fundamental than privacy. Such strategies might include such things as curfews, a requirement to apply for a permit to travel even a short distance within one's own country, arrest and detention without trial, and even torture.

CASE STUDY 11.3

The Ticking Bomb in Paris

Suppose a fanatic, perfectly willing to die rather than collaborate in the thwarting of his own scheme, has set a hidden nuclear bomb to explode in the heart of Paris. Police have been warned of what he intends to do and are on the lookout for him. The man is arrested as he attempts to board a train out of the city, but it is clear that he has already planted the device; he even taunts the police officers who are interviewing him, laughing and telling them they have very little time to save their loved ones. There is clearly no time to evacuate even a fraction of the people in the city, so the only hope of preventing tragedy is to torture the perpetrator, find the device, and deactivate it.

SOURCE: Based on a case provided in Henry Shue, "Torture," *Philosophy and Public Affairs* 7(1978), 124–143, p. 141.

Article 5 of the Universal Declaration of Human Rights states "No one shall be subjected to torture or to cruel, inhuman or degrading treatment or punishment." The United Nations Convention against Torture and Other Cruel, Inhuman or Degrading Treatment or Punishment (UNCAT) came into force in June 1987, and as of the end of June 2011, had been ratified by 147 states.[28] Yet the rise of terrorist attacks around the world has led a number of states to authorize the use of techniques, which have been widely condemned as torture, to help combat such attacks. When defending their actions against such claims, it has been common for such states to either deny that the methods they use are equivalent to torture, or to insist that the actions they are taking are necessary in the circumstances. For example, in late 1996, when the Israeli secret police successfully appealed to the Israeli High Court for permission to use "moderate physical pressure" in the interrogation of an Islamic suspect, an attorney acting for the state claimed that "No enlightened nation would agree that hundreds of people should lose their lives because of a rule saying 'torture' is forbidden under any circumstances."[29] Such claims are, in essence, an appeal to the idea of supreme emergency.

Ticking Bomb cases have often been used in philosophical discussions to illustrate situations in which the use of torture may be ethically permissible. To be clear, those who suggest that it may be ethically permissible to utilize torture in some circumstances are only ever suggesting its use in interrogational situations; they claim that it might be ethical to use torture as an aid in the gathering of important information, and are not suggesting that it ought to be used as a form of punishment.

The fictional ticking bomb in Case 11.3 (The Ticking Bomb in Paris) is essentially a type of supreme emergency, since the same sorts of conditions that applied to the wartime supreme emergency situation also apply here. For supreme emergency to apply in time of war, it is necessary that a state be a victim of aggression, facing military defeat, and that the consequences of that military defeat would be utterly disastrous. In Case 11.3, it is clear that those who will be harmed by the exploding bomb are innocent victims, who can thus be claimed to be the victims of aggression. Case 11.3 is somewhat different from a wartime situation of supreme emergency, since the ticking bomb case does not involve imminent military defeat in a war, when such defeat would lead to disastrous consequences. However, the ticking bomb case does involve an immensely serious and imminent threat, in the form of a possible nuclear explosion, where the result of "defeat," that is, the bomb detonating, will clearly be utterly disastrous. Thus, it does seem that there is a case for "breaking the rules," which in this situation does not mean violating the principles of discrimination or proportionality, but instead means torturing the perpetrator. In a case like this, most people seem to accept that torture is, if not ethically acceptable, at least excusable, or perhaps understandable.

As was the case in the wartime supreme emergency scenario, there are various conditions that would need to be met for a "ticking bomb" case to also be considered an example of supreme emergency. Only if these conditions are met would "breaking the rules" seem to be justified, for if all these conditions are not met, then it seems impossible to claim that this is, in fact, a case of supreme emergency. I suggested earlier that the six conditions that must be met for any particular situation to count as a supreme emergency are the same conditions as the ones that need to be met to go to war. In a "ticking bomb" scenario, for torture to be justified, it would need to be the case that (1) there is a just cause for violating the normal prohibitions against torture; (2) the intention in violating those prohibitions is to save the innocent people, and not merely to punish the suspected perpetrator; (3) violating the prohibition on torture is a last resort, so all other reasonable options have been exhausted; (4) the decision to use torture in such a case has been made by the appropriate authorities, which would at least mean very senior figures in the police force and the government; (5) a reasonable probability of success, where "success" refers to the probability of preventing the detonation of the bomb, rather than to the likelihood of getting some information out of the person being tortured; and (6) the harm done in violating the usual prohibitions on torture is proportional to the good achieved by torturing in this particular situation. Of course, in the theoretical case presented here, these conditions **are** met. There is a just cause, since countless people will die if the bomb explodes; the intention in torturing the perpetrator is to save those lives; giving the amount of time remaining until the bomb explodes there is no other option; there is a reasonable probability of success since the perpetrator knows where the bomb is, so if the information is revealed the bomb can be defused; and so on. This case (11.3: The Ticking Bomb in Paris) is deliberately constructed in such a way as to make torture seem reasonable in the circumstances. There is imminent and overwhelming harm to a huge number of people, the captive who will be tortured possesses the information that is needed to end that threat, and if the information is obtained the bomb can be defused and the threat ended. One of the main criticisms of a ticking bomb case like the one presented here is that real-life situations simply are not as straightforward as this. Situations like this are commonly contrived in fiction, but reality is never so neat. While situations are often depicted as "ticking bomb" cases, in real life it is very rare that it is known that there actually is a bomb, that there is no possible way to reduce the threat posed by a bomb, that it is known what the casualties are likely to be, that someone in custody is known to be the actual perpetrator who possesses the information necessary to defuse the bomb, that torturing the person who planted the bomb will actually reveal accurate information and will do so in a short period of time, and that gaining such information will definitely allow the bomb to be defused. But sometimes, perhaps, cases that are at least similar to this do arise in real life.

CASE STUDY 11.4

The Ticking Bomb in Sri Lanka

I sat in that swank hotel drinking tea with a much decorated, battle-hardened Sri Lankan army officer charged with fighting the LTTE (Liberation Tigers of Tamil Eelam aka the Tamil Tigers) and protecting the lives of Colombo's citizens. I cannot use his real name, so I will call him Thomas...."By going through the process of laws," Thomas patiently explained, as a parent or a teacher might speak to a bright yet uncomprehending child, "you cannot fight terrorism." Terrorism, he believed, could be fought only by thoroughly "terrorizing" the terrorists—that is, inflicting on them the same pain that they inflict on the innocent. Thomas had little confidence that I understood what he was saying. I was an academic, he said, with no actual experience of the life-and-death choices and the immense responsibility borne by those charged with protecting society from attack. Accordingly, he would give me an example of the split-second decisions he was called on to make. At the time, Colombo was on "code red" emergency status, because of intelligence that the LTTE was planning to embark on a campaign of bombing public gathering places and other civilian targets. Thomas's unit had apprehended three terrorists who, it suspected, had recently planted somewhere in the city a bomb that was then ticking away, the minutes counting down to catastrophe. The three men were brought before Thomas. He asked them where the bomb was. The terrorists—highly dedicated and steeled to resist interrogation—remained silent. Thomas asked the question again, advising them that if they did not tell him what he wanted to know, he would kill them. They were unmoved. So Thomas took his pistol from his gun belt, pointed it at the forehead of one of them, and shot him dead. The other two, he said, talked immediately; the bomb, which had been placed in a crowded railway station and set to explode during the evening rush hour, was found and defused, and countless lives were saved.

SOURCE: From Bruce Hoffman, "A Nasty Business," *Atlantic Monthly*, January 2002, pp. 49–52.

The situation illustrated in Case 11.4 (The Ticking Bomb in Sri Lanka) is certainly a ticking bomb, but the response to that ticking bomb is rather removed from the fictional situation illustrated in Case 11.3 (The Ticking Bomb in Paris). There is of course no way of knowing whether the story, as described by "Thomas" is actually accurate, so for the purposes of this discussion I will simply assume it is actually true. Many of the elements that are known for certain in the classical ticking bomb case are not known for certain here. The three terrorists are believed, but not known, to have planted a bomb. They are believed, but not known, to be the right people. The bomb is believed to be ticking, but this is not known for certain. To put things in blunt terms, three men, who may or may not be terrorists, may or may not have planted a bomb, which may or may not be ticking, and if the right leverage is applied they may or may not reveal information that may or may not allow the authorities to disarm the bomb, if it exists and is ticking.

Based on this, Thomas does not decide that it is appropriate to apply "moderate physical pressure" or "enhanced interrogation techniques"; he pulls out his gun and murders one of the men. I call it murder, since I simply cannot think of another word that is appropriate, given the situation at the time. It certainly was not warfare, since this was a man in custody who is no longer a part of an enemy's attempt to harm and who has no possibility of defending himself. It is not a justified execution, since at that point Thomas did not know whether the man was actually guilty of anything, and there had been no trial of any sort. The best possible case for defending Thomas's actions here is to claim that this killing was justified as a defensive act, that this man was threatening the lives of other people and that killing him saved the lives of the people who he was threatening. But in fact, this man is not actually threatening anyone, since the bomb is the threat, not the unarmed man. Killing the man does not directly end the threat either, since the bomb remains even after the man has been killed. The only reason that lives are saved is because of what the other men do; immediately offer information about where the bomb is. Their immediate response does seem rather at odds with Thomas's claim that these men are highly dedicated and steeled to resist interrogation. The only possible justification for Thomas's actions in this case is a utilitarian one, that his actions produced the best possible consequences in that they produced the greatest good for the greatest number of people. However, this is at best a highly questionable claim, since Thomas didn't even try any methods short of murder, even though other methods might have produced the same result, and done so without ignoring ideas like justice, fundamental human rights, the rule of law, or a military officer's duty to obey the law of the land.

Of course, it turns out that "countless lives were saved," although since the bomb did not go off, it is impossible to know how many deaths were actually prevented. Thomas obviously feels that what he did was appropriate; indeed he claims that the only way to fight terrorists is to inflict on them the same pain they inflict on the innocent. Of course, if his intuitions about a similar case turn out to be wrong, and he shoots someone who doesn't know anything, or was simply in the wrong place at the wrong time, then Thomas will be inflicting pain on the innocent himself. Acting in the way that Thomas did in this case involves breaking the law in the name of upholding law and order, murdering to fight against murder, and treating those merely suspected of being involved in terrorism as less than human.

Perhaps the biggest problem with a case like this, in the end, is that a single "success" story like this can and does get used to justify torture in the wide range of more ordinary cases that have nothing to do with ticking bombs or with saving many lives, but simply with acquiring information that may or may not be time sensitive, which may or may not be valuable, and which may or may not be able to be obtained by other means. If interrogational torture is permitted to deal with extreme situations, the practice can fairly rapidly become normalized and be used in routine cases to extract routine information. For example, the Israeli human rights organization B'Tselem estimates that over 85% of Palestinians who have been arrested on suspicion of involvement in terrorism have been subjected to one or more of prolonged sleep deprivation, prolonged sensory deprivation, prolonged maintenance of stressful body positions, exposure to extremes of temperature, humiliation, and physical abuse.[30] In simple terms, saving countless lives becomes saving some lives, then becomes saving one life, then becomes getting some useful data, which might, or might not, at some time in the future, allow a life to be saved.

The attacks against the World Trade Center and the Pentagon on September 11, 2001, were an enormous shock to the United States and to the people of many other countries around the world. Several senior U.S. politicians, including the Secretary of Defense Donald Rumsfeld and former New York City Mayor Rudy Giuliani, have asserted that the United States faced a supreme emergency following those attacks and that the prospect of terrorists getting their hands on weapons of mass destruction meant that the world had totally changed, and that all the laws of warfare needed to be rewritten to cope with the realities of this new world. As Orend points out, if the criteria that must be met for a supreme emergency to exist are examined, it is clear that the United States met only one after 9/11, in that it was the victim of an aggressive attack.[31] There was certainly no evidence that the United States was about to be defeated in this new conflict, nor that defeat would be catastrophic. Yet such arguments were certainly taken seriously by the U.S. administration; President George W. Bush even claimed that civilization itself was at stake in the conflict. So it is perhaps a little surprising, given that civilization itself was at stake, that the same administration decided to dispense with some of the very rules of armed conflict that were created to preserve civilized values during conflict, that is, to maintain some standards of decency and to protect fundamental human rights in time of war.

Accurate intelligence is important in any war. In the so-called war on terror, the most obvious source of intelligence was, and is, those captured during operations. To aid in the extraction of information from those captured during operations against Al Qaeda and the Taliban in Afghanistan, and then later in Iraq, the United States government authorized the use of "enhanced interrogation techniques," which could be used when interrogating illegal enemy combatants. Such techniques included such things as sleep deprivation, deprivation of food and drink, deprivation of sensory information, the use of stress positions, threatening with dogs, religious and sexual humiliation, exposure to extreme temperatures, and waterboarding. These techniques were certainly not being used to deal with actual ticking bombs but rather were being used to gather any and all possible information from those who were detained. Even after extensive criticism of the use of such techniques, both domestically and internationally, President Bush refused to rule out the use of such techniques.[32] However, one of President Obama's first actions after his inauguration was to issue an Executive Order requiring the CIA to use only those interrogation methods outlined in the Army Field Manual on Interrogations.[33]

A brief examination of some of the issues raised by the case that began this chapter (11.1: The Petraeus Letter to the Troops) seems a good way of summing up the issues that have been canvassed here, with regard to terrorism and torture, and in the previous chapter with regard to surrender and detention. The findings revealed in the surveys conducted by the Mental Health Advisory team in Iraq revealed a wide range of problems that were clearly of concern to General Petraeus, particularly with regard to the attitudes shown toward the treatment of noncombatants and their property, and toward torture. Given that officers and NCOs are supposed to set an example for their troops, it was interesting that although over 85% of those surveyed said they had received training that made it clear how to treat noncombatants, only 71% of soldiers and 67% of marines said that their officers and NCOs made it clear that mistreatment of noncombatants was not appropriate. Perhaps this helps to explain why considerably less than half of those surveyed were of the view that all noncombatants ought to be treated with respect.

What was clearly of concern to General Petraeus was the attitude of the troops to torture. Perhaps a lot of them had taken on board the idea that the United States faced a supreme emergency, or that new rules were required to fight the war on terror, for more than 40% of those surveyed felt torture should be allowed if it would save the life of a single soldier or marine and close to the same number thought it should be used it this would merely reveal important information about insurgents. Since many of them would have been aware of the CIA's use of "enhanced interrogation techniques" and the U.S. government's insistence that such methods were not torture, it would seem that many felt that the methods already being used did not go far enough. Petraeus was clearly of a different opinion, noting that the use of torture was illegal and that the use of torture produced intelligence of questionable value.

Above all, Petraeus emphasized the need to maintain standards, respect dignity, and do what is right. He noted that military personnel are warriors who train to kill and who must be violent at times. But the standards and values he expected his troops to maintain were what set them apart from the enemy. What he didn't say explicitly, but what is implicit in his letter, is that there is a difference between a warrior and a murderer. Both may kill, but a warrior, unlike a murderer, only aims to kill combatants, and treats all noncombatants with respect, both those who are detained and those in the community at large.

NOTES

1. "Military Ethics of Fighting Terror: An Israeli Perspective," *Journal of Military Ethics* 4(2005), 3-32, p. 4.
2. The authors argue that a state can act in a manner which terrorizes a particular population, but that such actions can be analyzed under the existing legal and ethical framework of just war theory. Thus a state which engaged in such a practice would be guilty of a war crime. However they do not discuss how such practices ought to be understood if they occur outside the bounds of traditional war.
3. Alex Bellamy, *Just Wars: From Cicero to Iraq* (Cambridge, U.K.: Polity, 2006).
4. This line has been used by many different people in many contexts, but the first use actually seems to come from a work of fiction; Gerald Seymour's novel *Harry's Game* (London: Corgi, 1999), originally published in 1975.
5. *Just Wars*, p. 136.
6. Consider, for example, the following quotation from then United Nations Secretary-General, Kofi Annan: "I think regardless of the differences between governments on the question of definition of terrorism, what is clear and what we can all agree on is any deliberate attack on innocent civilians, regardless of one's cause, is unacceptable and fits into the definition of terrorism" (Press conference with Iranian Foreign Minister Kamal Kharrazi, Teheran, January 26, 2002). Brian Orend also suggests that a defining feature of terrorism is that it involves the deliberate use of force against civilians (i.e., noncombatants). See *The Morality of War* (Peterborough, ON: Broadview, 2006), p. 69; whereas Michael Walzer states that terrorism involves "the random murder of innocent people," *Just and Unjust Wars* (New York: Basic, 1977) p. 197.
7. See Chapter 16 of *Just and Unjust Wars*.
8. See Chapter 5 of *The Morality of War*.
9. In his discussion of supreme emergency, Orend states that there are two conditions which must be met, which equate to the second and third conditions I have listed. The first condition is implicit in his discussion, since he notes that supreme emergency is only available to "a country victimized by aggression" (Ibid., p. 140). I have simply made that condition more explicit here.
10. Ibid.
11. As Orend points out, in this instance "Britain" effectively means the entire Commonwealth, since all of Britain's colonies and former colonies were also at war with Germany (Ibid., p. 148).

12. Quoted in Walzer, *Just and Unjust Wars*, p. 254.
13. Ibid., p. 253.
14. Ibid., pp. 261–263. Walzer highlights the bombing of Dresden in February 1945 as an example of an unjustified terror attack.
15. Ibid., pp. 263–268.
16. *The Morality of War*, pp. 142–143.
17. Ibid., pp. 146–157.
18. Ibid., p. 146.
19. Ibid., p. 156.
20. Ibid., p. 157. This idea also links back to the idea of probability of success. As Orend notes slightly earlier in his discussion (p. 156), if it is the enemy's military machine that poses the threat and you are about to be militarily defeated, how is killing enemy civilians going to help at this point in time? If the use of weapons of mass destruction is contemplated, why not use such weapons against the enemy's front line rather than on enemy civilians?
21. "Terrorism and International Justice," in James P. Sterba (ed.), *Terrorism and International Justice* (New York: Oxford University Press, 2003).
22. One chapter of his book *The Triumph of Practice over Theory in Ethics* (New York: Oxford University Press, 2005) is devoted to this issue. See Chapter 7: "International Terrorism and Iraq War II."
23. Sterba also discusses the Gaza Strip, from which Israel has since withdrawn, though Israeli military forces still control land and sea access to the Gaza Strip and the airspace over Gaza (see Case 5.1: Operation Cast Lead).
24. Another significant point that Sterba does not mention here is that Israel also has the support of the United States within the UNSC. The United States has consistently vetoed any UNSC resolutions critical of Israel's actions, particularly with regard to the Occupied Territories.
25. "Terrorism and International Justice," p. 215.
26. "Military Ethics of Fighting Terror," p. 4.
27. For a discussion of some of the issues raised by this type of practice, see Stephen Coleman, "E-mail, Terrorism, and the Right to Privacy," *Ethics and Information Technology* 8(2006), 17–27.
28. As of June 30, 2011, significant states that had signed the treaty but not ratified it included India, Laos, and Sudan. States that had never signed the treaty included North Korea, Iraq, Iran, Malaysia, Vietnam, Oman, the United Arab Emirates, Taiwan, Zimbabwe, Papua New Guinea, Angola, Tanzania, and the Central African Republic.
29. Quoted in Ross Dunn, "Israel Gives Go-Ahead For Torture," *Sydney Morning Herald*, November 16, 1996, p. 1.
30. B'Tselem, "Position Paper: Legislation Allowing the Use of Physical Force and Mental Coercion in Interrogations by the General Security Service" (Jerusalem: B'Tselem, 2000), p. 44.
31. *The Morality of War*, p. 145.

32. On March 8, 2008, President George W. Bush vetoed a bill that would have restricted interrogators to the use of only those techniques specifically authorized in the 2006 Army Field Manual.
33. Executive Order 13491 of January 22, 2009.

FURTHER READING

Allhof, Fritz. "Terrorism and Torture." *International Journal of Applied Philosophy* 17(2003), 105–18.

Bellamy, Alex. *Just Wars: From Cicero to Iraq* (Cambridge, U.K.: Polity, 2006). Chapter 7: Terrorism.

Coady, C.A.J. "Terrorism, Morality, and Supreme Emergency." *Ethics* 114(2004), 772–89.

Orend, Brian. *The Morality of War* (Peterborough, ON: Broadview, 2006). Chapter 5: "*Jus in Bello* #2: Supreme Emergencies."

Walzer, Michael. *Just and Unjust Wars.* (New York: Basic, 1977). Chapter 16: "Supreme Emergency."

Wolfendale, Jessica. *Torture and the Military Profession* (New York: Palgrave MacMillan, 2007). Chapter 5: "Military Torture"; Chapter 6: "Military Training and Moral Agency"; Chapter 7: "The Moral Psychology of Torture."

Wolfendale, Jessica. "'New Wars', Terrorism, and Just War Theory." In Paolo Tripodi & Jessica Wolfendale (eds.), *New Wars and New Soldiers: Military Ethics in the Contemporary World* (Farnham, U.K.: Ashgate, 2011).

DISCUSSION QUESTIONS

- Is the supreme emergency argument a valid one?
- Is terrorism ever a justified tactic?
- Can the use of torture ever be justified in real-life situations?

12

✦◯

Conclusion

The role performed by the military is unique in modern society. Military forces act to defend their state and its interests from external threats, and in fulfilling this role military personnel are given special moral permission to engage in acts of violence and destruction. Military personnel give up a range of their own individual rights to better protect the state that they serve. Thus, military personnel accept the duty to obey legitimate orders, thereby giving up the right to free action. Military personnel accept limitations on their freedom to criticize their own government, thereby giving up some of their right to free speech. Military personnel risk, and in some cases lose, their lives in the service of the state, thereby laying down their right to life. Such things have long been a part of military service. But modern military personnel also engage in many other tasks that traditional militaries did not. Modern military personnel may be deployed to serve in international peacekeeping or peacemaking operations, to fight irregular forces or against insurgent groups, and even to engage in armed humanitarian interventions that are aimed to protect the fundamental rights of those outside their own state.

As the defenders of the state, military personnel are authorized to act in ways that others are not. As was noted in Chapter 3, members of the military have the right, in some circumstances the duty, to deal out death and destruction, often not in strict self-defense. But as servants of the state military personnel are required to carry out their duties in accordance with international law and in compliance with the legitimate demands of the civilian government that controls the military. They must risk their own lives, and the lives of those who serve with them and under their command, when this is necessary to fulfill the overall defense mission. They must sometimes take the lives of others, but they act as warriors, not murderers, and thus there are limits on who they may kill, and how and why.

Given the pressures placed on military personnel, and in particular on those who lead them, it is perhaps unsurprising that the Mental Health Advisory Team

(MHAT) survey of personnel serving in Iraq (Case 11.1: The Petraeus Letter to the Troops) found that nearly a third of them had, during their deployment in Iraq, encountered ethical situations where they did not know how to respond.

The aim of this book has been to help those who have to deal with such situations to be better prepared for what they will have to face. Problems can arise for modern military personnel in an enormous number of ways, hence the range of topics discussed in this book. It is important to understand the relatively ordinary issues of military life, such as knowing what the role of the military actually is and the special moral demands this role may entail, as was discussed in Chapter 3. Given the possible life and death nature of such matters, the dilemmas of giving and following orders are also tremendously important, as was highlighted in the discussion in Chapter 6. Military personnel also need to understand when and why it may be legitimate to engage in armed conflict, both in traditional wars and in modern irregular wars, thus such issues are discussed in Chapters 4 and 5.

My aim in writing this book has been to assist those members of the military who have to deal with all of the ethical issues raised by complex modern operations. In particular, I have focused on the problems faced by those charged with the day-to-day conduct of such operations. For such people, the issues of *jus in bello* are likely to be of particular importance, hence the major focus on such issues in this book. Although there are obviously similarities between the *jus in bello* issues in different types of operations, there are also significant differences. Thus, the types of ethical issues that arise in traditional wars, as discussed in Chapter 7, are rather different from those in modern irregular wars, discussed in Chapter 8, or armed humanitarian interventions, as discussed in Chapter 9. However, in all these types of operations military personnel are likely to have to deal with issues that arise out of the need to deal with people who have surrendered to the military and have been taken into custody, which was discussed in Chapter 10. The problems of terrorism and counterterrorism also raise significant issues, particularly with regard to the treatment of those who are taken into custody during counterterrorism operations, hence the separate discussion of these issues in Chapter 11.

Military personnel in general, and military leaders in particular, may face a range of different ethical problems in the course of their duties. But perhaps the one underlying issue that must be addressed, at least in part, before a book like this can be considered in any way complete, is to explain why military personnel should even worry about trying to deal with these ethical problems. If law and ethics set different standards, why not simply follow the law? I would suggest that being a member of the military profession, known traditionally as the profession of arms, means adhering to the ethical standards of that profession, that is, the standards of *jus in bello*, rather than simply complying with the law. Thus, in any situation where law and ethics set different standards, a member of the military profession will follow the higher standard, inevitably the one required by ethics, rather than the lower standard, that of LOAC.

But this leads to a further question, which is why anyone should think that it is actually important to be a member of the military profession in the first place. So to conclude this book, I want to briefly address this problem, since doing so will, I hope, serve as a means of drawing together all of the problems I have examined.

COMPETENCE AND THE PROFESSIONAL

Those people who are engaged in practical tasks within society are often required to acquire a range of different skills to do their jobs. When such skills relate to safety standards, there is often a lot of focus on training people in these skills to ensure that they have reached a particular standard and are therefore competent to perform a particular task. Thus, it has become very common in recent times to find that a lot of military training, in particular pre-deployment training, is focused on ensuring that every person who will need to perform a particular task has been trained on how that task is to be performed, thus ensuring that each individual can have a little box next to their name ticked off and they can be marked as "competent" with regard to that task. In some respects, it seems competency has become the new gold standard.

If a person is considered to be a competent member of the military, at any rank or level of command, then this simply means that the person in question has the necessary skills to perform the job required. The particular skills that any individual member of the military will need to acquire will depend on the particular role that person fulfills within the military structure, but it is likely that a competent member of the military will have an ability to issue and/or carry out meaningful orders; an ability to use those weapons or weapon systems that relate to his or her role; an understanding of LOAC and of other laws relevant to the particular position which that person holds, such as those related to military discipline or the law of the sea; some specialized knowledge that directly relates to that person's job role, such as an understanding of infantry tactics, or navigation at sea, or navigation in the air; and so on.

But to be a **good** member of the military, perhaps to truly be a member of the military profession, it is not enough to merely be competent, that is, to have the skills that are required to do the job. Competency is necessary to be a member of the military profession, but it is not sufficient. To be a member of the military profession, rather than merely a competent employee of the armed forces, it is not only necessary for a person to have the required skills, it is also necessary for that person to use those skills in the right way and to achieve the right ends. The corollary of this is that there are at least three ways in which a particular person might be thought to be a **bad** member of the armed forces: to either lack the necessary skills to do the job, or to use those skills in the wrong way, or to use those skills to achieve the wrong ends.

For example, a naval officer who miscalculates the course that needs to be followed and ends up running his ship aground on a sandbar as a result of his lack of navigational skills, is clearly not a good naval officer, since he is lacking in competence in a vital area. However, a person can also possess all the necessary competencies but still not be a good member of the military profession. For example, an infantry Sergeant who has wonderful combat skills and commands great respect from his subordinates, but who encourages those subordinates, through his own actions, to think of all local noncombatants as insurgents who ought to be treated like animals, is not using his skills in the right way. This was exactly the sort of problem highlighted in some parts of the survey that was conducted by the MHAT team, reported in Case 11.1 (The Petraeus Letter to the Troops). Similarly, a logistics officer who has excellent negotiation skills, but uses those skills to fill her own pockets with bribes and kickbacks, may well be competent in all the right ways but equally clearly is not a good military professional, since she is using her skills to achieve the wrong ends, in this case personal enrichment, rather than the good of the state.

THE UNLIMITED LIABILITY CONTRACT

General Sir John Hackett famously noted that military personnel serve the state under a contract of "unlimited liability."[1] Since Hackett coined the term it has been used by many different people, who almost exclusively use the term to refer to the fact that military personnel agree to serve in the armed forces of the state, while knowing that such service inherently involves risk to life and limb.[2] But it is apparent, on closer examination, that there is a great deal more to the unlimited liability contract than this. In fact, the risk to life and limb is, in some strange sense, the easy part of the contract. Another part of this contract, perhaps less obvious, is that even while demanding of a member of the military that he or she risk life and limb on behalf of the state, the state puts limits on what that member of the military may do; limits that, at least in some cases, actually increase that risk. Along with this comes total accountability for one's actions in the service of the state, so that every action taken by every member of the military, especially in conflict, but also in times of peace, can be examined, and in some cases found wanting, by the state.

Consider the SEALs in Case 10.1 (Operation Red Wings), for example. They could, of course, have decided that the only way in which they could protect their own lives would be to kill the goat herders. But, as LT Murphy himself says in that case, if they were to do this, then they would be charged with murder. There are things that members of the military are not permitted to do, even in defense of their own lives. As Michael Walzer notes, members of the military are required, by LOAC and by the laws of their own state, to accept increased levels of personal risk to avoid harming people who are not combatants.[3] This restriction still applies if those noncombatants are angry, or unpleasant, or citizens of an enemy state, or POWs, or enemy military personnel who are *hors de combat*, or, as was the case in 10.1, possess information that is a threat to your own life. Even under conditions of extreme stress, in combat, when lives are on the line, every member of the military is still required, as part of the unlimited liability contract, to do the right thing and to be fully accountable for any mistakes made.

OF WARRIORS AND MURDERERS

The limits on what military personnel are permitted to do, even in defense of their own lives, are certainly a part of the unlimited liability contract under which members of the military serve the state. But these limits also represent something more, since they help to define what it is to be a member of the military profession. As has been mentioned several times in this book, it is perhaps by looking at the limits on what military personnel may do, on who they do **not** kill, that we can most easily distinguish the military professional from the killer; the warrior from the murderer. This fact was one of the things noted by General Petraeus in the letter he wrote in response to the release of the MHAT findings in 2007.

> We are, indeed, warriors. We train to kill our enemies. We are engaged in combat, we must pursue the enemy relentlessly, and we must be violent at times. What sets us apart from our enemies in this fight, however, is how we behave. In everything we do, we must observe the standards and values that dictate that we treat noncombatants and detainees with dignity and respect. (Case 11.1: The Petraeus Letter to the Troops)

It has to be admitted that when they are sent into an armed conflict, members of the military are being paid to kill. But military professionals are not merely hired killers in the service of the state, for there are things that military professionals will not do, even if ordered to do them by the state they serve. The World War II case of the German General Erwin Rommel is often cited in this context,[4] and is also sometimes used as evidence of the claim that one can be an honorable and professional soldier even in the service of an evil state. In response to a series of successful raids by British Commando units, on October 18, 1942, Adolf Hitler issued the so-called Commando Order, which stated that all Allied commandos encountered by German forces in Europe and Africa should be killed immediately, even if those commandos were in uniform or if they attempted to surrender. Rommel simply refused to issue this order to his troops; when he received the order, he burnt it.[5]

Some of the things that military professionals must do in the service of the state are far from pleasant. Combat is certainly not pretty. Yet perhaps for as long as there has been such a thing as combat and recognizable warriors battling within it, there have been codes of conduct that set limits on what those warriors could and could not do, limitations that had to be obeyed if one wanted to remain a warrior rather than a murder. As Shannon French notes, "For the warrior who has such a code, certain actions remain unthinkable, even in the most dire or extreme circumstances."[6] But if combat is so difficult and so dangerous, then why place limits on what members of the military can do in such an environment?

Perhaps one reason for placing such limits on military professionals is to protect them from psychological damage. For example, people researching the incidence of Post-Traumatic Stress Disorder (PTSD) among Vietnam veterans have found that the most severe cases of PTSD are likely to be found among those veterans whose experiences did not simply involve witnessing, or being a party to, acts of extreme violence, but rather among those who were either directly or indirectly involved in illegal, immoral, or dishonorable behavior in warfare.[7] As Shannon French puts it, "Warriors need a way to distinguish what they must do out of a sense of duty from what a serial killer does for the sheer sadistic pleasure of it."[8] In other words, the codes that limit the behavior of military professionals are there to try to ensure that the military professionals not only live through the battle, but can also live with themselves afterwards.

KNOWING AND DOING

To be a true military professional, a person needs to know what the right thing to do is when this is obvious, and be able to work out what the right thing to do is when the situation is more difficult. But merely knowing what the right thing to do is will not be sufficient for a member of the armed forces to count as a military professional. A military professional must not only know what the right thing to do is, they must also actually **do** the right thing. This relates to a distinction that was made right back in Chapter 1, between tests of integrity and ethical dilemmas. An ethical dilemma is a situation in which the difficulty lies in knowing what the right thing to do actually is. A test of integrity is a situation in which it is clear what the right thing to do is, but for whatever reason, it is difficult for the person involved to actually do the right thing. Sometimes these situations can overlap, so that it is hard to work out what the right thing to do is, and even then it is hard to actually do. But to truly be a member of the military profession, it is necessary to do the right thing, even when it is difficult; or as it is sometimes expressed, to choose the hard right over the easy wrong. A member of the military profession needs to be a person of integrity; a man or woman who does the right thing even when it is clear that he or she could get away with doing the wrong thing **and** even when there is pressure to do the wrong thing.

Military services inevitably have a range of resources that are designed to help their personnel know, or work out, what the right thing to do is: codes of conduct, standing orders, training courses on LOAC and ROE, and so on. But in the end all of these things are of no use unless the military personnel who must deal with difficult situations make the decision to do the right thing and then actually do it.

If you serve in the military, whatever position you hold, other people can help you to work out what the right thing to do is, but only you can do the right thing. In the end, how you actually conduct yourself as a member of the military is entirely up to you. Only you can chose whether you wish to become a member of the military profession or simply an employee of the state.

NOTES

1. General Sir John Winthrop Hackett, *The Profession of Arms: The 1962 Lees Knowles Lectures Given at Trinity College Cambridge* (London: Times, 1962), p. 63.
2. In Chapter 3 I noted the use of the term by Martin L. Cook in *The Moral Warrior: Ethics and Service in the U.S. Military* (Albany: State University of New York Press, 2004), p. 74. Cook uses the term in exactly the manner I have described here.
3. *Just and Unjust Wars* (New York: Basic, 1977), p. 305.
4. Michael Walzer uses this case as evidence of the distinction between *jus ad bellum* and *jus in bello*. See *Just and Unjust Wars*, pp. 38–40.
5. Ibid.
6. *The Code of the Warrior: Exploring Warrior Values Past and Present* (Lanham, MD: Rowman and Littlefield, 2003), p. 231.
7. Jonathon Shay, *Achilles in Vietnam: Combat Trauma and the Undoing of Character* (New York: Simon and Schuster, 1994), p. xiii.
8. *The Code of the Warrior*, p. 5.

APPENDIX

◆○

The Laws of Armed Conflict

The following is a list of the international treaties that make up the Law of Armed Conflict. After each treaty there is a note that says how many of the member states of the United Nations (UN) are party to it. In cases where more than two-thirds of the UN member states have ratified a particular treaty, states that have not ratified that particular treaty and are among the world's top military spenders are also noted.

It should be noted that the mere fact that a state has not ratified a certain treaty does not mean:

1. That the state is necessarily opposed to the content of that treaty. In some cases, a state may agree with the overwhelming majority of the content of a treaty, but object to a few phrases, which nonetheless prevent the state from ratifying the treaty as a whole. This is perhaps most likely to occur in those states that require the ratification of treaties to be approved by one (or more) of the houses in that state's legislative body.
2. That the state is not bound by that treaty despite not having ratified it. Some of these treaties, in whole or in part, may have the status of customary international law and are thus binding on all states, including those not party to the treaty.

All data is current as of June 17, 2011, at which point there were 192 member states in the UN.

- **Geneva Convention (I)** for the Amelioration of the Condition of the Wounded and Sick in Armed Forces in the Field. August 12, 1949.
- **Geneva Convention (II)** for the Amelioration of the Condition of Wounded, Sick and Shipwrecked Members of Armed Forces at Sea. August 12, 1949.

- **Geneva Convention (III)** relative to the Treatment of Prisoners of War. August 12, 1949.
- **Geneva Convention (IV)** relative to the Protection of Civilian Persons in Time of War. August 12, 1949.

All members states of the UN are parties to the Geneva Conventions (which are the only treaties on this list that Somalia is actually a party to). Only seven states are a party to every other treaty listed here: Austria, Bulgaria, Costa Rica, Germany, Netherlands, Slovenia, and Spain.

- **Protocol Additional to the Geneva Conventions of August 12, 1949**, and Relating to the Protection of Victims of International Armed Conflicts. **Known as Protocol I.** June 8, 1977. 169 parties. Of the states that are not party to this convention, the most significant is the U.S.A., a permanent member of the United Nations Security Council (UNSC). Other significant military spenders not party to this convention include India, Indonesia, Iran, Israel, Malaysia, Myanmar, Pakistan, the Philippines, Singapore, Somalia, Sri Lanka, Thailand, and Turkey.
- **Protocol Additional to the Geneva Conventions of August 12, 1949**, and Relating to the Protection of Victims of Non-International Armed Conflicts. **Known as Protocol II.** June 8, 1977. 164 parties. Of the states that are not party to this convention, the most significant is the U.S.A., a permanent member of the UNSC. Other significant military spenders not party to this convention include Angola, India, Indonesia, Iran, Iraq, Israel, Malaysia, Myanmar, North Korea, Pakistan, Singapore, Somalia, Sri Lanka, Syria, Thailand, Turkey, and Vietnam.
- **Protocol Additional to the Geneva Conventions of August 12, 1949**, and Relating to the Adoption of an Additional Distinctive Emblem **(Protocol III).** December 8, 2005. 56 parties.
- **Convention on the Rights of the Child**, November 20, 1989. 190 parties. The only UN member states not party to this convention are Somalia and the U.S.A..
- **Optional Protocol to the Convention on the Rights of the Child** on the involvement of children in armed conflict, May 25, 2000. 140 parties. Significant military spenders not party to this convention include Cameroon, Central African Republic, Cote d'Ivoire, Equatorial Guinea, Estonia, Ethiopia, Fiji, Gambia, Ghana, Indonesia, Iran, Iraq, Israel, Lebanon, Liberia, Malaysia, Myanmar, Niger, Nigeria, North Korea, Pakistan, Saudi Arabia, Somalia, Syria, United Arab Emirates, Zambia, and Zimbabwe. The U.S.A. is a party to this convention despite not having ratified the Convention on the Rights of the Child; although described as an Optional Protocol to the Convention on the Rights of the Child, it is technically a separate treaty.

- **Rome Statute of the International Criminal Court**, July 17, 1998. 114 parties. Of the many states that are not party to this convention, the most significant are China, the Russian Federation, and the U.S.A., who are all permanent members of the UNSC.
- **Convention for the Protection of Cultural Property** in the Event of Armed Conflict, May 14, 1954. 122 parties. Of the states that are not party to this convention, the most significant is the U.K., a permanent member of the UNSC. Other significant military spenders not party to the convention include North Korea, South Korea, Singapore, and Vietnam.
  - **First Protocol to the Hague Convention of 1954** on the prevention of the export of cultural property from countries occupied during time of war, May 14, 1954. 99 parties.
  - **Second Protocol to the Hague Convention of 1954** extending the level of protection given to cultural property of the greatest importance to humanity, and to cultural property in non-international armed conflicts. March 26, 1999. 60 parties.
- **Protocol for the Prohibition of the Use of Asphyxiating, Poisonous or Other Gases, and Warfare**, June 17, 1925. 135 parties. Significant military spenders not party to the convention include Myanmar, Singapore, United Arab Emirates, and Zimbabwe.
- **Convention on the Prohibition of the Development, Production and Stockpiling of Bacteriological (Biological) and Toxin Weapons and on their Destruction,** April 10, 1972. 162 parties. Significant military spenders not party to the convention include Egypt, Israel, Myanmar, and Syria.
- **Convention on the Prohibition of Military or Any Other Hostile Use of Environmental Modification Techniques,** known as ENMOD, December 10, 1976. 74 parties. Of the states that are not party to this convention, the most significant is France, a permanent member of the UNSC. Other significant military spenders not party to the convention include Indonesia, Iran, Iraq, Israel, Libya, Mexico, Myanmar, Saudi Arabia, Singapore, South Africa, Thailand, and Turkey.
- **Convention on Prohibitions or Restrictions on the Use of Certain Conventional Weapons Which May Be Deemed to be Excessively Injurious or to Have Indiscriminate Effects**, known as CCWC, October 10, 1980. 113 parties. To be a party to this convention, states had to agree to at least two of the component protocols. Significant military spenders not party to the CCWC include Afghanistan, Egypt, Indonesia, Iran, Iraq, Lebanon, Libya, Malaysia, Myanmar, Nigeria, North Korea, Singapore, Sudan, Syria, Thailand, Vietnam, and Zimbabwe.
  - **Protocol on non-detectable fragments (I).** 111 parties. The only states party to the CCWC but not Protocol I are Morocco and Senegal.

- **Protocol on prohibitions or restrictions on the use of mines, booby traps and other devices (II).** 93 parties. As amended on May 3, 1996 (Protocol II to the 1980 Convention). 96 parties. Largely superseded by the 1997 Anti-Personnel Landmine Treaty (below).
- **Protocol on prohibitions or restrictions on the use of incendiary weapons (III).** 107 parties. The only states party to the CCWC but not Protocol III are Israel, Monaco, Morocco, South Korea, Turkey, and Turkmenistan.
- **Protocol on Blinding Laser Weapons (Protocol IV to the 1980 Convention),** October 13, 1995. 98 parties.
- **Amendment to the Convention on Prohibitions or Restrictions on the Use of Certain Conventional Weapons Which May Be Deemed to Be Excessively Injurious or to Have Indiscriminate Effects (with Protocols I, II, and III),** December 21, 2001. 73 parties.
- **Protocol expanding the CCWC (Protocols I, II, and III),** to non-international armed conflicts. November 28, 2003. 70 parties.
- **Convention on the Prohibition of the Development, Production, Stockpiling and Use of Chemical Weapons and on their Destruction,** January 13, 1993. 185 parties. The only UN member states not party to this treaty are Angola, Egypt, Israel, Myanmar, North Korea, Somalia, and Syria.
- **Convention on the Prohibition of the Use, Stockpiling, Production and Transfer of Anti-Personnel Mines and on their Destruction,** September 18, 1997. 153 parties. This treaty largely supersedes Protocol II of the CCWC. However, some states that ARE party to Protocol II of the CCWC are NOT party to this Convention. Of these, the most significant are China, the Russian Federation, and the U.S.A., who are all permanent members of the UNSC; other UN member states in the same position are Cuba, Finland, Georgia, India, Israel, Laos, Mongolia, Morocco, Pakistan, Poland, Sri Lanka, and Uzbekistan. Significant military spenders party to NEITHER this convention nor Protocol II of the CCWC include Egypt, Iran, Lebanon, Libya, Myanmar, North Korea, Saudi Arabia, Syria, United Arab Emirates, and Vietnam.
- **Convention on Cluster Munitions,** May 30, 2008. 56 parties. Of the many states that are not party to this convention, the most significant are China, the Russian Federation, and the U.S.A., who are all permanent members of the UNSC.

BIBLIOGRAPHY

Al-Jazeera. "The Life and Death of Shaikh Yasin." *Al-Jazeera.net*, March 25, 2004.

Allhof, Fritz. "Terrorism and Torture." *International Journal of Applied Philosophy* 17(2003), 105–18.

Amidror, Yaakov. "Winning Counterinsurgency War: The Israeli Experience." Paper in the *Strategic Perspectives* series, Jerusalem Center for Public Affairs, 2008.

Aquinas, Thomas. *Summa Theologica*. English translation by Fathers of the English Dominican Province, in three volumes (New York: Benziger Bros. 1947)

Aristotle. *The Nichomachean Ethics*. Translated and edited by Roger Crisp (Cambridge: Cambridge University Press, 2000).

Bellamy, Alex. *Just Wars: From Cicero to Iraq* (Cambridge, U.K.: Polity, 2006).

Benson, Mary. *Nelson Mandela* (Harmondsworth, U.K.: Penguin, 1986).

Bentham, Jeremy. *An Introduction to the Principles of Morals and Legislation* (Oxford: Clarendon, 1907). First published in 1789, reprinted with corrections by the author in 1823.

Blumenfeld, Laura. "In Israel, a Divisive Struggle Over Targeted Killing." *Washington Post,* August 27, 2006.

Boot, Max. "Retaliation for Me, But Not for Thee." *Weekly Standard*, November 18, 2002.

Bowden, Mark. *Black Hawk Down: A Story of Modern War* (New York: Penguin, 1999).

Brecher, Jeremy & Smith, Brendan. "The Trials of Ehren Watada." *The Nation,* June 1, 2009.

Brickhill, Paul. *The Dam Busters* (London: Evans, 1952).

British Broadcasting Corporation. "Gaza Looks Like Earthquake Zone." *BBC News,* January 20, 2009.

B'Tselem. "Position Paper: Legislation Allowing the Use of Physical Force and Mental Coercion in Interrogations by the General Security Service" (Jerusalem: B'Tselem, 2000).

Bury, Patrick. *Callsign Hades* (London: Simon and Schuster, 2010).

Byers, Michael. *War Law: Understanding International Law and Armed Conflict* (New York: Grove, 2005).

Cahn, Steven M. (ed.). *Exploring Ethics: An Introductory Anthology*. 2nd ed. (New York: Oxford University Press, 2010).

Cave, Peter. "Israel Assassinates Ali Abu Mustafa," *ABC News–AM*, August 28, 2001.

Ceulemans, Carl. "The NATO Intervention in the Kosovo Crisis: March–June 1999." In Bruno Coppieters & Nick Fotion (eds.), *Moral Constraints on War: Principles and Cases* (Lanham, MD: Lexington, 2002).

Coady, C. A. J. "Terrorism, Morality, and Supreme Emergency." *Ethics* 114(2004), 772–89.

Coleman, Stephen. "Discrimination and Non-Lethal Weapons: Issues for the Future Military." In David Lovell & Igor Primoratz (eds.), *Protecting Civilians in Violent Conflict: Theoretical and Practical Issues for the 21st Century* (Farnham, U.K.: Ashgate, 2012).

Coleman, Stephen. "The Child Soldier." *Journal of Military Ethics* 10(2011), 316.

Coleman, Stephen. "Just War, Irregular War, and Terrorism." In Paolo Tripodi and Jessica Wolfendale (eds.), *New Wars and New Soldiers: Military Ethics in the Contemporary World* (Farnham, U.K.: Ashgate, 2011).

Coleman, Stephen. "The Problems of Duty and Loyalty." *Journal of Military Ethics* 8(2009), 105–15.

Coleman, Stephen. "E-mail, Terrorism, and the Right to Privacy." *Ethics and Information Technology* 8(2006), 17–27.

Commonwealth of Australia. *Report of the Board of Inquiry into the Fire in HMAS WESTRALIA on 5 May 1998* (Canberra: Defence Publishing Services, 1998).

Connell, F. J. "Double Effect, Principle of." *New Catholic Encyclopedia Vol. 4* (New York: McGraw-Hill, 1967).

Cook, Martin L. & Hamann, Phillip A. "The Road to Basra." In W. Rick Rubel & George R. Lucas (eds.), *Case Studies in Ethics for Military Leaders* 3rd ed. (New York: Pearson Custom Publishing, 2009).

Cook, Martin L. *The Moral Warrior: Ethics and Service in the U.S. Military* (Albany: State University of New York Press, 2004).

Coppieters, Bruno & Fotion, Nick (eds.). *Moral Constraints on War: Principles and Cases* (Lanham, MD: Lexington, 2002).

Coyne, John T. "Investigation to Inquire into the Circumstances Surrounding the Joint Task Force-6 (JTF-6) Shooting Incident that Occurred on 20 May 1997 Near the Border Between the United States and Mexico." United States Marine Corps.

Crawford, J.W., III. "The Law of Noncombatant Immunity and the Targeting of National Electrical Power Systems." *Fletcher Forum of World Affairs* 21(1997), 101–19.

Darack, Ed. "Operation Red Wings: What Really Happened?" *Marine Corps Gazette* 95(2010), 62–67.

Davison, Neil. *"Non-Lethal" Weapons* (Basingstoke, U.K.: Palgrave Macmillan, 2009).

Dennett, Daniel. *Elbow Room: The Varieties of Free Will Worth Wanting* (Cambridge, MA: MIT Press, 1984).

Dobos, Ned. "Is U.N. Security Council Authorisation for Armed Humanitarian Intervention Morally Necessary." *Philosophia* 38(2010), 499–515.

Dobos, Ned. "Rebellion, Humanitarian Intervention, and the Prudential Constraints on War." *Journal of Military Ethics* 7(2008), 102–15.

Dunn, Ross. "Israel Gives Go-Ahead For Torture." *Sydney Morning Herald*, November 16, 1996, p. 1.

Erlanger, Steven. "Weighing Crimes and Ethics in the Fog of Urban Warfare." *New York Times*, January 16, 2009.

Erlanger, Steven . "A Gaza War Full of Traps and Trickery." *New York Times*, January 11, 2009.

Fernandes, Clinton. "East Timor." In Clinton Fernandes (ed.), *Hot Spot: Asia and Oceania* (Westport, CT: Greenwood Press, 2008).

Ficarotta, J. Carl. "A Higher Moral Standard for the Military." In George Lucas et al. (eds.), *Ethics for Military Leaders*. 5th ed. (Boston: Pearson Custom, 2002).

Flynn, Sean Michael. *The Fighting 69th: From Ground Zero to Baghdad* (New York: Penguin, 2007).

Foot, Philippa. "The Problem of Abortion and the Doctrine of the Double Effect." *Oxford Review* 5(1967), 5–15.

Fotion, Nick. *War and Ethics: A New Just War Theory* (London: Continuum, 2007).

French, Shannon E. *The Code of the Warrior* (Lanham, MD: Rowman and Littlefield, 2003).

Gibbs, David N. *First Do No Harm: Humanitarian Intervention and the Destruction of Yugoslavia* (Nashville, TN: Vanderbilt University Press, 2009).

Ging, John. "Press Conference by Director Of Gaza Operations, United Nations Relief and Works Agency for Palestine Refugees in the Near East." United Nations Department of Public Information, News and Media Division, New York. January 6, 2009.

Gordon, Michael R. & Trainor, Bernard E. *The General's War* (New York: Little, Brown, 1995).

Gross, Michael L. *Moral Dilemmas of Modern War: Torture, Assassination and Blackmail in an Age of Asymmetric Conflict* (New York: Cambridge University Press, 2010).

Gross, Michael L. "The Second Lebanon War: The Question of Proportionality and the Prospect of Non-Lethal Warfare." *Journal of Military Ethics* 7(2008), 1–22.

Guthrie, Charles & Quinlan, Michael. *Just War: The Just War Tradition: Ethics in Modern Warfare* (London: Bloomsbury, 2007).

Gwynne, S. C., Faltermayer, Charlotte & Thompson, Mark. "Border Skirmish." *Time Magazine*, August 25, 1997.

Hackett, John Winthrop. *The Profession of Arms: The 1962 Lees Knowles Lectures Given at Trinity College Cambridge* (London: Times, 1962).

Hartle, Anthony E. *Moral Issues in Military Decision Making*. 2nd ed. (Lawrence: University Press of Kansas, 2004).

Herrick, Thaddeus. "Family to Receive $1.9 Million in Border Shooting/ Grand Jury Again Refuses to Indict Marine." *Houston Chronicle*, August 12, 1998.

Hobbes, Thomas. *Leviathan* (Oxford: Oxford University Press, 1965). First published in 1651.

Hoffman, Bruce. "A Nasty Business." *Atlantic Monthly*, January 2002, pp. 49–52.

Human Rights Watch. "Civilian Deaths in the NATO Air Campaign." Volume 12, no. 1, February 2000.

Human Rights Watch. *Needless Deaths in the Gulf War: Civilian Casualties During the Air Campaign and Violations of the Laws of War* (New York: Human Rights Watch, 1991).

Huntington, Samuel. "Officership as a Profession." In Malham M. Watkin (ed.), *War, Morality and the Military Profession.* 2nd ed. (Boulder, CO: Westview, 1986).

"IDF Releases Cast Lead Casualty Numbers." *Jerusalem Post,* March 28, 2009.

Jeffrey, Anthea. *People's War: New Light on the Struggle for South Africa* (Johannesburg: Jonathan Ball, 2009).

Kant, Immanuel. *Foundations of the Metaphysics of Morals* (New York: MacMillan, 1990). First published 1785.

Kant, Immanuel. "On a Supposed Right to Tell Lies from Benevolent Motives." First published 1797.

Kasher, Asa & Yadlin, Amos. "Military Ethics of Fighting Terror: An Israeli Perspective." *Journal of Military Ethics* 4(2005), 3–32.

Kashnikov, Boris. "The NATO Intervention in the Kosovo Crisis: Whose Justice?" In Bruno Coppieters & Nick Fotion (eds.), *Moral Constraints on War: Principles and Cases* (Lanham, MD: Lexington, 2002).

Kershnar, Stephen. "The Structure of Rights Forfeiture in the Context of Culpable Wrongdoing." *Philosophia* 29(2002), 57–88.

Kilcullen, David. "Twenty-Eight Articles: Fundamentals of Company-level Counterinsurgency." Written for the U.S. Department of Defense, March 2006.

Kleinig, John. "The Blue Wall of Silence: An Ethical Analysis." *International Journal of Applied Philosophy* 15(2001), 1–24.

Knickerbocker, Brad. "The Fuzzy Ethics of Nonlethal Weapons." *Christian Science Monitor,* February 14, 2003.

Koplow, David A. *Non-Lethal Weapons: The Law and Policy of Revolutionary Technologies for the Military and Law Enforcement* (Cambridge: Cambridge University Press, 2006).

Krulak, Charles C. "The Strategic Corporal: Leadership in the Three Block War." *Marines Magazine* 28(January 1999), 28–34.

Lavie, Mark. "Israeli Supreme Court Votes to Uphold Military's Policy of Targeted Killings." *New York Sun,* December 15, 2006.

Lejeune Leadership Institute. *Discussion Material for Small Unit Leaders: Issues of Battlefield Ethics and Leadership* (Marine Corps University, Quantico, VA: Lejeune Leadership Institute, 2008).

Levitt, Matthew. *Hamas: Politics, Charity, and Terrorism in the Service of Jihad* (New Haven, CT: Yale University Press, 2006).

Luttrell, Marcus (with Robinson, Patrick). *Lone Survivor: The Eyewitness Account of Operation Redwing and the Lost Heroes of SEAL Team 10* (London: Sphere, 2008).

Mackenzie, Nick. "Military Dispute over Casualties." *Sydney Morning Herald,* May 18, 2009.

MacLean, Alastair. *Force Ten From Navarone* (London: Fontana, 1994).

Mangan, Joseph. "An Historical Analysis of the Principle of Double Effect." *Theological Studies* 10(1949), 41–61.

May, Larry. "Superior Orders, Duress, and Moral Perception." In Larry May, Eric Rovie & Steve Viner (eds.), *The Morality of War: Classical and Contemporary Readings* (Upper Saddle River, NJ: Pearson Education, 2006), pp. 430–39.

McLennan, David. "Soldiers in Clear Over Deaths of Baby, Teen" and "Ready for Anything, Even Stray Toddlers." *The Canberra Times*, May 13, 2008.

McMahan, Jeff. "Preventive War and the Killing of the Innocent." In Richard Sorabji & David Rodin (eds.), *The Ethics of War: Shared Problems in Different Traditions* (Aldershot, U.K.: Ashgate, 2006).

Miller, Seumas, Blackler, John & Alexandra, Andrew. *Police Ethics*. 2nd ed. (St. Leonards, NSW: Allen and Unwin, 2006).

Myre, Greg. "In Loss of Leaders, Hamas Discovers a Renewed Strength." *New York Times*, April 25, 2004.

Norman, Richard. "War, Humanitarian Intervention and Human Rights." In Richard Sorabji & David Rodin (eds.), *The Ethics of War: Shared Problems in Different Traditions* (Aldershot, U.K.: Ashgate, 2006).

Oehring, George J. "Rights to Engagement." *The Bulletin* (A publication of The Army Lessons Learned Centre, Canada) (Vol. 7, No 2, October 2000), pp.11–13.

Opall-Rome, Barbara. "Israel: Airstrike Accuracy Doubled in 2 Years." *Defense News*, May 26, 2008.

Orend, Brian. *The Morality of War* (Peterborough, ON: Broadview, 2006).

Osiel, Mark J. *Obeying Orders: Atrocity, Military Discipline and the Law of War* (New Brunswick, NJ: Transaction, 1999).

Øverland, Gerhard. "High-Fliers: Who Should Bear the Risk of Humanitarian Intervention." In Paolo Tripodi & Jessica Wolfendale (eds.), *New Wars and New Soldiers: Military Ethics in the Contemporary World* (Farnham, U.K.: Ashgate, 2011), pp. 69–86.

Paul, Christopher. "As a Fish Swims in the Sea: Relationships Between Factors Contributing to Support for Terrorist or Insurgent Groups." *Studies in Conflict & Terrorism* 33(2010), 488–510.

Prosecutor *v.* Martić, No. IT-95-11-T, Judgement. (International Criminal Tribunal for the Former Yugoslavia, June 12, 2007).

Prusher, Ilene R. & Lynfield, Ben. "Killing of Yassin a Turning Point." *Christian Science Monitor*, March 23, 2004.

"RAF Doctor Jailed Over Iraq Refusal." *The Guardian*, April 13, 2006.

Rawls, John. *A Theory of Justice* (New York: Oxford University Press, 1971).

Robinson, Paul. "Introduction: Ethics Education in the Military." In Paul Robinson, Nigel de Lee & Don Carrick (eds.), *Ethics Education in the Military* (Aldershot, U.K.: Ashgate, 2008).

Robertson, Horace B., Jr. "The Obligation to Accept Surrender." *Naval War College Review* 46(Spring 1993), 103–15.

Rodin, David. "The Ethics of Asymmetric War." In Richard Sorabji & David Rodin (eds.), *The Ethics of War: Shared Problems in Different Traditions* (Aldershot, U.K.: Ashgate, 2006).

Rodin, David. *War and Self-Defense* (New York: Oxford University Press, 2003).

Rubel, W. Rick. "Leave No One Behind." *Journal of Military Ethics* 3(2004), 252–56.

Rubel, W. Rick. "Come Right." In W. Rick Rubel & George R. Lucas (eds.), *Case Studies in Military Ethics* (Boston: Pearson Education, 2004).

Rubel, W. Rick. "Come Right: The Sequel." In W. Rick Rubel & George R. Lucas (eds.), *Case Studies in Military Ethics* (Boston: Pearson Education, 2004).

Seymour, Gerald. *Harry's Game* (London: Corgi, 1999). First published 1975.

Shay, Jonathon. *Achilles in Vietnam: Combat Trauma and the Undoing of Character* (New York: Simon and Schuster, 1994).

Shue, Henry. "Civilian Protection and Force Protection." In David Whetham (ed.), *Ethics, Law and Military Operations* (Basingstoke, U.K.: Palgrave Macmillan, 2011).

Shue, Henry. "Torture." *Philosophy and Public Affairs* 7(1978), 124–43.

Silva, Romesh & Ball, Patrick. *The Profile of Human Rights Violations in Timor-Leste, 1974-1999.* Report by the Benetech Human Rights Data Analysis Group to the CAVR, February 9, 2006.

Singer, Peter (ed.). *A Companion to Ethics* (Oxford: Blackwell, 1991).

Sites, Kevin. "Open Letter to Marines: What Happened in the Fallujah Mosque." http://www.msnbc.msn.com/id/6556034/ns/world_news-mideast/n_africa/ (accessed May 2, 2011).

Smith, Hugh. "Conscientious Objection to Particular Wars." *War and Society* 8(1990), 118–34.

Sterba, James P. *The Triumph of Practice over Theory in Ethics* (New York: Oxford University Press, 2004).

Sterba, James P. "Terrorism and International Justice." In James P. Sterba (ed.), *Terrorism and International Justice* (New York: Oxford University Press, 2003).

Sterba, James P. "Reconciling Pacifists and Just War Theorists." *Social Theory and Practice* 18(1992), 21–38.

Stimson, Henry L. "The Decision to Use the Atomic Bomb." *Harper's Magazine* 194 (February 1947), 96–107.

Stockdale, James B. "A Vietnam Experience, Duty—Address to the Class of 1983, United States Military Academy." In Christopher Cox (ed.), *West Point's Perspectives on Officership* (West Point, NY: Thomson Custom Publishing, 2002).

Sweetman, John. *The Dambusters Raid* (London: Cassell, 2002).

Thompson, Janna. "Terrorism and the Right to Wage War." In Tony Coady & Michael O'Keefe (eds.), *Terrorism and Justice: Moral Argument in a Threatened World* (Melbourne: Melbourne University Press, 2002).

Thomson, Judith Jarvis. "The Trolley Problem." *Yale Law Journal* 94(1985), 1395–1415.

Thrasher, Zachary D. "Truth vs Loyalty: The Case of the Missing Flashlight." In W. Rick Rubel & George Lucas (eds.), *Case Studies in Ethics for Military Leaders.* 3rd ed. (Boston: Pearson Custom, 2009).

Tripodi, Paolo. "Deconstructing the Evil Zone: How Ordinary Individuals Can Commit Atrocities." In Paolo Tripodi & Jessica Wolfendale (eds.), *New Wars and New Soldiers: Military Ethics in the Contemporary World* (Farnham, U.K.: Ashgate, 2011).

Tripodi, Paolo & Wolfendale, Jessica (eds.), *New Wars and New Soldiers: Military Ethics in the Contemporary World* (Farnham, U.K.: Ashgate, 2011).

Uhler, Oscar & Coursier, Henri. *Commentary on the Geneva Conventions of 12 August 1949: Volume IV, Relative to the Protection of Civilian Persons in Time of War* (Geneva: ICRC, 1958).

United Nations. "Human Rights in Palestine and Other Occupied Territories: Report of the United Nations Fact Finding Mission on the Gaza Conflict" (Goldstone Report).

United Nations. "Report of the Commission of Experts Established Pursuant to United Nations Security Council Resolution 780" (1992).

United Nations. *Universal Declaration of Human Rights.* Adopted and proclaimed by United Nations General Assembly resolution 217 A (III) of 10th December 1948. http://www.un.org/Overview/rights.html

United States Department of Defense. "Final Report to Congress: Conduct of the Persian Gulf War," April 10, 1992.

Walker, J. Samuel. "Recent Literature on Truman's Atomic Bomb Decision: A Search for Middle Ground." *Diplomatic History* 29(2005), 311–34.

Walzer, Michael. *Just and Unjust Wars* (New York: Basic, 1977).

Western Australia State Coroner. *Inquest into the Deaths of Shaun Damien Smith; Phillip John Carroll; Megan Anne Pelly and Bradley John Meek (HMAS Westralia)* (Perth: Government of W.A., 2003).

Whetham, David (ed.). *Ethics, Law and Military Operations* (Basingstoke, U.K.: Palgrave Macmillan, 2011).

Whetham, David. "The Challenge of Ethical Relativism in Coalition Operations." *Journal of Military Ethics* 7(2008), 302–16.

Wolfendale, Jessica. "'New Wars,' Terrorism, and Just War Theory." In Paolo Tripodi & Jessica Wolfendale (eds.), *New Wars and New Soldiers: Military Ethics in the Contemporary World* (Farnham, U.K.: Ashgate, 2011).

Wolfendale, Jessica. *Torture and the Military Profession* (New York: Palgrave MacMillan, 2007).

Woodward, Sandy (with Robinson, Patrick). *One Hundred Days: The Memoirs of the Falkland Battle Group Commander* (Annapolis, MD: Naval Institute Press, 1992).

Zupan, Daniel S. *War, Morality and Autonomy: An Investigation in Just War Theory* (Aldershot, U.K.: Ashgate, 2004).

INDEX

Note: Entries in quotation marks refer to cases.

Printed in the USA/Agawam, MA
December 7, 2022

802199.008